"IMAGES, A Pictorial History of Columbus, Ga."
by
F. Clason Kyle
commemorates the 20th anniversary of the Historic Columbus Foundation, a non-profit organization dedicated to preserving the past in order to deserve the future.

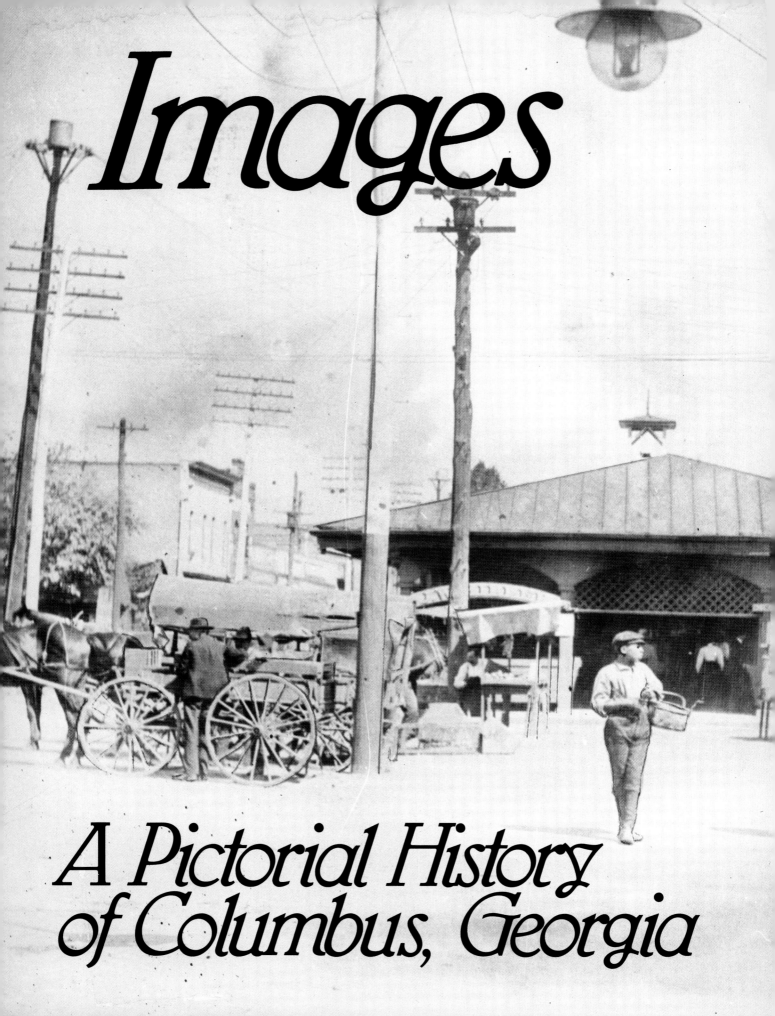
Images
A Pictorial History of Columbus, Georgia

by F. Clason Kyle

THE DONNING COMPANY/PUBLISHERS
NORFOLK/VIRGINIA BEACH

Dedicated to Miss Roberta Lawrence, my Columbus High School English teacher who said I was too smart to ever amount to anything. This volume may prove her 100 percent accurate.

And to the late C. Dexter Jordan, who squirreled away so much Columbus history, and who was always an encouraging friend and civic inspiration.

Copyright © 1986 by F. Clason Kyle

All rights reserved, including the right to reproduce this work in any form whatsoever without permission in writing from the publisher, except for brief passages in connection with a review. For information, write:
The Donning Company/Publishers
5659 Virginia Beach Boulevard
Norfolk, Virginia 23502

Edited by Diana L. Bailey

Library of Congress Cataloging-in-Publication Data

Kyle, F. Clason (Fleming Clason), 1929-
  Images: a pictorial history of Columbus, Georgia.
  Bibliography: p.
  Includes index.
  1. Columbus (Ga.)—History—Pictorial works.
I. Title.
F294.C7K944   1986   975.8'473   86-2134
ISBN 0-89865-451-3 (lim. ed.)

Printed in the United States of America

Contents

Preface • 7

Acknowledgments • 9

Chapter I:
1828—The Beginning • 13

Chapter II:
1829-1860—Taming the Frontier • 21

Chapter III:
1861-1870—The Rebellion and
Reconstruction • 47

Chapter IV:
1871-1900—Industrialization and
Growth • 71

Chapter V:
1901-1920—World War I and
Fort Benning • 123

Chapter VI:
1921-1949—Depression and
World War II • 173

Chapter VII:
1950-1985—To the Present • 217

Bibliography • 288

Index • 291

About the Author • 296

Preface

Tapestry: a heavy woven cloth with decorative design and/or pictures. Usually made of wool or silk.

Columbus is such a fabric. Its weave is of people and buildings, events and memories. Whether the fabric is rough or smooth, its design can be classified as good or bad, handsome or ugly, happy or sad. *Images* is an attempt to display the warp and woof on the loom that is our city. The result? A textile that shows the founding of the town, its growth and dominant patterns, a chain of many of its events (whether natural disasters or planned achievements), plus personalities who have embroidered their own highlights into the fabric of the community. The time span? From past to present, i.e. from 1828 to 1985.

A definitive history? No. Six excellent volumes about Columbus—*Columbus, Georgia, 1827-1865* by John H. Martin; Nancy Telfair's *A History of Columbus, Georgia, 1828-1928*; Etta Blanchard Worsley's *Columbus on the Chattahoochee*; Dr. Katherine Mahan's *Showboats to Soft Shoes*; Margaret Whitehead and Barbara Bogart's *City of Progress, 1828-1978*; and Dr. John Lupold's *Columbus, Georgia, 1828-1978*— have already been written. And Dr. Lupold also provided a thorough pamphlet on the city's industrial development for the Society for Industrial Archeology when their annual conference was held in Columbus in April of 1979.

So, for the serious student of local history, there is already a significant body of work. This pictorial collection, while prepared seriously, is designed to be interesting viewing and reading. I certainly hope you enjoy *Images*.

F. Clason Kyle

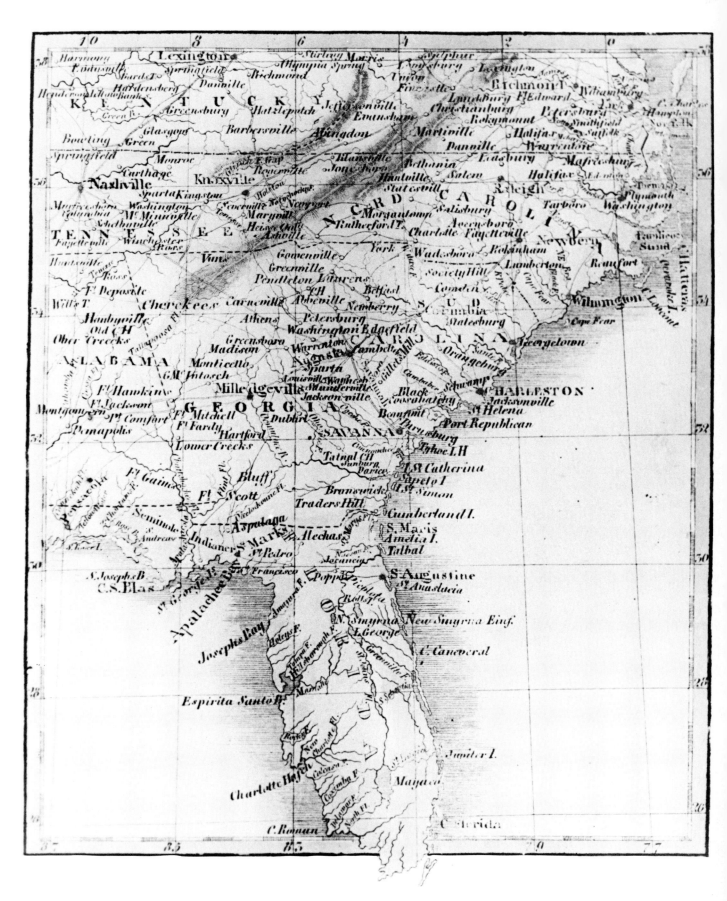

Acknowledgments

Most non-fictions of this ilk—I fain to dignify calling this work a "history"—commence with an apology for the author's inadequacy. Or should I buck such a well-established practice by stating boldly that I have done all the work myself and that it is 100 percent accurate in every way? Would that I could.

A community's 157 years of existence should be enough to convince the most accomplished and dedicated of historians that the task of preparing such a volume is monumental and probably insurmountable. As my mother said when told that a group of us whippersnappers were going to restore the Springer Opera House, "Since they're too young to know it can't be done, they'll do it." She proved to be only moderately correct: we were not really that "young," nor has our task been fully accomplished.

Back to this humble beg-off for even attempting such a project. My one legitimate claim to qualification to record a social history of Columbus in the first place was that on one side of my family I am descended from one of the five original commissioners, Dr. Edwin L. deGraffenried, and, on the other side of the family, from George Parker Swift, a textile pioneer in both Georgia and Muscogee County. Thus, my roots are closely allied and sentimentally attached to the tree that is our Columbus.

Anyone beginning such a project looks to see what foundation stones have already been placed upon which to build an illustrated chronicle, one that, from the outset, confesses to be not a total anything, not a complete record of births or deaths, constructions or demolitions, not a catalogue of events or legends, nor an encyclopedia of personalities, living or dead. It is, at its best, a cursory glance at "a very curious place," as Mrs. Basil Hall described the embryo town in 1828. How prophetic she proved to be!

(By the way, "A Very Curious Place" was a title that I thought of using, feeling that Mrs. Hall was using the word "curious" to denote the uniqueness and novelty in the way the community was being born and not as a "peculiar, laughably funny" place. However, as the completed volume is a series of quick impressions, glimpses, and reflections of people, places and episodes, *Images* results in being not only the best but also the most accurate title.)

This "historian" was trained in English and journalism, and I make the distinction between English and journalism before someone else does. A journalist in the United States employs at least a form of English and strives to get his facts straight. Therefore, a reporter is a present-tense historian, and yesterday's newspaper, purportedly fit for no more than wrapping up today's trash, becomes a vital source of local history as it turns yellow with age.

Already have I given credit to the foundation stones that served as my chief source of material, volumes about Columbus by Martin, Worsley, Mahan, Telfair, Lupold, and Whitehead and Bogart. Again I would like to extend my thanks to those proper scribes, three of whom have shuffled off this mortal coil. A more extensive bibliography follows this for those who care to delve more deeply into our town's loves and lores, its trends and foibles.

In addition to the two invaluable inspirations to which *Images* is dedicated, there were two other individuals who were constant and rewarding sources of challenge. My cousin, the late Jim Woodruff, Jr., was a consistent worker for the betterment of the city of Columbus. He was such a toiler that I could have told the story of a quarter of a century of the city's progress by just using pictures of him at meetings, groundbreaking ceremonies and greeting distinguished visitors. The other spur to excellence came from the late Edge R. Reid, who served as executive editor of the *Ledger-Enquirer* newspapers for most of my seventeen years there. He always questioned my copy and then stood loyally behind it and me. They inspired me to try to do my best.

What one regrets most about such a public offering as this book is that there remain research rocks unturned, persons you were told to contact whom you never did, attics you never explored, older folks you never interviewed, tales by family members you only half heard, microfilmed newspapers you never read.

Every effort has been made to identify the owners of the illustrations appearing in this book. Apologies are extended for any omissions in this respect. Appropriate acknowledgments will be made in any future printings.

If you want to know what the author is going to hate the most, it will be that first early morning phone call from the person whose father is misidentified in a group photo, or the person who calls to say that she (or he) could have identified all the people in the picture found on such and such a page. "Why didn't you call me?" If I had but known that only one more phone call would have solved the puzzle!

Two loyal typists have I had. (You see, I wright beautifully, but I cannot spel.) One was Laura Potuznik, a Fort Benning housewife who allowed motherhood to come between us and finishing the job together. The other was Beverly Taylor whose countless afternoons have been spent lending her able fingers to the improvement and clarity of "Kylestyle" prose. (And we only gossiped occasionally.)

Other staff members of the Historic Columbus Foundation—Barbara Stephens, Celia Page and Janice Biggers—were part of a marathon weekend when all the nitty-gritty was wrapped up before shipping "the baby" to Norfolk's Donning Company Publishers who had probably given up on ever seeing a finished product. Two other praiseworthy marathoners, Mary Margaret Byrne and Dr. Richard Bullock, popped in late on Saturday night of that weekend and asked if they could help any the next day. Indeed, yes, and for twelve solid hours they "hepped"—as we are inclined to pronounce it in Columbus. The moral of that is "don't volunteer." And, as a matter of fact, I haven't heard from either of them in quite some time.

Ever sensitive to my needs and quick to supply the seemingly impossible answers were Brady Wilson and Joan Emens of the W.C. Bradley Memorial Library; Callie McGinnis of the Simon Schwob Memorial Library, Columbus College; and Patricia Hardy and Gladys Sandoval of the *Ledger-Enquirer* newspapers' library and Dr. A. Elizabeth Taylor.

Particular appreciation must be expressed to the *Ledger-Enquirer* photographers, past and present, who snapped the bulk of the photos in *Images* and gratitude to the management of the *Ledger-Enquirer* for their wisdom in preserving such a valuable archive, a treasure-trove from which an entirely different version of Columbus could easily be produced. And probably a third volume as well. When I think of what I had to leave out because of print space limitations or sheer ignorance, I could cry. And I think I will. Tomorrow. At Tara.

Two final thanks. One to Joe Maher, who assisted in the quality reproduction of so many of the treasured but-lent "family album" photos and who thought nothing of spending hours locating certain tombstones in Linwood Cemetery.

And the other to my able "go-for," Roger Harris. Lucky is hardly the word for it when one acquires a Fulbright scholar as an assistant. Roger, too, has the love for Columbus, and he couples that with an agile mind and a merry laugh, the merry laugh coming even when things were at their worst. I can't say that *Images* would never have come out without his help, but he made its last three months a very pleasant period of creativity, culminating when, as Shakespeare put it, this literary effort was "snatched untimely from its womb."

Whom have I not thanked? The two most important institutions who sponsored this volume that benefits the Historic Columbus Foundation: the *Columbus Ledger-Enquirer* newspapers and the Trust Company Bank of Columbus. More than anything, I appreciate the faith they placed in my ability. My deepest gratitude to both organizations, especially banker Sam O. Franklin, III, and publisher Glenn Vaughn.

And to the readers of *Images*, here is the Columbus that I have known, my life period being almost exactly one third that of the city's legislated being. Here are its loves and legends, its dimples and some of its warts. In other words, its images.

F. Clason Kyle

Left to right, Dr. Richard Bullock, Roger Harris, Peter Cranton, and Mary Margaret Byrne were the gratefully received "heppers" who on a marathon work weekend graciously donated their time and expertise in order that Images *would meet the deadline to its publishers, the Donning Company in Norfolk, Virginia.*

GEORGIA,
Town of Columbus.

THIS will certify, that the Lot lying in the Town of Columbus, and State of Georgia, fronting on *Few and Jackson* Street, and numbered in the plan of said Town *three hundred and ten* containing an Half Acre, was this Day sold at Public Auction for the sum of *ninety one* Dollars and that *William Carr* having been the highest bidder, and having paid to us *eighteen* Dollars *twenty cents* being one Fifth part of the aforesaid sum. NOW provided the said *William Carr* or *his* Heirs or Assigns, shall pay to the Treasurer of the State of Georgia, the remaining Four-Fifths of the aforesaid sum, in Annual Instalments, or within sixty days after they become due respectively, then the said *William Carr* or *his* Heirs or Assigns shall be entitled to receive a Grant for said Lot, agreeably to the provisions of an Act of the General Assembly, " To lay out a Trading Town, and to dispose of all the Lands reserved for the use of the State near the Coweta Falls," &c. Assented to on the 24th of Dec. 1827.

WITNESS our hands this *24th* day of *March* 182*9*

Elias Beall
E. L. De Graffenried
Ulysses Lewis
James Van ___

Commissioners.

Printed at the Office of the 'ATHENIAN,' Athens (Georgia.)

Chapter I
1828
The Beginning

"A very curious place."

The writer was British. A retired naval captain, Basil Hall was travelling across Georgia with his wife and daughter. Their journey had been arduous, through wilderness and on roads that scarcely deserved to be called even trails. Besides a maid for the child, Hall also had a camera lucida with him, and this instrument ultimately would provide the first recorded view of the embryo town of Columbus when Hall's *Travels in North America* was published in Edinburgh in 1829.

For indeed it was Columbus that Hall evaluated both as "a very curious place" and later as "this singular place." After visiting the site and noting the sites around him, his estimates were of a city, legislated into being by the state of Georgia, as it was being carved from the primeval forest on the banks of the Chattahoochee.

As they crossed the river into the country of the Creek Indians on April 1, 1828, Hall wrote, "I could form no idea, from what I saw or heard, on the spot, how this strangely concocted town would get on...." Hopefully, Hall is somewhere that he can see that Columbus has been able to "get on" very well for the past 157 years!

The most significant fact about Columbus is that the city did not develop out of need or change. Instead, it was created by act of legislature, with Governor of Georgia John Forsyth signing the act on December 24, 1827. This made Columbus the last planned city of the thirteen original colonies.

A trading post and ferry had existed at the bend in the Chattahoochee below the river's fall line before the legislature, meeting at the state capital in Milledgeville, willed Columbus into being. A trading post and a pre-legislative past involving the nations of France, England and Spain, the events and personalities of those several centuries would be a volume of much local interest and would make exciting reading. *Images*, however, has chosen to begin its chronology with the formal founding of the city.

When the *Enquirer-Sun* and the *Columbus Ledger* united to publish a centennial edition to commemorate the 100th anniversary of the city, Loretto Lamar Chappell related a colorful and charming picture of the town's events from 1828 to 1865. Scion of pioneer settler families and former librarian at the city's public libraries, Miss Chappell commenced her brief local history with the information about the early days of the founding of the Colony of Georgia. And our history can begin with Miss Chappell's account.

She began:

When the members of the corporation, called "The Trustees for Establishing the Colony of Georgia in America," accepted from George II of England a grant of land, their reach did surely exceed their grasp. Then, Georgia extended from a northern point of the Savannah River to a point south of the Altamaha River, and from the Atlantic coast to the South Seas!

Of course, Georgians never governed so much as one-tenth of the vast territory assigned them. Indeed, the English civilization planted on the coast of Georgia in 1733, spread inland so very slowly that almost one hundred years elapsed before it reached the western boundary of a newly-defined and materially diminished Georgia.

When the Revolutionary War ended, white settlers held in Georgia only the strip of land lying between the sea and the Ogeechee River. Thereafter, white domination moved westward in successive waves, as every few years the Indians were persuaded to sign a treaty, surrendering land to the white people. Thus Georgia's western frontier was in 1782 the Ogeechee River, in 1790 the Oconee, in 1803 the Ocmulgee, in 1821 the Flint, and, at last, in 1827 the Chattahoochee.

The treaty, by which Georgia acquired from the Creek Indians the territory lying between the Flint and the Chattahoochee, was signed at Indian Springs in February, 1825 and before the close of 1827 the Indians had moved west of the Chattahoochee, leaving their lands for white settlers.

Legislators of the state of Georgia looked with favor on the vicinity of Coweta Falls in the Chattahoochee River. Marking that this was the head of navigation from the gulf and that here were excellent river crossings, they ordained that on the Coweta Reserve a trading town should stand, and that its name should be Columbus. In December 1827, a commission was appointed by the legislature to select the exact site and to divide it into building lots which were to be sold by the state.

The members of the commission, Ignatius Few, Elias Beall, Philip H. Alston, James Hallam and E. L. deGraffenried, with Sowell Woolfolk as secretary, met first on January 15th, 1828, at Milledgeville, then the capital of the state. Subsequent meetings were held on the Reserve at the Coweta Falls. Here the wise commissioners dwelt during the winter months of 1828 and throughout the spring. The surveyor, Edward Lloyd Thomas, and his little band of axmen and chainmen at once began their work. On raw, cold February days and the windy days of March, Thomas and his young assistants tramped through the forests and swamps by the Chattahoochee. They took measurements and ran lines, nor ever lost the vision of a beautiful and populous city, whose streets must be broad, whose provision for churches, schools and city hall must be generous.

On the morning of July 10th, 1828, at 9 o'clock a throng of merchants, professional men, planters, Indian traders and speculators stood before the house of William D. Lucas, their eager eyes lifted toward a window, wherein the auctioneer stood, ready to offer the first lot for sale. Within the room at the auctioneer's back waited the five commissioners and the secretary. At 11 o'clock the sales were closed and each successful bidder came forward to make an initial payment and to sign certain papers. At 2 o'clock in the afternoon the auction reopened, continuing until 5 p.m., when again purchasers were given an opportunity to comply with the state's terms of sale.

Every day from the tenth to the twenty-third of July the lively scene was re-enacted until four hundred and eighty-eight building lots and forty-five large gardening lots within the town had been sold. A number of extensive places beyond the city's limits had also found purchasers.

Immediately houses of boards or logs began to appear on the purchased lots. Many of the impatient settlers had, while awaiting the auction, built themselves small dwellings, which might be transported on rollers whither one would. Just a year and a half later there were in Columbus "seventy-five excellent and permanent frame buildings, twelve dry goods and grocery stores, one drug store and two commodious and extensive hotels."

John Forsyth, governor of Georgia in 1828, was one of the most distinguished men the state ever produced, even though he was born in Virginia in 1780. (Two of the city's original five commissioners, appointed by Forsyth, also were born in Virginia.) Before serving as governor, Forsyth had been the U. S. minister to Spain under John Quincy Adams and before that, both a congressman and a senator. Later, he would serve as secretary of state under both Andrew Jackson and Martin Van Buren, a major political coup not equaled until Dean Rusk in more recent times. Besides appointing the commissioners, Forsyth also personally supervised the embryo city's lot sale, which began on July 10, 1828. The sale lasted for two weeks, during which Forsyth and his retinue camped on the banks of the Chattahoochee River on the South Common, part of the Green Belt that surrounded the original city. Photograph courtesy of the Columbus Ledger-Enquirer *newspapers*

"Ordered, that Ignatius Few of Richmond, Edwin L. deGraffenried of Greene, James Hallam of Muscogee, Philip H. Alston of Elbert and Elias Beall of Monroe be appointed Commissioners to lay out and dispose the Town of Columbus at the Coweta Falls on the Chattahoochee, according to the provisions of an Act of the General Assembly assented to on the 24th inst., and that Commissioners attend at the Executive office of the 15 day of January next for the purpose of entering into Bond that they may proceed forthwith in the execution of their duty under said act." The above is from the Executive Minutes of the Governor, dated December 26, 1827. A descendant of Baron Christopher deGraffenried of Switzerland, who brought a group of people to the new world to escape religious persecution, Commissioner deGraffenried was a graduate of the University of Pennsylvania, and a friend of the American statesman-orator Daniel Webster. Moving to Columbus from Greene County, deGraffenried was one of the first four doctors in the town. Credited with the wide streets in the early city plan, Dr. deGraffenried established the first Temperance Society and called a meeting to establish the first Episcopal church in the community. He was especially active in the welfare and health of the Indian population in and around Columbus. He died December 7, 1871. The de Graffenried home was located on the southeast corner of First Avenue at Twelfth Street. The steeple in the lower right side of the photo is of the First Baptist Church. Photographs from the author's collection

Born in 1790 in Richmond County, Ignatius Few was one of the original five commissioners of Columbus. (His uncle William was a signer for North Carolina of the Constitution of the United States.) A former lawyer, Few converted to Christianity in 1829 and became a minister. He served for one year as pastor of St. Luke Methodist Church and one year as presiding elder of the district. In 1836, at the age of forty-six, Few left Columbus to found Emory College at the new town of Oxford, which was to be laid out by Columbus's original surveyor, Edward Lloyd Thomas. A deed, from the board of trustees of Emory to Seaborn Jones of Columbus, is for a lot in the town of Oxford, stipulating that the property will revert back to the trustees if "said Seaborn Jones or his heirs or assigns shall sell, or permit to be sold any inebriating liquor, or play or permit to be played any game of hazard on the aforesaid lot." The date is July 10, 1837. The total price of the lot was $300. Photograph courtesy of Emory University

British naval captain Basil Hall and his wife stopped here during their tour of America in 1828. Setting up his camera lucida in a clearing, he captured the accompanying scene of rude log structures scattered amongst the Georgia pines. The only other signs of civilization, save the lone laborer, are clumps of sawed-off tree stumps and a long signboard hanging from a tall verticle pole. Both Hall and his wife published books on their journey and wrote extensively in them of the embryo town which, when they were present, was "a city as yet without a name, or existence in law or fact." This comment is a trifle baffling, since the legislature had included a name when it authorized the creation of the community. Photograph courtesy of the Columbus Ledger-Enquirer *newspapers*

Although preaching was his real calling (nearly forty years of it by the time of his death on August 17, 1852), Virginia-born Edward Lloyd Thomas will be best remembered in Georgia for establishing the Alabama-Georgia boundary in 1826 (finally accepted by Alabama in 1840) and the planning and laying out of a site on the Chattahoochee which was to be called Columbus. Thomas's oldest son, called Truman, died of pneumonia while performing as a chain-bearer during the local survey, and was the first person buried in the cemetery provided for in the city plan. Nine years later, Thomas again surveyed for a new city in Georgia, this time the town of Oxford. In his will, he noted that he was free of the bondage of debt and recommended to his children that they follow his example if they wished to preserve serene minds and unruffled tempers. Photograph courtesy of the Columbus Ledger-Enquirer *newspapers*

Traditionally, the Walker-Peters-Langdon House is considered the oldest dwelling in Columbus and also one of the "prefabricated" houses about which Britisher Basil Hall wrote when he visited Columbus in 1828. He described a cluster of structures that were only about two or three weeks old and which had been "built on trucks—sort of low, strong-wheeled mechanism such as cannon are supported by—for the avowed purpose of being hauled away when the land should be sold." He also pointed out that there were at least "sixty frames of houses...lying in piles on the ground—and got up by the carpenters on speculation, ready to answer the call of future purchasers." The Walker-Peters-Langdon House is now a museum, owned and operated by the Historic Columbus Foundation. Photograph from the author's collection

In a private local collection is a rare piece of Staffordshire china, Staffordshire being the shire (or county) of England where notable pottery works, such as Minton, Spode, and Wedgwood, have existed since the Middle Ages. This piece of china is small, less than four inches across, and while its chief interest locally is historical, it previously had a utilitarian purpose: it was a cup plate. Within its fruit and flower border, is a view of Columbus taken from "Forty Etchings from Sketches Made with the Camera Lucida in North America in 1827 and 1828" by Captain Basil Hall, published in London in 1829.

The cup plate on the mid-nineteenth century dinner table afforded a resting place for the tea or coffee cup after the beverage had been poured into the larger deep saucer for cooling, a perfectly acceptable practice at that time. The series of American views by Enoch Wood were made in black, medium blue, light blue, pink, and mulberry. Therefore a whole dinner set would not necessarily be in a single color, but instead have plates in one color, platters in another and hollow-ware in yet a third. Photograph from the author's collection

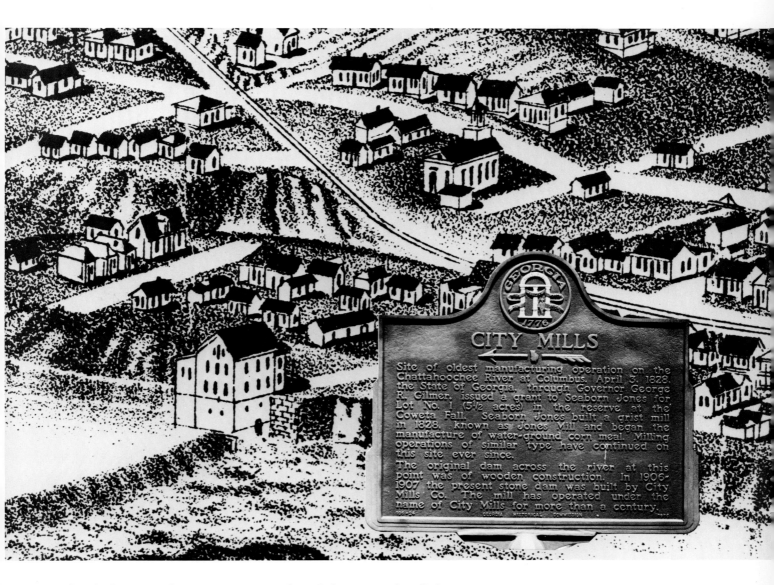

Credit for being the first man to harness the energy of the Chattahoochee is generally given to Seaborn Jones. He was a former aide-de-camp to Governor George Troup, and came from Milledgeville to the new town of Columbus. Jones built the first dam across the river and started the first real industry, City Mills, in 1828. This grist mill operation, Columbus's oldest business, has had a number of owners through the years, such as G. A. Pearce, Eelbeck Mills and currently Lloyd Bowers, and has claims to being the oldest continuously commercial gristmill in the United States. The corn mill at City Mills is the only locally-known, surviving building constructed by Horace King, the freed slave and master builder.
Photograph from the author's collection

Chapter II
1829-1860
Taming the Frontier

Last planned city of the youngest of the thirteen original colonies is an accurate designation for Columbus. Georgia as an English Royal Colony dates back to 1733 when General James Oglethorpe arrived with his followers aboard the Anne *to settle on the bluffs of what is now Savannah. Independence from the Crown was achieved, of course, in 1776, with Georgia achieving statehood when it became the fourth to ratify the Federal Constitution on January 2, 1778. Georgia seceded from that Union on January 19, 1861, the fifth state to do so, and was formally readmitted to the Union by the U.S. Congress on July 15, 1870. Its state seal, on one side with the motto of "Wisdom, Justice and Moderation," has been in use since 1799 with two exceptions: the period 1863-1865 when there was another seal, and in the period 1868-1871 when it was hidden by Secretary of State Nathan C. Barnett. In 1872, it was restored by Barnett to the state government. In 1914, the date on the seal was changed by legislative action from 1799 to 1776, to correspond with the date of the Declaration of Independence. Georgia's state flower is the Cherokee Rose, its state tree is the live oak, and its state bird is the brown thrasher. Its state flag, combining the state seal on a field of blue and the remainder being known as the Battle Flag of the Confederacy, was established by the Act of February 13, 1956. Photograph courtesy of the state of Georgia*

Five years after the Basil Halls' visitation, another European visitor—this time a Swedish scholar named C. D. Arfwedson—found a "flourishing town" where laborers "could not erect houses fast enough." The streets that the Halls had found indicated only by stakes and blazes on trees were "so filled with loaded wagons that it was next to impossible to pass...." Arfwedson commented on the residences as being mostly of wood and "some in the Grecian taste," but his most architecturally vivid remarks pertained to "the hotels, (which) are, perhaps, the worst buildings in town: I resided in one, the staircase of which bore a strong resemblance to a fire-ladder, and the bedroom, although provided with window frames, had no panes of glass in them."

Otherwise, Columbus was making good progress. A newspaper (the *Enquirer*) issued its first number during the last week in May of 1828. Columbus' first historian, John H. Martin, described the newspaper as "a weekly sheet of good size and fair appearance...." The first hotel had been built and was named appropriately, if not too imaginatively, the Columbus Hotel. Martin records that the lot that sold highest at the (founding) sale was one on the southwest corner of Broad and Crawford (10th) Street. It was bought by Messrs. Nicholas Howard of Greensboro and Peter Dudley for the sum of $1,855.

In addition to listing when the first bank was created in Columbus, Martin also recorded that the first ordinance of the municipal government was one requiring all houses on the streets and common to be removed and "forbidding all persons to cut down or destroy any tree on the river common."

A temperance society formed, a rude theater was constructed, and on the 14th of February the *Enquirer* said:

Columbus is rapidly advancing in improvements. Building is carried on in a style that would do honor to our populous cities, and with a rapidity scarcely equalled within our knowledge. Such is the progressive style that we frequently find large two-storied houses and well-cleaned gardens, in various parts of the town, where but a short time previously, we were rambling after game. Ramblers are not unfrequently surprised at finding their hunting ground so suddenly converted from a wilderness into cultivated fields or adorned by the labors of the architect and enlivened by traffic. We have dry goods and groceries in abundance, and all the difficulty in the way of good living is the want of the wherewith to purchase the commodities. Few of our citizens having the necessary cash or credit, are often reduced to deplorable straits. The absence of the grand sine qua non, *however, seems to be no barrier to the growth of the town.*

In 1830, the marshal reported a town population of 1,152 with a state census a few months later at 1,261. The population of Muscogee County was given at 3,507 of whom 2,262 were white. In 1831, figures for deaths were set at fifty-seven between June 1st and November 19th. Martin wrote, "Out of the above number, 40 have died of fever, three in child-bed and two from intemperance."

Speaking of intemperance, the early visitors to Columbus commented upon a number of "loose persons, on which account morals were at the lowest ebb." Arfwedson wrote, "Opposite to the town, on the Alabama shore, a number of dissolute people had founded a village, for which their lawless pursuits and atrocious misdeeds had procured the name Sodom. Scarcely a day passed without some human blood being shed in its vicinity; and, not satisfied with murdering each other, they cross the river clandestinely, and pursue their bloody vocation even in Columbus." He philosophized that it would take the removal of the Indians from this part of the country and for the state of Alabama to enforce the observance of her laws "and not till then will Columbus see her own population happy and tranquil, and civilization diffusing its light upon her citizens."

The celebrated Irish actor Tyrone Power, great-great-grandfather of the Hollywood matinee idol of the same name, also described in 1834 the "wild-looking village as composed chiefly of 'minions o' the moon,'" i.e. outlaws from the neighboring states.

Miss Chappell wrote:

Brave and ambitious was the citizenry of the little frontier town. For protection against possible incursions of the Indians, dwelling in Alabama, volunteer military companies were formed. During the day hundreds of Indians would visit the city, coming on peaceful errands and cheerfully complying with the law which bade them return to their own shore at nightfall. Much cotton was brought from the outlying plantations to the Columbus wharf, whence it was sent by steamboat to the Gulf of Mexico.

Scant, at first, were the opportunities for recreation. When the occasional visit of an itinerant preacher gathered the townsfolk together, their voices were glad in singing old hymns. The Fourth of July, when one might see the Frontier Guards in review and hear a bit of stirring oratory, was a grand occasion. Meeting of the Debating Society and the Temperance Society and jolly corn-shuckings enlivened the evenings.

By treaty in 1832, the Creek Indians ceded their lands in Alabama and agreed to move west of the Mississippi within five years of the treaty date. However, they soon regretted this action and, as an expression of bitterness against the white man in general, they began to molest the citizens of Columbus and people of the region. These troubles boiled to a climax in the Creek War of 1836 described by Miss Chappell:

In February, 1836, occurred at Bryant's Ferry, fifteen miles below Columbus, a fight between twenty-two white men and forty armed Indians. Two white men were killed and two wounded in this affair, known as the Battle of Hitchiti. Thereafter the Indians manifested their hostility by murdering white families which had settled in eastern Alabama, by attacking stage coaches and by firing upon river boats. They burned the bridges across the Big and Little Uchee Creeks.

In Columbus there was great excitement. The Columbus Guards had been organized during the previous year. Now three more volunteer companies were quickly formed. United States troops came to the aid of the white people of Georgia and Alabama, and a

The person who read the Declaration of Independence at the Fourth of July celebration in 1828—a tradition at that time—was Ulysses S. Lewis. On January 1, 1829, he was elected the first intendant of the infant town and, along with six commissioners, formed the local municipal government. The commissioners were Samuel B. Head, James Van Ness, Ira Scott, Simon L. Smith, George W. K. Dillard and Thomas G. Gordon. Subsequent intendants were James Van Ness, Sowell Woolfolk, Samuel Lawhorn, Allen Lawhorn and James C. Watson. In 1836, the first city government of Columbus was established and the titles of Intendant and Commissioners were changed to Mayor and Aldermen. On his gravestone is carved the information that Lewis was "a direct descendant of Fielding Lewis and his wife Betty Washington Lewis, a sister of George Washington." The Fielding Lewises lived at Fredericksburg, Virginia in the historic house known as Kenmore. Photograph courtesy of the Columbus Ledger-Enquirer *newspapers*

number of companies of the Georgia militia also arrived to share in the frontier warfare. Gen. Winfield Scott was in command of all military operations. His headquarters were in Columbus. Terrorized Alabama settlers came in hordes across the covered bridge, their household effects in hand. The proportionately small number of Indians, who were friendly to the white people, also gathered in or near Columbus.

The Indians, thoroughly defeated, began what has become known in history as the infamous "Trail of Tears," referring to the roundup of the regional Indians and their forced exodus to reservations west of the Mississippi.

The formation of a temperance society in 1829, a debating society in 1830 and both a northern and southern daily mail service in 1831 were but three indications that the new community was rapidly taking on the airs of a city. Another urban indicator was the fact that, according to Martin's History, "the Muscogee Bible Society was in active operation, supplying Bibles to the destitute." The two mail services, the northern one going via Macon, Milledgeville and Augusta and the southern one via Montgomery and Mobile, were augmented by a stagecoach line connecting Columbus with Macon via Thomaston and Forsyth. The fare was $8.50 and the journey, traveling in daylight hours only, took from a 7 a.m. departure on Friday to a noon arrival on Sunday. Advertisement from Worsley's Columbus on the Chattahoochee *(1951)*

Stage-Coach Line that came near site of Columbus in 1827 and earlier.

In a rough-hewn theater that had been built in four days by contractor Asa Bates, frontier trouper Sol Smith presented his acting company in "Pizarro," a drama dealing with South American Indians. For extras, Smith considered himself fortunate, at first, to engage a group of Creek Indians as Peruvian warriors. Smith paid fifty cents and a glass of whiskey to each of the twenty four Creeks who furnished their own bows, arrows, and tomahawks. Unfortunately for the success of the performance, the whiskey was "paid" and drunk in advance. The result was chaos, the performance a shambles. The next night, the same braves reappeared and were eager to perform in "Macbeth." However, Smith "most positively declined their valuable aid." The year was 1832. Drawing by Juan Carcache

May 29, 1828 was the date of the first issue of the Enquirer. *Its founder and editor was Mirabeau Buonaparte Lamar, of a distinguished and learned Georgia family that thought nothing of the burden such a name might hold or even worse that given to a cousin, Lucius Quintus Cincinnatus Lamar. After the death of his wife Tabitha and a congressional defeat by another Columbusite, Seaborn Jones, Lamar quit Columbus and the newspaper, taking the stagecoach for Montgomery on June 15, 1835 en route to Texas. There, Lamar would become the hero of San Jacinto, and in a few years, the second president of the Republic of Texas, following the hero of the Alamo, Sam Houston, into office. "The cultivated mind is the guardian genius of democracy," a Lamar quote, is still the motto of the* Enquirer. *Later a minister to Latin American countries, Lamar died at the age of 61 in 1859 and is buried in Richmond, Texas, although his wife is buried in Linwood Cemetery. Photograph courtesy of the* Columbus Ledger-Enquirer *newspapers*

The cottage of Mirabeau B. and Tabitha Lamar was near the Chattahoochee River, and the couple frequently strolled along the river banks in the evenings. On Tabitha Jordan Lamar's monument in Linwood Cemetery, Lamar inscribed that her death "has left him no other happiness than the remembrance of her virtue." Lamar composed the following poem, "At Evening on the Banks of the Chattahoochee" in her memory. Photograph from the author's collection

At Evening on the Banks of the Chattahoochee

I
Oft when the sun along the west
His farewell splendor throws,
Imparting to the wounded breast
The spirit of repose—
My mind reverts to former themes,
To joys of other days
When love illumined all my dreams,
And hope inspired my lays.

II
I would not for the world bereave
Fond Memory of those times,
When seated here at summer eve,
I poured my early rhymes
To one whose smiles and tears proclaimed
The triumph of my art,
And plainly told, the minstrel reigned
The monarch of her heart.

III
Enriched with every mental grace,
And every moral worth,
She was the gem of her bright race,
A paragon on earth;
So luminous with love and lore,
So little dimmed by shade,
Her beauty threw a light before
Her footsteps as she strayed.

IV
But all the loveliness that played
Around her once, hath fled;
She sleepeth in the valley's shade,
A dweller with the dead;
And I am here with ruined mind.
Left lingering on the strand,
To pour my music to the wind,
My tears upon the sand.

V
I grieve to think she hears no more
The songs she loved so well—
That all the strains I now may pour
Of evenings in the dell,
Must fall as silently to her,
As evening's mild decline—
Unheeded as the dewy tear
That Nature weeps with mine.

VI
Oh, if thous canst thy slumbers break,
My dear departed one,
Now at thy minstrel's call awake,
And bless his evening song—
The last, perchance, his failing art
May o'er these waters send—
The last before his breaking heart
Shall songs and sorrows end.

VII
I fain would let thee know, blest shade,
Though years have sadly flown,
My love with time has not decayed—
My heart is still thine own;
And till the sun of life shall set,
All thine it must remain,
As warmly as when first we met,
Until we meet again.

VIII
If I have sought the festal hall,
My sorrows to beguile,
Or struck my harp at lady's call,
In praise of beauty's smile—
Oh, still thou didst my thoughts control
Amid the smiling throng;
Thou were the idol of my soul,
The spirit of my song.

IX
Take, take my rhyme, O ladies gay,
For you it freely pours;
The minstrel's heart is far away—
It never can be yours.
The music of my song may be
To living beauty shed,
But all the love that warms the strain—
I mean it for the dead.

—Mirabeau B. Lamar

After receiving the $14,000 contract to build the first bridge across the Chattahoochee in 1832, John Godwin moved to Columbus from Cheraw, South Carolina, bringing with him an able assistant in the person of Horace King, a slave who had been born on September 8, 1807. As reward for his years of service and as a show of his affection, Godwin petitioned the Alabama General Assembly in 1848 to grant King his freedom. Although freed, King remained active in Godwin's bridge-building business and, after Godwin's death on February 26, 1859, erected a marble shaft over Godwin's grave that reads "This stone was placed here by Horace King. In lasting rememberance of the love and gratitude he felt for his lost friend and former master." It is said that after Godwin's death, King financially supported Mrs. Godwin and her children. The truss of bridges built by King is called Kingpost, a triangle with a supporting column in the middle. King died in the late 1880s and he and his wife are believed to be buried in the Godwin cemetery in Girard-Phenix City. For more on Horace King, please see page 69. Photograph from the author's collection

Begun in 1828 and completed in 1833, St. Elmo is said to be "one of the most exquisite examples of classic houses in America." Built by Seaborn Jones on the Old Stage Coach Road, the house originally was named Eldorado. In 1875, its name was changed to St. Elmo after the title of Augusta Evans Wilson's famed romantic novel, as the then owner thought a member of their family was the model for one of the characters in the book. (Mrs. Wilson was a niece of Mrs. Jones and this Victorian best-sellter was completed while the author was a guest.) Three stories tall, the house has massive (three feet thick and forty feet high) columns on three sides with eighteen-inch-thick exterior walls. Of the original outbuildings, only one remains: a dovecote and smokehouse combined. Many distinguished visitors were entertained at the house during its early years, such as James K. Polk, Millard Fillmore, Henry Clay, and Winfield Scott. Listed on the National Register of Historic Places, St. Elmo is now owned by Dr. and Mrs. Philip T. Schley. Painting by Wilbur G. Kurtz, 1961

In 1834, the trading town was taking on the airs and dimensions of a city. Events large and small included the founding of the Columbus Episcopal Association, the arrival in March of the first cargo of ice (seventy tons of it) for Columbusites to enjoy in the coming hot summer, and the exhibition of Chang and Eng, the original Siamese Twins. Born in Siam of Chinese extraction, these men were united between the xiphoid cartilages by a thick fleshly ligament. They lived from 1811 to 1874, being born only one year after Phineas Taylor Barnum, the American showman, who displayed them throughout the world. In the same year, Columbus had its first bank failure (the Bank of Chattahoochee) and the opening of its municipal race track. But more about the latter later. Photograph from Drimmer's, Very Special People *(1976)*

Indeed it was an honor to be conferred membership in the Columbus Guards. This military unit had entered state service in 1835 under Maj. Gen. Daniel McDougal and federal service on January 1, 1836, just in time for the Creek War. Its first captain in 1835 was John A. Urquhart, a physician and the first president of the local Temperance Society. With his picture at the top and the date reading "186__," it must be presumed that this honorary membership was one used during the War Between the States when Paul J. Semmes was the captain of the Guards, a position he had held since 1854. He was a third cousin to the Confederate hero, Raphael Semmes, who was commander of the CSS Alabama. *One of the best-drilled companies in the nation, the Columbus Guards under Semmes served as honor guard to Jefferson Davis at his inaugural in Montgomery, Semmes firing the first salute with the Columbus field piece "Red Jacket." During the civil conflict, the Columbus Guards took part in thirty battles and were present at Lee's surrender at Appomattox. Semmes was mortally wounded at Gettysburg in 1863 and was buried in Virginia. Later, his body was returned to Columbus and buried in the W. S. Shepherd lot in Linwood Cemetery. His monument has been decorated annually by the Ladies Memorial Association of Columbus. John Forsyth, Jr. was captain of the Guards in 1849, and Philip T. Schley in 1845. Ware (another physician), S. Armstrong Bailey, and John E. Davis presumably also served as captains of the unit. The Columbus Guards served voluntarily in the Indian*

War of 1836, the 1846 war with Mexico, the War Between the States, the Spanish-American War, on the Mexican border in 1916-17, and became inactive after the First World War. It surrendered at Appomattox on April 9, 1865 with but two officers and eleven men. Photograph from the author's collection.

"A situation wildly beautiful" was how Irish actor Tyrone Power described the river front of Columbus when he visited in 1835. He observed "several dwellings of mansion-like proportions and others of similar character in progress." (Later this street would be known as "Golden Row," with the most golden of the houses being the residence of Columbus's first mayor, John Fontaine. Columbus became a city by an act of General Assembly, with the first mayor and council being elected on January 2, 1836. Fontaine was descended from a distinguished French family and is listed as a cotton merchant in Columbus in 1829. He died at the age of seventy-six, in 1866, only one year after the War Between the States. His handsome Greek Revival house, pictured here, survived on Front Avenue into the 1930s when the street became totally commercial.) On his visit, Power concluded that Columbus was exceedingly lawless: "...affrays ending in blood are said to be frequent, apprehensions few, acquittals next to certain in event of a trial." But he didn't think the traveler ran much risk, in fact "to a stranger the rudest of these frontier spirits are usually civil." He also described passing through Sodom (present-day Phenix City) but "few of its denizens were yet stirring; they are composed chiefly of 'minions o' the moon,' outlaws from the neighboring states." (The quote "minions o' the moon" is from Shakespeare and naturally would be known by an actor.) Power's account of his southern journey was published after his death, the vessel on which he was returning to Europe being lost at sea. The twentieth century movie actor by the same name was a great great grandson. *Photograph from the author's collection*

The successful Victorian novelist Augusta Jane Evans was born May 8, 1835 at Wildwood, the Muscogee County home of her grandfather, John Howard. The first woman writer in the United States to earn $100,000 from sales of her works, she enjoyed public acclaim as a best-selling authoress and in later years was the social lioness of Mobile, Alabama. At the age of fifteen she wrote her first novel, Inez: A Tale of the Alamo, *in an effort to better the family's ailing fortunes. She gave it to her father, Matthew Evans, as a Christmas present.* Beulah, *her second novel, she dedicated to her aunt, Mrs. Seaborn Jones of Columbus. Her most famous novel,* St. Elmo, *was published in 1866, and its huge success made her a literary celebrity and one of the most widely read novelists of the nineteenth century; the novel has been called the most popular novel ever published until* Ben Hur. *Other novels by her were* Vashti *(1869),* Infelice *(1875), and* At the Mercy of Tiberius *(1887). In 1868 she married Lorenzo Madison Wilson of Mobile. She died on May 9, 1909, that Southern port city's most esteemed literary and social figure. Photograph by W. A. Reed; courtesy of Special Collections, Ralph B. Draughon Library, Auburn University*

Built by the Georgia Militia in 1813 and named for David Brydie Mitchell, Georgia governor at the time, Fort Mitchell was located on the old Indian trail from Augusta, Georgia to Saint Stephens, Alabama. Besides being a popular duelling ground, the military installation served as headquarters for John Crowell, the U. S. Indian agent from 1821 to 1836. From time to time, as many as four batteries of artillery and two companies of U. S. Infantry were garrisoned there, guarding the frontier against the not-infrequently-hostile Indians. It was at Fort Mitchell that the Marquis de Lafayette had entered the Creek Nation in March of 1825 on his triumphant goodwill tour of America, demonstrating his patriotic affection for George Washington. And it was also here that the Creek Indians engaged in their last stick-ball game east of the Mississippi before their forced removal to the western reservations in 1836. This drawing of Fort Mitchell was redrawn from one sketched by the noted Alabama historian Peter Brannon.

John Crowell was Alabama's only congressman when President James Monroe appointed him United States Agent to the Creek Indians, a position he held from 1821 to 1836. He made his headquarters at Fort Mitchell and his plantation was nearby. Born in Halifax County, North Carolina, Crowell spent his post-agent years until his death in 1846 in the enjoyment of the sport of the chase and the turf, his horses winning prizes and purses of great value. One of Crowell's horses, "John Bascombe" (born during a camp meeting and named for a preacher), won a three-mile race in Columbus in 1835 against J. J. Harrison's "Volney." Later in Augusta, Georgia, he beat General Wade Hampton's famous racer "Argyle" in handsome style. In the spring of 1836, the nineteenth century version of the Triple Crown came when he defeated "Post Boy," considered the premier horse of North America. There being no flat cars or trucks to carry him, John Bascombe had walked from Fort Mitchell to the Union Course on Long Island for the May 31, 1836 race. Reprinted with permission of the Jockey Club, N.Y.

"A most alarming character" was how a Macon newspaper described the situation around Columbus in the spring of 1836, a situation created by attacks upon steamboats, upon the stages running between Columbus and Montgomery, and the burning of outlying plantations and bridges. The attackers were Creek Indians, rebellious over the treaty of 1832 with the federal government that had bound them to be removed within five years from the Alabama territory to their new home west of the Mississippi. To this near-war crisis was dispatched one of the military heroes of the time, General Winfield Scott, who made the Oglethorpe Hotel in Columbus his headquarters. A few sharp skirmishes were sufficient to quell the murderous ardor of the marauding Indians and, by July, Scott was on his way to direct what has become known as the infamous "Trail of Tears," the removal of the North Georgia/North Carolina Cherokees to the West. Photograph from the author's collection

Dead at age thirty two was James Walker Fannin Jr. Not just dead, but shot to death in a massacre, in Goliad, Texas, of 330 soldiers who had been captured at the battle of Caleto on March 20, 1836. A week after capture, General Antonio Lopez Santa Anna ordered the execution of the volunteers who had been fighting for Texas's independence from Mexico. "Remember Goliad" would be a rallying cry to go with "Remember the Alamo," as many young Columbusites such as Fannin (who briefly attended the United States Military Academy at West Point), left Georgia for the action in Texas. The historical marker at the BPOE building on Second Avenue identifies that Fannin was a member of the local Elks lodge before he became a mercenary, adventurer, and corpse. Fannin County in North Georgia was created from Gilmer and Union counties in 1854 and named for the massacred hero. Painting by Samuel F. B. Morse; courtesy of the Dallas Historical Society collection

A father and son combination had a profound influence upon Methodism in Georgia and both served at one time or the other as pastor of St. Luke, the community's oldest congregation. Dr. Lovick Pierce, seated, was called the "Nestor of Southern Methodism," Nestor being, according to Greek legend, the oldest and wisest of the Greeks in the Trojan War. After serving as an army chaplain in the War of 1812, Pierce graduated from the University of Pennsylvania and set up practice as a physician in Greene County, Georgia. However, he returned to the regular ministry in 1823 and became the foremost preacher in the state. Born February 3, 1811, son George Foster Pierce won honors on graduation from the University of Georgia in 1829 and within ten years was the most popular pulpit orator of any denomination in Georgia. The first president of Georgia Female College (later Wesleyan College) in Macon, the oldest women's college in the United States, Pierce left the pastorate at St. Luke in 1848 to become president of Emory College. He was elected bishop on the first ballot in his church's General Conference in 1854. According to historian James W. May, "For 30 years, Bishop Pierce gave aggressive and conservative leadership to his denomination." Dr. Lovick Pierce lived to the age of ninety five. Bishop Pierce died at the age of seventy three. Courtesy of Mr. and Mrs. Lovick Pierce Corn

Mistippee

Yoholo-Micco

Although few traces now remain, this area was once an important center of southeast Indian culture. The Creek capital, Coweta Town, to which Gen. James Edward Oglethorpe came in 1739 to sign a treaty with the Creeks, was located in Alabama slightly southwest of the site of Columbus. As the white settlements grew, however, the pressure on Indian tribes to give up their ancestral lands increased. The Treaty of 1832 allowed the Indians to sell their lands in Alabama and go west or stay in Alabama. Some went voluntarily. Despite the promises of the treaty, by 1836 white settlers were determined to move the Indians out. The Indians, unhappy over broken promises, were becoming hostile. The U. S. government took the side of the whites. This led to a tragic episode in our national history as infamous as the "Trail of Tears." The U.S. Army assembled some 1,600 warriors of the tribes of the Creek Confederacy, along with their wives and children, at Fort Mitchell, Alabama, in July 1836. They marched them west along the old Federal Wire Road to Montgomery, where the Creeks were loaded onto steamboats and shipped down the Alabama River to New Orleans, then up the Mississippi River to their desolate new home, the Oklahoma Territory. The conditions of the journey were brutal, and many of them died. In recent years, members of the Yuchi, an important tribe of the Creek Confederacy, have returned periodically to the Columbus Museum of Arts and Sciences, where they have shared their tribal customs and their ancestors' stories of life in this area and of the "Trail of Tears" with local audiences. Pictured here are representatives of some of the tribes that made up the Creek Confederacy. They have adopted elements of European dress and blended them with tribal costume. Courtesy of the McKenney-Hall Portrait Gallery of American Indians

Even to this day, tourists have found that the "best" hotel in town is best only by comparison. James Silk Buckingham, a professional world traveller and writer, found this to be the case when he visited in 1839, stopping at the Oglethorpe House (now the site of the Flowers Building on the northeast corner of 12th Street and First Avenue). Not only finding it impossible to awaken the slaves who supposedly worked the establishment, he observed in his book, The Slave States of America, ... *"but though built not more than four or five years, it (the Hotel) had all the defects of a much older building. The doors of the rooms were many of them shattered, hinges and locks out of repair, windows broken and sashes and blinds out of order without any attempt being made to remedy all this." His bed fell to pieces when he pulled it from the wall, its support having been removed. Photograph from the author's collection*

"...An actor in that glorious struggle which demonstrated that a brave people are capable of self-government." So reads a notice in a November 3, 1841 issue of the Columbus Enquirer *on the death of Samuel Cooper, dead at the age of eighty-seven. The "glorious struggle" referred to is not the War Between the States, but the American Revolution! According to the obituary, Cooper was born in Maryland, fought in many battles, particularly Brandywine, Germantown and Stony Point, and settled in Georgia about fifty-one years later, "where in both peace and war, he has been marked by all who knew him for a staunch, unwavering spirit of independence and honest principle in all his actions." Cooper's headstone is in a private and gravely-overgrown burial ground behind Mike Montarella's grocery store on the northeast corner of Miller and Warm Springs roads. Besides Cooper, other Revolutionary soldiers interred and/or marked in Muscogee County include William Scurlock, Daniel Higdon, Philemon Hodges, Richard Christmas, and William Patrick. Photograph courtesy of the* Columbus Ledger-Enquirer *newspapers*

Named for the newly-inaugurated president, the "Harrison Freshet" in March of 1841 marked the time when the city bridge went a-sailing. There had been days of torrential rain and a rapid rise of the river, a river soon loaded even with whole "trunks of trees with their roots entire." According to Martin's History, one end of the city bridge floated off its pier and dropped down river. "Never was there a more majestic sight than the departure of that notable bridge on its remarkable voyage." The voyage was of an eight-mile length to Woolfolk Plantation, "where it took up new moorings in the center of a large cotton field on which the river had never before been known to encroach." Subsequently, John Godwin received City Council approval to build a new bridge, having it ready for crossing by the 20th of July. Drawing by Kent Wilson, 1985; from the author's collection

Little red brick school houses are as basically American as the Bill of Rights, as fundamental as "In God we Trust" and as admired for their spartan simplicity as Greek Revival is revered for its columned splendor. Such an edifice, now stuccoed and painted white, exists in Columbus and is considered the oldest building in continuous use as a school facility in the state of Georgia: the library of Wynnton Elementary. The structure was built in 1843 by a consortium of John Banks, James Chambers, Van Leonard, A. H. Flewellen and William Wynn who desired their children to be educated. In 1890-91 when the school was the male part of Wynnton College, the school catalogue pointed out that the college afforded "all the advantages of the city, while every temptation is removed. There is not a saloon within a mile and a half of the grounds." Photograph courtesy of the Columbus Ledger-Enquirer newspapers

Fire! This four-letter work struck more fear into the hearts of early Columbus settlers than any other. Houses and businesses were especially vulnerable to such destruction by this means because they were generally built of wood. On March 15, 1842 Columbus suffered its first major conflagration, starting in a frame building on the west side of Broad Street and destroying many businesses, up to $100,000 loss with little insurance. Although there had been a volunteer unit dating from May 21, 1831, it wasn't until 1843 that the Columbus Hook and Ladder Company was organized. The funds for a fire engine, which arrived by steamer, were acquired by public subscription. According to Martin's History, "The company, numbering about 75 members, turned out to receive it and convey it to the engine house. They were in uniform and made a fine appearance. ...At the first fire which occurred after the arrival of the engine, the company turned out promptly, but the scarcity of water prevented the efficient working of the engine." Photograph courtesy of the Columbus Ledger-Enquirer *newspapers*

In the second photo, the inscription on the silver horn reads, "Presented by Vigilent Fire Co. #2 to Henry T. Hall as an acknowledgement of his valuable service to the Fire Department. Columbus, Ga., Dec. 25, 1849." The decades later helmet on the right belonged to the fire station located in the Springer Opera House. Photograph from the author's collection

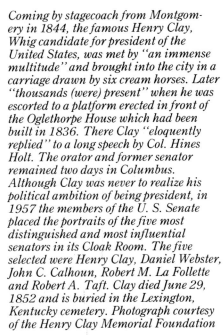

Coming by stagecoach from Montgomery in 1844, the famous Henry Clay, Whig candidate for president of the United States, was met by "an immense multitude" and brought into the city in a carriage drawn by six cream horses. Later "thousands (were) present" when he was escorted to a platform erected in front of the Oglethorpe House which had been built in 1836. There Clay "eloquently replied" to a long speech by Col. Hines Holt. The orator and former senator remained two days in Columbus. Although Clay was never to realize his political ambition of being president, in 1957 the members of the U. S. Senate placed the portraits of the five most distinguished and most influential senators in its Cloak Room. The five selected were Henry Clay, Daniel Webster, John C. Calhoun, Robert M. La Follette and Robert A. Taft. Clay died June 29, 1852 and is buried in the Lexington, Kentucky cemetery. Photograph courtesy of the Henry Clay Memorial Foundation

Most youngsters don't commence a trip around the world at age fifteen, but Boston-born Henry T. Hall did just that. He landed in Pensacola, Florida, proceeded to Apalachicola and thence by steamboat to Columbus. By 1843, he had amassed enough money by cotton factoring to have a sidewheeler built in Pittsburgh specifically for the Chattahoochee. As a salute to his native state, Hall dubbed the steamer Lowell, which is unusually prophetic as Columbus eventually was dubbed "the Lowell of the South" when it became a major textile community. With a capacity to load 1,800 bales of cotton and transport fifty passengers, the Lowell carried a crew of forty-three with a weekly payroll of $472. This vessel sank below Fort Gaines two years later, on March 4, 1845, but Hall's ardor for Columbus as a potential shipbuilding center wasn't dampened too seriously, for he began the construction of the Wave in 1856 and the vessel provided service for a number of years. Many Hall descendants live in Columbus today; he was the father of the late Mrs. W. C. Bradley. Photograph courtesy of the Historic Columbus Foundation; from the collection of Judge and Mrs. Henry Hall Hunter, Jr.

In 1846, Columbus again came down with the Mexican fever. Ten years before, many of its male citizenry had gone off to fight for Texas Independence, men such as Fannin and Lamar. This time, it was a declared War with Mexico. Columbus was selected by Governor George Washington Crawford as headquarters for an infantry regiment and he came to review the troops. The governor might well have remembered the 5th of January, 1828, when he had fought a duel with another Augustian, Thomas E. Burnside, across the Chattahoochee at Fort Mitchell. Crawford had a distinguished career, being elected to the state legislature, to Congress, twice to the governorship, to the position of Secretary of War under President Zachary Taylor (the hero of the Battle of Buena Vista where, against heavy odds, his troops defeated those under Santa Anna) and president of the Georgia Secession Convention in 1861.
Photograph courtesy of the Columbus Ledger-Enquirer newspapers

In 1950, City Manager J. A. Willman and Mrs. Burrel Cole unveiled a marker erected by the Columbus Town Committee of the National Society of the Colonial Dames of America in the State of Georgia of the "route of the first telegraph wire connecting North and South (which) entered Columbus, Ga. near here (on Victory Drive), July 1848." The Morse Telegraph Line ran from Washington, D. C., to New Orleans, a distance of 1,716 miles, the longest in the world at that date. A Columbus man, Daniel Griffin, was president of the southern branch of the line and later president of the company. A local legend holds that the celebrated inventor Samuel F. B. Morse, then an itinerant painter, visited Griffin and they rowed across the Chattahoochee to see Griffin's friend, Stephen M. Ingersoll, who was using a signals system on a plantation telegraph line to communicate by wire with his overseer and field hands. Griffin resigned from the presidency when his friend Ingersoll received no recognition for the code system, recognition that went to Morse instead. Photograph courtesy of the Columbus LedgerEnquirer newspapers

When James Knox Polk, the first "dark horse" or little-known presidential candidate, was elected president in 1844, the houses of local Democrats were illuminated "and (there were) other demonstrations of Delight," according to Martin's History. So, it is not surprising that when the ex-president visited here on March 15, 1849, he was brought into the city in a carriage drawn by four horses while his family followed in another carriage, also drawn by four horses. The Oglethorpe House was the site of a large dinner in his honor, with many speeches and toasts, while Mrs. Polk and her nieces supped in council chamber with ladies of the city. The first president not to seek re-election, Polk died of cholera three months to the day after his visit to Columbus. Photograph courtesy of the National Infantry Museum

New York born William H. Young came to Georgia in 1824 when he was seventeen years old. Twenty-seven years later, after Young had lost and made a fortune or two, he established the Eagle Manufacturing Company, commencing to realize what he had foreseen as a young man, that Columbus was destined to be a textile manufacturing site because of its immense water power. In 1860, the Eagle purchased the Howard Manufacturing Company, which had been established in 1847. Over two million dollars in gold and silver coin were deposited in the Bank of Columbus during the War Between the States (the bank of which Young also was president) by order of the Secretary of the Confederate Treasury, C. G. Memminger. After the war, with Young as treasurer and his brother-in-law R. M. Gunby as president, the company was reorganized with a name typifying its rebirth, the Eagle and Phoenix Manufacturing Company. When Young became president in 1883, the mill had some two thousand operatives. Pictured here is Young's home, Beallwood, located on the Hamilton Road in north Columbus, which burned in 1896, three years after the death of its owner. Photograph courtesy of the Columbus Ledger-Enquirer *newspapers*

"With the hospitalities of the city." Thus does Martin's History of Columbus refer to the "cordial reception" received by Millard Fillmore, thirteenth president of the United States (1850-1853), when he visited here with his former Secretary of the Navy, John P. Kennedy, in April of 1854. According to Martin, the bill of expense for the entertainments for Fillmore and Kennedy came to $1,007.10 with city council paying $728.10 and the balance "by the sale of tickets to a soiree." Photograph courtesy of the National Infantry Museum

On a cold February night, the 25th of the month, in 1856, one of the greatest writers of his generation (only Charles Dickens was really any competition) gave a lecture in Columbus. William Makepeace Thackeray verbally drew a sardonic portrait of one of England's four Hanoverian kings named George. The gathering was in Temperance Hall, whose cornerstone had been laid on December 22, 1849, and which for many years was the civic, social and cultural center of the life of the community. Located on the west side of First Avenue between Twelfth and Thirteenth Streets, Temperance Hall served as the first school for Negroes when, seven years after the War Between the States, the city began providing public education for black children. Novelist Thackeray was on his second tour of America and provided Columbus with its most urbane evening until an Irish lecturer and playwright, Oscar Wilde, came on a visit in 1882. Thackeray's "take" for his week of lecturing in Savannah, Macon and Columbus came to only five hundred dollars, but these were "real" dollars as compared to the dollars of the 1980s. Photograph courtesy of the Columbus Ledger-Enquirer newspapers

In the years 1850-1856, Frederick Law Olmsted (1822-1903) travelled extensively in Europe and in the United States, observing methods of agriculture and landscape gardening. Visiting Columbus, he found the local stagehouse to have bad food, stupid inattentive waiters and the inn to be extremely dirty. Better did he find the "courtesy to strangers," and "the real hospitality of disposition of the people of near Columbus." America's greatest city park, Central Park in New York City, is the work of Olmsted, along with Calvin Vaux, and more than eighty public parks throughout the Unted States. A specialist in natural landscape resources in the construction of urban parks and recreational grounds, Olmsted's other major achievements include the U. S. Capitol grounds, San Francisco's Golden Gate Park and the landscaping for the World's Columbian Exposition in Chicago in 1890-93. Drawing by Peter R. Cranton, 1985; from the author's collection

Beneath Linwood Cemetery's tallest obelisk-statue, marked "in memory of our brother and Uncle Charles," lies a naturalized citizen. Charles Burrus had been born in Marlenheim in the Alsace region (sometimes a part of France and sometimes a part of Germany) in May of 1825. An excerpt from the document making his U. S. citizenship official reads: "And the said Charles Burrus having thereupon produced the Court such evidence, made such declaration and renunciation; and taken such oaths as are by the said Acts required: Thereupon, It was ordered by the said Court, that the said Charles Burrus be admitted, and he was accordingly admitted by the Court, a CITIZEN OF THE UNITED STATES OF AMERICA. In Testimony Whereof, I have hereunto set my hand, and affixed the Seal of the said Court, this 17th day of November in the Eighty-first year of the Independence of the United States [1857]. EDMUND H. WORRILL, Judge S.C.C.C." Burrus died on October 26, 1878 and is buried in the Springer Family lot. Photograph from the Frank D. Foley Jr., collection

Religion, especially in the form of revivals, were exceedingly popular in 1858, with all the local churches having revivals at the same time. The result? Some five hundred "heathens" converting to one denomination or the other. Not to be outdone, the Jewish community of some twenty families in 1859 consecrated a temporary place of worship at Fourth Avenue and Tenth Street, building a brick Temple Israel there in 1886. Among the worshippers during the War Between the States was the family of Lazarus Straus, a Bavarian who came to this country in 1852 and settled in Talbotton in 1854. In 1862, he moved his family and mercantile business to Columbus. For three years, they remained in Columbus before moving to New York, where sons Isidor, Oscar and Nathan made the family name nationally famous as the chief brains and money behind the phenomenal growth of the R. H. Macy Company among the other distinctions they held as bankers and diplomats. The final line of the marker reads, "The Straus family is honored, not for its wealth, but for its outstanding contribution to the American way of life." Photograph courtesy of the Columbus Ledger-Enquirer *newspapers*

Although they were the second denomination to organize, the First Baptist Church has the oldest religious structure in the city. In the original plan of the town, lots were set aside for future congregations. In 1830, the Baptists built a wooden structure for $800. Ten years later, they erected a second sanctuary, this time of brick and costing $18,000. The third church, pictured here, was built in 1859, again of brick. Although the building was essentially Greek Revival, it had a Gothic steeple. In 1896, after renovations, this steeple was removed. In 1909, the front of the building was once again remodeled, resulting in the Doric-columned portico that today fronts Twelfth Street. Various families in the congregation contributed to the erection of the six granite columns. First Baptist's second house of worship became the First African Baptist Church and was served by white preachers until 1862 when the Rev. Henry Watson became the church's first black pastor. Today, the city's first congregation (Saint Luke United Methodist) and the First Baptist share an entire city square in downtown Columbus. Photograph courtesy of the Columbus Ledger-Enquirer *newspapers*

With a population of 9,621, Columbus received its first city directory in 1859-60. It was printed and bound locally by the firm of Thomas Gilbert and Company. The city had only one bank but there were fourteen barrooms. There were forty-five grocers, the largest retail group, but not far behind were thirty-two lawyers. There were three photographers, two bookstores, five druggists, four cotton factories, two flour mills, two gunsmiths and one hairdresser. A further survey reveals that Columbus had three daily newspapers, eleven churches and five Masonic Lodges. There were three slave depots, four tinsmiths, five watchmakers, four hotels, three ice dealers, two iron works and three music stores. Only one ornamental plasterer was listed. There also was one cigar manufactory, nine confectioners, one crockery dealer and twenty-six dry-goods houses. There were fifteen physicians, five restaurants and two marble works, one of which was this one located on Broadway across from the Pease home. This handsome residence was torn down in the early 1940s. Photograph courtesy of Herb Cawthorne, Camera One

An idealized landscape quite worthy of many a romantic painter would be this view of Columbus. Obviously, the couple with child has strolled up one of the hills on the west side of the Chattahoochee River, probably above where now is the Girard Cemetery. If the drawing were reversed, the trio would be on Ingersoll Hill and the husband would be pointing up river toward the old Clapp's factory. Photograph from the author's collection

Song of the Chattahoochee

I

Out of the hills of Habersham,
Down the valleys of Hall
I hurry amain to reach the plain,
Run the rapid and leap the fall,
Split at the rock and together again,
Accept my bed, or narrow or wide,
And flee from folly on every side
With a lover's pain to attain the plain
Far from the hills of Habersham,
Far from the valleys of Hall.

II

All down the hills of Habersham,
All through the valleys of Hall,
The rushes cried Abide, abide,
The willful waterweeds held me thrall,
The laving laurel turned my tide,
The ferns and fondling grass said Stay,
The dewberry dipped for to work delay,
And the little reeds sighed Abide, abide,
Here in the hills of Habersham,
Here in the valleys of Hall.

III

High o'er the hills of Habersham,
Veiling the valleys of Hall,
The hickory told me manifold
Fair tales of shade, the poplar tall
Wrought me her shadowy self to hold,
The chestnut, the oak, the walnut, the pine,
Overleaning, with flickering meaning and sign,
Said, Pass not, so cold, these manifold
Deep shades of the hills of Habersham,
These glades in the valleys of Hall.

IV

And oft in the hills of Habersham,
And oft in the valleys of Hall,
The white quartz shone, and the smooth brookstone
Did bar me of passage with friendly brawl,
And many a luminous jewel lone
—Crystals clear or a-cloud with mist,
Ruby, garnet, and amethyst—
Made lures with the lights of streaming stone
In the clefts of the hills of Habersham,
In the beds of the valleys of Hall.

V

But oh, not the hills of Habersham,
And oh, not the valleys of Hall
Avail: I am fain to water the plain.
Downward the voices of Duty call—
Downward, to toil and be mixed with the main,
The dry fields burn, and the mills are to turn,
And a myriad flowers mortally yearn,
And the lordly main from beyond the plain
Calls o'er the hills of Habersham,
Calls through the valleys of Hall.

—Sidney Lanier

Not counting a log cabin in which some strolling players were accomodated during Columbus's founding days, the Springer Opera House was the sixth theater in which live performances were given: the Sol Smith (where the Indians went on a rampage); the Crawford Street (Tenth Street, between Broad and First), which burned in 1853 after a life of sixteen years; the Lyceum, built in 1840 on the southwest corner of Broad and Thirteenth; and, within a few years, the Concert Hall, directly across Broad on the southeast corner of Thirteenth. On December 22, 1849, the cornerstone was laid to Temperance Hall that was to serve the city for many years and in many ways. It was at Temperance Hall on October 13, 1860 that the manager of Canning Dramatic Company accidentally shot one of his actors, an actor who eventually became more celebrated (or damned) for his actions in a box at Ford's Theater in Washington than for any of his performances on that stage: John Wilkes Booth. Actually Temperance Hall operated throughout the War Between the States, with a steady stream of concerts (professional and amateur), plays, etc., serving the double purpose of providing entertainment and war fund benefits. Photograph from Harper's Pictorial History of the Civil War

This overview of Columbus was drawn from the Alabama side of the Chattahoochee River and shows the city in the early 1860s. In the right foreground is one of Horace King's covered bridges spanning the river; there was also another "good" bridge that would permit Columbusites to travel back and forth between the two states; and there were two railroad bridges. Three railroads terminated here and two others were considering making the city the "end of the line." The artist chose not to include in his sketch several of the largest buildings of "public importance" in the city. Among them, the court house (considered one of the best of its class in the state), the "extensive" factories and the Perry House, which was "one of the largest and most commodious Hotels in the interior of the whole country." Citizens of the time enjoyed an active social life, with nine churches (some known even then for their architectural beauty), a Masonic Hall, an Odd Fellow's Hall, and the Sons of Malta or Temperance Hall. There were five fire companies, three military companies, four weekly and three daily newspapers, excellent schools, an orphan asylum, "a stirring musical association" and a Young Men's Christian Association. In addition, they had 151 stores in which to shop! The city was well lighted with gas, and the river, within two miles, had a fall of 132 feet with water power sufficient to supply forty thousand buildings; "works to supply the excellent waters of the Chattahoochee" within the city limits "were about to be started." Three steamboats were built in Columbus with the capacity to carry fifteen hundred bales of cotton, and they ran the river from the Gulf of Mexico to Columbus from five to eight months during the year. The soil of Columbus was described as "sandy and overlies the cretaceous formation, though the bed of the river from here many miles up is of primary rock." The population was 7,316, "of these, 2,341 were negroes." Photograph courtesy of the Columbus Ledger-Enquirer newspapers

HARPER'S WEEKLY.
A JOURNAL OF CIVILIZATION.

Vol. V.—No. 259.] NEW YORK, SATURDAY, DECEMBER 14, 1861. [SINGLE COPIES SIX CENTS.
$2 50 PER YEAR IN ADVANCE.

Entered according to Act of Congress, in the Year 1861, by Harper & Brothers, in the Clerk's Office of the District Court for the Southern District of New York.

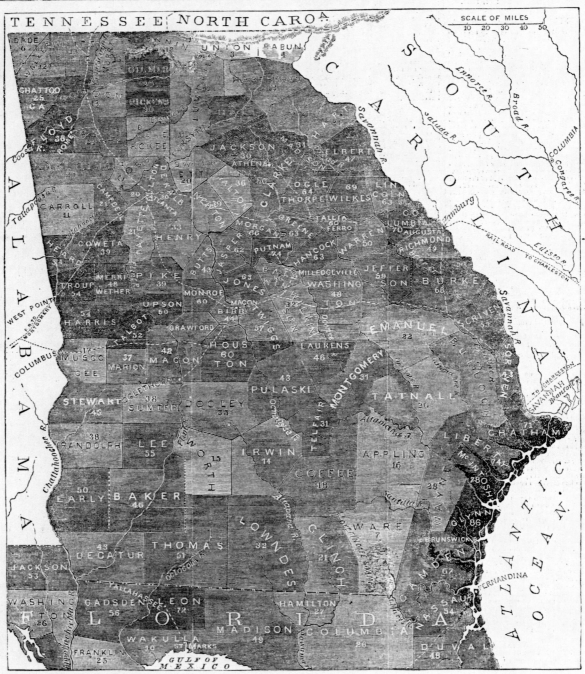

A CHART MAP OF GEORGIA, SHOWING THE PERCENTAGE OF SLAVES IN EACH COUNTY.—[SEE NEXT PAGE.]

Chapter III
1861-1870
The Rebellion and Reconstruction

At certain times in history, particular issues have become burning ones. Such was the case regarding slavery when Harper's Weekly: A Journal of Civilization *published a map of Georgia, showing the percentage of Negro slaves in each county. Created by the state legislature in an act of December 11, 1826 from the Creek Cessions of January 24 and March 31, 1826, Muscogee County is shown on the map as having a 17 percent slave population, indicating more of an industrial population than an agricultural one. On the other hand, the coastal counties of Glynn, Camden, McIntosh, Liberty and Chatham had the highest percentage, as high as 86 percent for Glynn. The north Georgia counties of Rabun, Union, Fannin, Murray, Whitfield and Dade had the smallest slave population, as low as one percent in Rabun. Muscogee's neighboring counties south along the Chattahoochee, such as Stewart, Randolph, Early and Decatur, were all in the middle range: 38 percent for Randolph and up to 50 percent for Early. Counties containing the fall-line cities of Macon in Bibb and Augusta in Richmond had percentages of 44 and 49 respectively. Note the subscription price of* Harper's Weekly *was $2.50 per year in advance, or six cents per copy. Map from* Harper's Weekly *(December 1861)*

Cities apparently are like people: they both seem to reach maturity after age twenty-one. In fact Columbus was all of thirty-three years old when she was forced to accept responsibilities linked with a conflict later to be known as the War Between the States.

Its steady growth in population, its industrial development, its water power and its basic isolation were the four major factors that contributed to the important role that Columbus was to play in the next four years, the war years. The city performed its role so well that its pet villain, Union Gen. James H. Wilson, writing in his autobiography, *Under the Old Flag*, identified Columbus as "the last great manufacturing place and storehouse of the Confederacy."

In Act One, Columbus donated her sons to the Southern Cause and converted her industries to the manufacturing of the instruments of war. A map, drawn by George Burrus in 1928, located nearly eighty industrial sites actively engaged in some manner of supporting the Confederate war effort. According to Col. I. W. Avery, a Confederate cavalryman and historian, "Every Georgian will take pride in the fact that the city of Columbus, Georgia, furnished more manufactured articles of every kind to the Confederate Quartermaster's department than any place in the Confederacy, except Richmond, which had all the protection and fostering care of the government. This superiority was not relative according to population, but absolute, producing more clothing, shoes, hats, cooking utensils, axes, spades, harness and other goods."

Act Two saw the gathering cloud of doom that forecast the death of the Confederacy as the deceased and injured list grew longer and longer. And Act Three found the enemy not only on the family doorstep but also occupying the loveseat in the parlor.

On Easter Sunday, April 16, 1865, Columbus was captured by mounted forces under the command of the aforementioned General Wilson in an engagement that has been described as the "last battle of the war," a war that officially had ended a week before when Robert E. Lee had surrendered to Ulysses S. Grant.

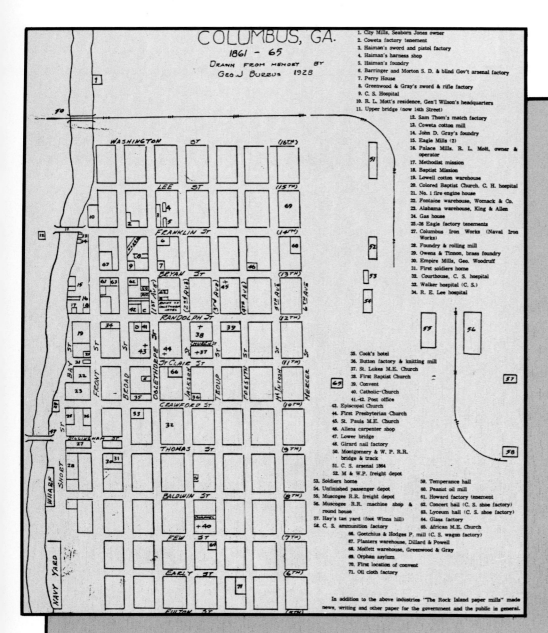

industrial development in the three decades before 1860 enabled it to become one of the major producers of war goods in the Confederacy." Photograph courtesy of the Columbus Ledger-Enquirer newspapers

Columbus, GA. 1861-65 Drawn From Memory. By Geo. J. Burrus 1928

In addition to the above industries "The Rock Island Paper Mills," made news, writing and other paper for the government and the public in general. A- No. 5 Fire Co.—A 2-No. 2 Fire Co.—B. Daily Sun—C. Times & Sentinel—D. Enquirer—E. Fire Co. No. 3.

The Columbus (Clapps) Mfg. Co. 3 miles above the city, made osnaburgs, jeans for uniforms, yarns, cotton batting, leather, shoes, and corn meal.

A Columbusite's Recollections Reprinted Exactly As He Wrote Them

In a comparison between the North and the South, the former enjoyed overwhelming advantages going into the ill-named Civil War. The North comprised a total of twenty-three states, including the border ones of Maryland, Kentucky and Missouri, and a population of 20,700,000 people. In contrast, the South had a population of 5,450,000 free citizens and over-three-and-a-half million Negro slaves. In manufacturing firms, the North had a superiority of ten to one, a three to one superiority in railroad mileage, a two to one superiority in manpower, a thirty to one superiority in arms production and an incontestable supremacy in finance and commerce. The agricultural South's only claims were a boast of superior officers, men more accustomed to outdoor life, the sterling goals of fighting for home and freedom and a grim determination to maintain announced independence to the last—plus the fatal delusion that European textile markets were totally dependent on Southern cotton. In a quote from Columbus, Georgia in the Confederacy by Diffie W. Standard, the celebrated landscape architect Frederick Law Olmsted termed Columbus "the largest manufacturing town south of Richmond." The accompanying map, drawn from memory by George J. Burrus in 1928, locates nearly eighty industrial sites actively engaged in some manner of supporting the Confederate War effort. Columbus possessed the essential characteristics for war industry, a substantial body of available labor, water power and a spirit of enterprise which encouraged new industry, Standard said, adding "The advance that Columbus had made toward

Columbus as it was during the war 1861-65

In this story I will give the recollections of a boy of the various manufacturing interests as they were at that time. Everybody was engaged in recruiting the army for the defense of the South and it was largely done by the soul-stirring music of the drums and fife. Consequently, they were in demand, and as the supply was limited and no more to be had from the North, we had to look elsewhere for them. At that time there was a music store conducted by Brands & Koner, situated near the site of J. A. Kirven Co. They commenced the manufacture of drums and fifes and supplied as many as needed. Matches was a needed article also. Mr. Sam Horn at the Alabama end of the 14th Street bridge established a plant for the manufacture of matches. The Cavela factory at the Ga. end of the bridge where Muscogee Mill No. 1 now stands made white goods, yarns, etc. Next below stood a large six-story building, called the Carter factory, it was never used for any purpose that I can recall until, John D. Gray & Co. established an iron foundry about the year 1862 for the making of castings, syrup kettles, etc. The Eagle Manufacturing Co., with two mills, occupied a part of the present plant, of the Eagle & Phoenix Co. They manufactured cotton cloth and wool jeans, the latter was mostly used for uniforms for the army. The Palace Mills stood near where Mill No. 3 now stands. Where corn meal and some flour was ground for army and home consumption. Greenwood and Gray occupied the warehouse (now occupied by Sol Loeb Co.) for the storage and sale of cotton and contained 7000 bales when it was burned in 1864 by an incendiary who was subsequently mortally wounded in a fight with a R. R. engineer named Thomas Campbell, and before he died confessed to burning the warehouse, post office and the buildings from White's Book Store to the store now occupied by the "Ladies Habadasher." And the night he died was to bring the Eldorado Saloon now occupied by the "Newark Shoe Co." and J. F. Scarbrough. The Lowel warehouse occupied present site. With the yard shedded contained 15,000 bales of cotton. Foutaine warehouse now the upper part of the W. C. Bradley Co. warehouse, was occupied by Warwick & Co. and contained 7000 bales of cotton. Adjoining on the south was the "Alabama Warehouse" King and Allen properties with 20,000 bales. The Naval Iron Works (now Columbus Iron Works) Maj. Warner in charge. Manufactured various articles for the Navy, including cannons. Here the breech loading cannons, which now lies in the basement of the Court House, was made. And said to be the first attempt in the South. It proved to be a failure. Just across the street where the planning mill of the "Columbus Iron Works" now stands, was the rolling mills and a large machine shop. The rolling mill was visited every night by a good crowd as it was a novelty and interesting sight to see the men putting the red hot scraps through the rollers and making bans of iron to be manufactured in various needed articles. In Girard at Lloyds Corner, was the nail factory, where nails were cut from bans of iron, turned out at the rolling mill, "The Empire Mills," Geo. W. Woodruff, proprietor corner Front and 9th streets was busy day and night grinding corn for the army and home consumption. Down on the Commons below 5th St. and near the river, was a small brass foundry owned and operated by Owens and Tinnon. An oil cloth factory owned by Brans & Koner was situated on the corner of 3rd Ave. and 4th St. Their product was largely used to make army equipment. Such as belts, cartridge boxes, etc. A glass factory was built at the corner of 7th St. and 2nd Ave. but proved a failure. The ammunition factory or Arsenal was situated near the Macon division of the Central R. R., and 10th Ave. where the Columbus R. R. crosses the Southern R. R. Hay's Tan Yard at the foot of Wynnes hill. The Confederate wagon shops occupied the present site of the YMCA building and grounds, Capt. Johnson, Supt. At the old Presbyterian Church, where now stands the 10th St. School was a knitting mill and button factory. Peanut oil mill on 1st Ave. north of Murrah building. Shoe manufacturing plants on both SE and SW corners of Broad St., about 500 or more men were employed here mostly negroes. Mr. Tibbetts a cripple was the Supt. Wooden soled shoes as well as leather was turned out here for the army. Government shops occupied corner of 1st Ave. and 14th St. (south side). Here was situated a planning mill and shop for the manufacture of ammunition cases. Blacksmith shop for various forging and a large foundry for various castings including cannons.

Just across the street (north) was the celebrated Haiman Bros. plant where sabres, bayonets, pistols and accoutrements were manufactured, also harness. They occupied from the center of the block running north and south from 14th St. to the present site of the "Southern Overall Co." On the southern part of the site of the Ga. Mfg. Co. stood the shops of Greenwood & Gray where sabres and Mississippi Rifles were manufactured under the supervision of J. P. Murray for many years a noted gun smith of this city. The grindstone question was a serious one with the Haimans in the early part of the '63. Grindstones was used for grinding and polishing sabres etc. and the stone could not be had as they were a northern product. Some one cried "Uncle." The stone was found in Russell County, Ala. about 2 miles from the city, that answered admirably.

John Keller (brother-in-law of the Haimans) had a lampblack and oil cloth factory on Second Ave. near 23rd St. The new Arsenal buildings were located along the back of the "Montgomery and West-Point R. R." just west of Linwood Cemetery, and was only finished a short time before Gen. Wilson's visit, and all the above mentioned property and were burned by the raiders with a very few exceptions.

The Moffett warehouse occupied the site on 6th Ave. from "Dimon? Grocery Co. to 13th St. Greenwood and Gray, proprietors containing 15,000 bales of cotton. Above the city at that time was the City Mills at the present site which made meal and flour when they had wheat.

Rock Island Paper Mill Co., from which a great deal of paper used by the CS government was made here. It was situated on the Alabama side of the river, a short distance above the Bibb Mills. The Columbus (Clapps) factory was situated on the well known site. They wove cotton and woolen goods and in connection with the same had a grist mill which was noted for the fine quality of corn meal ground there. Also a tan yard and shoe manufactory. They also owned the bridges across the river, as there were two islands at the bridge site, it took three bridges to span the river. A short one in the center and two longer ones on the Alabama and Georgia banks, but there were no piers needed for the bridges. It is hardly necessary all the last mentioned properties were also burned. The Walker Hospital was located at the "Commercial Hotel" site. Lee Hospital at corner of 12th and Broad Sts. (Garrard Building). Another in the Sammis? and Rooney building where the Grand Theater is now located. Bankes Building. East side Broad above 13th St. (3 story building) was also a hospital. The Court House and the negro Baptist Church corner of Front and 11th St.

The Caines Convalescent Camp was situated from 19th St. north to 20th St. and from 2nd Ave. to the branch on the eastern boundry. First soldiers home was on corner of 9th and Broad Sts. on the site where now stands the office of the Empire Mills.

"The Soldiers Wayside Home" stood where station No. 4 of the Fire Dept. now stands. Geo J. Burrus Columbus, Ga Nov. 30th, 1928

On June 27, 1865, the *Enquirer-Sun* carried an account of the battle and the following is a condensed version of that account:

The Confederate troops consisted of two regiments of the Georgia State Line, Waddell's Battery, some of the forces of Generals Buford and Wofford, a small number of Georgia reserves, and the organized company for local defense, besides a number of citizens of Columbus and a few hastily collected reserves from Russell County, Alabama, numbering in all about two thousand. The outer fortifications of the city were abandoned for lack of men to defend so long a line, and the troops were drawn into a line of rifle pits, extending from Dr. Ingersoll's hill to the upper bridge and including the Opelika Railroad and two fortifications near the ends of the trenches in which batteries were placed. The lower, or city bridge, was not encircled within the line, but the planks on the Girard end had been torn up, and every preparation was made to fire the bridge in the event of an attempt by the enemy to force its passage.

The first appearance of the Federal troops was about 2 p.m. when their advance drove in the Confederate pickets on the Hurt's or lower Crawford bridge. At Crawford, the force had divided, advancing upon the city by two roads. The Confederate pickets retreated into the town, closely pursued by the Federals, who were within good rifle range, and firing briskly. Their advance however was checked, largely by the battery on the hill near the upper bridge. A portion of this party made a dash at the lower bridge, but was stopped by the torn flooring. The order to fire the bridge was then given, and it was soon wrapped in flames. In the execution of this order, Capt. C. C. McGehee acted with conspicuous bravery.

From this time till dark, no attack was made by the Federals, though it was evident that they were arriving in considerable numbers, as they showed themselves in small squads on most of the hills commanding a view of the city and of the Confederate line of defense. The Confederate batteries attempted to shell the hills on which these demonstrations were made, but with little success. Almost the entire Federal force seems to have been cavalry, and they had but a few, apparently not more than two or three, pieces of artillery with them.

The night was clear but dark. At almost 8 o'clock the Federals, dismounting their men, made a vigorous charge upon the Confederate line. It was met steadily and repulsed, as was a second attack. Soon, however, it was discovered that some Federals had managed to slip through the thin line of defenders and to gain and hold the Girard end of the upper bridge, actually in the rear of the line of defense. It is supposed that this was done by the use of some of the ravines near the railroad bridge, the invaders afterwards coming down along the bank of the river. This maneuver interfered seriously between the headquarters in the city and the defenders in the trenches. Communications were so interrupted that it became impossible to carry on effective operations at the outer lines, and they were abandoned. A rush for the bridge ensued, and friend and foe, horsemen and footmen, artillery wagons and ambulances were jammed together in its narrow avenue, which was as dark as Egypt. How it was that many were not crushed to death in this tumultuous transit of the river seems incomprehensible.

Brave attempts were made to rally the Confederate troops, but they were hopelessly outnumbered and resistance soon ceased.

A very large quantity of cannon, small arms, ordnance and commissary stores fell into the hands of General Wilson, and were destroyed, and with them the gunboats. He also destroyed fifteen locomotives, two hundred and fifty cars, the railroad and foot bridges, 115,000 bales of cotton, four cotton factories, the paper mills, the navy yard, arsenal and armory and many other buildings. Thus was laid in ruins our prosperous little city.

In his autobiography Wilson wrote, "It will be recalled that up to that time, the Confederate authorities had been burning all the baled cotton within reach of our columns, whether it belonged to the Confederate Government or to the Southern people. It was the only product of the South that would sell for gold, and it was at that time worth over a dollar a pound, for the simple reason that it was required by the entire civilized world, and yet with insensate folly, the Confederates were destroying it as though it were food or military supplies necessary to meet our daily wants. So as they took this view of it, I willingly helped them."

In a paper entitled the "Last Battle of the Civil War," which was presented at the organizing or first meeting of the Columbus Historical Society, held on

If today's symbol of success is being on the cover of Time *magazine, then an appearance on the cover of* Harper's Weekly: A Journal of Civilization *(published in New York City) would have been the mid-nineteenth century equivalent. In all their glory, it was on the cover of the January 5, 1861 issue of* Harper's *that the Georgia delegation in Congress appeared. According to the front page, the ten gentlemen, six with some form of beard or goatee, had been photographed by Mathew Brady (1823-1896), the most famous lens-man of the decade, and then their likenesses converted to a drawing by Winslow Homer (1836-1910), the most famous of the artists who served as correspondents during the War Between the States. (Homer's later fame lay in his watercolors, which reflect a preoccupation with the sea and are among the most powerful and expressive images of late nineteenth century American art.) Two of the delegates, Martin Jenkins Crawford and Alfred Iverson, were from Columbus. Crawford served in the U. S. House from 1855 until he resigned on January 23, 1861—four days after Georgia adopted its secession ordinance and eighteen days after his sketch appeared on the journal's cover. Iverson had represented the Second Congressional District in Washington from 1847 to 1849, been a judge of the Muscogee Superior Court, and as a States-Rights Democrat, had been picked by the Georgia Legislature in 1855 to replace the Whig William Crosby Dawson in the U. S. Senate. Iverson, who could have easily been appointed to the Confederate Cabinet if he had so desired, resigned from the U. S. Senate five days after Crawford and returned to the war-energized Columbus. Crawford was a member of the Confederate Provisional Congress from February 1861 to February 1862, and before that had served on an eight-member committee that helped Thomas R. R. Cobb write the Confederate Constitution. After failing in a peace mission, Crawford organized the Third Georgia Cavalry Regiment and later served on the staff of Maj. Gen. Howell Cobb. Both Iverson and Crawford are buried in Linwood Cemetery. From* Harper's Weekly *(January 1861)*

February 10, 1915, Charles Jewett Swift noted that according to Edward F. Winslow, the Union officer assigned by Wilson to the command of the defeated city, the amount of cotton destroyed at Columbus was 125,000 bales. Giving a valuation to this of a dollar a pound and an average of five hundred pounds to the bale, the value of the whole lot was $62,500,000.

Swift ended his paper, a treatise designed to establish the claim that the Columbus engagement was indeed the last battle of the War Between the States, in this fashion:

"If we are not already a reunited people," he wrote:

"The time will come when the Civil War must take its place as a vestige of the law of the inevitable; be regarded as the means of a permanent unity of peace and concord; and that its travails were the foreordained price of our greatest national destiny; and for the home-coming to be lastingly sweet. In these views, the appointed area in Columbus will stand apart as decisively historic ground. The battles and sieges towards its attainment were of such magnitude and greatness of purpose that beside them the arms and men of which Virgil sung are pigmies in the balance, and insofar as they are exceeding, they will be for the story of a greater epic than The Siege of Troy.

Swift may not have been totally objective in his evaluation of the April 16, 1865, event, but his historical broadside did contain this summation of the reconstruction that followed the devastation of the city. He wrote, "But, withal, Columbus has emerged from the desolation in which she was left, and like Job, from her vestment of sackcloth and from her heaps of ashes, has soared on electrified luminous wings phoenix-like to Jove."

The city's factories were to respond to the absence of hostilities in a most healthy fashion. The conversion from a peacetime economy to a wartime one had been accomplished with a singleness of patriotic purpose. Equally compelling was the need to convert from the wartime economy tack to a peacetime economy with a resoluteness born of the desire to survive.

This faith in the future would be born out by two non-natives to Columbus: former New Yorker W. H. Young, who undertook the rebuilding of his textile factory by adding a new mill in 1866, and by a European named F. J. Springer, who undertook the building and opening of an opera house by 1871. Both constructions, one dedicated to business and the other to the arts, were towering testimonials to the expected phoenix of the city!

The provisional government at Montgomery had been in power but a few days when it appointed a former Columbusite, John Forsyth, Jr., of Alabama, Martin J. Crawford of Columbus and A. B. Roran, ex-governor of Louisiana, as commissioners to the government in Washington for the purpose of opening negotiations upon all questions growing out of the present revolutionary movement. Son of the governor of Georgia who had been present at the birth of the city of Columbus, Forsyth had been a founding member of Trinity Episcopal Church in 1835, local postmaster from 1845 to 1849, first lieutenant of the Columbus Guards in the Mexican War of 1846 and president of the first Gas Light Company of Columbus in 1852. Forsyth was living in Mobile and was editor of the Mobile Register *when he was appointed to the peace commission. The Confederates presented their credentials to William H. Seward, who had expected to be president but had had to accept the position of secretary of state instead. Seward required them to cool their heels for nearly a month and ultimately refused to grant them an audience with Lincoln. He further refused to recognize the government under which the Southerners acted, wouldn't admit the right to establish it, and told them that they and all their constituents were then, as they had been before, still citizens of the United States. They replied that it was now their "melancholy duty to return home and tell their government and their countrymen that their earnest and ceaseless efforts on behalf of peace had been futile and that the government of the United States meant to subjugate them by force of arms." The date of the final communication between Seward and the commissioners was April 10, 1861. The firing upon Fort Sumter in Charleston harbor commenced two days later. The "force of arms" that was to be known as the War Between the States was underway! From the author's collection*

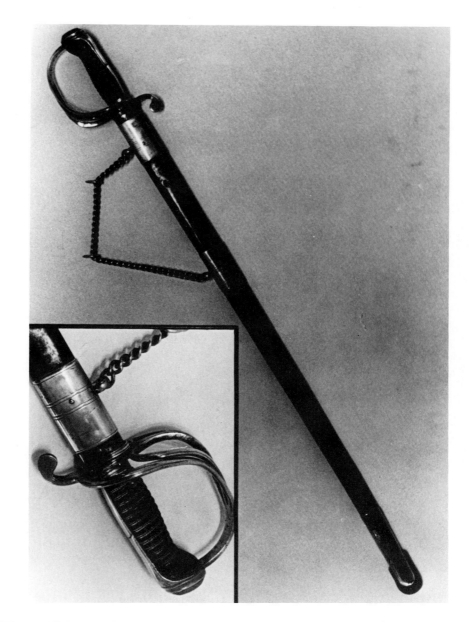

This sword belonged to Maj. James Fleming Waddell of Seale, Alabama, and later of Columbus. His artillery battery was one of the units engaged in the defense of Columbus during the Wilson Raid. The unmarked sword probably was manufactured by the largest sword maker in the Confederacy, Louis Haiman and Bro. of Columbus. One weapons authority has remarked on the scarcity of known Haiman swords by saying that in the future "some swords now termed 'maker unidentified' will be established as the product of this establishment" which by 1863 was credited with producing 250 swords and cutlasses a day. Louis Haiman and brother Elias came to this country from Colma, Prussia, in the early 1800s and opened a small tinshop in Columbus. Loyal to their adopted state, Louis ran the factory during the war, with Elias going to Europe to send materials through the blockade. According to historian W. A. Albaugh III, the first sword made by Haiman was presented to Col. Peyton H. Colquitt, who was afterward killed at Chickamauga. The sword was one of the finest in all the Southern Army, being inlaid in gold. Colquitt was married to Julia Hurt, daughter of Joel Early Hurt of Dinglewood. An advertisment ran in the Columbus Times on November 17, 1861, which read: "Swords! Swords" the Best quality of swords are now made and for sale at the 'Confederate States Sword Factory' Columbus, Ga. by L. Haiman and Bro. who have large contracts for the Confederate Govt. They will furnish officers swords with belt for $25 or for $22 where as many as four are ordered in one lot. Every sword is tested according to rules laid down in the manual of War." Photograph from the author's collection

The former executive officer of the Virginia *during its celebrated battle with the enemy's* Monitor *was Lt. Catesby ap R. Jones, right. In the summer of 1862, Jones was ordered to Columbus to assume command of the gunboat* Chattahoochee *which was nearing completion at Saffold in Early County. Three-masted and schooner-rigged, the* Chattahoochee *had been specially designed for the shallow waters of the Flint, Apalachicola, and Chattahoochee rivers and required a 110 to 120-man crew. Because of damage from a boiler explosion in 1863, the* Chattahoochee *was at Columbus being refitted for action when the Wilson Raid occurred and the crew fired the vessel to prevent its capture. The other prominent officer stationed in Columbus was James H. Warner, bottom, who had been chief engineer of Gosport, Virginia, when hostilities began and was one of the highest ranking chief engineers in the Confederate Navy at its inception. Therefore, he was very valuable in organizing and directing what was termed "the nucleus of ordnance establishment." Warner took over the most important installation in Columbus, the Iron Works, converting it into a naval facility that operated twenty-four hours a day with a total of 400 employees, principally supplying boilers and engines for Confederate warships under construction at Charleston and Savannah. Additionally, it cast cannons and constructed gunboats, such as the* Muscogee. *A third capable Confederate States naval officer was Lt. Augustus McLaughlin, upper right, who served locally as the commander of the C. S. Navy Yard and Station. Photographs courtesy of the James W. Woodruff, Jr., Confederate Naval Museum*

Saint James African Methodist Episcopal Church was organized in 1863. This congregation was originally called "Old Asbury," the name given by worshipers shortly after the Emancipation Proclamation. The present church is built on land granted by act of the Georgia Legislature in 1873. It was erected in 1876 under the pastorate of Rev. Wesley J. Gaines at a cost of $20,000. It is of frame construction with exterior walls of solid masonry and handmade bricks. The graceful central tower and flanking turrets were added in 1886 during the ministry of Rev. L. L. Thomas. The church has been called the finest example of Victorian Gothic Revival in Columbus and Saint James AME ranks as the second oldest church of the denomination in Georgia. Photograph from the author's collection

According to Martin's history, Columbus Council, first in August and again in September, had appropriated the sum of $5,000 to the Columbus Ambulance Corps "for the benefit of exiles from Atlanta after the capture of that city." During this closing period of the war, Columbus became a Confederate hospital center, with facilities for 1,500 beds, occupying eight buildings on Broadway (including two former saloons) and the county courthouse. A prominent physician was Dr. Francis Orray Ticknor, who besides his healing ways had a gift for poetry. He penned the touching poem, "Little Giffen of Tennessee," based upon the actual case of the youngster Isaac Giffen (only sixteen years old) whom Ticknor cared for and later took to his handsome home, Torch Hill, for convalesence. Giffen went back to war and, as the Ticknor family never heard from him again, it is sadly presumed that he died in a subsequent battle. After the war, Ticknor resumed his private practice. Two collections of his poems, both published after his death in 1874, received favorable comment from critics. Photograph from the author's collection

LITTLE GIFFEN OF TENNESSEE

"Out of the focal and foremost fire,
Out of the hospital walls as dire;
Smitten of grape-shot and gangrene,
(Eighteenth battle, and he sixteen!)
Spectre! such as you seldom see,
Little Giffen, of Tennessee.

"'Take him and welcome' the surgeon said;
'Little the doctor can help the dead!'
So we took him; and brought him where
The balm was sweet in the summer air;
And we laid him down on a wholesome bed—
Utter Lazarus, heel to head!

"And we watched the war with bated breath—
Skeleton Boy against skeleton Death.
Months of torture, how many such?
Weary weeks of the stick and crutch;
And still a glint of the steel-blue eye
Told of a spirit that wouldn't die.

"And didn't. Nay, more! in death's despite
The crippled skeleton 'learned to write'.

'Dear Mother,' at first of course; and then
'Dear Captain,' inquiring about the men.
Captain's answer, 'Of eighty-five,
Giffen and I are left alive.'

"Word of gloom from the war, one day;
Johnston pressed at the front, they say.
Little Giffen was up and away,
A tear—his first—as he bade goodbye,
Dimmed the glint of his steel-blue eye.
'I'll write, if spared!'
There was news of the fight;
But none of Giffen. He did not write.

"I sometimes fancy that, were I King
Of the Princely Knights of the Golden Ring,
With the song of the minstrel in mine ear,
And the tender legend that trembles here,
I'd give the best on his bended knee,
The whitest soul of my chivalry,
For 'Little Giffen of Tennessee'."

—Francis Orray Ticknor

Only two years before the start of the War Between the States, the French did it—built the first iron-clad warship, that is. Completed in 1859, the Glorie *had four-and-a-half inch iron plates which were backed by heavy timber. When the Columbus Iron Works improvised its version of the* Glorie, *the resulting Confederate vessel was 225 feet long, fifty-nine feet wide and vested in four-inch iron plates, backed by two feet of wood. Officially named the* Jackson *for Mississippi's capital, the warship was known locally as the* Muscogee. *This rare photo shows the steam-powered ram, designed on the lines of the* Virginia *that fought the Union's* Merrimac *in the first battle between ironclads, after it was "successfully launched...and now sits calmly upon the Chattahoochee as a duck upon a pond."*

The Columbus Enquirer *prophetically had described the* Muscogee *as a sitting duck, and that was exactly how she eventually encountered the Union enemy. The Wilson Raid came out of the west and not up the river which the* Muscogee, *with its four seven-inch and two six-and-one-quarter inch guns, had been designed to defend. Thus, the* Muscogee *never got to fire a shot in its own defense or in that of the city of Columbus. The Union troops set fire to the vessel and the flaming* Muscogee *floated twenty-five miles downstream and sank. Rescued a century later from its watery grave, the burned hulk is on exhibit at the James W. Woodruff Jr. Confederate Naval Museum on Fourth Street (U. S. 280) and the Oglethorpe Bridge. Photograph courtesy of James W. Woodruff, Jr., Confederate Naval Museum*

Shown in a 1930s photograph, the Martin J. Crawford house faced Thirteenth Street between Second and Third avenues and was demolished in 1949, approximately one hundred years after its construction. A local tradition has it that one of the last meetings of the Confederate Cabinet was held at the house, attended by Crawford, who then was head of a cavalry unit; Alexander Stephens, vice-president of the Confederacy; and Gen. Robert Toombs. A former U. S. congressman, Stephens had been a happy Confederate who gradually lost his enthusiasm for the conflict and was among Confederate commissioners who discussed peace with President Lincoln and William H. Seward in February of 1865. Stephens was arrested at his home, Liberty Hall, in Crawfordville and served four months in prison but was never indicted or tried. Stephens was re-elected to congress after Southerners were again permitted to hold such positions and, at the age of seventy, was elected governor of Georgia. However, he died on March 4, 1883, after only four months in office. Also a former U. S. congressman, Toombs (1810-1885) was a wealthy lawyer from Wilkes County who served in several capacities, both political and military, during the War Between the States. Fleeing to Europe after the war, Toombs returned home in 1867, but he was not imprisoned or indicted. He never applied for a pardon and, therefore, was never again able to hold office. Both photographs courtesy of the Columbus Ledger-Enquirer *newspapers*

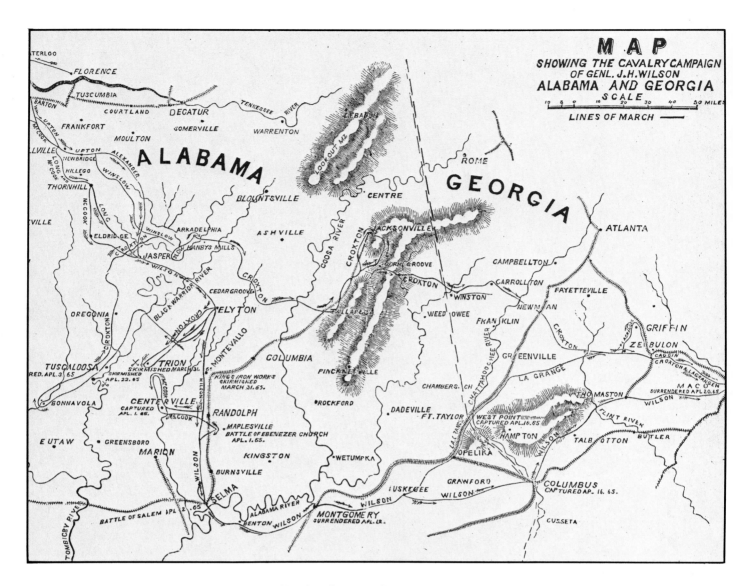

Wilson's Raid can easily be compared to Sherman's famous (or infamous) March to the Sea, which had occurred in November of '64. Wilson's cavalry corps—the largest mounted during the war—began its devastating swath by capturing Selma on April 2nd, Montgomery on April 12th, Columbus on the 16th and Macon and Gen. Howell Cobb on the 20th, ending the Yankee invasion that had begun some five hundred miles away in north Alabama. James P. Jones, professor of history at Florida State University, states in his book, Yankee Blitzkrieg, that, "His Selma Campaign of 1865 was his (Wilson's) most valuable legacy to latter-day practitioners of the art of warfare. On this expedition he demonstrated for the first time that a massive, highly mobile strike force—the forerunner of the mechanized battalions of the twentieth century—would be used to overwhelming effect." Overshadowed by such momentous events as the fall of Richmond, Lee's surrender and Lincoln's assassination, the raid played not only a significant role in the death of the Confederacy but, as a cavalry force acting without accompanying infantry, deserves a place in the history of mounted warfare. Bruce Catton, in This Hallowed Ground, termed the raid as "a true mechanized infantry, in the modern sense, except that their means of locomotion consumed hay and grain rather than gasoline." Drawing from Harper's History of the Great Rebellions (March 1865); from the author's collection

An oft-told end-of-the-war event at Trinity Episcopal Church regards the 6 a.m. Easter service on April 16, 1865, conducted by Stephen Elliott, first Episcopal bishop of Georgia. According to historian Worsley, Elliott had rented what in the twentieth century is called the Yonge-Key-Tyler place in Wynnton and was refugeeing there with his family. The Holy Communion was very solemn, with many of the men in uniform and all of the women in tears. The last battle was about to begin and, for the homefolks, it was to be an unsuccessful one. Senior warden Daniel Griffin assisted Bishop Elliott in hiding the morning collection, which this author remembers his grandmother saying went into "the hollow of a tree." The author also remembers hearing her say that "the money was never found—not that it was worth much, anyway!" Bishop Elliott was one of three founders of the University of the South at Sewanee, Tennessee, in 1857. As senior bishop of the Episcopal Church in the Confederacy, Elliott was instrumental, according to historian Hubert Bond Owens, in "the amicable reunion" of (Episcopal) churches North and South which was consummated soon after hostilities "ceased." He died suddenly at age sixty-one, after having served as bishop of Georgia for more than twenty-five years. Photograph courtesy of Mrs. Robert Carter

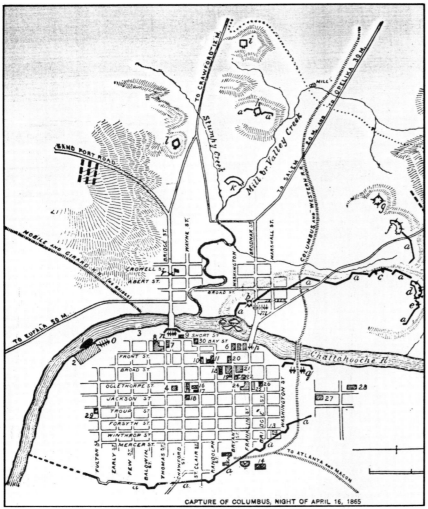

CAPTURE OF COLUMBUS, NIGHT OF APRIL 16, 1865

The boast of Col. Leon von Zinken, the German-born militaryman in command of the major portion of the field troops defending Columbus, was that "If tem tam Yankees come, I make vun hell of tam fuss." Indeed, sound without much fury proved to be an apt description of what has been referred to both as the Last Battle of the Civil War and as the Last Battle of the Civil War East of the Mississippi. This is not meant to be a condemnation of the conduct or fighting ability of the Confederate troops but more of a tribute to what Gen. James H. Wilson describes as "the splendid gallantry and steadiness of General Winslow and all the officers and men engaged in the night attack." Many of the rebels were inexperienced and untested in battle and some were even city defense units. When, through a successful maneuver, Federal troops suddenly appeared at the Girard end of the Fourteenth Street bridge behind the Southern soldiers, it is not surprising that confusion turned to near riot as friend and foe alike stampeded through the dark, unlighted bridge span. According to Wilson, "The rebel force (over 3,000 men)...could not believe that they had been dislodged from their strong fortifications by an attack of 300 men."

59

The man who captured Columbus wasn't the run-of-the-mill soldier. Born near Shawnee Town, Illinois, on September 2, 1837, James Harrison Wilson graduated from West Point in 1860. Five years later, as he led a bruising cavalry raid through Alabama and Georgia, capturing Selma, Montgomery, Columbus and Macon, Wilson was but twenty-eight years old and already held the rank of brevet major general. He had been breveted major for gallant conduct at Fort Pulaski in 1862 and participated in the battles of Antietam and South Mountain. Wilson subsequently acquitted himself with distinction on battlefields at Chattanooga and the Battle of the Wilderness. In September of 1864, he was transferred to the command of the cavalry of the Mississippi Division and was conspicuous at the battles of Franklin and Nashville. Then came the Georgia-Alabama raid, climaxed with the capture of Jefferson Davis. Wilson was appointed lieutenant colonel in the regular army but resigned in 1870 to engage in railroad engineering and management. At the outbreak of the Spanish-American War, he commanded a division in Puerto Rico as a major general. Before retiring in 1910 with the rank of brigadier general, he had commanded troops both in the occupation of Cuba and the American and British troops at the battle of the Eight Temples in China against the Boxers, the secret Chinese Society that attempted in 1900 to drive foreigners out of China and to force native converts to renounce Christianity. In 1902, he represented the United States Army at the coronation of Edward VII. He died in 1925. Drawing from Harpers History of the Great Rebellion *(March 1865); from the author's collection*

Wilson recorded that, "in addition to 125,000 bales of cotton, much of it belonging to the Confederate government, Gen. Edward F. Winslow destroyed 20,000 sacks of corn, fifteen locomotives, 250 freight cars, two bridges over the Chattahoochee River, the machine shops, round houses and railway supplies, one naval armory and shipyard, two rolling mills, with all their machinery, the Confederate arsenal and nitre works, two powder magazines, two iron works, three foundries, ten mills and factories engaged in making cotton cloth, paper, guns, pistols, swords, shoes, wagons and other military supplies and over one hundred thousand rounds of artillery ammunition, together with immense quantities of small arms, military accoutrements and army clothing of which no account could be taken." The drawing shows the rebel munitions being rounded up on the river bank. Wilson's figures regarding the number of bales of cotton, sacks of corn, locomotives and freight cars might be slightly exaggerated but such was the military and economic might of Columbus during the War Between the States. Wilson evaluated, "When it is remembered that these operations gave to us the city of Columbus—the key to Georgia, four hundred miles from our starting-point, and that it was conducted by cavalry, without the inspiration from the great events which had transpired in Virginia—it will not be considered insignificant, although (somewhat) shorn of its importance." The devastation evoked by Federal troops was later criticized but the news that Gen. Robert E. Lee had surrendered to Gen. Ulysses S. Grant at Appomattox Court House on April 9, 1865, had not reached Columbus or Wilson in time to prevent the battle and subsequent demolition from occurring. Photograph courtesy of the Columbus Ledger-Enquirer *newspapers*

"This house never went out of the Union" is a Columbus tradition. When Union Gen. James H. Wilson needed a headquarters after the battle of Columbus, the owner of this dwelling is proported to have said that the Union (and not the Confederate) flag had always flown in his heart. So Wilson accepted the hospitality of Randolph Lawler Mott, whose son John was adjutant on the staff of Gen. Henry L. Benning, giving credence to the claim that many families had members who fought on opposite sides of the war. Believed to have been built in 1844, the three-story plus cupola brick house was originally the residence of Mrs. James S. Calhoun, nee Nancy Howard. Later the residence of Daniel Griffin, president of the Southern Telegraph Line, the house was sold by Griffin to Mott in 1856. Griffin had beautified the grounds, adding a wall along Fourteenth Street with towers at each end. Among the flowers that he probably imported was a camellia (the best known of a genus of ten to eighty species being the camellia japonica of East Asia) that in the twentieth century became known as the "Lindsay Neill." The ornamental shrub (with blossoms that are widely ranging in variety from almost solid red to splashed with white) was named for the textile executive who propagated it while employed at the Muscogee Maufacturing Company. Fieldcrest Mills, the current owners of the property, continues to use the ante-bellum structure as its local administrative office, as had Muscogee. Photograph courtesy of the Columbus Ledger-Enquirer newspapers

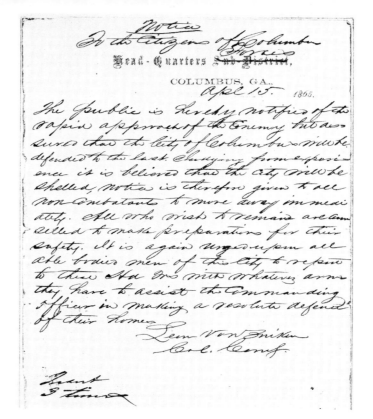

"Notice To the Citizens of Columbus (from) Head-Quarters Forces, COLUMBUS GA, Ap 15, 1865. The public is hereby notified of the rapid approach of the Enemy but [is] assured that the City of Columbus will be defended to the last. Judging from experience it is believed that the city will be shelled [;] notice is therefore given to all non-combatants to move away immediately. All who wish to remain are to make preparations for their safety. It is again urged upon all able bodied men of this city to report to these Hd Qrs with whatever arms they have to assist the Commanding Officer in making a resolute defence of their homes. [signed] Leon von Zinken, Col[onel] [of the] Conf[ederacy]." Photograph courtesy of the Dexter Jordan collection

After the capture of Columbus, word reached General Wilson that Confederate President Jefferson Davis and members of his cabinet were in flight from the last of the capitals of the Confederacy, Danville, Virginia. After Charlotte, North Carolina, Davis abandoned his railroad car and, with an escort of cavalry, took off into the countryside heading in a south, southwesterly direction, probably for Texas or Florida. A Harper's Weekly illustration, "sketched on the spot by an English artist," shows Davis bidding farewell to his escort two days before his capture. Born in Kentucky but raised in Mississippi, Davis had been graduated from West Point in 1828, the year that Columbus was founded, appointed and twice elected senator from Mississippi, served as secretary of war under Democratic President Franklin Pierce and was serving as senator again when his state seceded from the Union. He was captured on May 10, 1865, about a mile north of Irwinsville in south Georgia, ending the official and military history of the Confederacy. Imprisoned in Fort Monroe on a treason charge, Davis was never brought to trial, but he did receive harsh treatment while imprisoned. Noted Civil War historian Bruce Catton judged that "he had done the best he could do in an impossible job, and if it is easy to show where he made grievous mistakes, it is difficult to show that any other man, given the materials available, could have done much better. He had great courage, integrity, tenacity, devotion to his cause and, like the Old Testament Sisera, the stars in their courses marched against him." Photograph courtesy of the Columbus Ledger-Enquirer newspapers; drawing from Harper's Weekly

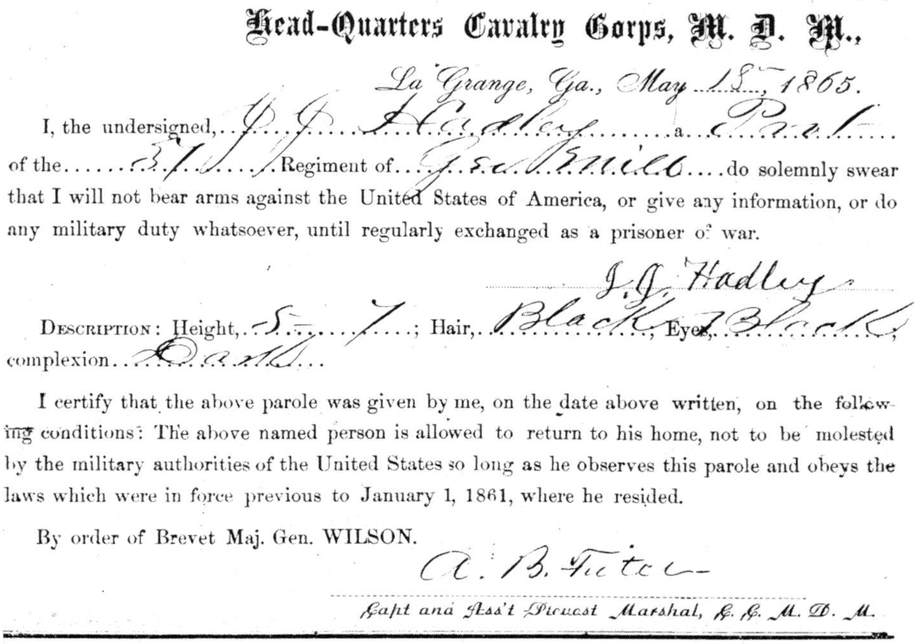

Head-Quarters Cavalry Corps, M. D. M.,

La Grange, Ga., May 18, 1865.

I, the undersigned, *J. J. Hadley*, a *Pvt.* of the *3.1.* Regiment of *Ga. S. C. Mill.* do solemnly swear that I will not bear arms against the United States of America, or give any information, or do any military duty whatsoever, until regularly exchanged as a prisoner of war.

J. J. Hadley

DESCRIPTION: Height, *5 7*; Hair, *Black*, Eyes, *Black*, complexion *Dark*.

I certify that the above parole was given by me, on the date above written, on the following conditions: The above named person is allowed to return to his home, not to be molested by the military authorities of the United States so long as he observes this parole and obeys the laws which were in force previous to January 1, 1861, where he resided.

By order of Brevet Maj. Gen. WILSON.

A. B. Fitch
Capt and Ass't Provost Marshal, C. C. M. D. M.

Former Confederate soldiers were made to sign a pledge not to bear arms against the United States of America. J. J. Hadley was such a former Johnny Reb. Additionally, Hadley, described as being five feet, seven inches tall, having black hair, black eyes, and a dark complexion, had to swear that he would not "give any information, or do any military duty whatsoever, until regularly exchanged as a prisoner of war." In return, Capt. A. B. Fitch agreed that "The above named person is allowed to return to his home, not to be molested by the military authorities of the United States so long as he observes this parole and obeys the laws which were in force previous to January 1, 1861, where he resided." Photograph courtesy of the Columbus Ledger-Enquirer newspapers

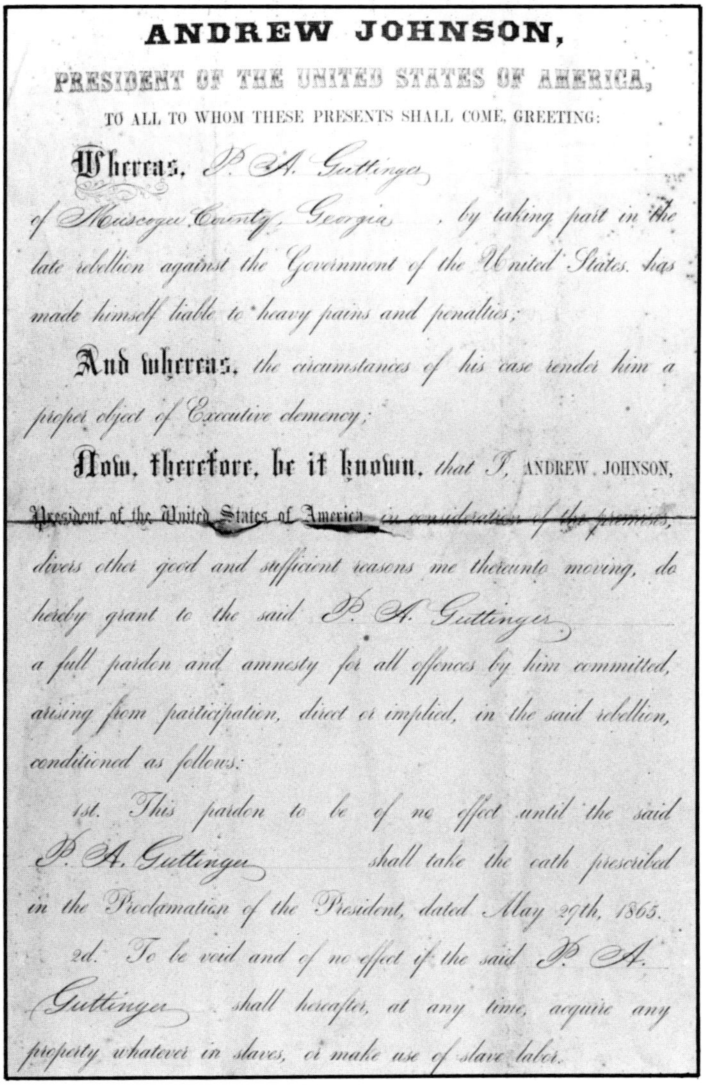

ANDREW JOHNSON,
PRESIDENT OF THE UNITED STATES OF AMERICA,
TO ALL TO WHOM THESE PRESENTS SHALL COME, GREETING:

Whereas, *P. A. Guttinger* of *Muscogee County, Georgia*, by taking part in the late rebellion against the Government of the United States, has made himself liable to heavy pains and penalties;

And whereas, the circumstances of his case render him a proper object of Executive clemency;

Now, therefore, be it known, that I, ANDREW JOHNSON, ~~President of the United States of America in consideration of the premises,~~ divers other good and sufficient reasons me thereunto moving, do hereby grant to the said *P. A. Guttinger* a full pardon and amnesty for all offences by him committed, arising from participation, direct or implied, in the said rebellion, conditioned as follows:

1st. This pardon to be of no effect until the said *P. A. Guttinger* shall take the oath prescribed in the Proclamation of the President, dated May 29th, 1865.

2d. To be void and of no effect if the said *P. A. Guttinger* shall hereafter, at any time, acquire any property whatever in slaves, or make use of slave labor.

In the archives of the Frank D. Foley family is this proclamation of "full pardon and amnesty" for family ancestor P. A. Guttinger from Andrew Johnson, who ascended to the presidency after Lincoln's assassination. Courtesy of the Frank D. Foley Family

The first firm to demonstrate the remarkable recovery that was to be made by the industrial sector of Columbus after the War Between the States was the Eagle and Phenix Manufacturing Company, R. M. Gunby, president, and W. H. Young, treasurer. The Eagle Manufacturing Company, with Young as president, was burned by the troops under General Wilson. This mill Number One, built in 1866, with a new name to indicate rebirth, still stands and is the oldest structure in the complex of buildings stretching from Twelfth and Fifteenth streets along the Chattahoochee, excepting the circa-1840 Mott House which Fieldcrest Mills uses as the administrative headquarters for its local operation. Fieldcrest acquired Muscogee Manufacturing Company from its local owners in 1963 and the Eagle and Phenix Mills from Reeves Brothers in 1978. Photograph courtesy of the Columbus Ledger-Enquirer *newspapers*

"The Ladies Memorial Association, like the Phoenix, rose from the Soldiers' Aid Society which was consumed in the fires that burnt the Confederacy. The parent organization was born under the altar, in the Baptist Church of Columbus, on May 21, 1861, and its object was to perform a woman's part in the service of her country in time of war." So wrote Anna Caroline Benning, in the preface to a history of the origin of Memorial Day. Daughter of the famed Confederate general, Miss Benning was, in 1898, the only surviving founding member of the society. The Ladies Memorial Association was born following a visit by some Columbus ladies who, postbellum, were tending the graves of soldiers who had died while in Columbus hospitals. April 26th was adopted as the date when the most spring flowers in this area bloom. Memorial observances began in 1866, with exercises held at Saint Luke Methodist Church, attorney and Confederate veteran James N. Ramsey delivering the first oration. The decorating of the Confederate graves in Linwood Cemetery has continued to this day. (See related photograph in Chapter VI.) Photograph courtesy of the Columbus Ledger-Enquirer *newspapers*

In October of 1867, 229 pupils, bright-eyed and eager for knowledge, answered the bell that rang in the local public education system. The father of the system was John McIlhenny, an Irish-born Philadelphian who had come to Columbus in 1857 and had stayed for twenty years, during which time he was manager of the local gas plant, joint owner of both an iron foundry and a cotton mill, a director on many boards and mayor of the city for three terms. He donated $1,000 for the purchasing and equipping of a school building. Photograph courtesy of the Columbus Ledger-Enquirer *newspapers*

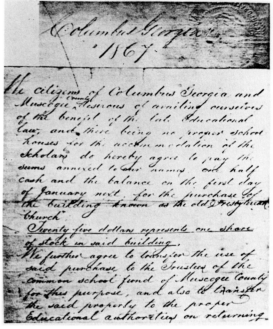

Called "Columbus Male Public School Number One," the first free educational facility was in the former First Presbyterian Church whose congregation had recently occupied their new Romanesque-style edifice on the corner of First Avenue and Eleventh Street. Martin's history of Columbus states that the first Presbyterian Church building was dedicated on October 22, 1831, and was located at Second Avenue and Tenth Street, now the site of Fire Station Number Five, where a larger church with a frame bell tower was built in 1845. This was the structure that became the first white male school building. Photograph courtesy of the Columbus Ledger-Enquirer *newspapers*

"We citizens of Columbus Georgia and Muscogee County desirous of availing ourselves of the benefit of the late Educational law and there being no proper school houses for the accommodation of the scholars do hereby agree to pay the sums annexed to our names, one half cash and the balance on the first day of January next, for the purchase of the building known as the old Presbyterian Church.

... Twenty-five dollars represents one share of stock in said building. We further agree to transfer the use of said purchase to the trustees of the common school fund of Muscogee County for this purpose and also to transfer the said property to the proper educational authority on returning to us the amount paid." A list of contributors followed. The petition is dated at the top, Columbus, Georgia, 1867, and a seal affixed. Photograph courtesy of the Columbus Ledger-Enquirer *newspapers*

The first Columbus Public School Superintendent, a position he was to hold for seventeen years (1867-1884), was George M. Dews. His salary was set at $1,800 and included a house on the school premises. (A quarter of a century later, the salary of the school superintendent was the same, minus a house in which to live.) After his election, Dews asked permission to tour other educational facilities, desiring "as far as possible to make it so that the best public school system of the North [be] now the one operating in Columbus." In a resolution by the school trustees after his death in 1891, Dews was described as one of its wisest, bravest pioneers of educational interests of the South, and as "one of our city's noblest benefactors in that it was he who laid so wisely and well the foundation on which the Public Schools of Columbus now so firmly stand." The Columbus Enquirer-Sun *described him as "a man of modest mien, sterling integrity and generous impulse." He died at Forsyth, Georgia, after several years of ill health spent on his farm on the Savannah River, and is buried in Linwood Cemetery. Photograph courtesy of the* Columbus Ledger-Enquirer *newspapers*

Massachusetts-born, George Parker Swift I wasn't a "carpetbagger" when he organized Muscogee Mills in 1867 on the site of the old Coweta Manufacturing plant, which had been destroyed when Wilson burned the city. A historical marker states that he had been born in Fairhaven Massachusetts, on September 1, 1815, son of a whaling captain, and had moved to Georgia in the early 1830s and started the Triune Mills at Waymanville in Upson County. Swift's mill prospered there but was destroyed during the War Between the States. His descendants have continued in the textile business for four generations. A great, great grandson, George (Sonny) Swift founded Columbus Mills, a carpet firm, in Columbus in 1958. In this 1958 photo, George P. Swift III, a former Muscogee Mills president, and his grandson, George P. Swift V. admire the historical marker to their ancestor. Photograph courtesy of the Columbus Ledger-Enquirer *newspapers*

The Georgia Home Building, known in more recent years of the twentieth century as the "White Bank," has been a local landmark since its construction began in the late 1850s. It was not completed until after the War Between the States. Although its fabricator is unknown, various authorities list it as having been brought up river in sections from both Pittsburgh and from Italy. However, the quality of its design and attractiveness is unquestioned. In 1976, the First National Bank, then owners of the property, received a Certificate of Commendation from the Friends of Cast Iron Architecture for having "maintained this unusual structure and continued it in use, one of the largest iron-fronted buildings in the South and one of the most handsome." Of a prototype available through the celebrated Badger Iron Works of New York, the building was credited by historian Etta Blanchard Worsley as having been designed by Samuel Hatcher of Columbus, and today it is listed on the National Register of Historic Places. Photograph from the author's collection

In the wee small hours of March 31, 1868, five masked men (who may have been attending a masquerade ball at a nearby residence) entered a black brothel across from the Perry House (later the Racine Hotel). There, according to Telfair, they shot to death George W. Ashburn, a "scalawag" or "low class white Southerner" known for "his cruelty to Negroes" who was "successively dismissed by all who employed him." A native of North Carolina, Ashburn, upon moving to Columbus in 1867, became active in the Republic (Radical) party and was elected to represent Muscogee County at the Constitutional Convention in December of that year. All during his stay in Columbus, Ashburn was known (and despised) by the local citizens for taking advantage of the social unrest of the period following the War Between the States. Following the murder, arrests were made, prisoners released, more arrests made, and some four hundred townsfolk posted bond at the Bank of Columbus for those charged. While jailed, the defendants (all prominent local citizens) were subjected to great indignities. Some were even "hot-boxed" at Fort Pulaski near Savannah. Finally, fourteen men faced a military commission that convened at McPherson Barracks in Atlanta on June 29, 1868. The able-but-ailing Alexander Stephens, former vice president of the Confederacy, headed the defense counsel. The trial continued until July 21, 1868, the day that the Georgia Legislature passed the resolution ratifying the Fourteenth Amendment, an action clearing the way for the state to be readmitted to the Union and thus ending the period of military authority. This closed the Ashburn case. The following day, the prisoners returned to Columbus where a large crowd of anxious and indignant, but thankful, citizens greeted them at the depot. Photograph courtesy of the Columbus Ledger-Enquirer *newspapers*

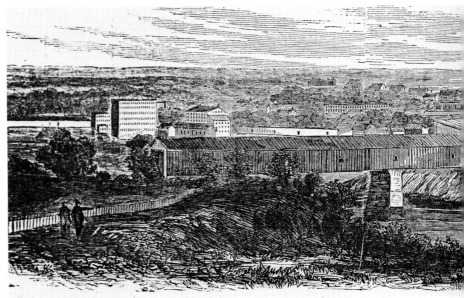

"The noblest work of God, an honest man." This is how Horace King was referred to by one writer evaluating his service of two terms as Russell County Representative in the State Legislature of Alabama after the War Between the States. (When King's name had appeared on the ballot, he had refused to run, but he was elected nevertheless.) A slave who was freed in 1848 by John Godwin of Cheraw, South Carolina, King had come to Columbus with Godwin to build the city's first span across the Chattahoochee. He later rebuilt this Lower Bridge at Dillingham Street after it was destroyed during the Federal raid and he also participated in the 1858 Upper Bridge construction at Fourteenth Street and built two covered bridges at Eufaula. In the Girard Cemetery of Phenix City, he erected an affectionate marker over the grave of Godwin, who had died in 1859. King died in 1887, and he and his wife are believed buried in the Godwin Cemetery plot. This photo of the Dillingham Street Bridge bears the date "Built 1870" but it had been constructed within a year or two after the War Between the States. The covered span lasted until its concrete replacement in 1910. An ad for Chancellor's (mens furnishings) appears over the Alabama portal, so the photo was made post-1880s. Photograph courtesy of the Columbus Ledger-Enquirer newspapers

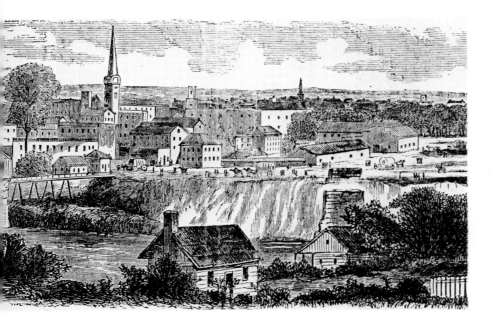

This engraving was made by a staff artist, Theodore R. Davis, for Harper's Weekly and appeared in that publication September 10, 1868, along with the following comment: "Columbus, before the war, was one of the most thriving cities in Georgia. The cotton factories that gave very considerable wealth and importance to that place were nearly all destroyed by General Wilson at the time of his raid. This destruction was the occasion of very great suffering to the operatives. It is situated on the Chattahoochee, and is handsomely and regularly laid out. The population is over 10,000." The two most striking features in the sketch, made from the Alabama side of the river, show that smoke is once more belching from several smokestacks, indicating that industrial recovery had begun, and that the Dillingham Street Bridge, which had burned, had been rebuilt. The tall spire in the center probably belongs to the First Presbyterian Church. From the author's collection

Chapter IV
1871-1900
Industrialization and Growth

The opening on February 21, 1871, of the Springer Opera House represented as solid a faith in the future of the city as any financial commitment to industry.

Francis Joseph Springer had been born in the Alsace and had emigrated to Columbus before the War Between the States. The elegant and sophisticated structure that Springer built was obviously not in a boom period. Springer wisely estimated that a theater would not support itself on box office receipts; therefore, he encircled his opera house with a hotel (as much for revenue as for soundproofing) and also included a saloon, a restaurant and a grocery, each obviously designed to subsidize his affection for the theater.

Columbus was a theater town from its founding days, but the performing arts came into their own with the building of the Springer, a theater to which every great name of the late nineteenth and early twentieth century American theater would flock. Lecturing here in 1882 was the celebrated Oscar Wilde, and he was not the only luminary from the other side of the Atlantic. But Americans dominated the Springer stage. The legendary Edwin Booth played here in 1876 on his first southern tour after the war. He had been reluctant to make the tour because, as he wrote in a letter to the Springer manager, of "the awful act of his brother." Both Edwin and his erratic, brilliant brother, John Wilkes Booth, had visited Columbus in happier days before the war and had been guests of the Moses family at their plantation, Esquiline.

Joseph Jefferson, another famous nineteenth century actor, appeared at the opera house in his great role of *Rip Van Winkle*. James O'Neill, father of the playwright Eugene O'Neill, played the Springer in his famous role as *The Count of Monte Cristo*. Mrs. John Drew, the grandmother of the Barrymore clan, was the first of a long line of that family to grace the stage of the Springer when she starred in *She Stoops to Conquer*.

In addition to drama, the Springer can boast that John L. Sullivan, the boxing champion, gave a boxing

The first among several banks to be organized following the War Between the States was the cast-iron and stained glass Merchants and Mechanics Bank which received its charter in 1871. In 1876, the National Bank of Columbus became operational and was located in the cast-iron Italian Renaissance style building which still stands at the corner of Eleventh Street and Broadway. The First National Bank, as it is known today, consists of many mergers over the years, including the 1953 joining together of the Merchants and Mechanics Bank with First National. Though local banks have had some name changes since the 1870s, there has been a Key family member in the picture since 1916 when James Biggers Key became a vice president at the M & M Bank. He became president in 1919 and served in that capacity until 1939 whereupon his son, Jack Botts Key, became president. After the 1953 joining together of the M & M Bank with First National, Jack B. Key served as president of First National until 1963. His son, James Williams Key, became president of the bank in 1972, serving until 1980 when he was elected chairman of the board, the position he currently holds. Collectively the three Keys have served a total of fifty-two years as president—certainly a local record! Photograph courtesy of the Columbus Ledger-Enquirer *newspapers*

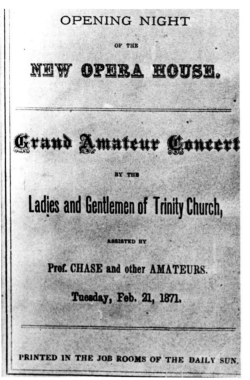

exhibition here in the 1890s. This was also the place that the great political orators came to speak, including the silver-tongued William Jennings Bryan.

But that is not the end of the Springer story. This rather remarkable building will be met again. And again.

Columbusites went to the theater at the Springer, and they also found entertainment at Villa Reich, a new world version of an old world facility. Frederick Reich and his family had emigrated to the United States from Germany, and his place of amusement was designed after the Korsal in Bad Nauheim, a celebrated gambling house. However, the Villa was unlike the Korsal in that it was not a gaming place, more of a place for games: sporting events, picnics on the ground, masquerade balls, roller skating, a dancing school and calisthenics, soirees and amateur plays.

Street lights lit the way to these diversions beginning about 1880. According to Etta Blanchard Worsley in *Columbus on the Chattahoochee*, the streets in Columbus were lighted by gas lamps on tall poles. The policemen lit these lights. By 1883, there were ninety-nine gas lamps on the corners of the streets and

The opening entertainment at the Springer Opera House on February 21, 1871, was a "Grand Amateur Concert By The Ladies and Gentlemen of Trinity [Episcopal] Church." The official opening occurred a week later, when the celebrated Katie Putnam hopped into town in the title role of "Fanchon, the Cricket." One day during her engagement, her brass band was playing outside the theater and frightened Mr. James P. Adams's mule so that it bolted, destroying his wagon. According to the Columbus Enquirer, *Mr. Adams successfully sued ticket seller Mathews for $80. The opera house and hotel complex was built by Francis Joseph Springer who, before the War Between the States, had emigrated to Columbus, with a stop in Cincinnati, Ohio, from his birthplace in the Alsace region of Germany. That such an elegant and beautiful structure was built only six years after "the late unpleasantness" attests to the remarkable economic recovery made by Columbus during the Reconstruction period. Photographs courtesy of the Springer Opera House*

Georgia representatives to Congress were excluded from their seats when, in March of 1869, Georgia failed to adopt the Fifteenth Amendment, forbidding the disfranchisement of a citizen on account of race, color or the fact that he had been a slave. The Federal troops returned and Georgia, still under its carpetbagger governor Rufus B. Bullock, began its second reconstruction. This lasted until July of 1870 when the amendment was rammed through and Georgia once again was a member of the Union. The corrupt regime of Bullock as governor of Georgia came to a close with his flight from the state in October of 1871. At a special balloting in December of that same year, James Milton Smith (pictured here), Twiggs County-born but a Columbus lawyer since 1846, was elected to the high office and commendably guided the state back to law and order. Smith (1824-1890) probably lost his bid for a second term by not commuting the death sentence of a white woman convicted for murder, the only other such hanging sentence since 1806. He said, "Society demands that crimes shall be punished and criminals warned and false humanity that starts and shudders when the axe of justice is ready to strike, is a dangerous element for the peace of society." An officer in the Confederate Army as well as a member of the Confederate Congress, Smith later was judge of the Chattahoochee Circuit Superior Court. Although he was twice married, he died without issue and is buried in Gainesville, Georgia, where he lay in an unmarked grave for thirty years. *Photograph courtesy of the* Columbus Ledger-Enquirer *newspapers*

Originally based in the late 1860s at the southwest corner of Broad and Ninth streets, Franklin L. Lummus moved his plant in 1871 twenty-three miles east to Juniper, Georgia. There the ginning operation remained until 1898 when the firm's product demand outgrew the rail and water power facilities at Juniper, and the company returned to Columbus. From Lummus Cotton Gin Company, the name was changed to Lummus Industries, Inc., today a company which ships its products to over seventy countries. Lummus is the world's largest manufacturer of complete cotton ginning systems and the only independently-owned manufacturer of cotton ginning machinery. *Photograph courtesy of the* Columbus Ledger-Enquirer *newspapers*

an official lamplighter. When this number grew to a total of 127 fixtures in 1887, the lamplighter had a salary of $286.10 a year. However, modern technology in the form of electricity abolished this position as electricity was used exclusively three years later.

Another old-timey job, that of the mounted policeman, died out by the turn of the century. Edmund Wesley Joines was the first mounted police officer, serving on the force from 1876 to 1883. His faithful steed? Minnie.

Nearly three peaceful decades in Columbus brought with it the birth of a number of business institutions that became landmarks of commerce for nearly a century. Names like Kirven's, Rosenberg's, David Rothschild Company, Schomburg's, Chancellor's, Harvey Lumber Company, W. C. Bradley Company, the Southern Railway System, and the Fourth National Bank had their beginnings (with more or less the same names) during this period.

Columbusites played at a newly created park named Wildwood where fishing, swimming, boating on the lake, baseball and dancing in the pavilion were popular activities. One got there on a trolley route called the Dummy Line, and as the moon peeped through the tall pines, one also "pitched a little woo," if one was lucky enough to have an amicable companion.

Columbus expanded its railroad fingers out in all directions, put on a series of street fairs and watched as the Doric columns to the city's second Muscogee County courthouse toppled and the site leveled to make way for the third courthouse, a red brick structure whose dome was to be topped by a blindfolded figure of Justice.

Columbusites also were continuing their romance with war or, to be more accurate, romance with military men.

You cannot somehow or other sink a United States battleship in the harbor of Havana and couple this with accounts in the "yellow press" of Spanish atrocities without arousing the wrath of the American people. So it was that the U. S. sided with Cuban nationalists in their quest for independence and, on April 25, 1898, returned Spain's declaration of war.

This war was over and the peace treaty signed before Christmas of 1898. It brought fame as the leader of the "Rough Riders" to Theodore Roosevelt, provided for Spain's withdrawal from Cuba, and ceded Guam, Puerto Rico and the Philippines to the United States. It also brought a temporary military post to north Columbus, on vacant land between Second Avenue and Hamilton Road, ending just south of Swift Spinning Mills. Camp Conrad's purpose was to serve as a garrisoning post for several thousand troops before their service was needed in either Cuba or Puerto Rico.

Columbus matrons immediately formed the Soldiers' Aid Society and followed this equally fast by a flurry of social activity, as they correctly presumed this was the chief need of the far-from-home soldier.

It was at this point that a paraphrasing of the MacArthurian motto of "Old soldier's never die, they just get called back to duty" could have been applied. Such was the case of one James H. Wilson. That name sounded familiar to the townsfolk of more than thirty-five years of age, for that had been the time lapse since James H. Wilson had been the invading Union general who had devastated the city in 1865. Wilson had been called back into active duty at the age of sixty years and came from Macon on a special train to make an inspection of Camp Conrad. There was no dinner given in his honor but, by historical accounts, he was treated "respectfully."

A native of Hanover, Germany, Carl Frederick Schomburg (right) came to this country at the age of nineteen. He served a year of apprenticeship as watchmaker and jeweler in New York before coming to Columbus where, in 1872, he began what is now Columbus' oldest jewelry store. He was succeeded in the business by his son, Frederick Herman Schomburg, Sr., (left) and by his grandson Frederick Herman Schomburg, Jr. Two great-grandsons, Charles Frederick Powell and Frederick Collins Schomburg are also associated with this 113-year-old business that now has its store on Auburn Avenue. Photograph courtesy of the Columbus Ledger-Enquirer *newspapers*

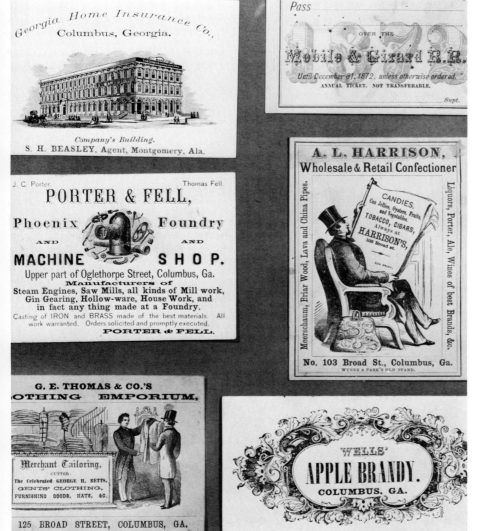

Business cards of a century ago were exceedingly more decorated than they are today and they were larger than those presently in vogue. An English orphan, Thomas Gilbert was taught the printing trade by Thomas De Wolf of Connecticut who founded the Columbus Daily Sun *in 1854. Gilbert later became a partner of De Wolf. Eventually Gilbert established a firm which did quality printing, including Martin's history of the early city, for almost one hundred years. A collection of calling cards, numbering nearly two hundred, by Gilbert shows that restraint in advertising wasn't a characteristic of the merchants in Columbus in 1872. Also, they provide a social and economic window to the past, particularly to the reconstruction past of the city. Photograph courtesy of the* Columbus Ledger-Enquirer *newspapers*

Another family business that remains active in 1985 is the Chancellor Company. Its founder, Alexander C. Chancellor, was not only a bookkeeper in the firm of Thornton and Acee but owned an interest as well. That was in 1873. By 1875, the store was operating under the name of Chancellor and Pearce. In the next decade, it became A. C. Chancellor Company and, in 1931, the Chancellor Company. The business has remained in the same block of Broadway since its establishment and essentially in its original location. Street numbering systems have caused changes in the address, such as listing for a store at 78 and 1108 Broad. The accompanying photo shows the founder, A. C. Chancellor, third from the left, standing in front of the store with a sign that reads 1132-1134. The city directory for the years 1902 to 1912 indicates the company was at that address. Today the men's clothing store is operated by J. Edgar Chancellor, great-grandson of the founder. Photograph courtesy of the Columbus Ledger-Enquirer *newspapers*

The man for whom Fort Benning was named was a Columbus attorney, Henry Lewis Benning. Born April 2, 1814, in Columbia County, Georgia, and married to Mary Howard Jones, daughter of Seaborn Jones who founded Columbus' first industry: City Mills. Benning was a graduate of Franklin College, which became the University of Georgia, and a judge of the Georgia Supreme Court. Entering the service of the Confederacy as a colonel of the Seventh Regiment of the Georgia Infantry, he soon was made a brigadier general, was in a number of the most famous battles that involved the Army of Virginia and was affectionately called "Old Rock" by his troops. After his distinguished military career, Benning returned to his family and his law practice in Columbus where he died July 10, 1875. Photograph courtesy of the Columbus Ledger-Enquirer *newspapers*

Taking its name from the rise where the Indians of the area lit signal fires, Torch Hill was the residence of Francis Orray Ticknor (1822-1874). Ticknor has been described as a country doctor with a large practice who wrote poetry and played the flute to amuse himself and friends. However his war poetry, especially his best-known poem, "Little Giffen," and other martial airs such as "The Virginians of the Valley," "Loyal," "Unknown," and "Our Left," should have won for him a high place in American literature. Photograph from the author's collection

J. Albert Kirven was a $20-a-week clerk in a dry goods store before, with $500 of his own money and $2,500 borrowed from his sister, he purchased a notions and dry goods store that recently had declared bankruptcy. The year was 1876. Two moves and a decade later, Kirven and his brother-partner, Richard, settled into 1136-1138 Broadway, addresses which still serve as the muchly-expanded— nearly seventy thousand square feet— store's Broadway entrance. Descendants of the founder still direct the operations of Columbus' oldest department store. This photo of the founders and employees was taken in 1892. Photograph courtesy of the Columbus Ledger-Enquirer *newspapers*

The renowned impresario of the circus, P. T. Barnum, dubbed him Gen. Tom Thumb and publicized him as an 11-year-old dwarf from England. In truth, he was born Charles Sherwood Stratton on January 4, 1838, in Bridgeport, Connecticut, and was not quite five years old when Barnum hired him. The general grew to the impressive height of forty inches and weighed a total of forty pounds. In 1863, Stratton (Thumb) was married to another circus midget, Lavinia Warren, in an elaborate wedding ceremony at Grace Episcopal Church in New York and they became international celebrities. Together, the Thumbs appeared at the Springer on March 31, 1876, and he alone returned again on March 15, 1883. Mrs. Thumb came once more to Columbus and the Springer on January 10, 1891, eight years after his death. Photograph from Drimmer's Very Special People *(1976)*

Although driven into acting exile by his brother's assassination of President Lincoln, Edwin Booth was out of retirement by 1876 when he "Hamlet"ed at the Springer on February 15th of that year. Thus Columbus was privileged to see him in his greatest role, termed by one critic "the best of its generation." If not the finest, Booth was the most popular actor of his time and the best paid, sometimes more than $10,000 a week. His Grammercy Park home in New York is the leading theatrical club in the country, and several of its early actor-presidents played the Springer. Courtesy of the Springer Opera House

Columbus Female College had a short but happy life from 1877 to 1884. Located on the southeast corner of Third Avenue and Fifteenth Street, facing Third Avenue, the college had strict rules of behavior. Its catalogue contained the following: "No day pupils will be allowed to attend 'balls' or 'germans' or take 'drives' with young men, or engage in any diversion that unfits her for her college duties. No girl can be a society belle and a school girl at the same time; she is sure to 'hold to the one and dispise (sic) the other.'" Its seventh annual register stated that the college had a chapel, recitation room and main building and all were connected, with heating and ventilation throughout, so that it was "not necessary for a young lady to be out of doors during rainy, disagreeable weather." Its catalogue stated: "To send a girl off to school with a trunk filled with costly clothing is most unwise. Calico or muslin dresses for summer and flannel or worsted dresses for winter, are every way costly enough and sufficiently comfortable." The college burned in 1884 and it was not rebuilt. Its faculty consisted of G. R. Glenn, Mental and Moral Science; Rev. Howard W. Key, Natural Science and Mathematics; and J. Harris Chappell, A. B., Latin, History and English Composition. Photograph courtesy of the Columbus Ledger-Enquirer *newspapers*

Scherenschnitte is a Swiss-German word that means "scissor-cutting." Love letters, legal records and religious subjects, all were popular grist for the domestic art form. Examples date in the United States from the mid-1600s, with splendid scherenschnittes, *such as the one pictured here, being executed late in the nineteenth century. Leonora Watkins McGehee's cutout was a present for her husband, and probably was done in 1876 to have it ready for him on New Year's Day, 1877. Done on tablet paper (close inspection reveals fine blue lines) and mounted on brown osnaburg cloth, Mrs. McGehee's* scherenschnitte *represents truly intricate work, coupled with extreme patience. Her husband, Allen C. McGehee, according to granddaughter Leonora Woodall Nilan, "was one whose maxim was that a man should never marry until he owned a home AND a cemetery plot!" Photograph from the author's collection*

Because a court had returned a verdict of one cent in favor of the man suing him for libel over an editorial about lawlessness in Russell County, the publisher of the Columbus Enquirer, *William E. Salisbury, carried a pistol one April morning in 1878. He never got to use it. At the depot in Seale, Alabama, then the county seat of Russell County, Salisbury was shot in the back and died within twelve hours on April 21, 1878. A highly respected citizen, soldier, and banker as well as editor, Salisbury's funeral procession stretched from his Broadway residence all the way to Linwood Cemetery. The central park on Broadway containing the Confederate Monument is named in his honor. Photograph courtesy of the* Columbus Ledger-Enquirer *newspapers*

Instead of the statue of a Southern soldier facing north that adorns many Confederate monuments, the Columbus marker is an obelisk topped by a funeral urn draped in mourning. Erected in 1879, the Confederate Monument is dedicated to the local soldiers, more proportionately per population than from any other Southern community, who marched away in 1861 to serve as Johnnie Rebs. Initially, the family of M. M. Moore and neighbors decorated the marble shaft each April 26th. This duty is now performed by the local chapter of the United Daughters of the Confederacy. Shortly after its placement, a fence with turnstiles was installed around the monument to keep out the neighborhood cows that customarily grazed in the area. Photograph from the author's collection.

Taking four years to build, the cross-topped, lofty-spired Church of the Holy Family was dedicated on May 2, 1880. Its architect was Daniel Matthew Foley, who was born in Dublin, Ireland, in 1811 and who designed sixteen other churches around the United States. The first Roman Catholic church, that of Saints Philip and James, was granted one of the original four church lots in Columbus by the General Assembly in 1931. A "humble edifice" was built on the east side of Second Avenue at Seventh Street in 1835. This property was sold after the Church of the Holy Family was built. An early pastor of Saints Philip and James, Father Michael Cullinan, died in 1877 while work was underway on the Byzantine-Gothic church. It had been his request that he be buried in Columbus. His body was returned from Savannah and is interred on the east side of the main entrance of the Church of the Holy Family. Photograph from the author's collection

Fine and flossy were many of the steamboats that plied the Chattahoochee River through the long decades when boating was a large and important industry in Columbus. Pictured is the steamer Rebecca Everingham *of the Central Line of Steamers, Samuel J. Whiteside, general agent; George B. Whiteside, secretary and treasurer. The legend accompanying this photograph states: "Built at Columbus, Ga., 1880. Plies on Chattahoochee, Flint & Apalachicola Rivers. Length 4 ft., Beam 28 ft. Depth of Hold, 5 ft. 3 in. 28 State Rooms." The* Rebecca Everingham *burned at Fitzgerald Landing, slightly north of Thompson's Landing, in the early morning of April 3, 1884. Eight people lost their lives in this tragedy, considered to be one of the two worst tragedies in the history of the river. Photograph courtesy of the* Columbus Ledger-Enquirer *newspapers*

Columbus had a population of 10,123 when the first telephone exchange began service to forty-two subscribers on April 21, 1880. (Another twenty-one were added by October 19.) The speed with which this service became a part of the everyday life of Columbus seems remarkable since Alexander Graham Bell had invented the telephone only four years before. In its first fifty years, the original $1,000 physical plant investment grew to an estimated $650,000 value and the number of subscribers to approximately seven thousand. In 1984, there were 78,852 subscribers at a cost of $88 million and 1,434,000 daily calls handled, compared to the six hundred per day by the first two operators. In 1977, Southern Bell celebrated its ninety-seventh anniversary of service to Columbus subscribers. Here, Jasper Dorsey, Southern Bell vice president for the state of Georgia, looks on while Mrs. Henry B. Crawford, a descendant of one of the original subscribers, "answers" an early model telephone. The voice at the other end asked, "Number, please?" Photographs courtesy of the Columbus Ledger-Enquirer *newspapers*

Whatever the official name of the firm, the name of the picnic site was always "Clapp's Factory." And for decades beginning with the Gay Nineties and ending with World War I, "Clapp's Factory" was the city's favorite picnic site. In 1834, Martin's history refers to the Columbus Merchant Mill being completed three miles north of Columbus and run by James Shivers and Company. In 1849, came the Columbus Factory, with its incorporators (and brothers, by birth or marriage) Charles D. Stewart, John Fontaine, Henry D. Meigs, J. R. Clapp and George Stewart. This mill, three or four miles north of Columbus, was burned on General Wilson's command. In 1866, the factory was rebuilt and officially incorporated as the Columbus Manufacturing Company. In 1880, this mill had 4,296 spindles and 134 looms. Its officers were J. Rhodes Browne, president; A. Illges, secretary; and R. B. Gunby, treasurer. This three-storied ghost factory burned on March 19, 1910, and its property was purchased by the Stone and Webster Company. Photograph courtesy of the Columbus Ledger-Enquirer *newspapers*

On September 7, 1881, Sidney Lanier, Georgia's most famous poet before James Dickey, died at Lynn, North Carolina. Born in Macon on February 3, 1842, Lanier practiced law with his father in Macon after graduating from Oglethorpe University in Milledgeville. He served in the Confederate Army and was captured while commanding a naval blockade runner. In 1873 he moved to Baltimore and lectured at Johns Hopkins University. It is difficult at times to prevent whole generations of Columbusites from reciting all eight verses of his famous poem, "Song of the Chattahoochee." Photograph courtesy of the Columbus Ledger-Enquirer *newspapers*

A house without a tower in 1881 (the year that Joseph Simpson Garrett built this one at the corner of Second Avenue and Fourteenth Street) would be like building one today without a jacuzzi! Better than four stories high, its upper windows offered a splendid view of downtown Columbus. Garrett brought his family to Columbus at the end of the War Between the States and opened a whiskey and tobacco establishment, the first in the city. Garrett and Sons prospered and eventually moved to Baltimore where it became the Garrett-Williams Company. (Garrett and Sons is shown as a six-story building in the advertising inserts around the 1886 bird's-eye view of Columbus.) After Prohibition, Garrett served eight years as postmaster in Columbus from 1897 to 1905. He died December 19, 1923. One of his sons, George J. Garrett, developed the famous July fox hound strain and is regarded as the dean of southern fox hunters. About the tower: Garrett senior had gas fixtures installed in the tower as a whim and, perhaps because of this whim, the tower was destroyed in a fire and never replaced. Drawing by T. Michael Howard; courtesy of Virginia Garrett Ellis

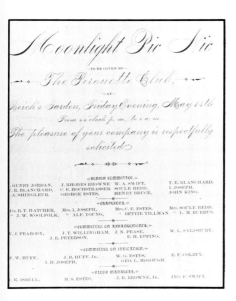

Columbusites in the 1880s danced, skated, partied and picnicked in a setting more European than west Georgian. This is not surprising as the Villa Reich was modeled on the famous Korsal of Bad-Nauheim, the birthplace of Frederick Reich who had immigrated to America (and ultimately to Columbus) six years before the War Between the States. Occupying the entire block between Fifth and Sixth streets and between Broadway and Front Avenue, Villa Reich boasted ornamental gardens with a bandstand and a main building that contained a 50-x-100-foot ballroom. After Reich's death in 1892, the amusement place was closed, and wings of the central casino structure were dismantled to serve as sides of smaller dwellings. Street Scene photograph courtesy of the Columbus Ledger-Enquirer *newspapers; program from the Frank D. Foley collection*

"And the mills are to turn..." goes a line from Sidney Lanier's "Song of the Chattahoochee." The river in the celebrated poem's title can be seen streaming past the Eagle and Phenix Cotton and Woolen Mills at Columbus in this drawing which appeared on page 124 of an April 16, 1881 supplement to the popular *Frank Leslie's Illustrated Newspaper.* The artist is identified as Walter Goater. Another drawing (at right) is of a view looking east on Twelfth Street with the belfrys of the First Baptist, Saint Luke, and Trinity churches clearly identifiable, as are the two spires of the First Presbyterian Church. On page 123 of the same supplement are ten sketches of "modern [cotton] machinery" in operation in Atlanta, but the machinery would have been identical to machinery in use in Columbus' textile temples.

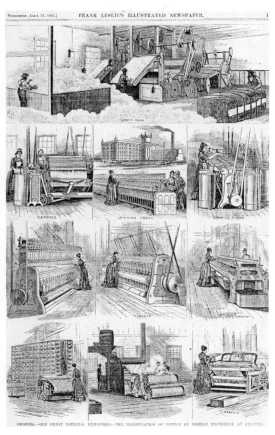

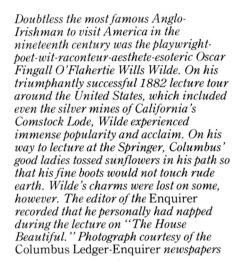

Doubtless the most famous Anglo-Irishman to visit America in the nineteenth century was the playwright-poet-wit-raconteur-aesthete-esoteric Oscar Fingall O'Flahertie Wills Wilde. On his triumphantly successful 1882 lecture tour around the United States, which included even the silver mines of California's Comstock Lode, Wilde experienced immense popularity and acclaim. On his way to lecture at the Springer, Columbus' good ladies tossed sunflowers in his path so that his fine boots would not touch rude earth. Wilde's charms were lost on some, however. The editor of the Enquirer *recorded that he personally had napped during the lecture on "The House Beautiful." Photograph courtesy of the* Columbus Ledger-Enquirer *newspapers*

Five times the bell bonged out its fearsome message. "A fire in the Fifth Ward," a street vendor cried to his customer. A few blocks east, the fire engine headed off to find the conflagration. High up in the ninety-foot bell tower at the intersection of Eleventh Street and Broadway, the bell had indicated only the ward, not the particular street nor the house number. The tower was erected in 1882 only to be taken down in 1905. The iron fence that enclosed the bell was moved to 820 Third Avenue. It was the custom for Mr. Carl Schomburg to ring the bell each day at 11 a.m. in order that clocks and watches throughout the city could be checked for their accuracy. Later, he would maintain the city clock in the First Presbyterian Church after 1891, passing the duty on down to his son, Fred. Photograph courtesy of the Columbus Ledger-Enquirer *newspapers*

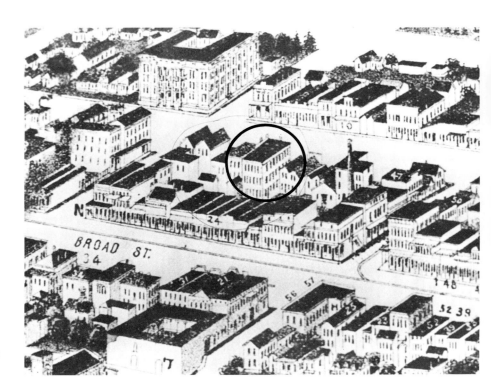

According to the rites and customs of the Masonic fraternity, Columbus Guard's Capt. Philip T. Schley had laid the cornerstone to Temperance Hall on December 22, 1849, with Masons, Odd Fellows, Sons of Temperance and Cadets taking part in the ceremonies. Three stories tall, one hundred feet long and sixty feet wide, Temperance Hall was the largest building in town and served the community in many ways. First, it had been an entertainment center. Then, when floods of wounded Confederate soldiers washed into the city, it became a hospital. Two more uses were to come. In 1872, the public school system in Columbus established a school there for black children. This lasted until 1875 when the school board bought the African Methodist Church building on Sixth Avenue for $800, converting the brick structure into classrooms and building a two-story frame school building for $1,462.85. But Temperance Hall was yet to serve one more function before its demise. Excelsior Mills, begun by William A. Swift and G. Mote Williams, had its first looms in Temperance Hall in 1882 before the business expanded and was incorporated the next year as Swift Manufacturing Company. Today, the property is the open parking area between the Empire Building and Home Federal on First Avenue. Photograph courtesy of the Columbus Ledger-Enquirer *newspapers*

"Red Jacket" came home in 1884. This small brass cannon was first used in firing a salute of five hundred guns when Georgia seceded from the Union. Later it fired salvos at Jefferson Davis' inauguration in Montgomery. When Wilson's troops approached Columbus in April of 1865, members of the Columbus Guards threw it into the Chattahoochee to prevent its capture. Four years later, it was raised on the fluke of an anchor and sold as junk. Acquired by a New York armorer, Red Jacket was eventually returned to the Columbus Guards. Alas, vandals stole it in 1930. Taking it to the river bank, they attempted to fire it, and its barrel burst. Alva C. Smith, secretary-treasurer of the Columbus Historical Society, found all of the pieces and had the gun mended. Photograph courtesy of the Columbus Ledger-Enquirer *newspapers*

The Boston-Savannah Steamship Company had among its fleet of vessels one named the City of Columbus. *The 2,200-ton iron hull was propelled by a 1,500-horsepower compound engine, with fore and aft auxiliary sails on two masts. She had been built by John Roach and son in Chester, Pennsylvania, and launched June 19, 1878. She was 275 feet long and 38½ feet in the beam. Termed a "floating palace," her grand saloon was one hundred feet long. With forty-two staterooms on two decks, she was licensed to carry two hundred passengers. Out of the 132 officers, crew and passengers aboard, 103 did not survive the night of January 17, 1884, when the ship wrecked at Gay Head Light on Martha's Vineyard. The brass knob from the vessel's deck fittings is owned by a Columbus citizen, Ret. Col. Ralph Tibbets, a grandson of one of the twenty-nine fortunate survivors. The ship's name plate is preserved in the Mystic Seaport Museum. Both photographs courtesy of the* Columbus Ledger-Enquirer *newspapers*

A lot was going on in Columbus in January of 1884. Theatergoers were to be exposed to two great names of American drama, as the Springer Opera House ads proclaimed. Minnie Maddern (later to be Mrs. Fiske) was booked to appear in The Puritan Maid *on January 23 for the benefit of the Columbus Public Library, and Joseph Jefferson on January 26 in his muchly acclaimed role of Bob Acres in Richard Sheridan's famous play,* The Rivals. *Reserved seats for the latter show were listed as $1.50 for reserved seats, gallery reserved $1 and gallery fifty cents. Besides the legitimate stage, there was to be a free art exhibition "of first-class oil paintings at 148 Broad Street," an auction complete with "Prof. Fowler" as lecturer. And Theo M. Foley was to have "Very Desirable Property" at auctions, with "terms very liberal—made known on day of sale." Photograph courtesy of the* Columbus Ledger-Enquirer *newspapers*

It will be of no surprise to Columbusites that a native son would be known to the sophisticated world of New York as "Mr. Taste." William Odom was born in Columbus in 1886 to "an impoverished Southern gentlemen of a father (who) was a speculator on the cotton market who had a side line in trotters," as described in a 1983 article in House and Garden. *Odom probably would have followed his two brothers "onto the race track, where both made names as jockeys and trainers," except for a childhood riding accident. During his five years of convalescence, he decided instead on a musical career and went north to New York around 1904 to study conducting. "According to Stokowski (Leopold Stokowski, noted symphony conductor), he lacked the necessary stamina, "and so enrolled instead in the New York School of Fine and Applied Arts (soon to change its name to the Parsons School in honor of its director Frank A. Parsons); he joined the Parsons School staff in 1909. In 1916 Odom published an ambitious two-volume* History of Italian Furniture, *which is still regarded as the most authoritative work on the subject. The Roaring Twenties saw interior decorating come into its own and the best elegant examples were in a large measure due to the "arbiter elegantium," the "never very celebrated and now almost forgotten" Georgian, William Odom. However, according to a 1946 issue of* House and Garden *magazine, "there is hardly a decorator practicing today but at some time, directly or indirectly, fell under the spell of William Odom." The magazine continued to admire his work and felt his influence so great it again carried editorial commentary on him in the May 1983 issue. But, of course! Photograph courtesy of Conde' Nast Publications and* House and Garden *(May 1983)*

Before 1885-86, Columbus streets and avenues bore the names of distinguished personages, not numerical designations. In his original map of the city, Edward Lloyd Thomas named the streets for the current governor of Georgia, Forsyth; for the founder of the state, Oglethorpe; for the first president of the United States, Washington; for his mother's maiden name, Covington; for either one of the original commissioners or for the uncle of the same commissioner, Few; for a famous Revolutionary Officer, Mercer; for a former Georgia governor, Troup; for a Creek chief, McIntosh, etc. Three streets bore more geographical names, such as Bay because it ran along the river, Broad because it was that, and Bridge because it led into the river span. One street the

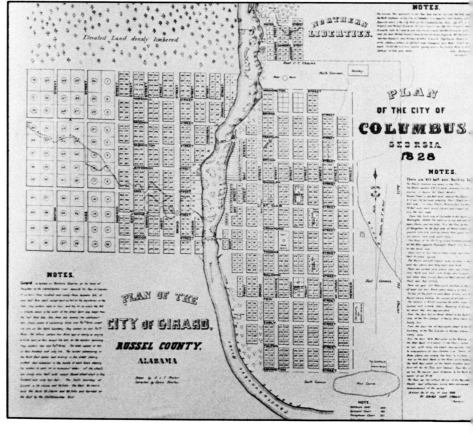

surveyor named for his father (or for himself but who's to say?). And of those original streets, only that one has survived. An extension of Thomas Street exists in a predominantly black residential area east of the original city. Photograph courtesy of the Columbus Ledger-Enquirer *newspapers*

A 13540 The Market, Columbus, Ga.

Tenth Street School, Columbus, Ga.

The City Market was for many years one of the liveliest places in town. Farmers from all over the Chattahoochee Valley brought their produce to sell, and housewives—or often their cooks—thronged to find vegetables and fruits at their freshest. An 1872 city map shows the market taking up about half the block of Oglethorpe Street (now First Avenue) between Crawford (Tenth Street) and Saint Clair (Eleventh Street). By 1886, another map reveals that the market had by then taken up most of the block and had added a handsome three-story tower crowned with a cupola. This photograph was probably made sometime in the 1890s. The date of the demolition of the market is unknown. Photograph courtesy of the Columbus Ledger-Enquirer newspapers

The year 1887 saw the completion of the Tenth Street School on a site formerly occupied by the second church of First Presbyterian's congregation, a structure dedicated on January 25, 1845. Known as the Columbus Male Public School, the new educational facility was on the northeast corner of Tenth Street and Second Avenue. Since 1934, when the school was torn down, two different fire station buildings have been built on the site. According to Etta Blanchard Worsley in Columbus on the Chattahoochee, the streets in Columbus were lighted by gas lamps on posts beginning about 1880. Policemen lit the lamps. By 1883, there were ninety nine gas lamps on the corners of the streets and an official lamplighter had been employed. When the number of lamps grew to 1271 in 1887, the lamplighter's salary was set at $286.10. But three years later electricity was used exclusively for street lighting. Photograph courtesy of the Columbus Ledger-Enquirer newspapers

Accomodations on the Pactolus, one of the many steamboats which made the river trip between Columbus and Apalachicola, Florida, were quite elegant. Cabins were comfortable and the dining salon of the steamboat, photographed in 1887, was typical of the post-War Between the States ships, spacious and decorated in steamboat gothic or carved gingerbread with chandeliers and carpets. Other amenities on the five-and-one-half-days trip included officers in caps and braid and the best cooks around. These steamers were sometimes used for boat parties complete with bands, midnight suppers and champagne. And chaperons! The table appointments were sumptuous. In this photo, three or four cruets of condiments such as oil, vinegar, etc. are spaced at regular intervals down the table, and tall water glasses are at each plate, as are the eating utensils. A stove is at the far end of the room and in the foreground is the obviously proud maitre d'hotel. One of the finest and most elegant of all steamboats, the Pactolus, was built in Jeffersonville, Indiana, a major shipbuilding port which built many ships for the Chattahoochee. It was owned by Capt. S. J. Whitehead of Columbus and was dismantled at Chattahoochee, Florida, "in its old age," according to the 1956 issue of Industrial Index. The information comes from a broadcast about the Chattahoochee River steamboats as given in August 1942 over radion station WRBL during its "Historical Hour" then being featured on Sunday evenings. The part of "Old Timer," who gave the information, was read by W. C. Woodall, newspaper editor and historian, and the interviewer was Miss Gertrude Handley, a beloved pianist and entertainer of the era. Photograph from the Georgia Department of Archives and History

The successor to Villa Reich as Columbus' playground came in 1887 when construction began on forty-five acres of land, bordered on the north by Garrard Street, on the south by Seventeenth Street, on the east by Forest Avenue, and on the west by Eighteenth Avenue, for conversion into Wildwood Park. For the next thirty years, this outdoor amusement center was where citizens fished, swam, boated, picnicked, sported, gamed, danced to the music of Mike Rose's Italian orchestra, hunted Easter eggs, and marveled at a small zoo. Pleasure seekers traveled there via the Belt Line, a seven-mile-long railroad whose engines ran on coke to eliminate dirty smoke. Both photographs courtesy of the Columbus Ledger-Enquirer *newspapers*

A burial occurred at Linwood Cemetery in August of 1888. The deceased was a druggist who had been born in Knoxville, Georgia, in 1831, moving with his family to Columbus in 1844. After studying pharmacy at "an eclectic school of medicine" in Macon, he returned to Columbus where he married Anna Eliza Clifford Lewis. At the Eagle Drug and Chemical Company, he served refreshments, many of them his own creations. One favorite cordial, called "French Wine Coca," is generally regarded as the ancestor of a popular soft drink today. He died on August 16, 1888, but his drink lives on at the rate of two hundred million sold per day. His name? John S. Pemberton. The drink? Coca-Cola. (See also the Pemberton photo on page 263.) Photograph courtesy of the Historic Columbus Foundation collection; photograph from the author's collection

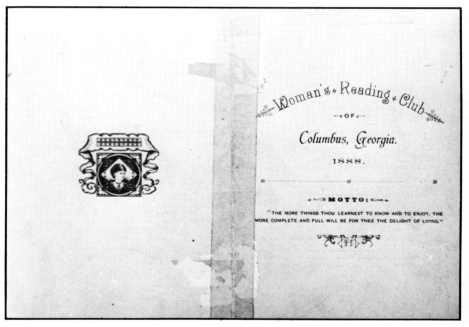

Early in February of 1888, a small group of ladies met in a room filled with musty books; the tomes constituting Columbus' only claim to a library. They listened while the librarian, Miss Anna Hull, described her dream of a club where friends would meet to study and improve their minds. Her plan was received with enthusiasm and, a few days later, they met again at the home of Misses Anna and Theresa Griffin. This time they formed the Woman's Reading Club, the first organized woman's club in Columbus and the first in the state of Georgia with a constitution and bylaws. Mrs. Helen L. Spencer (Mrs. Samuel) was the first president. Their motto was "The more things thou learnest to know and to enjoy, the more complete and full will be for thee the delight of living." Photograph from the author's collection

There was a parade, speech-making and firing of the Confederate cannon Red Jacket when the Chattachoochee Valley Exposition Company opened its 1888 Exposition on November 15. The magnificent grounds and buildings—the main one a two-story structure, three hundred feet long and one hundred feet wide and designed to hold between four thousand and five thousand people—had been rated by the Atlanta Constitution *as "alone worth a trip to Columbus." Seven years later, the* Enquirer-Sun *of April 18, 1895 contained a report that the fences and buildings on the exposition grounds "are rapidly decaying and falling down." It would be 1917 before another agricultural exhibit and carnival would be held in Columbus. Photograph courtesy of the* Columbus Ledger-Enquirer *newspapers*

Little Fannie Joseph was surely one of a privileged few in Columbus seen being strolled around town in a carriage of such ornate wicker splendor. A nice decorative and customizing touch was the letter "J," which is in plain view just above the left rear wheel. Fannie's father, Isaac Joseph, was president of a successful line of steamboats which travelled the waters of the Chattahoochee-Apalachicola-Flint river system and owner of the 1840 Joseph House at 828 Broadway. This house, now the offices of attorneys Martin, Calhoun and Davidson, was inhabited by Joseph family members for over one hundred years and was listed on the National Register of Historic Places in 1969. Photograph courtesy of the Columbus College Archives

The year was 1889 and 1414 Second Avenue was the place. Robert Winship Woodruff's birth made the date and address memorable. The grandson of George Waldo Woodruff who purchased the Empire Mills in Columbus in 1862, Robert Woodruff moved to Atlanta and assumed the presidency of the Coca-Cola Company at the age of thirty-three. He remained a dominant force behind the company for over a half-century during which time Coca-Cola became an international household word. Known for decades as Atlanta and Emory University's best "unknown" benefactor, "Mr. Anonymous," Robert Woodruff was honored for his contributions to Columbus with the placement of a marker identifying his birthplace and recognizing him as an "honored citizen, noted industrialist and philanthropist, a Georgian of universal friendships and acclaim." Photograph courtesy of the Columbus Ledger-Enquirer *newspapers*

The Harmony Club, in its four locations, has been a part of the Columbus scene since 1889. When first making application for its charter in June of 1889, the Harmony Club was called the Harmony Circle and its officers included: Sol Loeb, president; A. Schield, vice-president; Julius Friedlaender, secretary; and M. Julius, treasurer. The first location of the Harmony Club was on the second floor of a wholesale shoe store on the corner of Eleventh Street and Broadway. At that time the club was mainly a card club, having two dances a year. From that location, the club moved to the Beach home on the southwest corner of Twelfth Street and Fifth Avenue. In 1952, the club purchased land and built a new club on the Airport Thruway and utilized this location until October of 1984. The newest location is being built on Macon Road. Photograph courtesy of the Columbus Ledger-Enquirer *newspapers*

Bonsoir *or* bonvoir. *"Goodnight" or a slightly fractured "Goodsight." The beautiful script identifying this social club was so ornate that the "v" could have been an "s" and the "s" could have been a "v." Whatever, the scene is the front drawing room of the celebrated Bullard-Hart House at 1408 Third Avenue, with musicians seated left and right in what was designated as, appropriately enough, the music room. The Bonsoir-Bonvoirers were obviously about to enjoy a dance. The 1890 house was built by Dr. William Lewis Bullard, designed by L. Thornton and Company of New York and decorated by LeRolle Company, also of New York. The outstanding Second Empire house is a seemingly endless array of textures and architectural details. Walls of lincrustia walton (a fabric of embossed silver, copper and gold), pressed leather, a three-story unsupported staircase, a thirty-foot chandelier, art nouveau tile work, composite columns and stained glass are special features that make this National Register property a tour de force of Victorian details. Today, Dr. and Mrs. Lloyd Sampson own the house, using it as did the Bullards, both as a residence and a medical office. Photograph from the Sewell Brumby collection.*

The Golden brothers, T. E. and J. P., opened a small foundry and machine shop at the corner of 6th Avenue and 13th Street. In 1889, they were joined by a local businessman, A. Illges, and became incorporated. In the same year, the company moved to their present location, where the firm now occupies a whole block, paralleling the railroad yards. The company shifted from cupola melting to an electric furnace in 1974, and today (1985) is the oldest operating foundry in the city.

While Louis Haiman's company had begun to beat its swords into plows, the Columbus Iron Works was perfecting an ice machine to replace its cannon line, there seeming to be few customers now for the latter product. The great numbers of war-related items that were being manufactured by the Iron Works during the War Between the States led to the technology which enabled the company to produce its most distinctive product, the ammonia-absorption ice machine. One of the company's first cooling machines, based on A. Muhl's ether process, was sold in Montgomery, another in Cuba. But by the 1880s, the Iron Works, guided by H. D. Stratton, was successfully marketing an absorption ice machine for national and international sales.

George W. Mathews, Jr., founded Columbus Foundries, Inc., in 1971 and served as first president of the fledgling firm. He has since been elevated to chairman of the board with Jay W. Alford replacing him as CEO. Mr. Mathews founded the company to produce ductile iron castings, which are utilized in the truck and automobile manufacturing industry. Although it is the most recent foundry to come into existence in Columbus, this firm has followed the success enjoyed by its forerunners.

As early as the 1840s, members of the Slade family were at the forefront of educational interests in Columbus. Sladeville Hall, which stood at 1417 Fourth Avenue and served as a highly regarded academy for fifty years, was the Rev. Thomas B. Slade's school for local boys and girls. In a June 15, 1890 Columbus Ledger *article, it was called "the grandest institution of learning in Western Georgia...where many of our mothers and grandmothers courted the Muses." During the 1890s and early 1900s, Capt. J. J. Slade, son of the Rev. Thomas Slade, carried on the family's proud tradition by establishing a boarding school in his home, Saint Elmo, where it is said that pupils came from as far away as New Orleans to study and live. Seen here boating on Saint Elmo Lake, just to the rear of the classical mansion-school with the same name, were two of the schoolmistresses Slade (at right on bridge and at extreme right in canoe), accompanied by several fellow oarswomen and lots of lilypads. Their bateau was named, appropriately enough, the* Belle of the Land. *Photograph courtesy of the* Columbus Ledger-Enquirer *newspapers*

Institutions such as churches, hospitals and libraries are generally thought of as venerable places to be respected. But to "enjoy" an institution is almost unheard of. Well, Alex Mitchell's at 1216 Broad was such an institution. It brought joy and delight for almost eighty years to the citizenry of Columbus. Many were attracted to the store by the whistle from the roasted peanut warmer that sat in the front door facing the street. Fresh fruit and hard candies were other stock items. Mitchell was an emigrant from Sparta, Greece, who made his way to Columbus when he heard there were no candy stores here. In 1889, he opened his business with $60 in his pocket and, after the next day's sales, hungry Columbusites bought $90 worth of what became known as dixie chip and flapper food. (Dixie Chip was thick, pink fudge laced with half-cooked peanuts and Flapper Food was a Mitchell version of heavenly hash, i.e. marshmallows, pecans and chocolate.) After the senior Mitchell died in 1940, son Evans Mitchell carried on the enterprise until retiring in 1968 at age sixty-nine. At age eighty-six, Mitchell still whips up a batch of his favorite candy, peanut brittle. Photograph courtesy of the Columbus Ledger-Enquirer *newspapers*

When annexed to the city of Columbus in 1889, Rose Hill was less of a suburb (in the twentieth century sense of the word) and more of a collection of nearly a dozen large estates. The neighborhood had acquired its title through the good services of one homeowner, Mrs. James C. Cook, who so loved roses that she planted them not only in the garden of her home (Rosemont) but around the intersection of Talbotton and Hamilton roads. Her neighbors followed suit until the proper name for the area was appropriately easy. Pictured without a rose in sight is Rose Hill School, which served into the twentieth century. Both photographs courtesy of the Columbus Ledger-Enquirer *newspapers*

In 1891 fire damaged the First Presbyterian Church at the corner of First Avenue and Eleventh Street. As its main tower was being rebuilt, jeweler and church member Carl Schomburg proposed that the city of Columbus purchase a $500 clock for the tower, agreeing to install the clock and maintain it free of cost to the city during his lifetime. Purchased was one by the noted American clock manufacturer, Seth Thomas, with four dials that required winding each week. Schomburg kept his part of the bargain until he retired in 1930. At that time, his son, Fred H. Schomburg, Sr., took on the chores of the city clock maintenance until it was electrified after World War II. Photograph from the author's collection

From 1886 to 1892, Columbus had a native son as representative in the congress, Thomas W. Grimes. With the federal court system expanding, there developed the possibility that one might be located here. Indeed, President Harrison, to whom Grimes was a personal friend, announced in 1891 that Columbus would be the site of one of the new courts, specifically the western division of the northern district of Georgia. But where to house it? Chosen was the southeast corner of First Avenue and Twelfth Street and included the local post office as well as the courtroom and other necessary facilities. Four years later, the red brick building was completed. Next door on the right can be seen Trinity Episcopal Church, that congregation's second sanctuary. The first judge of the new district was William T. Newman. Another district was formed in 1926. Photograph courtesy of the Columbus Ledger-Enquirer *newspapers*

John Wellborn Root was born in Lumpkin, son of Sidney and Mary Root, July 10, 1850, and died January 15, 1891, in Chicago, where he was one of the pioneers of the Chicago School of Architecture that gave birth to the skyscraper. In Chicago, Saint Louis, San Francisco, Cincinnati, Kansas City and Atlanta are examples of Root's designs, said to be the ultimate in creativity, imagination and originality. He died after being named the consulting architect for the World Columbian Exposition in Chicago in 1890. At his request the appointment was changed to include his partner, Daniel H. Burnham. He is credited with the site selection and basic plans for the fair. He designed the fine arts building that is Chicago's permanent Museum of Fine Arts. Photograph from Donald Hoffman's The Meanings of Architecture: The Writings of J. W. Root *(1961)*

The Deep South's oldest rivalry of Georgia versus Auburn or, as some prefer it, Auburn versus Georgia, was born in Atlanta's Piedmont Park on February 20, 1892, before a crowd of close to two thousand spectators. This is how that first football team at Auburn looked. In 1925 the site of the rivalry was moved to Memorial Stadium in Columbus where it became the excuse for extensive partying throughout the city until 1958. Players pictured, left to right, front row are: C. L. Hare, Professor C. H. Barnwell, Dorsey, R. B. Going, Lupton. Second row: Stevens, H. H. Smith, H. T. Debardeleben, Professor A. F. McKissick, Culver, A. D. McLennan. Third row: W. E. Richards, A. W. Herren, S. J. Buckalew, F. M. Boykin, G. W. Dantzler, U. A. Culbreath, R. Y. McRae, E. H. Graves, R. W. Greene, D. E. Wilson, C. H. Smith. Back row: Professor George F. Atkinson, Bob "Sponsor" Frazier (the mascot) and Dr. George Petrie—the first coach and "father of Auburn football." Photograph courtesy of the Auburn University Archives

Wiley Williams became chief of police in 1893 and is credited with being one of the finest police chiefs in the country. He is pictured with his troops, his lieutenants, and several civilian officials. The clearly lettered photo identified the personnel as: 1. J. B. Key, Chairman Police Committee, 2. R. W. Page, Police Commissioner, 3. E. S. McEachern, Chairman Police Commission, 4. Chief Williams, 5. Lieutenant Ryckeley, 6. Lieutenant Reynolds, 7. W. C. Woodall, 8. W. Britt, 9. John M. Compton, 10. H. Newsom, 11. W. Dukes, 12. M. Moon, 13. W. McMichael, 14. R. Kunsberg, 15. Sar. Ellison, 16. Sar. Perry, 17. Wm. Gray, 18. J. R. Beahn, 19. C. R. Cooley, 20. F. R. Reese, 21. J. C. Lowe, 22. G. W. Cannon, 23. T. D. Bartlett, 24. B. H. Willis, 25. T. E. Moore, Det., 26. J. P. Layfield, 27. J. R. Thompson, 28. W. E. Tillery, 29. C. W. Bennett, 30. C. H. Voight, 31. J. T. Moore, 32. R. C. Harper, 33. L. L. Lawson, 34. J. R. Cornett, 35. H. M. Snell, 36. W. J. Davidson, 37. L. F. Watkins, 38. J. E. Copeland, 39. W. G. Smith, 40. John Foran, 41. James Palmer, 42. C. C. Green, 43. C. J. Willis. Photograph courtesy of the Columbus Ledger-Enquirer *newspapers*

Although this photograph of the James H. Hawkins family was snapped out-of-doors in 1893, evidence of stiff Victorian propriety is here to be found by a close observer. One could assume that the handkerchief and folded fan of Mrs. Hawkins (the former Sarah Ann Samantha Avant of Talbot County) were not likely placed in her lap after wiping perspiration from her brow or stirring the breeze about, but instead were there to conceal the unmistakable proof of her delicate condition. Even the siblings on either side of her were lending a hand in the "cover-up" of the sister who would arrive later that year. Mr. Hawkins, oblivious to his wife's modesty, was a native of Columbus who was reared in Meriwether County by maternal grandparents, but returned to Muscogee County to raise his children. They are (front row left to right) Belle, Mary Elizabeth, Annie (back row left to right) John Clifford, unidentified beau with umbrella, Leola, and Evans. Photograph from the Roger T. Harris collection

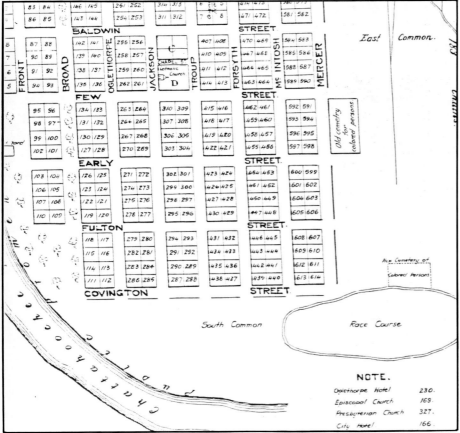

The Columbus Enquirer-Sun *and the* Columbus Ledger *(not then in joint ownership) collectively printed a centennial issue for the city's hundredth birthday. Included in the edition was a map of the city based upon the Edward Lloyd Thomas original, one showing a race course at the southwest corner where the original South and East commons met. An 1893 article in the* Enquirer-Sun *described this oval as "the oldest continuously used race track in America." The article stated that the present (1893) track was "laid out on almost the identical ground as the old one," which the story stated was established fifty-nine years before. This date agrees with Martin's history in which he recorded the 1834 opening of the race course. The year 1834 was also the first that Columbus "enjoyed the luxury of ice." The newspaper article stated that, although the buildings (there) "have been destroyed several times, the mile track has always been ready for use." Research regarding the validity of this 1893 claim to "the oldest continuously used race track in America" produced no confirmation or denial of the title. However, several references pointed out other tracks as being older. Perhaps the operative word is "continuously." Both photographs courtesy of the Columbus Ledger-Enquirer newspapers*

The city's first central station hydro electric plant came into being in 1894 when the Columbus Railroad Company leased the structure projecting out into the Chattahoochee and limited water power use from the City Mills. Installed were four sixty-eight-inch vertical Samson Leffel turbines, with several more added a couple of years later. Until 1902, this station supplied all of the city's commercially-transmitted electricity. After the North Highland Dam was constructed in 1902 and all the power companies merged under the Stone and Webster Company in 1906, the Columbus Railway Station became a very minor producer of current. Some generating equipment is still operative on the property. Photograph courtesy of the Columbus Ledger-Enquirer *newspapers*

Among the many prominent families who had cottages at Warm Springs when it was the most popular (and nearest) of summer spas was the Joseph family. (Mr. Joseph was president of a steamship line whose vessel, the Fanny Ferne, was well known.) Many persons trained to Warm Springs, known to the Indians for its healing capacities, but with the advent of the automobiles this former mode of transportation faded. However, as late as the 1920s, the unpaved forty-five-mile-long road could reduce even the most stalwart of businessmen-fathers to weeping, frustrated tire-changers. It was a member of the Joseph family who introduced Franklin D. Roosevelt to the Spring's medicinal capabilities in 1927. In this August 24, 1894 picture, the Joseph family is shown occupying the handsome Warm Springs "tallyho," the occasion is identified as "Papa's 62nd birthday." Photograph courtesy of the Columbus College Archives

City Hospital, Columbus, Ga.

The earliest bird's-eye view of Columbus (1872) fails to include the South Common, now occupied by the ball park, the City Auditorium and Memorial Stadium. Nor did its later companion, an 1886 aspect. So the first depiction of medical facilities in Columbus is of the second City Hospital and not of the earlier one where, in 1841, Mrs. Cassy Ann McGehee was superintendent and the clientele consisted of town drunks, charity cases and those with contagious diseases, hence the name, "Pest House." Resembling more an elaborate private residence than a public facility, the new healing house was built in 1894 for a cost of $8,250, with an operating cost, in 1896, of $100 a month. Patients then, as now, had a not-too-encouraging view of Linwood Cemetery, as the new hospital was on the East Common across from the burial ground. The hospital was considered "well-furnished and arranged, with all necessary comforts and conveniences." Note the one-story, brick operating room with the glass skylight. Columbus' third hospital, four-storied and with 290 beds, was completed in 1915 on the site of the old Cowdery home. Both photographs courtesy of the Columbus Ledger-Enquirer newspapers

Railroad building became the barometer of economic good times in the two decades following the War Between the States. Getting people in and out of the city became the concern of many well-known members of the Columbus business community. Especially did G. Gunby Jordan, a pioneer in banking, hydroelectric power and textiles, turn his energies toward railroading. The Georgia Midland and Gulf Railroad, incorporated in 1885, was operational by 1887 to McDonough, as well as to Opelika. By 1894, this company was a victim of the depression and in receivership until 1896. Sold to Jordan and three others, it was reorganized as the Georgia Midland Railroad. Later that year, the G.M.R. was acquired by the Southern Railway Company headed by Samuel Spencer, a Columbus native. Jordan is shown in a 1918 photo with his grandson and namesake on his lap. The younger G. Gunby Jordan is dressed in an overseas cap and coat, a patriotic gesture to World War I. Photograph courtesy of the Columbus Ledger-Enquirer *newspapers*

Four years before the National American Woman Suffrage Association met in Atlanta in 1895, Helen Augusta Howard, the youngest of twelve children, had founded the Georgia Woman Suffrage Association at her family home "Sherwood Hall." Although the Georgia state chapter initially contained only the founder, her four sisters and her mother, there soon was a membership large enough for Miss Howard to issue an invitation to the national group to convene in Atlanta. After the meeting of ninety-three delegates from twenty-eight states, Susan B. Anthony, the famed reformer and advocate of women's rights, visited the Howards for three days. The Columbus female rights champion died in 1934 in New York, but is buried in Linwood Cemetery under a tombstone that reads "Altruist, artist, philosopher and philanthropist." And Susan B. Anthony ended up on the face of a U.S. coin. Photograph courtesy of the Columbus Ledger-Enquirer *newspapers*

Shakespeare wrote that "Orpheus with his lute made trees and the mountain tops that freeze bow themselves when he did sing." That was good enough a recommendation for a group of fifteen Columbus women to organize a music club in his name in November 1895. Miss Mary Unity Kivlin, one of the city's leading musicians, envisioned an organization which would study the history of music and its masterworks. The first meeting on January 25, 1896, consisted of her paper on the club's objectives, an essay on Beethoven, and instrumental selections. The Orpheus Club is the oldest music club in the state of Georgia, the second oldest in the Southeast, and preceded its affiliate, the National Federation of Music Clubs by three years. Courtesy of the Columbus Museum of Arts and Sciences

Close scrutiny of an 1895 photo of Broad Street in Columbus reveals that almost every man has on a hat or cap of some sort. The one female, lower right, has on a long skirt and what appears to be a hip-length cape. Although there is a pile of bricks stacked in the median to the left of the blurred street car, the street is bare dirt. Also in the middle of the street can be discerned an oxen team, along with a number of horse or mule-powered drays and rigs. There is a retracted awning over the front entrance to the Fourth National Bank, located on the Tenth Street corner of the Rankin Hotel. Other recognizables include David Rothschild and Company, the bell tower at the intersection of Broad and Eleventh streets and the decorative iron balcony of the hotel. Photograph courtesy of the Columbus Ledger-Enquirer newspapers

"Then, thence forward and forever free." So proclaimed President Abraham Lincoln on January 1, 1863, abolishing slavery in the United States. On the thirty-first anniversary of issuancy, 1895, an Emancipation Celebration was held in Columbus under the auspices of the Chattahoochee Valley Emancipation Proclamation Association, with "all citizens of Columbus and adjacent Counties" being "cordially invited to participate in the grand celebration. We sincerely hope that all Colored Organizations will take an active part in the Parade." According to the broadside, among those assisting the committee were professors W. H. Spencer and S. R. Marshall. Although black children had been receiving both public and privately-supported education in Columbus since 1868, it was not until 1930 that Columbus had its first public black high school. Named in honor of Spencer, who served fifty years in the public school system as teacher, principal, and general supervisor of all black schools, the original Spencer High School was located at 800 Tenth Avenue. Later this school was known as Marshall Junior High, and the Spencer name was transferred to a new high school on Shepherd Drive in 1953. And then, in 1978, the name again was assigned to a new high school, this one off of Victory Drive. Spencer lived in this house on Fourth Avenue at Eighth Street from 1912 until his death in 1925. The neo-classical residence was placed on the National Register of Historic Places in 1978. Both photographs from the author's collection

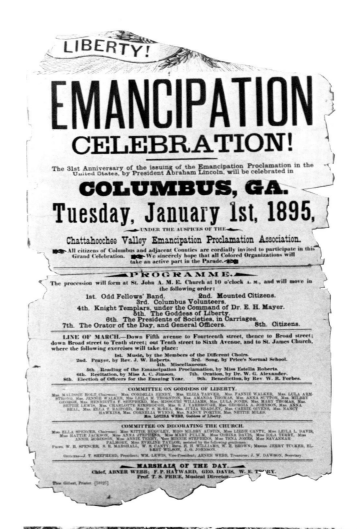

Booker Taliaferro Washington spoke to the Georgia Teachers' Association meeting in the Springer Opera House on June 20, 1895. He had held the position of president of Tuskegee Institute since it was founded in 1881. At its beginning, the school for blacks had two small buildings, no equipment and very little money. According to the Encyclopedia Britannica, at Washington's death, Tuskegee had more than one hundred well-equipped buildings, some fifteen hundred students, a faculty of nearly two hundred teaching thirty-eight trades and professions, and an endowment of approximately $2 million. In other words, the school was a monument to Washington's life work. Born in a slave hut in Franklin County, Virginia, Washington's appearance in Columbus was only a couple of months before his speech at the Atlanta Exposition where, on September 18, he said, "In all things that are purely social we can be separate as the fingers, yet one as the hand in all things essential to mutual progress." When discussion is held regarding race relations, the years 1895 to 1915 are generally referred to as the "Age of Booker T. Washington." Harvard University gave him an honorary degree in 1896, Dartmouth in 1901, and, in 1939, the city of Columbus conveyed its official recognition of the famed educator's importance by naming its first urban renewal project in his honor. Photograph courtesy of the Columbus Ledger-Enquirer *newspapers*

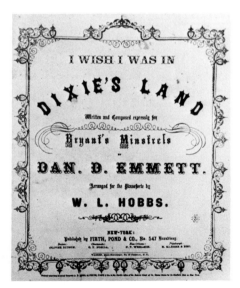

Daniel Decatur Emmett was born October 29, 1815, in Mount Vernon, Ohio. As a burnt-cork character and musician, he built a reputation that led him to being a top performer and composer in the popular minstrels of the day. On two-day notice in 1859, he composed a lively "walk-around" that was an instant success. Its popularity swept the Confederate States, where it was adopted as the national air. In 1895, he made a farewell tour with the celebrated Al G. Fields Minstrels, playing the Springer on September 30 where his reception on stage was tenderly tumultuous. A composer of such other songs as "Old Dan Tucker," "Turkey in the Straw" and "The Blue Tail Fly," Emmett, who died June 28, 1904, is still best known for that quick tune for which the publishers paid him $300: the anthem of the Old South, "Dixie." Both photographs from the author's collection

Muscogee County's third courthouse in seventy-five years was completed in 1896, the second of three to occupy the block between Ninth and Tenth streets and between First and Second avenues. The first county courthouse, a rude wooden structure, had been located in the 1500 block of First Avenue, but it burned while the second courthouse was being built in 1838. Domed and topped by a statue of Justice, the ten-columned (five on the north portico and five on the south) structure of red brick cost $55,979.40, with $7,500 added "in the interest of safety." A fountain and a bandstand ornamented the well-treed front lawn and removed was a forbidding brick wall which had enclosed the previous courthouse. Both photographs courtesy of the Columbus Ledger-Enquirer *newspapers*

COURT HOUSE, FOUNTAIN AND SQUARE.

Caroline Carter is illustrative of how important the Mammy role was to the Southern family. A Mammy was an integral part of the family and was dearly loved by her charges. As the children grew, she became interested in their social life and watched their weddings with pride. In this 1896 photo, Caroline is surrounded by her charges, descendants of the pioneer Biggers family. Front row, left to right, William Pease Biggers, Carrie Estides Biggers (Hatcher) in Caroline's lap, Bascom Hill Biggers, and James Joseph Walton Biggers. Back row, left to right, James Norman Biggers, Helen Pease Biggers (Rogers), and Susie Lee Biggers (Rogers). A Mammy was considered a blessing to all.

Commonwealth was a Christian experiment in community living that was born in 1896, chartered in Muscogee County in 1898 and died shortly after the turn of the century. Founded by a Congregational minister named Ralph Albertson of Springfield, Ohio, and located about halfway between Columbus and Upatoi, the primitive colony had a sawmill, barns, blacksmith shop, dining hall, print shop, school, bachelor's hall, farm buildings, a cotton mill which opened in 1899 to manufacture towels, plus an orchard of ten thousand Japanese plum and peach trees. Rundown plantation lands, summer heat and winter frost, a typhoid fever epidemic, dissension within its ranks and rumor of free-love behavior tolled its knell. Only one French Canadian family named DeBrabant remained in the community after the less than two dozen survivors decamped for Long Island. Descendants can be found today in the local telephone book. A 1907 map of Muscogee County locates Commonwealth as being south-southeast of Midland and due west of Upatoi. Photograph courtesy of the Columbus College archives.

Man's inhumanity to man is universally well known. And a demonstration of it in Columbus tragically occured on June 1, 1896, when two Negroes, one charged with rape and the other with attempted rape, were taken by a lynching mob, shot and hung from a tree in the middle of Broadway, just south of Eleventh Street. Although both deeds were done in broad daylight, no one who was a part of the brutality was ever punished. The names of the two men murdered were Jesse Slayton and Will Miles. The former had been on trial in the temporary courthouse and the other had been in county jail waiting to be retried after a mistrial when mob rule overcame civil law and order. Photograph from the author's collection

Columbus' oldest religious congregation is Saint Luke United Methodist. Initially, the congregation of, according to historian Etta Blanchard Worsley, "fifty-four white members and seven colored" met in a "log structure on the southwest corner of the present lot." Next, in 1831, came a brick structure, the first brick Methodist church in the state of Georgia. A larger structure was required by 1846 for the rapidly growing congregation (415 whites and 375 colored) and additional members dictated the construction of a Romanesque-style sanctuary, with cornerstone-laying ceremonies occuring in 1897. This fourth house of worship for Saint Luke burned on Mother's Day, May 10, 1942. The present church (and fifth structure on the same south half of the city block that was set aside in 1827 by the Georgia Legislature for church occupancy) was dedicated on Mother's Day, May 9, 1949, "To the glory of God and the Service of Man." Photograph courtesy of the Columbus Ledger-Enquirer *newspapers*

A new suit (or uniform as the case may be) is certainly reason enough for having one's picture taken. The Columbus Police Department was no exception. Here members of the department posed in 1903 on the north steps of the Muscogee County Courthouse in their new uniforms. The hatted gentleman in the front row with his right hand in his waistcoat is the city's mayor, the Honorable Lucius Henry Chappell. Dubbed the "Father of Modern Columbus," Chappell was elected mayor in 1897 and held the office for two successful tenures: 1897-1907 and 1911-1913. He earned this accolade due to the many improvements in city services which were accomplished during his times in office, such as street curbing, paving and parking programs, a movement to build municipal waterworks, the construction of the first reinforced concrete bridge across the Chattahoochee River, the completion of a public library, fire stations, schools, a city jail and a municipal building. Also among his accomplishments were the location and return to Columbus of the small field pieces known as "The Ladies' Defender" and "The Red Jacket." (See Chapters IV and V.) Photograph courtesy of the Columbus Ledger-Enquirer newspapers

Siege guns of the type called "Brooke," named for the Confederate naval officer John Mercer Brooke who adapted them from the Union's Parrott gun, formerly dotted the city of Columbus. This one still guards a Confederate grave area in Linwood Cemetery, but two of its kin caused quite a stir in August of 1897. These cannon had lain more or less undisturbed (except when one was buried and then exhumed) in an area adjacent to the railroad yard since the War Between the States. Suddenly, the nearly 25,000-pounders were ordered to be loaded onto railroad cars and shipped to the Confederate Cemetery in Franklin, Tennessee. No one liked that idea, especially Mrs. J. W. Barber of 13 Seventh Street, who thought that they were her late husband's property. The issue—and it became quite a local issue—was finally resolved with the two Brookes being moved to the north lawn of the Muscogee County Courthouse where they remained until the government center was built. Why were they here in the first place? For defense of the city? For use aboard the Confederate ram the Jackson (alias the Muscogee)? Or were they en route to Charleston to be mounted on the CSS Columbia? One can only guess. Where are they now? They now reside at the Confederate Naval Museum, along with the Muscogee. Photograph courtesy of the Columbus Ledger-Enquirer newspapers

The short-fought Spanish-American War, with its "Remember the Maine" battlecry, prompted the establishment in the fall of 1898 of Camp Conrad in North Highlands as a garrisoning post for several thousand troops before service in either Cuba or Puerto Rico. The Soldiers' Aid Society was formed and a flurry of social activity swept over Columbus, a city always eager to entertain the troops. Maj. General James H. Wilson, the same Federal officer who had led the raid on Columbus at the conclusion of the War Between the States, made an inspection tour of the camp and his presence added an unusual dimension to the local scene. By historical accounts, he was treated "respectfully." Photograph from the author's collection

Around the turn of the century, 1899 to be exact, a new idea in entertainment struck Columbus: the street fair. Designed to bring thousands of folks to the heart of the business district, the initial effort seems to have been well attended, as the accompanying photo attests. (Note that every space on the ferris wheel is occupied!) The week-long fall fair was to provide entertainment, but also was thought of as a boost to the mercantile area and the stores went all out in their decorations. In fact, the Georgia Home building is bedecked in banners. Perhaps the ferris wheels and side shows attracted more business than did the stores, because, in a couple of years, the fairs were once more relegated to the fair grounds near the South Common. A sign reminiscent of the older days in Columbus is that, far right, of the "Old Reliable," a celebrated institution of refreshments for a long period of time. Photograph courtesy of the Columbus Ledger-Enquirer newspapers

The David Rothschild Company, founded in 1886, continues to be a major part of the Columbus business community as it approaches its one hundredth anniversary downtown. Pictured here are Rothschild family members, Irwin (on extreme right) and Nathan (second from right near street,) standing before the company's second location at 1029 Broadway. It is believed that this photo was snapped around 1898, since that is the first year that "David Rothschild's, wholesale dry goods, notions, and manufacturer of pants and shirts" is listed at this address in the city directory. For its three-story-high elaborate cast iron facade, the building was impressive then as well as now, particularly since it is presently only one of two such facades that have remained in continuous use on Broadway. The White Bank, at the corner of Broadway and Eleventh Street, is the other structure boasting a facade of cast iron. Now housing Kravtin's Novelty Shop, the Rothschild Building was listed on the National Register of Historic Places in 1980. Photograph courtesy of the Columbus Ledger-Enquirer newspapers

On October 4, 1898, a dinner was held to honor the "Columbus boys of the 1st Georgia Regiment, U. S. Volunteers, on their return home from service in our late unpleasantness with Spain." The address of welcome was delivered by the Honorable Thomas J. Chappell, the occasion taking place at the Rankin House, a hotel on Broadway. The menu was as follows: "Soup and Consomme a la Royal; Fillet of Sole, Tar-Tar Sauce and Potato Croquettes; Kalamazoo Celery, Sliced Tomatoes and Queen Olives; Young Turkey and Chestnut Dressing, Spring Lamb and French Peas, Prime Ribs of Western Beef, Cutlets of Philadelphia Capon and Sauce Bechamel; De Resistance, Sou Bosomme, Thirty-eights and Fourty-fours; Terrapin in Cases and Ox Champignon; Belle Fritters and Sauce Anisette, Shrimp Mayonaise and Potato Salad; Asparagus Tips, French Peas, String Beans and Sweet Potato Croquettes; Tutti Frutti Ice Cream and Mixed Cakes; Cream Cheese, Saltinas, Coffee, Milk, Iced Tea, Fruits and Cigars." Obviously, the Columbus boys deserved and got the best of all menus! Photograph from the author's collection

Lane Cake

This famous Southern recipe was originated by the late Emma Lane and "improved upon" recently by her granddaughter, Emma Law, of Savannah, Georgia.

Emma Lane's original cake won its first prize for best cake at a competition in Columbus, Georgia, in 1898, and it has been a local favorite ever since.

This cake is much better *if it sits overnight.*

3-¼ cup sifted cake flour
2 tsp. baking powder
1/16 tsp. salt
1 cup butter
   (at room temperature)
2 cups sugar
2 tsp. vanilla
8 egg whites
1 cup milk
Lane Cake Filling
   (see below)
Boiled White Frosting

On wax paper, sift dry ingredients. Cream butter, sugar and vanilla. Add egg whites in four additions, beating after each. Fold in flour mixture alternately with milk; begin and end with dry ingredients. Turn into four ungreased 9-inch round layer cake pans lined on the bottom with wax paper.

Bake in preheated 375 degree oven until edges shrink slightly from sides of pans and tops spring back when gently pressed with finger, or cake tester inserted in center comes out clean (about twenty minutes). Cool on wire racks about five minutes. Turn out of pans; remove wax paper. Turn right side up. Cool completely.

Put layers together with Lane Filling. Cover top and sides with boiled frosting. Cover and store in a cool place. If refrigerated, bring to room temperature before serving for best texture.

Lane Filling*
8 egg yolks
1 cup sugar
½ cup butter
   (at room temperature)
1 cup seedless raisins,
   chopped fine
1/3 cup bourbon or brandy
1 tsp. vanilla

In a 2-quart saucepan beat the egg yolks; add in sugar and butter. Cook, stirring constantly, over moderate heat until quite thick. Remove from heat, stir in raisins, bourbon and vanilla. Cool slightly; use as directed in cake recipe.
From The Savannah Sampler Cookbook *by Margaret Wayt DeBolt with Emma R. Law*

Was it ineptness or revenge that explains why much of the fancywork that Victorian ladies made looks less than wonderful, horrible in fact? The ineptness was something the housewives couldn't help perhaps, but the revenge might have been aimed at the Victorian husband who thought his wife's proper place was in the parlor. Popular Victorian fancywork included doing bead-spatter-shell and fretwork, decorating lampshades and performing Berlin work, so called because Berlin was where the printed canvasses were made. (Today, Berlin work is more accurately called petit point or needlework.) And inevitably, there was the memorial picture or wreath, of which one of the latter hangs at the Rankin House Museum. This wreath, donated by Mrs. Charles Dimon to the Historic Columbus Foundation, is a fine example of the period when it was fashionable to clip strands of hair from the deceased and work them into a design to serve as a reminder of the departed to the surviving loved ones. This wreath is highly elaborate, incorporating seed pearls and glass beads into the intricate floral design. Quite obviously, a strong strain of melancholy, bordering on the bizarre, pervaded much Victorian literature and was carried over into the homestead as well.

Rare is the old group photo that has a complete personal identification! Pictured is the second grade of Columbus High School under the tuteledge of Professor Alderman in 1899. They are, top row, left to right: Joe Reese, Guy Garrard, Ed McEachern, Robert Farrish, B. O. Brinson, Lon Wickam, Shep Thweatt, F. H. Schomburg, Park Dexter, F. L. Wickham, and T. E. Waters. Second row, left to right: Herman Hicks, Florence McGruder, Annie Lindsay, Alice Bradley, Emmie Allen, Mira Bullard, Eula Henry, Emmie Blanchard, Ella Martin, Sadie Hunt, Susie Williams, and Louise Birdsong. Bottom row, left to right: Daisy Kurniker, Emmie Wolfson, Berta Britt, Hallie Fulford, Florence Kaul, Sadie Loeb, Annie Kirven, Etta Blanchard, Wattie Yonge, Katherine Mitchell, Minnie Lee Bartlett, Lillie Kaufman, and Sadie Wolfson. Photograph courtesy of the Columbus Ledger-Enquirer *newspapers*

This swan boat was not a float in the city's Centennial Parade in 1928 but of a vintage more than thirty years earlier. It presented Miss Annie Leonard Garrard, queen of the 1899 Street Fair, and her maids. (Lloyd G. Bowers, cotton broker who developed Overlook, is recognizable as the middle one of Miss Garrard's outriders.) The identities of the parade participants in the second photo are lost. For this festival, the buildings were highly decorated along Broadway where a ferris wheel and amusement area were assembled. There was a depression at that time, and it was hoped by the merchants that, drawn into the heart of the mercantile district, visitors once there would stay to buy. However people were more inclined to play than to shop and, as annual events, the street fairs died after a few years. Photograph from the Frank G. Lumpkin collection; photograph from the Historic Columbus Foundation Collection

"Gather ye rosebuds while ye may," the much-quoted line from the popular Robert Herrick poem, could easily be the title of this turn-of-the-century group portrait. The title, however, would not be derived only on the basis of the flowers that are featured so prominently in the photograph, but also because the "Rosebuds" was the name given to the six young Columbus women who are shown here holding their bouquets. The six friends, who ultimately assisted one another in the making of each one's wedding gown, are shown here in the company of five eligible beaux. Unfortunately, only three of the Rosebuds are positively identified in the photo; they are (second, third, and fourth from left, respectively): Janie Bruce (Freeman), Nora Walton (Bickerstaff), and Clara Bruce (Jones). The other three Rosebuds were Odelle Pearce (Hunt), Sarah Nisbet (Bullock), and Lizzie-Olive Hunt (Caffey). Photograph courtesy of Nora Bickerstaff Eakle

Besides the large pavilion for dancing or skating that was located in Wildwood Park, there was another dance facility called the North Highlands Casino. The casino, reachable by trolley from downtown Columbus, was a large two-story building located near the junction of Hamilton and Talbotton roads. In this 1900 photo, the casino forms the background for the group picture and contains a sign that a vaudeville company is to appear there on July 9th. The first name of the company is impossible to verify, but it seems to be Handy, the name of a famous black composer. According to Fred H. Schomburg, Sr.'s memoirs, "A company of young ladies drilled against the Columbus Guards during my first year in the company." The identifications on the back of the picture are from left to right, presumably beginning with the Columbus Guards, Lt. Ed Wells, W. F. Newman, Sgt. Louis Hennis, Sgt. Jno. C. Coart, C. L. Schomburg, Phillip Kunsberg, Ralph Coleman, Jim Devore, Willis Holstead, Herbert Harris, Brannon Bussey, Dan McEachern, Arthur Levy, F. H. Schomburg, Richard Deignan, F. M. Sommerkamp, Charles Woolridge, Louis H. Wolfson, Will Wise, George L. Sheram, Robert Patterson, Lt. Peter Preer, Mrs. Charles Hunt, Misses Bruce, Chase, Mitchell, Williams, Bruce, Etheridge, Hunt, Wood, Averett, Holstead, Lucy McDonald, Willie Bell Walker and Placie Watt. Photograph courtesy of the Columbus Ledger-Enquirer newspapers

It was in December of 1900 that this group of enthusiastic onlookers gathered for the laying of the cornerstone at Rose Hill Baptist Church, on the corner of Hamilton Road and Twenty-second Street. Originally constituted as the Second Baptist Church in an upstairs room at 1244 Broad Street on April 13, 1879, the congregation adopted the name Rose Hill Baptist in 1899. In 1968 the membership dedicated a new brick sanctuary on the lot adjacent to that one on which the 1900 structure stood. In April of 1985—eighty-five years after its completion—the old brick sanctuary (shown in the accompanying photo), whose cornerstone is featured in the crowd scene, was demolished so that a parking lot could be established in its place. Photograph courtesy of the Columbus Ledger-Enquirer newspapers; photograph courtesy of the Clarkie Davis Skelton collection

Whereas today's teenagers receive automobiles (if they have indulging parents), yesterday's youngsters (admittedly of a slightly younger age) received a billy goat to pull a crude box attached to four wobbly wheels. Doubtless the envy of his block was John T. Davis whose father owned Davis Wagon Factory, located on Tenth Avenue where the Tom's Foods Limited plant is today. John had a considerably more elaborate rig, complete with a padded seat beind the driver's, and not one but two white goats! Papa Davis used John T. to advertise his logo; note the Davis name on the side of the wagon. The fortunate youngster was photographed in front of the Davis residence, 1526 Third Avenue, about 1900. Photograph courtesy of Clarkie Davis Skelton

Old photos are either closely guarded family treasures or in carefully filed archives such as those of the Columbus Ledger-Enquirer *or Columbus College. Occasionally, though, pictures are found. And found in the most unlikely of spots. This turn-of-the-century photo of telephone cable being laid down the middle of Broadway was found in a Second Avenue house being demolished in 1974. Shiver's Wrecking Company noted that when they walked across a particular rug, they heard the crackle of breaking glass. Investigation revealed more than two hundred glass photographic plates, the majority of which were of Columbus scenes with the remainder being of Hot Springs in Arkansas and a small town in Oklahoma. Shiver's sold the collection to Herb Cawthorne and Spencer Garrard, proprietors of Camera One. Amazing, n'est-ce pas, what people will sweep under the rug! Photograph courtesy of Herb Cawthorne and Spencer Garrard*

Chapter V
1901-1920
World War I and Fort Benning

Macon's Mrs. Archelaus Augustus Drake, nee Mary Blackmar of Columbus, wrote five days after her eighty-fourth birthday in 1978 that she was the "Queen of the Brownies on the float for Blanchard and Booth's Dry Good Store." The occasion was one of the three street fairs that were born in downtown Columbus in 1899 and which died after the 1901 efforts. Crowds attended the parade and the evening ball, but forgot (while having a good time) to do what had been expected of them, i.e., buying in the local stores! The fancy-dressed members of her court were all neighborhood friends: top row, left to right, Dana Blackmar, Stewart Ticknor, Mary Blackmar (Drake), Mercer Blanchard and William Huff; bottom row, left to right, Edwin Huff, Albert Dozier, Paul Blanchard, George Kyle and George Williams. Photograph courtesy of the Columbus Ledger-Enquirer *newspapers*

The 1873 directory of the city contained a prediction that "Columbus is destined to become one of the largest manufacturing cities in the South."

The author of the city profile termed its citizenry as "alive to a sense of their advantages." Chief among those, of course, was the Chattahoochee River, and "Columbus has," he said "without a doubt, the easiest controlled water power on this continent." The scribe later quoted "a distinguished engineer" as remarking that "there is hardly two miles between here and West Point (thirty-eight miles) where a cotton factory could not be easily built and operated."

The profile recorded that "Columbus has averaged the erection of a cotton factory every year (since 1865) and it has been done almost exclusively with Southern money." The author also reduced by nearly one-half the amount of cotton that General Wilson said was destroyed in the post-War-Between-the-States raid, mentioning the year 1865, "when four mills and 60,000 bales of cotton were burned by the Federals."

That chief advantage, the Chattahoochee, had first been tapped when Seaborn Jones utilized a dam for the grinding process at his City Mills in 1828. Other industries likewise had utilized the river for their particular operations, but it was not until 1900 that a major producer of electricity would be developed. This was the North Highland Dam, said to have been the first large-scale dam built in the South. A dozen years later the Goat Rock Dam was completed by the Columbus-based Hardaway Construction Company for the Stone and Webster Corporation, a Boston, Massachusetts firm which bought out the Columbus Power Company. Hardaway also would build another multi-million dollar dam, this time at Bartlett's Ferry, for Stone and Webster in 1926. These backed-up waters have provided a second-home haven for many west Georgia and east Alabama families.

Subsequent river electrical development would earn for Columbus the title, "Lowell of the South," Lowell, Massachusetts being the major textile company of the North.

Bottled soft drinks were an up-and-coming business in the early 1900s. One beverage, for which Columbusites have a deep and abiding affection, was born in the basement of the old Hatcher Grocery Company on Eleventh Street between Broadway and First Avenue. In that basement, Claud (without an "e") Hatcher, a registered pharmacist, developed the first *bona fide* Columbus soft drink creation to achieve status—Royal Crown Ginger Ale.

The Hatcher Grocery Company was a built-in distribution system and the Hatcher soft drink business was on the way. Hatcher and his father organized the Union Bottling Works, and in 1907 the grocery firm moved to a Tenth Street and Tenth Avenue location that became the site of an international soft drink headquarters. In time, Hatcher followed with a line of fruit-carbonated drinks called "Melo" and another called "Chero Cola." Corporate name changes, Hatcher's death and a new chemist by the name of Rufus Kamm resulted in an early 1930s cola that became best known by its initials, "RC," which has a local pronunciation of "Aura See."

Actually, Columbus has a deep and abiding affection for and close ties to another liquid. Moonshine? No, not moonshine, although that concoction has its devotees, but Coca-Cola. That drink, of course, is a volume in itself and at this writing of 1985, it is still making history, particularly in the new product world of advertising!

As previously mentioned, Columbus has had a long-term romance with soldiers and soldiering. World War I would cause a lasting marriage between the city and the military, a wedding that naturally began with a proposal, only this proposal was in the form of a cablegram to the War Department from no less than Gen. John Pershing.

Pershing recommended that "instruction of divisions in the United States be conducted with a view of developing the soldiers physically and in knowledge of sanitation, inculcating high standards of discipline, producing superior marksmanship both on the range and in field-firing exercises in large bodies." In other words, establish an Infantry School. And on September 12, 1918, the War Department decided to transfer the three sections of the Infantry School from stations in Oklahoma, Ohio and Camp Hancock near Augusta to a site just east of Columbus on the Macon Road (in what is today's residential Briarwood). This was a momentous day for Columbus, a rewarding day to the many people actively engaged in endeavoring to attract a military post, however temporary, to this community. The classification "training school" gave no hint of what it would ultimately mean to the area.

Among the names prominently mentioned as responsible for the temporary cantonment's placement in the Columbus area have been M. Reynolds Flournoy, John A. Betjeman and A. F. Kunze: the hard work involved in getting the military installation more than indirectly taking the lives of Flournoy and Betjeman. One of the modern bridges that spans the Upatoi Creek at the Main Post approach to Fort Benning is named for Betjeman, the only civilian so recognized by designation of a plaque or marker.

Only a fortnight (that's British for two weeks) plus one day elapsed between the time that Col. Henry E. Eames had the seemingly dubious honor of being designated the first commandant of an unnamed installation that wasn't built and the arrival of its first tenants, i.e. troops. Under the direction of Maj. J. Paul Jones' forceful direction, an army of carpenters, plumbers and ditch-diggers turned the Alex Reid farm into a by-then-named Camp Benning in the record time of seven days, finishing four days before the first 400 troops arrived before breakfast on October 6, 1918.

Those initial eighty-five acres, of course, proved too small, and in late October of 1918 the War Department approved Eames' proposal to relocate the Infantry School of Arms onto a tract south of the city where some 115,000 acres were condemned in Muscogee and Chattahoochee counties. Part of the land condemned was 1,782 acres and a large home known as Riverside, the plantation of Arthur Bussey. This property was purchased for $439,000, Bussey being pursuaded to accept "half the load" of his asking price.

Camp Benning, however, had a near brush with extinction in 1919 when a peacetime and economy-minded Congress began calling for the abandonment of the many newly established cantonments. An order came on January 17, 1919 that said "to abandon Benning and salvage the equipment."

This round was won by Major Jones, the construction quartermaster. Jones was a builder; it pained him to have to destroy. So, Jones, aided by Webster's Dictionary, interpreted the word "salvage" as used so much in army parlance to mean "save." Therefore, he ordered all the buildings painted and preserved, i.e. "saved." It was doubtlessly this action that caused the visiting secretary of war to announce that Benning was "a gem in the junk pile of cantonments." Jones had been faithful to his country's laws, obedient to his

A five-story tower, a crenellated roof line, arched windows in the H. H. Richardson fashion, red brick with terra-cotta and granite embellishments are features of the Central Fire Station and Police Headquarters, located on First Avenue near Tenth Street at the same location as the present police station. The early twentieth century four-storied structure bears a startling resemblance to the Communal Palace in Siena, Italy, the seat of local government built between 1297 and 1310. The local fortress-like building was torn down after World War II. Next door to the fire station-headquarters was the Verandah Hotel, which was torn down in 1966. Photograph courtesy of the Columbus Ledger-Enquirer *newspapers*

When flood waters on February 27, 1902 destroyed the Fourteenth Street bridge that Horace King had built in 1870, the Hardaway Costruction Company, founded in the 1890s, replaced it with the latest in bridge-building construction: namely a steel-truss bridge with a wooden floor on concrete piers. The pipe on the bridge was probably that of a water main coming into the city from a creek in Lee County beyond Ingersoll Hill. Note that the electric street car is crossing the bridge on the English (left) side of the span, as one is coming from Columbus. Photograph courtesy of the Columbus Ledger-Enquirer *newspapers*

order and had a new respect for the dictionary.

Floods, overcrowding and construction problems earned for Benning the affectionate title of a peacetime Valley Forge. But January 1920 proved a banner month for the personnel there. On the 30th, the camp received an order authorizing the redesignation of the "School of Arms" as the "Infantry School." And on February 20th, Congress approved a plan to retain and further develop Camp Benning as a permanent installation.

But just wait until January 9, 1922, in the next chapter!

Besides "fain(ing) for to water the plains" as Sidney Lanier has the voice of the Chattahoochee sing, the river's sandbars and snags were treacherous to many a steamboat and paddle wheeler. Among the most graceful of the tri-steam vessels was the Naiad *(water maid.) Built in Columbus by Charles Blain and commissioned September 20, 1884, she burned at Blountstown, Florida, on February 26, 1902, but not before she gained the distinction of being in service longer than any other boat on the Chattahoochee. The* Naiad *was named for a class of water nymphs in ancient mythology fabled to dwell in, preside over and give life to lakes, streams, springs, fountains and presumably rivers. Photograph courtesy of the* Columbus Ledger-Enquirer *newspapers*

The wilderness area along the banks of the Chattahoochee north of town where generations of Columbusites had festive picnics and the traditional site of the together-in-death-rather-than-separated-in-life plunge by the Coweta maiden and her Cusseta brave lover (or was it a Cusseta maiden and her Coweta brave lover?) was changed radically when a large textile plant with twenty thousand spindles was built by Bibb Manufacturing Company. And this romantic spot vanished completely when the North Highlands Dam, the largest in the south at the time, was finished in 1902. Photograph courtesy of the Columbus Ledger-Enquirer *newspapers*

The Gibson girl was a pop goddess before the term was invented. But, as she was created by the artist, Charles Dana Gibson, the Gibson girl was more than just a society beauty. She was an athletic, outdoor type, poised and intelligent, much like the legendary Langhorne sisters of Virginia, one of whom Gibson married and on whom he patterned his creation. Young women of the 1890s and early 1900s hastened to copy the Gibson girl's pompadour, her elegant posture and her mode of dress. This September 1902 photo shows a local group who styled themselves the "Butterflies." Sans romantic wide-brimmed hats to display butterfly bows atop their towering pompadours, they are listed on the back of the picture as: Eula Kirven, Jeanette Martin, Mary Gordon, Ethel Illges, Vera Dozier, Ruth Martin, Marie Burrus, Jamie Butts, Lyra Garrett, Jessie Henry, Katherine Pearce, Belle Salisbury, Josie Blankenship, Louise Lott, Eiver Johnson, Edna Levy, Alice Johnson, Helen Garrard. The photo's owner, Jeanette Martin, later Mrs. Josiah Flournoy, is second from the left on the back row, but, alas, she failed to designate her system of identification. Photograph courtesy of the Helen Flournoy Huff Hudson collection

With Columbus native George Foster Peabody in attendance, the world's only all marble YMCA was dedicated in December 1903. Several years before, Peabody and his two brothers had offered to donate $35,000 for a "Y" building if the local organization would furnish a lot and raise $10,000 for an endowment. Financier-banker, humanitarian and philanthropist, Peabody attended night school at a "Y" in New York City while a young man, and this experience gave him a lifetime interest in education, especially for lower income groups. Photograph courtesy of the Columbus Ledger-Enquirer *newspapers*

A forerunner to the Columbus Little Theater (now the Springer Theater Company) was the Columbus Dramatic Club which presented a number of plays, including this 1903 cast for Because She Loved Him So, *to provide uniforms for the City Guards and other benefits. The players were, bottom row, left to right, Clifford Swift and James Woodruff. Second row, left to right, Peter Preer, Allene Tupper, Dozier Fuller, Etta Blanchard, Tom Hudson, Emmie Blanchard. Standing, left to right, Harry Bruce, Leonora Swift, R. E. Pou, George Waddell, Catherine Tupper, John Illges, Guy Garrard, MacDougald Dexter, Miss Hoflin, unidentified. Catherine Tupper became the wife of Gen. George C. Marshall, soldier-statesman. Photograph from Worsley's* Columbus on the Chattahoochee *(1951)*

Business was brisk on a probably hot summer afternoon in 1904 at the corner of Twelfth Street and Broad. Awnings were lowered against the sun, white dresses predominate on the female pedestrians and all the males in view sport hats. Horse and buggy seems to be the major form of transportation, although the couple in the middle of the street is doubtless headed for the streetcar transfer station just out of the picture to the right. One gentleman is about to mount his trusty bicycle and, leaning against an inverted Confederate cannon imbedded in the cement sidewalk, is a fashionable youngster in a cap and tie. The three-story brick building on the corner was the Third National Bank, founded in 1888 with G. Gunby Jordan as president. It merged in 1930 with the Columbus Savings Bank to become today's Columbus Bank and Trust Company. W. C. Bradley served as president of both banks as well as the merged organization from 1921 to his death, July 26, 1947. Photograph courtesy of the Columbus Ledger-Enquirer *newspapers*

The wording on an historic marker beside Victory Drive is but a blur to motorists whizzing by. Those who stop to read about the Hero's Memorial discover that, in the adjacent Porterdale Cemetery, is the grave of Bragg Smith over which the City of Columbus erected a marble memorial to commemorate his outstanding deed of heroism. The text reads: "Erected by the City of Columbus to mark the resting place of Bragg Smith who died on Sept. 30, 1903, at the age of 32, in the heroic but fruitless effort to rescue the City Engineer from a caving excavation on Eleventh Street." "Honor and fame from no condition rise. Act well your part, there all the honor lies" is carved on the reverse of the marker. Photograph courtesy of the Columbus Ledger-Enquirer *newspapers*

An association to provide free kindergarten care for underprivileged children, plus a school for kindergarten teachers, was born in 1895 largely through the efforts of Mr. and Mrs. George C. Duy, pictured here. The concept and its practice was officially adopted into the local public school system in 1905, the first such classes in the state of Georgia. Miss Edwina Wood, an 1899 graduate of the kindergarten school, became its director in 1900 at a salary of $270 per annum. In addition to holding the position of director for twenty-one years, she was the first woman member of the school board. The photographs of the Duys date from 1880. Motivated by compassion for the little "dinner toters," the children of mill workers who daily carried lunch pails to their parents, the association established three kindergartens in the spring of 1895 with two experienced teachers, Miss Edith Woodruff and Miss Winfred Barlow of Louisville, Kentucky, who were brought to Columbus in the fall to conduct the program and to set up a training school for teachers. The association, which became Goodwill Industries in 1921, provided its free service via a myriad of fund-raising events. Both photographs courtesy of the Columbus College archives

It took an act of Congress, but in 1904 the "Ladies' Defender" came home to Columbus. This petite but lethal muzzle loading cannon was cast here in 1861 from brass contributed by patriotic Columbus women from their domestic furnishings and utensils, i.e., pots and pans. Used about a year by the Confederate artillery, it was captured at the Battle of Shiloh in Tennessee on April 6, 1862, and probably was used by Federal troops against the Rebel forces. It was exhibited as a war trophy in a Chicago armory for a while after the between-brothers conflict and, later, was on the National Cemetery grounds at Shiloh. When this photo was taken, the "Ladies' Defender" was on the north lawn of the Muscogee County Courthouse, but today the field piece is on display at the Columbus Iron Works. Photograph courtesy of the Columbus Ledger-Enquirer *newspapers*

Credit for owning the first auto in Columbus goes to Leon A. Camp, who with his twin brother, Wilson, ran a bicycle shop. With the birth of the automotive industry, these establishments became the logical dealership sites. Pictured with his wife Lily Spencer Camp, Leon is at the helm of his 1904 (or '05) Locomobile Steamer. The Camp brothers used the unpaved and steep street up Ingersoll Hill as a testing ground of their cars for their prospective customers. Among these was a railroad engineer, who half way up the incline spied a gauge on the dashboard and asked what it was. "Steam dial," replied a Camp. With that, the engineer noted that the gauge read 400 and as this was twice what, in his estimation, was considered a safe rate, leaped from the moving machine and sprinted away, yelling that the steamer was about to blow up. Needless to say, he didn't buy. Leon A. Camp also had the distinction of being the first person charged here with reckless driving. His vehicle came unstuck from the sandy intersection of Twelfth Street and Broad, ran up on the side walk and pinned a startled but unharmed pedestrian against a building. However, a window in the building was broken. The case against Camp was dismissed later, as his lawyer won a dismissal on the grounds that there were no Georgia laws covering reckless driving or speeding. The anti-auto judge pounded the bench and said some should be passed. They were! Photograph courtesy of the Columbus Ledger-Enquirer *newspapers*

Established in 1892, the Chase Conservatory of Music had its spacious new home by 1904. Located on the southwest corner of Third Avenue and Tenth Street, the conservatory contained teaching studios, a lobby, and a 401-seat auditorium, as well as living quarters for the Chase family. Its platform stage was large enough for several grand pianos or an orchestral group. The founder of the conservatory, George Williams Chase, was born in Brooklyn, New York, on October 11, 1834, and died in Columbus on October 3, 1910. An 1857 newspaper ad indicates that he was teaching in Columbus at that time, later entering the Confederate army as a bandmaster. Sons Louis and George Chase and other members of the family ran the conservatory for many decades. In its heyday, prior to World War I, the conservatory had a faculty of thirteen-to-sixteen instructors and a student body of over 350. Dr. Katherine Hines Mahan, in her definitive volume on a century of musical development in Columbus (1828-1928), Showboats to Softshoes, *evaluated that "a diploma from Chase Conservatory was equivalent to one from Wesleyan (Macon) or New England conservatories." The conservatory was torn down in the 1960s. Louis Chase composed a march dedicated to the newspaper and the* Enquirer-Sun *published it on June 23, 1901. Photograph courtesy of the* Columbus Ledger-Enquirer *newspapers*

When Don Johnson, a noted Columbus photographer, made this photograph (sometime before 1905 because the old Bell Tower is still standing and after 1889 because the building in which is today's Tavern on the Square was constructed then), a load requiring sixteen oxen, yoked in eight pairs, was indeed a sight to see and to record. The names listed on the back of the photo are T. E. Blanchard, Chas E. Allen, Frederick Land, John C. Martin, Jake Joseph, Henry Fillingim, William H. Young and Felder Pou, but who is who is anyone's guess. The April 18, 1928 edition of The Industrial Index (Columbus Centennial Number) identifies the Pou Harness Company as the building in which William Makepeace Thackeray slept on the second floor when he visited Columbus in 1856. Photograph courtesy of the Columbus Ledger-Enquirer newspapers

Dedicated to the concept of vocational training for the common man was the Industrial High School, its cornerstone being laid on June 22, 1906, in the newly-opened subdivision of Waverly Terrace. To G. Gunby Jordan and Carlton B. Gibson, respectively the president of the school board and the superintendent of the school system, goes the credit for this facility, the first vocational high school in the nation operated by a public school system. Besides the more traditional classes, boys and girls obtained specialized occupational instruction on an 8 a.m. to 4 p.m. schedule for eleven months, thus completing in three years the work usually spread over a four-year curriculum. Photographs courtesy of the Columbus Ledger-Enquirer *newspapers*

The year 1906 saw the opening of Columbus' first planned subdivision. On December 1, 1983, that subdivision became Columbus's second historic district. At the turn of the century, the approximately twenty-five acres that became Waverly Terrace lay on the northern outskirts of what then was Columbus. The Jordan Company, headed by G. Gunby Jordan, began surveying the land in 1905. By 1929, most of the homes there had been completed and many of them survive in good condition to this day. The architectural styles in Waverly Terrace are varied, including crafts-bungalow, Spanish mission, late Victorian, neoclassical and Georgian Revival, and utilizing materials of wood, stucco and brick. One of the chief architects working in the area, according to W. Presley Tutherow who served as the sparkplug for the National Register recognition, was Thomas W. Smith. Tutherow and his family live in the home that Smith built at 2850 Hamilton Road, as seen in the top photo and showing the Confederate cannon that originally adorned the area. The Jordan Company printed an elaborate fifty-four-page brochure, entitled "The Home Book," touting the attractiveness of living in Waverly Terrace, coupled with the advantages of living in Columbus. The interior of the residence of Mr. Henry Sprang, above, is a splendid document for decorators or historians interested in mid-twenties furnishings and their arrangement. Both photographs courtesy of the Jordan Company

This bronze statue by the noted sculptor Daniel Chester French, whose most famous work is of A. Lincoln in Washington, D. C., was erected by the employees of the Southern Railway Company to honor their fallen leader, Samuel Spencer. Born in Columbus in 1847, Samuel Spencer graduated from the University of Virginia in 1869 with a degree in civil engineering after serving in the Confederate Army. Married to a daughter of Gen. Henry L. Benning, Spencer early developed an interest in railroading and ultimately was the president of six railroad companies. On Thanksgiving Day in 1906, Spencer was on his way to join friends for a hunt when one of the trains of a line of which he was president had a wreck and he was killed. He was the first president of the Southern Railroad. In 1970, the statue was relocated from Atlanta's Terminal Station to the southside of Brookwood Station in Buckhead, where Spencer sits with his back to his beloved railroad tracks and, alas, is forced to gaze down upon eight lanes of Interstate 85. Photograph from the author's collection

The annual New Year's dinner, "complimentary to superintendents, overseers and heads of department of Eagle and Phenix Mills and the Girard Cotton Mills" was held on January 3, 1906, at the Racine Hotel. The Eagle and Phenix Quartette gave a musical selection for four songs, and the menu consisted of "Apalachicola Oysters on half shell, Consommé en Tasse, Celery, Pim Olas, Sliced Tomatoes, Broiled Fresh Shad, Shoestring Potatoes, Stuffed Quail, Chestnut Dressing, French Peas, Asparagus Tips, Eagle & Phenix Salad, Tutti-Frutti Ice Cream, Assorted Cake, Toasted Wafers, Fromage Roquefort et Camembert, Coffee." Is it any wonder that the E. and P. styled itself modestly as "America's Greatest Mills?" Photograph courtesy of the C. Dexter Jordan collection

Where one hangs one's hat is generally regarded as home. On October 15, 1907, occurred the formal opening of the city's first truly permanent residence for books. Made possible through a grant of $30,000 from the Andrew Carnegie Foundation, the brick and limestone two-story structure was located on Broadway, just north of Muscogee Manufacturing Company, in an area known as Mott's Green, a portion of the green belt that had surrounded the original city when it was laid out in 1828. The first "public library" in Columbus belonged to a prominent druggist and pioneer citizen, Robert Carter, formerly of Virginia, who made available his personal volumes to other book lovers in an area at the rear of his pharmacy on Broadway near Twelfth Street. A Columbus Public Library Associaton came into existence in 1880 with a small collection of books, not the 431,000 volumes that comprise the present collection of the W. C. Bradley Memorial Library and its area branches in its capacity as the Chattahoochee Regional Library. The water in the foreground is not a part of the 1907 landscaping scheme, but is the unruly Chattahoochee River behaving in an undisciplined way. Photographs courtesy of the Columbus Ledger-Enquirer *newspapers*

Passengers alighting from the open electric trolley at Broadway and Twelfth Street were greeted by newsboys hawking the latest edition of the Ledger. *The year? 1907. If the female passengers, all wearing white hats, chanced to glance up and over their shoulders, they'd be greeted by a sign that urged them to "Cook with Gas." Many of the men sported straw boaters. A banner across the front of the transfer station advertised a "Show at Wildwood To-Night," Wildwood being the in-town-but-outdoor resort popular from 1890 to 1919 with both young and old. Photograph courtesy of the* Columbus Ledger-Enquirer *newspapers*

In 1870, October 25th to be precise, a newspaper article ran as follows: "Cook's Hotel, formerly kept by Hatch Cook, and subsequently by Wynne and Shivers, and Mr. Stubblefield, has changed name and hands. It is now styled the Rankin House, and is kept by Professor J. W. Ryan, so well-known as the popular proprietor of the Ruby Restaurant. The house has been thoroughly refitted and refurbished recently, and is now as neat, tidy and comfortable as when new." Under the 1908 proprietorship of A. and R. Reid, tokens were available "good for 12 ½ cents in trade." This was a "one bit," as in the more-used phrase of "two bits" and standing for $.25 or a quarter. The "bit" goes back to the real (or one-eighth of the Spanish peso) and worth 12 ½ cents normally. When pillar dollars were cut into four segments (cut money) each segment passed as "two bits," a modern colloquial usage in the United States. Both photographs courtesy of the Columbus Ledger-Enquirer *newspapers*

One of the marvels of his time, or any time for that matter, was "Blind Tom." Born a slave at Solitude, the Bethune plantation in east Muscogee County, Thomas "Blind Tom" Wiggins (1843-1908) early in life displayed a rare musical ability to reproduce perfectly on the piano any sound he heard, including classical compositions, thunderstorms and the song of birds. This prodigy was encouraged by the Bethune family who led him to perform his piano feats in both northern and southern cities and, later in life, on tours of Europe before royalty. He died in Hoboken, New Jersey, in 1908 and, in 1976, a commemorative headstone was placed at his previously unmarked grave at Westmoreland, the country estate of Mr. and Mrs. Fred Dismuke at Midland, Georgia. Both photographs courtesy of the Columbus Ledger-Enquirer *newspapers*

Love among the ruins would be an appropriate title for this photo of old Clapp's Factory, located near the present-day Columbus Water Works, only in the early twentieth century, couples went "acourting" or picnicking, nothing as flagrant as "loving." The first mill on the site was built in 1849. Burned by Wilson during his Columbus raid, the factory was rebuilt after the war using second-hand machinery from Louisville, Kentucky. But his operation was short-lived and the abandoned factory burned in 1910. A later company, the Chattahoochee Falls Company, owned by A. Illges, J. Rhodes Browne and others, was absorbed into Stone and Webster and the Columbus Electric and Power Company. The property would be near the present dam that forms Lake Oliver. Photograph courtesy of the Columbus Ledger-Enquirer newspapers

Professional baseball has been a regular fixture on the local sports scene since 1909 when the city joined the South Atlantic League. Jim (James Claudius) Fox, a gangling first baseman with the Atlanta Crackers, was secured to manage the club and he led it to three pennants within a six-year period. Fox, a native of Randleman, North Carolina, remained a citizen of Columbus until his death. In 1936, the Saint Louis Cardinals adopted the "Foxes," as they were known, and operated a farm club here for twenty years, or until 1955. Five more pennants were won during that time. Golden Park had been named for T. E. Golden, one of the early baseball enthusiasts and club officials, and was built in 1926 in two weeks by contractor Charlie Frank Williams after a considerable squabble developed over whether or not the newly completed Memorial Stadium was suitable. Photograph courtesy of the Columbus Ledger-Enquirer newspapers

Growth and change are ever present with the congregation of the First Baptist Church. Its original twelve members— four men, seven women and a male slave—established the Ephesus Baptist Church of Christ in 1829. Four years later it was renamed the Baptist Church of Columbus and, finally to proclaim its age in the community, it was changed to First Baptist Church. Its present structure, built in 1859, has had a number of structural modifications and additions, including the erecting in 1909 of six doric columns, donated by various member families, across its Twelfth Street facade. Bearing the distinction of being the oldest sanctuary in downtown Columbus, the church houses a congregation of 2,700. Photograph courtesy of the Columbus Ledger-Enquirer *newspapers*

"The attractions are too numerous to mention, but they were all good, and the Military Maids in their drill against a crack squad from the famous Columbus Guards is itself worth three times the price of admission." Covering themselves with glory were the Amazon Military Maids. The date was April 29, 1909, and the Society Circus, of which they were one of the acts, was a benefit for the Y.M.C.A. at the Springer Opera House. The maids consisted of, from left to right, Lucile Peacock, Lucile Ball, Effie McDonald, Susie Dozier, Lilly Carson, Hettie Garret, Clyde O'Neal, Nan Howard, Bessie Perkins, Marie Murray, Ann Compton, Kathleen Ball, Ethel Scarbrough, Emmie Ball, Gladys Gibson, Louise Billings, Gertrude Berry, and Eunice Gordy. The one gentleman on the end of the bevy of beauties was Fred H. Schomburg, who, according to the newspaper's reviewer, filled "the position of drilling officer 'to the queen's taste.'" The reviewer continued, "We have not space here to comment upon every detail of such a full program, but suffice it to say that Mrs. Osburn and Mr. Dowd, who were joint managers of the entertainment, have reason to be proud of the success attained." The Society Circus (and the Amazon Military Maids) performed again on May 19, 1909, for the Knights of Pythias who were conventioning in Columbus. Photograph courtesy of the Columbus Ledger-Enquirer *newspapers*

This picture was taken in October of 1909 from the rear of D. F. Wilcox and Company's insurance office at 1149 Broad Street. The lighting system has been changed from gas to electric but most clerical work was still being done from standing desks. On the walls are old insurance companies' advertising signs, plus a Southern Railway calendar on the right. Two iron columns support a dome in the middle of the ceiling and the middle front door has been lowered with a transom put in at the top. The gentlemen in the picture are, left to right, William C. Pease, Jr., at the roll-top desk, Frank G. Lumpkin (wearing a derby) and E. K. Cargill. Photograph courtesy of the Columbus Ledger-Enquirer *newspapers*

About the turn of the century, the Lloyd Bowers family blazed a small set of golf links, with tomato cans for cups, in the fields and orchard adjacent to their splendid Wynnton residence, the Elms. As local interest in the Scottish game grew, so did the recognition of a need for a club devoted to the sport. In 1909, sixty acres of Louis Garrard's Wildwood property was leased for such a use, with Lloyd G. Bowers becoming the club's first president. Today, the elaborate clubhouse of the Country Club of Columbus, surrounded by its eighteen-hole manicured golf course, swimming pool and tennis complex, is a far cry from those early neighborhood links or from the C.C.C.'s first brown-stained frame clubhouse. The second clubhouse is seen behind Frederick B. Gordon and eight members of the "Faithful Twelve," members' wives who assisted with club events in 1923. Photographs courtesy of the Columbus Ledger-Enquirer *newspapers*

The only Spanish moss growing in Columbus is found in abundance on trees above the river in Bibb City. On August 29, 1909, Bibb City incorporated and elected its first government, with the superintendent of the Bibb Mill, Walter Rigby, as its mayor. A planned community, such as had been successful around other company mills in Georgia, Bibb City had been created to provide a variety of social, educational and recreational activities for the residents, most of whom were either employees of the mill or family members of employees. The corporation originally owned everything except for a few stores in the village. However, in 1964, the houses were offered and sold to the residents and employees. Photograph courtesy of the Columbus Ledger-Enquirer *newspapers*

Old-timers still talk about Profumo's ice cream as the best they ever ate. And it had cost as little (or as much) as $.05 for a bowlful! Francis Xavier Profumo had been born in Genoa, Italy, in 1837, immigrating to the United States at the age of twelve (or thirteen) and coming to Columbus. He was the proper age to see service during the War Between the States and did so in the Confederate Army. In 1867, he married Columbusite Henrietta Hoffman and, in 1872, opened his own confectionary store at 12-14 Tenth Street. In business until his death in 1910, Profumo's most celebrated dish was that flavorsome sweet which, in an early form of take-out service, was available in pint and quart containers that were returned when empty (probably to be filled up again!). He is seen in the accompanying photo with his daughter Mary, who apparently did not inherit his blue eyes. The firm closed upon his death, and the recipe for the delicious cold dessert remains a closely-guarded family secret to this day. Photograph courtesy of the Frances Profumo collection

According to Cecil Darby, revered former sports editor of the Columbus Ledger, *"The old Columbus Young Men's Christian Association's basketball team wrote one of the most glorious and inspiring chapters in this city's sports history. It wasn't what you would call virtually unbeatable. It was unbeatable, period, going 19 games without a loss in 1910. (And that was the second undefeated season it had enjoyed in a space of three years.) It wasn't the Southern YMCA championship this team won and it wasn't the Southern Amateur championship. It was the Southern championship, won by taking on all comers and defeating same." Standing, left to right, were, Chester Newman, Tom Lewis, Coach W. L. Dowd, Dana Kilcrease, Harold Lyon. Seated, left to right, were Capt. Tippo Peddy, "Bud" Massey, Alonzo Dozier and Leonard Pease. Pease was the last member of this illustrious team to die; that was in 1972, sixty-two years after their memorable achievement. Photograph courtesy of the* Columbus Ledger-Enquirer *newspapers*

The War Between the States had ended nearly one-half of a century before this portrait was taken of Confederate veteran Col. Robert M. Howard and his great-nephew Howard Bickerstaff, Jr. The occasion for their being dressed so similarly was that of a Confederate Veterans' reunion on October 19, 1910, in Columbus. Nora Walton Bickerstaff, mother of eight-month-old Howard, wrote on the back of the original photograph that "both [were] wearing Confederate Gray as when Uncle Bob presented his grand nephew as mascot for Camp Benning at the Springer Opera House." It was Mrs. Bickerstaff who made the miniature version of the Confederate uniform for her son. Photograph courtesy of the Nora Bickerstaff Eakle collection

Members of the Columbus High School graduating class of 1912 are shown in their class picture of October 1911. The students are posing in front of the 1898 building which was Columbus' first public high school. They are, back row, left to right, Albert Peacock, Richard Slade, John Dolcater, Lillian Glenn, Jean Keene, Ethel Rogers (?), Rosa Rothschild, Angie Mae Miller, Mary Lewis Holt, kneeling, left to right, Abram Illges, Shelton Price, Susie Blackmar, Glennie Mae Fortson, Marjorie Kaufman, Mamie Vent Riech, Annie Jungerman, Mary Lou Downing, Carrie Matson, seated on ground, John Turner, Belle Munroe, Alberta Sommerkamp, Annie Forest Heath, Ruth Weekley, Lula Belle Cannon. This Eleventh Street and Fourth Avenue schoolhouse was used as an educational facility for over eighty years and in 1984 was successfully adapted for use as law offices by the firm of Kelly, Denney, Pease, and Allison. Photograph courtesy of the Columbus Ledger-Enquirer newspapers

Something the growing community of Columbus had heard rumored became fact on November 18, 1886 when a new newspaper began publication. And it was a newspaper with a difference. Not only was it an afternoon newspaper, something unusual in the South, but it was printed on pink paper. Founded by the husband and wife team of Edward T. and Elia Goode Byington, the Ledger *began life at 8 West Twelfth Street. One of its first reporters was Virginia-descended-but-Alabama-born Rinaldo William Page. Twenty-six years later, Page was the sole proprietor of the newspaper and head of a publishing empire with newspapers in Florida as well as in North Carolina. Photograph courtesy of the* Columbus Ledger-Enquirer *newspapers*

The gathering of the clan on holiday occasions was a good excuse for a family photo. A number of local firms specialized in these posed shots, notably Jungermann and McCollum Studios. This is a McCollum portrait of the Flournoy family gathered before their high Victorian residence on Carter Avenue. The back of the photo has the mark of "July 1911," so possibly it was taken before a Fourth of July barbeque. Helen Flournoy Huff Hudson identified the family members in 1985 as: left insert, Flournoy Hamburger; right insert, Gordon Flournoy; top row (left to right): George Hamburger, Isabel Hamburger, Rebecca Hamburger, Hatcher Flournoy (perched at the base of the post), Reynolds Flournoy, Walker Flournoy, John Manley Flournoy and Josiah Flournoy. The middle row consists of four people: Leila Priestly Flournoy, Maude Flournoy Dixon, Marshall Dixon and, being held in her lap, baby John Dixon. The front row consists of (left to right): Frank Flournoy, Priestly Flournoy, Josiah Flournoy, Helen Flournoy (the identifier), Jeanette Martin Flournoy, Mattie Hatcher Flournoy, Mary Reynolds Flournoy, John F. Flournoy and Mary Hannah Flournoy. The little girl in white with the bangs is Mary Passailaigue, nee Flournoy, who grew up to be a noted Columbus artist. Photograph courtesy of the Helen Flournoy Huff Hudson collection

Shortly after the War Between the States, Horace King, with the John D. Gray Construction Company, rebuilt the wooden covered bridge that the Federal troops had destroyed in the spring of 1865. That particular river span lasted until 1911, when the city of Columbus awarded a contract to the Hardaway Contracting Company, a local firm eventually to achieve not only a national but an international reputation for excellence, for a new Lower Bridge, also to be built at Dillingham Street. Visible in this 1911 photo of the new bridge is the J. T. Knight Scrap Metal Company, the iron frame of the Gas Light Company of Columbus and the south steeple of the First Presbyterian Church. Photograph courtesy of the Columbus Ledger-Enquirer *newspapers*

Carelessness on the part of the crew and capriciousness on the part of the Chattahoochee resulted in this turn of the century "sinking" of the Columbus-built Queen City. *A rapid rise in the river and a crew who failed to check its low-tied mooring lines kept the ship from floating up with an unexpected rise in the river. This was the sight that greeted its returning crew from a night out on the town. Naturally, the* Queen City *unsunk itself when the river went down again. Considered by the late insurance executive and former riverboat clerk and purser Fred L. Wickham to be the "best all-round boat that ever sailed the Chattahoochee," the fare to Apalachicola aboard the* Queen City *and many of the other boats was $9 for a week of relaxation and comfort, meals included. With its cabin and hull salvaged from the* Amos Hays, *the* Queen City *was dismantled at the Columbus wharf sometime after 1911. Thus, it was born and died here. Photograph from the author's collection*

A penny's worth of art is how the first paintings of the Columbus Municipal collection were acquired. The year was 1911 and the first art show for school children in Columbus was presented in a vacant downtown store. The show was arranged by Charles Frederick Naegele, a noted portrait painter living in Marietta, Georgia. An admission fee of ten cents was charged and the children voted on the painting they liked best. They also wrote little essays on their favorite painting and Naegele awarded an honor pin for the best essay. Frequently, the admission fees didn't cover the cost of the paintings, but, when informed of the circumstances, the artist allowed the paintings to be bought for what had been collected. The paintings (this one is by H. Bolton Jones and is entitled "South Egremont, Mass.") hung in the Public Library as long as the library was located in downtown Columbus. In more recent years, the Jones landscape has been at the Columbus Museum of Arts and Sciences, and the other two, a marine scene by Charles P. Gruppe and a landscape by W. Merritt Post, were destroyed in a fire at the Christian Fellowship Association in 1969. Photograph courtesy of the Columbus Museum of Arts and Sciences

Area citizens, as well as countless persons across the country, were distressed to read that Isidor Straus, a former local resident and a former representative from New York in the U. S. House, had been among those drowned when the Titanic sank on April 15, 1912. The "unsinkable" steamship, called "the largest and most sumptuously furnished ocean liner ever to sail," was on its maiden voyage from Southampton, England, to New York when it struck an iceberg off the banks of Newfoundland shortly before midnight on April 14th and less than three hours later carried more than 1,500 people to their deaths beneath the waters of the Atlantic. Straus, a native of Bavaria, had come to America in 1854 with his parents; it was in Talbotton that they would settle and his father, Lazarus Straus, would establish a mercantile business (followed by a similar concern in Columbus). Later, after the War Between the States, the elder Straus would establish a crockery and glassware business in New York, which, under the leadership of his son Isidor, would continue to prosper and eventually become one of the world's leading department stores: Macy's. The body of Isidor Straus was subsequently recovered from the Atlantic and interred in the family vault in Beth-El Cemetery, Brooklyn, New York. Pictured is a business card "presented by" Nathan Straus (Isidor's brother) which features L. Straus & Son's New York address—and a reference to the founder's being "Late of Columbus, Ga." Shown in this 1958 photo, taken at the dedication of the Straus Home Site marker in Talbotton, are left to right, Nathan and Jack Straus, out-of-state descendants of Lazarus Straus and cousins of Columbus native Jack B. Straus. Photograph courtesy of the Columbus Ledger-Enquirer newspapers

A native of Terrell County and a graduate in pharmacy, Claud (without an "e") Hatcher (1876-1933) was in the wholesale grocery business when he recognized the growing local demand for bottled carbonated drinks. So he invented one, calling it Royal Crown Ginger Ale. Later he pefected another calling it Chero Cola. This soft drink's popularity necessitated, in 1912, the founding of the Chero Cola Company, which grew into the Nehi Corporation and, in 1959, into the Royal Crown Cola Company. This latter firm's most successful product, developed by the company's chemist Rufus Kamm, was affectionately known by its initials, R. C., which is pronounced locally as "Aura See." With one more name change and two corporate moves, Royal Crown Companies is no longer home-officed in Columbus, but uses Chicago for the base of its multicompanied, international operations. Photograph courtesy of the Columbus Ledger-Enquirer *newspapers*

Fascination with a new-fangled gadget named the "nickelodeon" led a Harris County native, Roy Elmo Martin, (1885-1948), to owning and operating the largest chain of movie theaters in the southeast. His first permanent theater was the Bonita which he acquired in 1912.

"Work while other men play" was his slogan and, through the years, he continually added to his chain of theaters and real estate holdings. In 1927, Martin built what was then one of the largest theaters in the south, the 2,700-seat Royal Theater, now the Three Arts Theater.

After his untimely death in an airplane accident, his two sons, R. E. Martin, Jr. and E. D. Martin, continued the development of the Martin Theater empire until the company merged with Fuqua Industries in 1968. Photograph courtesy of the Columbus Ledger-Enquirer *newspapers*

According to music historian Dr. Katherine H. Mahan, "From about 1892 to 1910, no wedding, dance, large reception, riverboat excursion or other party was complete without the Mike Rose Orchestra or 'Italian Band' as it was also called." So, more than likely, the Mike Rose Orchestra was playing for this dance, with its formal dance card, held July 15, 1912 at the pavilion in Wildwood Park. Belonging to "Miss Gordy," the dance was for "Miss Beard, Miss Browne, Miss Bruce, Miss Hicks, Miss Rogers and Miss Shafor." "Miss Gordy" was obviously popular: she did the two-step with "Lamar," the waltz with "Lummus," the two-step with "Harley," the waltz with "Prather," sat out the next waltz, did the two-step with "Hollis," the waltz with Lewis ("Pee Wee"), sat out a waltz, did the two-step with "Claud Scarbrough," sat out another waltz, waltzed with "Howard," did the two-step with "Charlie" and sat out the final waltz before going "Home Sweet Home." Rose died January 14, 1922, and is buried in the Columbian Masonic Lodge lot at Linwood Cemetery. According to Dr. Mahan, "The band of the Columbus Musicians Protective Association, Local number 253, F. and A. M., which Rose helped to organize, played at the graveside." Both photographs courtesy of the Columbus Ledger-Enquirer *newspapers*

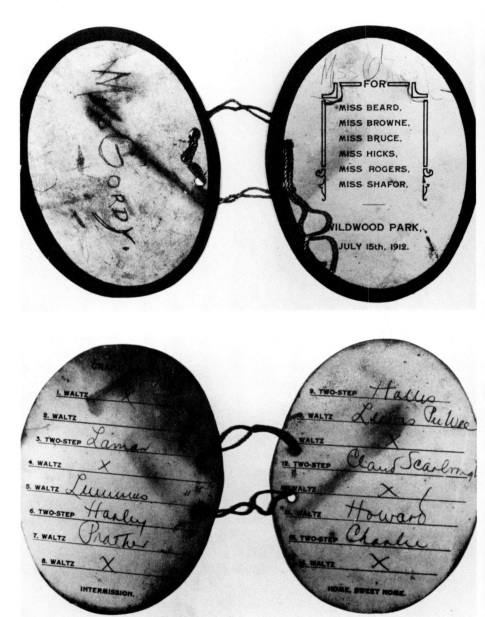

The taming of the Chattahoochee began when City Mills threw the first dam across the river in 1828. This restrainer was followed in the 1840s by the dam at the present Fourteenth Street Bridge and by the North Highlands Dam in 1902. When the Hardaway Construction Company finished the Goat Rock Dam thirteen miles north of the city, this marked the beginning of large-scale interconnection of the Columbus Power Company with Georgia and Alabama cities to the north. The 1912 dam forms a 940-acre lake, a 70-foot high concrete gravity structure, a 193-foot intake section, a 973 ½-foot spillway and 390 feet of non-overflow sections. Photograph courtesy of the Columbus Ledger-Enquirer *newspapers*

The Bachelors is one of the area's oldest social organizations, having been founded in the early years of this century. The 1913 Christmas Ball, pictured here, took place at the old Muscogee Club, which was located in the 1200 block of Broadway. The Muscogee Club was an exclusive city club for gentlemen. Ladies were present only on special occasions. Roast oysters were a club specialty. The club had once been the elegant home of the Hanserd family. Some idea of the architecture can be gained from the elaborate pedimented doorway and the acanthus leaf medallion in the ceiling. The Bachelors had garlanded the ballroom with southern smilax, a fashion of the era. Photograph courtesy of the Columbus Ledger-Enquirer *newspapers*

THRONATEESKA FISHING CLUB JUNE 1913

Doubtless it was the lure of the Chattahoochee that drove Columbus businessmen to organize fishing clubs in those ever-so-peaceful years before World War I. One such club was called the "Thronateeska Fishing Club," organized in 1913, with a clubhouse in Iola, Florida. Here members pose in a bateau called The John Edward *with the* W. C. Bradley *in the background. Left to right, in the back row, are Toombs Howard, (unidentified), Elliott Waddell, Tom Wade, Jim Woodruff, Clifford Swift and George Berry. In the front row, left to right, are John Illges, (unidentified), Hamlin Ford and Paul Wright. Neither of the black men on each end is identified. The name for the club came from the Indian version of the Flint River, a name given up decades before because the first whites in the area could not pronounce the first syllable of the appellation. According to Dr. John Goff in* Placenames of Georgia, *the Indian for Flint "began with a voiceless ell, a surd letter that exists in neither English nor Spanish...In fact the Creek Indians did not have an* r *in their language and experienced as much difficulty pronouncing that letter as we had with their vexatious voiceless ell." Photograph courtesy of the* Columbus Ledger-Enquirer *newspapers*

The Enquirer-Sun *in its morning edition of March 15, 1913, only totaled up "property damages conservatively" of nearly one hundred losers "at a little more than $200,000." This damage came from a "most terrific cyclone" that devastated a path through the heart of the business and residential district of Columbus the previous morning at 3:30 a.m. The newspaper termed the storm as "the only one of a serious nature within a period of twenty-nine years....Most remarkably miraculous not a single person in the path of the storm was injured in Columbus except a negro, whose house was completely demolished at the corner of Fifth Avenue and Fourteenth Street, and he sustained only slight bruises about the shoulder and body, perhaps a half dozen persons altogether were slightly scratched and scathed by being struck by particles of flying glass." The photos show the destruction on the west and east sides of First Avenue between Twelfth and Thirteenth Streets. Both photographs courtesy of the* Columbus Ledger-Enquirer *newspapers*

"Dinner toters" were a unique social and educational problem in Columbus' textile mill communities. Children were paid $.25 per week to carry lunches, sometimes as many as ten per day, to mill workers. Such tasks took longer than the usual one hour for lunch at regular schools, so these were children not getting an education. As they went around in the mills they helped tend the machines which often were running at noon, and so they learned the work long before they were of proper age to be employed. Here, nearly one hundred "dinner toters" wait outside Eagle and Phenix Mill for its gate to open. At right, bare feet, gingham dresses, straw bonnets and broad smiles make up the uniform of the female youths. Photograph courtesy of the University of Georgia Libraries

Eighteen-and-a-half Twelfth Street was the address for The White Company in its infancy. Here, on February 3, 1914, J. Linton White posed with his merchandise. The address is explained in that the Morton Realty Company was located in the rear. The White Company and White's Book Store had several downtown addresses before relocating in Cross Country Plaza and presently has a branch at 5252 Hamilton Road which specializes in office supplies. Photograph courtesy of The White Company

A never-say-die ship was the M. W. Kelly. *Built at the famous Howard Shipyard in Jeffersonville, Indiana, the* Kelly *measured 140 feet by 32 feet by 4 feet and had been designed expressly for the Chattahoochee River trade. Capt. A. A. Marcum was her master in 1906, and Fred L. Wickham was her purser. U. S. inspection records at Apalachicola show that the* Kelly *hit a snag in Frances Bend on January 6, 1902, and sank. The damage was listed as $20,000 to the steamer and $500 to its cargo. But the* Kelly *wasn't lost. It went into service once again, only to sink near Eufaula in 1906. Again, the* Kelly *was resuscitated and plied the river once more. However, the end wasn't far off. Her demise came at the Columbus wharf in 1908. Dismantled locally, the* Kelly's *cabin was installed on the* City of Eufaula, *which, alas, burned at Neal's Landing in 1914. A part of the* Kelly's *hull can still be seen in the river when the water level is low. Both photographs courtesy of the* Columbus Ledger-Enquirer *newspapers*

For many years following November 22, 1915, when various circuses played Columbus, delegations of circus personnel would make a pilgrimage to a large marble memorial located in Riverdale Cemetery. A collision north of the city caused ten cars of the Con. T. Kennedy Shows to derail and burst into flame. When the heat died down, rescuers sifted through the ashes and recovered the charred remains of eight people and numerous animals. The loss in circus equipment was estimated at more than $100,000. The mass funeral was held at First Baptist Church and the funeral procession moved to the burial ground as the circus band played "Rock of Ages." The circus tent-shaped monument has not been spared vandalism: note the missing carved rope atop the tent. Or was it souvenir-seeking? No difference. Photograph from the author's collection

Apparently the entire school system was participating in a Broad Street parade in 1915. In fact, they seemed to outnumber the viewers of the parade. But it had brought the vehicles to a halt, including the street car in the median. The traffic pattern on Broad is interesting: it seems to run opposite to what it does today. In the English fashion, cars are heading north on the west side of the street and south on the east side of the street. In this 1200 block of Broad, the tallest building, with the American Theater next door, now the Rialto, is occupied by Sternberg Carpet House, now a Goodwill Industries store. Photograph courtesy of the Columbus Ledger-Enquirer *newspapers*

It was in 1915 that Columbus' Rose Hill Lodge No. 480 of the I.O.O.F. (Independent Order of the Odd Fellows) posed for this group photograph. A fraternity which "neither allowing nor requiring any conduct or sentiment of its members inconsistent with man's duty to his country or his God," the Odd Fellows advocated service to mankind—among whom were "the widows and orphans, from whom, in their dark hours of distress, the Order has taken away or relieved the pangs of afflictions, to show that it is most worthy of the ardent support and encouragement of the wise and good of every land." The Roll of First Officers included G. B. S Medlock, Noble Grand; J. B. Brown, Vice-Grand; L. Y. Corley, Recording Secretary; J. T. Black, Financial Secretary; C. T. Smith, Treasurer; H. R. Murphy, Conductor; R. Howard Hendrix, Warden; C. H. Woodall, Inside Guardian; J. H. Carpenter, Outside Guardian; A. B. Brown, Captain Degree Team. Photograph courtesy of Roger T. Harris

With an original membership of sixteen, the Muscogee Chapter of the American Red Cross was organized January 14, 1916, making it the oldest chapter in the state of Georgia. With the entry of the United States into World War I, the dramatic growth of the local chapter, totaling some five thousand members by 1918, reflected the importance of the national organization to the families of the men serving on active duty or on the battle front. Besides rolling bandages, knitting sweaters and meeting troop trains, Mrs. Marshall Morton organized a local motor corps, units which proved of invaluable assistance when the Spanish influenza epidemic struck the city. In the photo, left to right, are Mrs. Dozier Pou, Mrs. Rhodes Brown, Mrs. Willis Battle, Miss Virginia Chappell, (unidentified), Miss Betty Carter, Mrs. T. Charlton Hudson, Mrs. Morton, Mrs. Barschall Andrews, Mrs. Walter Holden, and Miss Mary Slade. In the back row, left to right are (unidentified), Miss Ellen Compton, and Miss Jenny Crowell. When the local Red Cross chapter was organized, it was associated for a year with the District Nurse Committee. But when World War I came, the District Nurse Committee became the Public Health Nurse Association, with Mrs. John T. Fletcher being elected chairman, a post she would continue to hold for some thirty-three years. An early concern of the association was the alarming (and increasing) number of cases of tuberculosis in the community. The first services provided were "trained nurses whose duty it is to visit the sick in need of nursing care, to care for them at their homes and to teach the families they visit the simple rules of nursing and hygiene." Photograph courtesy of Margaret Garrard DesPortes

One of the highlights of the school year for many years was the annual May festival held at Wynnton School. Queen of the 1917 festival was Pauline Johnson (Feimster). Surrounding her in the court were: (1) Unidentified (2) Charles Neal (3) Newsome Cooper (4) Brownie Small (5) Anna Dozier (6) Dorothy Clason (7) Pauline Johnson (8) Eunice Turner (9) Florence Geeslin (10) Lydia Belle Chapman (11) Hatcher Flournoy (12) Charles Turner (13) Clarence Kendrick and (14) Unidentified. After their grand procession in made-by-the-mothers costumes, the group posed on the lawn of the First Baptist Church. Photograph courtesy of the Pauline Johnson Feimster collection

Water can be the raison d'etre for a city's birth, as was the case for Columbus in its location on the east bank of the Chattahoochee River. In its earliest years, water for Columbus had been piped through a system of hollowed-out tree logs from Leonard Springs on the property of Wildwood. A later system brought water from springs located in the east Alabama hills north of Phenix City. However, the disastrous Fifth Avenue fires of 1895 and 1912 were blamed on an insufficient supply of water. A suit involving breach of contract by the Columbus Water Works Company to supply adequate and wholesome water and one enjoining the city of Columbus from building its own waterworks system began in 1903. Ultimately, it was argued in the Supreme Court of Georgia on February 4, 1911, the case having had a life in the courts of more than eight years. Next came the question of whether to use artesian water or water from the river, with the latter winning out. The beautiful and efficient new waterworks plant was built near the former site of Clapp's Factory, just north of the then city limits on River Road, and completed in 1916. Photograph courtesy of the Columbus Ledger-Enquirer *newspapers*

This January 1916 photo shows Tenth Avenue looking south from the Wynnton Road. The vehicle is northbound and about to turn east into Wynnton. For 1985 readers, the high board fence would be the property now occupied by the local office of Royal Crown Cola. The ditch is more than just a ditch. It is Weracoba Creek and is now covered by the four lanes of Tenth Avenue. Barely to be seen to the left of the creek are railroad ties. The tracks are still there. Photograph courtesy of the Clarkie Davis Skelton collection

Temperance, debating and benevolent societies had been with Columbus since its earliest days. Yet it was not until the Rotary Club was organized in 1915, with the Rev. L. R. Christie as its first president, did the city have anything resembling today's men's service clubs. This 1917 photo of members of the Rotary was taken in front of the First Baptist Church. Present for the photo session were (with numbers corresponding to the accompanying sketch): 1. R. Curtis Jordan 2. C. A. Sears 3. Charles A. Johnson 4. Milo Clason 5. G. Gunby Jordan 6. L. C. Wells 7. Roland B. Daniel 8. Hans Mosen 9. W. W. McKenzie 10. Arthur Bussey 11. John C. Martin 12. Harry L. Williams 13. Charles M. Woolfolk 14. Wilson M. Camp 15. unidentified 16. Al F. Kunze 17. John P. Illges 18. Toombs Howard 19. Charles E. Turner 20. James Johnson 21. David Rothschild 22. Fred H. Schomburg 23. F. Edward Lummus 24. Howell Hollis 25. Joe Julius 26. Thomas W. Peters 27. James B. Everidge 28. Rev. Joseph A. Thomas 29. John B. McCollum 30. Roy Neal 31. Charles E. Lorenz 32. Thomas P. Wade 33. Dan Joseph 34. J. Edgar Chancellor 35. D. J. Guest 36. Herman Hicks 37. Fred G. Storey 38. Marshall Morton 39. W. J. Wood and 40. Clifford Jenkins. *Photograph courtesy of the* Columbus Ledger-Enquirer *newspapers*

ROTARY CLUB
COLUMBUS, GEORGIA.
1917
 INDICATES CHARTER MEMBER

The cornerstone of Shearith Israel Synagogue was laid on July 25, 1916, the first permanent place of worship for the Jewish community. After thirty-five years on the corner of First Avenue and Seventh Street, the congregation moved to Macon Road where a handsome brick structure was dedicated in 1951. Photograph courtesy of the Columbus Ledger-Enquirer *newspapers*

Born in Columbus in 1894, Eugene Jacques Bullard would, as a youth, leave his native America to go to France, where he joined the French Foreign Legion and became the first black combat aviator to serve in World War I. After a glorious career as a pilot with the famed Lafayette Flying Corps, Bullard opened his own nightclub in Paris' Montmartre and years later, during Hitler's reign of terror, became active in the French underground. Bullard eventually worked his way back to the U.S., where he lived in Harlem and worked as an elevator operator at Rockefeller Plaza. He died in 1961, having to his credit the distinction of receiving the Croix de Guerre, France's highest military decoration. He was buried among other French war veterans in a Flushing, New York, cemetery. Photograph courtesy of the Smithsonian Institution

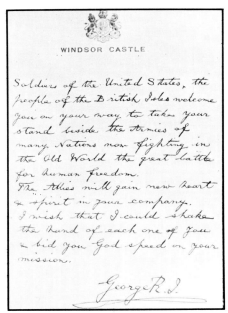

In the possession of Distinguished Service Cross-winner Terrell Wingfield Hill (1898-1941), who served with the American Expeditionary Force in France, was this salutation by England's King George V, written on Windsor Castle stationery in his own hand. "Soldiers of the United States, the people of the British Isles welcome you on your way to take your stand beside the Armies of many Nations now fighting in the Old World the great battle for human freedom. The Allies will gain new heart and spirit in your company. I wish that I could shake the hand of each of you and bid you God speed on your mission." Both photographs courtesy of the Helena Dismukes Hill collection

Hardly two months remained of World War I when Lt. Charles S. Harrison of the 328th Infantry, 82nd Division of the American Expeditionary Forces was killed in action while leading his platoon in the daylight raid of September 12, 1918, on the defenses of the enemy near Norroy, France. In the face of heavy machine-gun fire, Harrison exposed himself "without thought or regard for his safety and by doing so inspired his men with his spirit of bravery and fearlessness, enabling them to accomplish their mission, although at the sacrifice of his own life." The posthumous citation for heroism concluded, "Such deeds are evidence of that spirit of heroism which is innate in the highest type of the American soldier and responds unfailingly to the call of duty, whenever and wherever it may come." The local Post 35 of the American Legion was subsequently named in his honor. Photograph courtesy of the Columbus Ledger-Enquirer *newspapers*

The need for additional encampment facilities to train troops for the American Expeditionary Force, coupled with aggressive salesmenship by the local Chamber of Commerce and wholehearted community support, secured for Columbus a military post in the closing days of World War I. Named for Confederate Gen. Henry L. Benning, the campsite was some three miles east of Columbus on the Macon Road, approximately where the Cross Country-Columbus Square shopping centers are today. The first troops arrived October 6, 1918. Almost immediately, that initial eighty-five-acre site proved inadequate and the troops were moved to a vast tract of land, including the Woolfolk-Bussey plantations, some nine miles southeast of the city. These temporary buildings and tents housed the first troops to come to the original Camp Benning. U. S. Army photograph courtesy of the Columbus Ledger-Enquirer *newspapers*

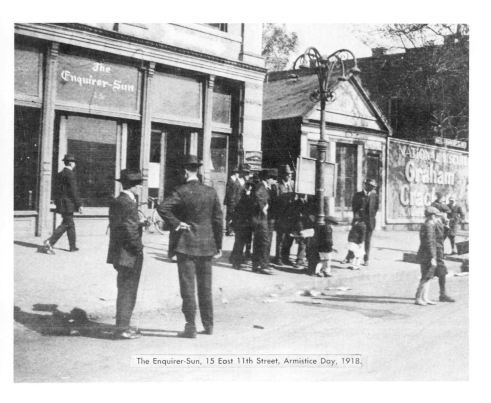

The Enquirer-Sun, 15 East 11th Street, Armistice Day, 1918.

In 1948, the Columbus Enquirer *published a special edition, commemorating the 120th anniversary of its founding. In that issue, it published this photograph showing a crowd standing in front of a bulletin board on which had been affixed a news dispatch telling of the signing of the armistice ending World War I. According to the story accompanying the photograph, it was taken on November 11, 1918 by Tom Wade, division freight agent of the Central of Georgia, whose office was just across the street from where the* Enquirer *was then located, at 15 East Eleventh Street. "'Mr. Wade,' the story continues, 'says that a few minutes later many people had gathered. The men in the foreground are identified by Mr. Wade as Robert H. Barnes (left) and Elliott Waddell.'" Observant readers will note that everyone in the photograph, including the small children near the lamp post, are wearing head covers: the men are in hats and the boys have on visored caps. Note also the large wooden billboard of the National Biscuit Company for "Graham Crackers," and the four-pronged street light. Photograph courtesy of the* Columbus Ledger-Enquirer *newspapers*

By April 1919, when this arch in the middle of the 1100 block of Broadway welcomed troops home from World War I, Columbus had experienced a number of highs and lows regarding Camp Benning. Its trainees had been moved to a vastly larger tract of federally-condemned land, yet the war had ended, bringing about the military cutback syndrome that usually follows hostilities. Would the new camp survive? A delegation of citizens was dispatched to lobby in Washington for its permanence, a move that proved successful when a directive out of the War Department designated Benning as the site of the Infantry School. Photograph courtesy of the Columbus College archives

A victim of the First Pershing Flood was the steamer W. C. Bradley, here pictured being loaded with bales of cotton at the Columbus Wharf. Built at Columbus in 1900, the W. C. Bradley had been in service for nineteen years when the raging Chattahoochee ripped it loose from its local moorings, and it sank a few days later at Burdock's Landing. The deluge was so named because it coincided with a visit by Gen. John J. "Black Jack" Pershing to inspect the camp he had advocated. The general's car, concluding a long journey from Washington, D. C., had to be driven across Upatoi Creek on the railroad bridge because the road's low span was completely inundated. As a test of the bridge's stability, a trainload of civilians preceded the general's vehicle. By the time Gen. John Pershing paid a second visit to the post, it had achieved permanent status, being designated as Fort Benning on February 8, 1922. Pershing's visit a month later again coincided with such extreme inclemency that the swollen creeks and river were dubbed the Second Pershing Flood in his honor. The general is remembered for saying that he had always thought the Columbus area would make a good Army base, but he was beginning to think it could also be used by the Navy. Both photographs courtesy of the Columbus Ledger-Enquirer newspapers

Webster's defines polo as a game of Oriental origin played by teams of players on horseback using mallets with long flexible handles to drive a wooden ball across a grass field and between goal posts. To citizens of Columbus before World War II, polo was defined as "French Field on a Sunday afternoon." Introduced to the United States in 1876 by James Gordon Bennett, publisher of the New York Herald, *polo was being played in Persia (Iran) during the first century A.D. and may be the oldest organized sport of any kind. It was introduced locally in 1920 on French Field when a group of horsemen began competitions which lasted until the start of hostilities in 1941. Horses were plentiful in those early days at Benning as there were still cavalry units on post, some not motorized until the start of World War II. One Columbus matron remembers that "following the matches, one went to the Officer's Club for the cocktail hour, had dinner, and danced until midnight." In very recent years, this exciting recreation has been revived among Columbus-Fort Benning equestrians. Photograph courtesy of the* Columbus Ledger-Enquirer *newspapers*

Opened in 1893 as a four-table delicatessen by an Italian immigrant, Spano's had become a dining institution by the time this photo was taken in 1920. Its founder, Angelo Spano, right, with his son Angelo, Jr., became one of the city's most beloved and oft-quoted citizens for his rare ability to corrupt his adopted tongue into pearls of wisdom and indisputable fact. Besides the local diners, many celebrities ate well at Spano's, including Al G. Fields who brought his famous minstrel show into the Springer Opera House (just across First Avenue) in order to celebrate the occasion at Spano's. The restaurant had three generations of family operation before it closed in March of 1979 following the renovation of Rankin Square. Photograph courtesy of the Columbus Ledger-Enquirer *newspapers*

In a hat with a veil, a glove on her left hand and her right hand bare to shake, Eleanor Roosevelt accompanied her husband on his vice-presidential campaign in 1920. Four years later, this healthy and vital Franklin Delano Roosevelt would be stricken with the crippling disease of polio while vacationing at Campobello, an island off the coast of Maine. He would hear of, come to investigate and find strength at nearby Warm Springs, whose healing waters had been revered by the early Creek Indians and more recently known to turn-of-the-century Columbusites. Many of the latter group had summer cottages at the popular spa, with its celebrated Meriwether Inn and handsome carriage. Both photographs courtesy of the Columbus Ledger-Enquirer *newspapers*

Said to have been the oldest city official in the United States for length of service at the time of his death, Montague M. Moore died on November 4, 1920. He had become clerk of the city council on July 6, 1863, during the War Between the States, after service with the Confederate Army from which he had been honorably discharged due to ill health. Moore, who is pictured here on the right, was eighty-three when he died, and it is believed that three-fourths of the entire minutes of city council were in his handwriting. Note the high desk and chair, the ceiling fan, and the combination gas and electric chandelier. Photograph courtesy of the Columbus Ledger-Enquirer *newspapers*

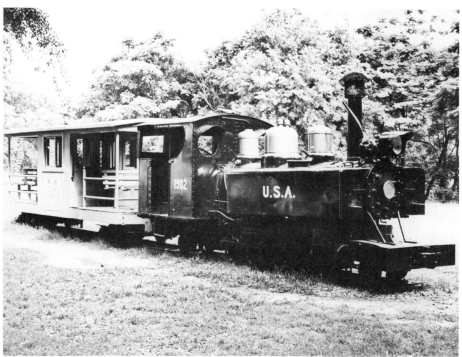

For an honorable length of service time, from 1920 to 1946, this tiny steam engine and coach transported troops from Fort Benning's main post to distant rifle ranges on the military reservation. During that time, it carried an estimated thirteen million passengers a total of more than three-and-one-half-million miles. Known affectionately as the "Chattahoochee Choo Choo," the vintage workhorse is not to be confused with the narrow gauge railroad line that ran from downtown Columbus and which was used chiefly by civilian workers on the main post. U. S. Army photograph courtesy of the Columbus Ledger-Enquirer *newspapers*

The first president of the United States of America to pay a visit to Camp Benning was Warren G. Harding. The date was October 27, 1921, and the fledgling military post had yet to be designated a permanent installation. The commandant's home, the former Arthur Bussey plantation known as Riverside, was the site of the ceremonial visit. In addition to city officials, a delegation of ladies from the City Federation of Women's Clubs went down to greet Mrs. Harding. The First Lady was celebrated for always wearing a hat and veil and, perhaps a bit maliciously, was reported to have worn them even during meals! The first two ladies on the left in this photo are, unfortunately, unidentified; however, the other nine in their company were, (from left to right), Miss Daisy Ticknor, Mrs. J. B. Knight, Miss Elaine Hammond, Mrs. Harding, Mrs. Charlton Battle, Miss Louise Randall, Mrs. Thomas Blanchard, Mrs. Katherine Hocker, and Mrs. Ethel Dusenberry. Photograph courtesy of the Columbus Ledger-Enquirer *newspapers*

Chapter VI
1921-1949
Depression and World War II

A total of forty months had passed since that crisp day in October of 1918 when Miss Anna Caroline Benning had raised the first flag over the cantonment named after her father, the Confederate general and local attorney Henry L. Benning. The suggestion for the name had come from Mrs. J. E. Minter, a prominent member of the United Daughters of the Confederacy in Columbus.

But on January 9, 1922, came the official order designating the fledgling post as a permanent fort. Benning had come of age, and with it Columbus gained a valued, consistent and considerate friend, a truly good neighbor.

It would be well nigh impossible to separate the growth of Fort Benning from the growth and life of Columbus during these three decades. The city that had labored so diligently to acquire a major military installation was equally eager to embrace the activities at the post, activities both socially and financially rewarding.

From the beginning, physical facilities lagged far behind the curriculum and the instruction. In 1920, funds for the installation of the first water and sewage systems were approved. Construction of the first permanent building, Service Club Number One, promised a brighter convivial future.

In 1922, the first permanent-type housing construction program got underway for officers and non-commissioned officers. In addition to housing, railroad shops, two steel-trussed bridges across the Upatoi Creek, and a gymnasium were constructed during this year.

Early in 1924 began the preparation of an overall plan for the future construction and arrangement of Fort Benning. This was the first organized plan drawn up for the Infantry School as an establishment of a permanent nature.

The Depression had a deadening effect on the activities of the school but proved a boon to the appearance of the post. Because civilians needed employment, the WPA was set up, and because many

173

public buildings and works were required, the PWA was organized.

New construction rose all over the post, everything from barracks to tank sheds, from chapel to guardhouse. Among the buildings dedicated in 1934 were the three bachelor-officer apartment groups named Lewis, Green and Collins Halls.

The present main officer's mess, costing nearly $100,000, was opened to its members on July 12, 1934. Plans for this building had been formulated as far back as 1924, when the club was housed in a small frame structure crowded among the classroom buildings.

The $6,352,000 WPA-PWA allotment also provided the necessary funds to build the Infantry School building. In 1934, classes were still being conducted in buildings of wooden and tarpaper construction. The Infantry School building, one of the most important of the entire construction program, was ready for occupancy on July 12, 1935. The structure, although only three stories high, has floor space equalling that of an average ten-story office building.

The major portion of permanent buildings on the post was completed in 1935, but additional structures were finished during the next two years. Construction of the new main post theater was begun on May 7, 1937 and completed in September 1938, providing the post with an attractive modern theater with a seating capacity of 1,504 people.

During the 1920s and '30s, the training at the Infantry School was curtailed to such an extent that, in 1937, there were fewer than six thousand officers and enlisted men stationed at Fort Benning. Compare this to the more than ninety thousand stationed there in 1945!

As the United States strengthened its forces following the outbreak of World War II in Europe, the Infantry School expanded to meet the growing need for trained leaders by the Army.

It was during this period that many officers, later to become household names through their brave exploits in World War II, were stationed at Fort Benning. To name a few, there were President Dwight D. Eisenhower; Generals of the Army George C. Marshall and Omar N. Bradley; Generals J. Lawton Collins, Joseph Stilwell, Mark Clark, Courtney H. Hodges, Alexander M. Patch, Simon B. Buckner, Manton S. Eddy, W. Bedell Smith, N. F. Twining, A. C. Wedemeyer, J. E. Dalquist and G. H. Weems.

One of the most colorful figures to bear American arms in World War II was at Fort Benning in 1940. Gen. George S. Patton, who sparked the Third Army's spectacular advances against the Nazis, commanded the Second Armored Division when it was stationed at The Post.

A construction program involving the expenditure of over a half-million dollars was announced in April of 1940, basically for road and sewage projects and wooden buildings to house additional troops. Also in April of that year was organized a test platoon of paratroopers, and the Army's first airborne combat unit, the 501 Parachute Battalion, was organized in September of 1940. In July 1941, the Infantry School opened its first Officer Candidate School, with the last World War II class graduating on December 9, 1946. During this period, 66,141 second lieutenants had been graduated. On November 1, 1949, all units and activities of Fort Benning were gathered under one command to form the Infantry Center.

But things were also happening in Columbus. Franklin Delano Roosevelt came to town in 1928 to deliver one of his famous "Happy Warrior" speeches on behalf of presidential candidate Al Smith. Smith was not elected, but Roosevelt was, in 1932, frequently visiting what became the Little White House at Warm Springs before and during World War II. In 1938, he paid an official call on Columbus and Fort Benning with First Lady Eleanor riding beside him in the open touring car. Mrs. Roosevelt, however, was not with him when he died at Warm Springs on April 12, 1945, a death mourned throughout the world, but especially in the Chattahoochee Valley where he was regarded as a good neighbor.

(FDR was a man who had his detractors as well as admirers. It would be agreed, though, that where the personal gesture of consideration was concerned, he was without peer. An example of this involved the late Cason Callaway's discovering, while dressing for a white-tie evening at the D. C. White House, that he had not packed white buttons. Could he borrow a set, he asked of the president's valet? Alas, came the reply, FDR himself had only one set. Thus, an embarrassed Callaway went to the reception with white tie and black buttons. His embarrassment was eased when he spied one other guest similarly accessoried improperly—the President of the United States!)

As has been noted, the construction work at Fort Benning was a godsend to the local labor pool, as the textile economy in Columbus was badly damaged by the Depression. And there was steady construction work in the city, such as the Royal Theater, which

In 1921 Columbus acquired its first motor-driven ladder truck. Since its earliest days, the city had had organized firefighters, the Columbus Hook and Ladder Company being formed in 1843 and remaining as a volunteer unit until 1896 when it became a fully-paid department of city government. The handsome rig pictured is by American-LaFrance, of Elmira, New York, the pioneer manufacturer of "modern" firefighting equipment. Note its solid rubber tires, hand-crank siren, electric headlights and the steering wheel that is on the right side. The vehicle had chain drive and chemical apparatus. The driver is M. M. Guerry; beside him is S. C. Stewart. Standing are, left to right, W. J. O'Toole, M. L. Landers (foot on ground), T. C. Turner, H. W. Cook and Chief O. E. McLaughlin. The photo was made at Fire Station Number Four on Sixth Avenue next to the depot. The now-demolished covered train station shed can be seen in the rear. Photograph courtesy of the Columbus College archives

In 1921 Columbus had a mayor and sixteen aldermen, two from each of the eight wards into which the city was divided, a type of government that many enterprising citizens felt should be "modernized" into the commission-management form. The state's General Assembly amended the city's charter and the citizens ratified the action, eliminating the previous ward system. Elected to the five-commissioner board was Miss Anna H. Griffin. A daughter of the pioneer stagecoach operator Daniel Griffin, she was an intelligent and capable leader in the suffrage movement and highly respected in the community. A span of fifty-seven years would elapse before another woman would be elected to the city's governing body. Mrs. Edna Kendrick was elected to Columbus Council in 1978 and is serving her second term. A business woman, Mrs. Kendrick has been active in Georgia's National Democratic Committee, the Daughters of the American Revolution and was chairman of the civic group that brought Columbus Iron Works Convention and Trade Center to fruition. Contemporary photograph by Richard Thomason; both courtesy of the Columbus Ledger-Enquirer *newspapers*

opened on April 30, 1928. Designed by T. Firth Lockwood of Columbus, the Royal (now known as the Three Arts Theater) was the crown jewel in the theater empire of the late Roy E. Martin. Built at the cost of a quarter of a million dollars, Martin was hailed for this "outstanding example of sheer enterprise and faith in Columbus."

Speaking of theaters, the Springer, which we have met before, continued as a legitimate theater through World War I and well into the 1920s. Then, the Great Depression began to make itself felt, and finally—and most effectively—killed off the road shows. As road shows had been the lifeblood of the Springer and other theaters like it around the country, these entertainment emporiums adapted to the times and became movie houses. Likewise the Springer adapted. It also began its long slide into near oblivion and near demise.

About this time, actually on August 25, 1930, a Columbus businessman, who had been born on a remote farm in Alabama and reared in equally remote Texas, achieved deserved recognition in "Time" magazine with a story entitled "The Farm Boy Who Became Peanut King." Tom Huston, for that was the name of the farm boy, would lose his peanut business through ventures into frozen foods, and he would leave Columbus, never to return until in his casket. He made his way to Florida where he recouped his fortune (this time in pet products). He continued to invent, moving into horticulture and abstract art, where he "painted with a camera instead of a brush." This quote is from a tender but well-considered salute written by Huston's widow, Columbus native Minnie Bullock, for the *Ledger-Enquirer's* Sesquicentennial Edition. She concluded, "He (Tom) was a sower of seeds who never stayed around for the harvest. His restless mind, the tool of his talents, never found a resting place. It was his glory and his defeat. But, the seeds he planted in Columbus have flourished into a business that is a benefactor and a blessing to the entire community."

(Like the Springer, we will also come across Tom's Toasted Peanuts a few decades down the pike.)

In a move that predated the consolidation of the city and county governments by exactly twenty-one years, the Columbus Public Schools and the Muscogee County School System commenced joint operation as a single unit on January 1, 1950, the first consolidated school system in the state of Georgia. The joining of the city and county governments also would be the first in the state of Georgia and one of only sixteen in the entire country.

He was born in Corsica (now Blooming Grove), Ohio in 1865. In 1891 he married Florence Kling DeWolfe. In 1898 he was elected to the Ohio Senate and to lieutenant governor in 1903. In 1914, he was elected to the United States Senate and to the presidency in 1920. Therefore, October 27, 1921 may not have been the most important date in the life of Warren G. Harding, but that was when he visited Fort Benning, along with his official party. Harding, front row with his cane under his chin, sat next to Brig. Gen. Walter H. Gordon, who was only some six weeks into his posting as the third commandant of the Infantry School. Harding died in San Francisco on August 2, 1923, before the Teapot Dome and other scandals of his administration became public. No autopsy was performed and the exact cause of his death is not known. Photograph courtesy of the Columbus Ledger-Enquirer *newspapers*

Somewhat in the manner of house moving, monuments in Columbus don't always remain in perpetuity where they are initially planted. An example is the better-than-six-foot-granite stone and bronze plaque known as the Oglethorpe Marker. After several moves in recent years, it has come to rest in what is the Founder's Area of the Promenade. The plaque reads "Kennard's Trail or Ferry, Here General (James) Oglethorpe crossed the Chattahoochee River and at Coweta Town, southwest of this point, signed the famous treaty with the Indians, August 21st, 1739." The monument was erected by the Oglethorpe Chapter of the Daughters of the American Revolution in 1922. The founder of Georgia, Oglethorpe needed a passively friendly or simply non-hostile relationship with the confederation of Indian tribes to serve as a buffer for his English-speaking settlers, menaced as they were by the Spanish from the south and the French from the west. The diplomat-soldier-statesman broke bread with the Indians in their own town, smoked their peace pipe and achieved his mission after a tedious journey from Savannah across the wilderness that was the early colony. Photograph from the author's collection

From behind the potted palms came the unmistakable sounds of the Lester Lanin of the Chattahoochee Valley...Mike Rose's Italian Band. Rose's aggregation was one of the most popular musical groups in this area from the time of its founding around 1892 until Rose's death in 1922. He was born Michele Fiedarone in Paterno, Italy, in 1854. When he came to Columbus he shortened his last name to Rose. He gathered other Italian musicians into the orchestra he had founded. During the years the group was active: no wedding, dance, large reception, riverboat excursion or any other party was complete without the Mike Rose orchestra. In addition to a busy schedule all year long in Columbus, the musicians were much in demand elsewhere. The orchestra often moved for the summer to Warm Springs or to one of the other spas that once dotted Meriwether County to play for dances at the hotels. The orchestra is pictured on the lawn at Warm Springs in 1892. Mike Rose is in the center with baton upraised. The orchestra's harpist, Joseph Brescia, is pictured beside his harp. The young woman beside Brescia is his wife, Mary Agnes, and the little girl holding a straw hat is their eldest child, Marie (later Mrs. John T. Bryant). The others in the picture are not identified. Photograph by J. A. Forsyth; courtesy of Marie Brescia Bryant

Not untypical but probably a bit more elaborate than most are these housing facilities at Fort Benning in the early 1920s. With scrap lumber, tar paper and lots of ingenuity, many families erected their own quarters, later selling them to their replacements when restationed. There were some unusual rules, such as a four-room house had to be occupied by a family of four. If you were a child short, you had to produce one within a twelve-month period. This ruling harvested so much anxiety (and so many children) that it was later rescinded. One veteran Benning alumnus recalled their tent home had a "floor" covered with scraps of tar paper, which was subsequently painted, shellacked and waxed before it was "suitable" for the rugs they had brought back from their previous post in the Orient. Photograph courtesy of the Columbus Ledger-Enquirer *newspapers*

In a community replete with unusual monuments, such as the King-Godwin and Bragg Smith markers, none is more unique than the granite boulder on the main post at Fort Benning, with its bronze tablet inscribed: "He Made Better Dogs of Us All." This tribute is to a canine, whose birthday is a question mark, but who, on August 29, 1923, was found poisoned. Called "Calculator" because "he put down three paws and carried one," this slightly-crippled dog daily hitched rides for over a three-year period from the Ralston Hotel corner to Benning and back again with the officers and non-commissioned who car-pooled from their civilian living quarters to their military duties. Saddened friends, privates and generals alike, sent funds from stations around the world to have the six-foot-tall and three-foot-round monument erected in his memory. Photograph courtesy of the Columbus Ledger-Enquirer *newspapers*

In front of a residence in the 200 block of Twelfth Street that was more akin to the antebellum architecture of Savannah than that commonly found in Columbus, William E. Joy opened his first florist shop. The year was 1922. Ten years later, Joy built an art deco-influenced, curved-fronted building at the intersection of Thirteenth Street and Thirteenth Avenue that is occupied now by the Sho-Place. A native of Blanchport, New York, Joy's first business interest in Columbus wasn't flowers, but the five-and-dime business, opening the first F. W. Woolworth store here in 1912. Joy served as president of Florist Transworld Delivery (FTD) from 1940 to 1946, instituting overseas floral delivery during his tenure. In 1951, he established Mid-South Steel Building Company of Atlanta and sold it to Atlantic Steel in 1954. He retired from the florist business in 1960. At the time of his death at the age of ninety-six in 1980, Joy was the oldest member of the Kiwanis Club of Columbus having been in the club for fifty-six years. Photograph courtesy of the Columbus Ledger-Enquirer *newspapers*

The year could be 1906, or 1921, or 1923 in which the reference "Sousa, the great band leader, was interested in trap shooting and was entertained by the Columbus Gun Club, and I took part in the shooting on the lower end of Broadway," appears in Frederick H. Schomburg, Sr.'s memoirs. On all three of those occasions, John Philip Sousa and his famous band played the Springer Opera House. Born in 1854 in Washington, D. C., the cradle of patriotism, it is not unexpected that Sousa became the composer of such a flag-waving song as "Stars and Stripes Forever," and other stirring marches. Sousa founded his band in 1892 after having played violin in a special orchestra that accompanied Jacques Offenbach on his U. S. tour and after having been Marine Band leader from 1880 to 1892. Sousa died in 1932. Photograph courtesy of the Springer Opera House

A bit of graphic art that links the name of the manufacturer to the height of female fashion (knee high) is utilized in a full-page ad in the Columbus Industrial Index's centennial issue of 1928. In 1907, Claud Hatcher, a pharmacist, added the Union Bottling Works to his family's wholesale grocery business at the corner of Tenth Street and Ninth Avenue. As the grocery business closed, the new enterprise of soft drinks boomed and Hatcher organized the Chero Cola Company in 1912 and began franchising bottlers in other cities. In 1924 the company began marketing NEHI drinks, introducing Royal Crown in 1934. Photograph courtesy of the Columbus Ledger-Enquirer newspapers

179

Little Italy might have been an appropriate name for the area around First Avenue and Tenth Street. Profumo's confectionary and Spano's restaurant were located on Tenth, and in the middle of the 1000 block of First Avenue was situated Giglio's specialty market. Owned and operated by Frank Giglio, who was born in 1876 in this country but whose parents were natives of Italy, his was more than just a grocery store. Ask for it, whether it was buffalo meat, bear steaks or rattlesnake meat in cans, Giglio's had it or would get it. A former employee revealed that there was an informal company motto of "If it creeps, crawls, grows or flies, we've got it." The accompanying photo will attest to the claim that annually the store was the best-decorated for Christmas in the city. Giglio died in 1945. Photograph courtesy of the Columbus Ledger-Enquirer *newspapers*

"Gentlemen, if you will produce the authority and show me that I am in error, I will change my ruling every five minutes. I desire to rule the correct law and not merely my individual opinion." The speaker was Judge William Augustus Little, born in Talbot County November 6, 1838. He died on February 27, 1924, after a distinguished legal and political career that included three elections to the House of Representatives from Muscogee County. He was twice chosen by that legislative body to be its speaker. Attorney general of Georgia, a state Supreme Court justice and a judge of the Chattahoochee Circuit, he was appointed by President Grover Cleveland to the position of assistant attorney general of the United States. Photograph courtesy of the Columbus Ledger-Enquirer *newspapers*

For a total of seventy-seven years, this handsome, three-story brick building belonged to the Fraternal Order of Odd Fellows. Then, in 1925, it was demolished to make way for a modern, $30,000 brick and limestone structure with lodge rooms on the second floor and three stores on the first floor. In the 1000 block of First Avenue on the east side, the Odd Fellows Hall had been built in 1848, about three years before Temperance Hall. Note that two of the posters on the rail fence are advertising a movie called Saucy Baby *which was billed as a comedy coming to the Queen. Photograph courtesy of the* Columbus Ledger-Enquirer *newspapers*

An Edward L. Mooney portrait of Mrs. Albert Hillhouse Shepherd, nee Anne Elizabeth Smythe (1813-?), hangs at the Columbus Museum of Arts and Sciences. In 1924, Col. W. S. Shepherd bequeathed his home Hillhouse, to the Ladies' Educational and Benevolent Society of the City of Columbus, an organization dedicated to caring for destitute and orphaned girls and dating back to 1840. Shepherd's will contained the stipulation that the name of the society become the Anne Elizabeth Shepherd Orphans' Home as a memorial to his mother. The home occupied Hillhouse until 1965 when, with Mrs. M. C. Jennings as president, the home was moved to its present site on Double Churches Road. The facilities, capable of housing twenty-four people, were used in the mid-1970s to accommodate boys as well as girls, but financial restrictions have caused the home to revert to the care of females exclusively. Both photographs courtesy of the Columbus Ledger-Enquirer newspapers

A 1925 aerial view shows the new cuartel, a Spanish word for station or barracks, that was under construction at Fort Benning. Finished and dedicated that same year were Doughboy Stadium, a memorial to infantrymen who were killed during World War I, and Gowdy Field, named for Hank Gowdy, the first major league baseball player to volunteer for service in World War I. Likewise, in Columbus, a memorial stadium, also dedicated to World War I veterans, was under construction. Photograph courtesy of the Columbus Ledger-Enquirer newspapers

On April 2, 1926, owner-editor Julian L. Harris was notified that the Enquirer-Sun *had won the Pulitzer Prize, journalism's highest award, for its opposition to the Ku Klux Klan. The prize committee termed it a "brave and energetic fight." The public announcement came on May 3, 1926. Son of Joel Chandler Harris, the creator of the famous Uncle Remus stories, Harris had taken on the "Invisible Empire," as the Klan was known, and had won. He had given battle through his editorials to the KKK when the other papers and editors-publishers in the state were ignoring its existence. The Pulitzer Prize's public service award jury felt that the newspaper's campaigns were "conducted without regard to personal safety or loss of circulation, and have been a stimulus to the improvement of the social and political life in the South." The* Enquirer-Sun *was born of a merger in January 1874 between the* Enquirer, *founded in 1828 by Mirabeau B. Lamar, and the* Daily Sun *which was first published July 30, 1855. Photograph courtesy of the* Columbus Ledger-Enquirer *newspapers*

It was a national event when A. O. Blackmar II and his wife, the former Mary Ann Blood of Charlton, Massachusetts, celebrated their diamond wedding anniversary in 1926. The New York Times *had record of only four other couples, prior to the Blackmars, in the entire United States who had taken such a lengthy matrimonial voyage. Having married when they were twenty-one and twenty respectively, Blackmar was ninety-seven and she was ninety-six when they observed their seventy-fifth anniversary. A newspaper account of the time reported Mrs. Blackmar as believing that moderate living and regular, temperate habits had been the secret to her longevity. He attributed his to heredity, adding "I have never been especially careful of my health. For years, I was a steamboat man and the work at that time was hazardous." Born in Savannah in 1830, he had been brought to Columbus at age five by his father. Active in insurance and banking, Blackmar had been on the board of trustees of the Columbus School System for seventeen years, had been both alderman and mayor pro tem and, for two years, had served as city treasurer. He lived to be almost 100 and his wife died at age 101 in 1932. Photograph courtesy of the* Columbus Ledger-Enquirer *newspapers*

In 1926, the completed Bartlett's Ferry Dam was West Georgia's largest hydroelectric plant, capable of producing 80,000 horsepower. Twenty miles north of Columbus, Bartlett's Ferry's 120-foot high, 900-foot long dam was constructed by the Hardaway Construction Company and backed up a reservoir of nearly 6,000 acres, with a shore line of 150 miles. This lake was officially named for R. M. Harding, the general manager of the Columbus Electric and Power Company which had also built dams across the Chattahoochee at North Highlands and at Goat Rock, harnessing the falls of the river that, from earliest Columbus' founding days, had been recognized as energy potential for a vast industrial complex. The impounded waters, stretching some ten miles upriver, quickly developed as a pleasure site for Columbusites who took advantage of boating and fishing activities, building many weekend cottages along its wooded shores. Photograph courtesy of the Columbus Ledger-Enquirer newspapers

Streetcar tracks ran down the median of Broadway, there was a traffic signal in the middle of the street at Twelfth, and Model A's and Model T's seemed to outnumber the spectators of this parade in 1925-26. The Merchants and Mechanics Bank, located between Payne Clothing Company and Flournoy Realty Company, has two of its upper lobby windows open for ventilation. To the left of Martin Furniture Company can be seen a long balustrade with six tall lanterns. This was the terrace of the private Muscogee Club, famous for its oyster pan roasts. The club was located in the old John Hanserd house. Also visible in the picture, on curbside just to the right of the traffic signal, is a three-way watering trough for horses, people, and dogs and cats. It (or one like it) is now located at the intersection of Eleventh Street and Broadway. Photograph courtesy of the Columbus Ledger-Enquirer newspapers

Edward Lloyd Thomas' plan for Columbus provided for a four-block-wide swath of greenbelt along its northern and eastern boundaries, with the Chattahoochee River delineating its western and southern limits. With the arrival of the railroads in the 1850s, the undeveloped East Common became the expedient site for the terminal and rail yards. Columbus was principally contained in its downtown blocks until 1925 when the Thirteenth Street viaduct, claimed as the longest structure of its type in the south (1,888 feet of reinforced concrete), leaped the railroad yards and opened a commerce corridor. Financed by the Central of Georgia, it was built by Davis Construction Company of Atlanta. That same year, in 1925, John Nolen, city planner from Cambridge, Massachusetts, made a comprehensive design for the city, a progressive plan that was never implemented. Three years earlier, the city had annexed the Wynnton area, and, with the subsequent railroad yard underpass, Columbus sped to develop the hills and dells east of the original city. Photograph courtesy of the Columbus Ledger-Enquirer *newspapers*

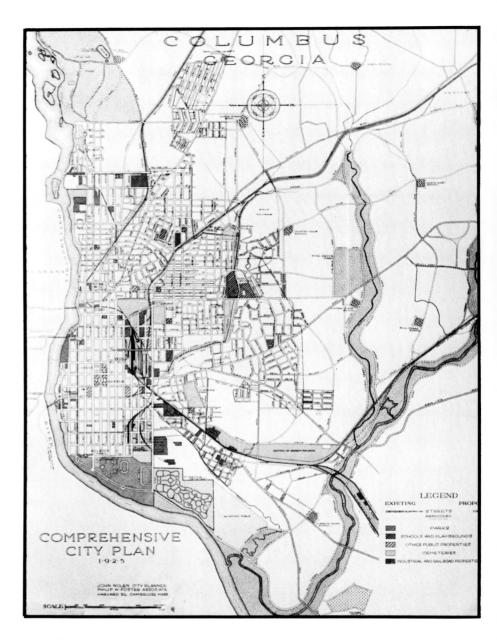

Standing on the front steps of the classic Greek Revival Third Avenue residence known as the Lion House because of the pair of cast iron kings of the jungle that guard the dwelling's entrance, is the original Cotillion Club. This local debutante group is still active in social circles, with its new members being presented at an annual ball during the Christmas season. The 1927 members are, standing on the sidewalk: left, Jeanette Baldwin (Mrs. Harold Lummus), right, Florence Banks (Mrs. Henry Coley); seated at left, Eliza Ott (Mrs. Alfred H. Parham), Adelaide Koonce (Mrs. J. Douglas Neill, Jr.); seated right, Edith Berry (Mrs. Gordon Mallory), Sarah Bussey (Mrs. L. Neill Bickerstaff); standing, front row, Ethel Holden (Mrs. William Howard), Ermine Trulock (Mrs. Tom Hannah), Marjorie Cargill (Mrs. Lawrence Petri); standing back row, Georgia Howard (Mrs. Maurice Latta), Betty Chipley (Mrs. Walter Hudson), Ann Deaton (Mrs. Joe Neal) and Charlotte Storey (Mrs. Edward A. Cummings). Photograph courtesy of the Columbus Ledger-Enquirer *newspapers*

The Lyric Theater in the late 1920s was located on the south side of Twelfth Street between Broad and First. Adjacent to it, with the sign that reads "Books," was The White Company. Across the street was the Stag Billiard Hall. A few doors away was another "parlor," this one featuring not only "billiards," but "soda," "cigars," and "shines." Imagine being able to get your shoes shined, what a luxury! S. H. Harris was in the travel business in the corner of the Flowers Building on the corner of First Avenue and Twelfth Street. Of course, towering over everything in downtown Columbus was the ten-story Ralston Hotel, ground for which had been broken in 1914. Named for J. Ralston Cargill, a former president of the board of trade, the Ralston was the civic club meeting center of the community and its mirrored ballroom was the scene of many social occasions. Managed for twenty-seven years by Oscar L. Betts, Jr., who specialized in what he termed "P.R." (personal reconaissance) in keeping his guests happy, the Ralston closed as a hotel in 1975 and became the Ralston Towers, an apartment complex for senior citizens. Photograph courtesy of the Columbus Ledger-Enquirer *newspapers*

For three days in April 1928, normal business activities of the city took at least second place to activities surrounding the city's celebration of its first one hundred years of existence as the last planned city of the thirteen original colonies. This observance included a battalion-in-defense demonstration at Fort Benning, an historical pageant held nightly at Memorial Stadium, a Confederate Memorial Day Observance with exercises held in the Springer Opera House followed by salute firing at Linwood Cemetery, a noon centennial-military parade and an evening coronation of Miss Dorothy Gloer as "Miss Columbus" and the judging of the county queens. A street festival on Broadway with bands playing for dancing and a Queens' Ball at the Country Club concluded the celebration. The photo at left shows Miss Columbus on her float with her court. First place in the float competition went to Fort Benning and second to Wynnton School. The other photo shows the Columbus Electric and Power Company float, behind which can be seen a number of electric streetcars stabled in the vacant lot south of the car barn. (Power for the streetcars was generated by nearby City Mills dam.) Pictures of various textile mills in Columbus decorated the side of the float, plus signs touting the importance of electricity. The front of the float was a large horse's head and front legs. Both photographs courtesy of the Columbus Ledger-Enquirer *newspapers*

The Unwritten History of Columbus

*Told Most Interestingly by Mr. Blackmar
The Ledger: Columbus, Georgia,
November 7, 1920*

Quite a treat was in store for the members of the Oglethorpe Chapter D.A.R. on Thursday afternoon last, when Mrs. A. O. Blackmar and Miss Betsy Blackmar were joint hostesses.

On this occasion Mr. A. O. Blackmar, Sr., honored the chapter with a sketch of Columbus about 85 years ago, when he first came to this city to make his home.

Mr. Blackmar is perhaps the oldest living citizen of Columbus. He is remarkable both physically and mentally. He is a most entertaining speaker and possesses much personal magnetism.

Through his courtesy, the article is given below:

Ladies: My contribution to the program today relates mainly to my remembrance of current events, that happened in the early history of our city. Vatel in his law of nations, says the first impressions made on the mind, are of the utmost importance for the remainder of life.

Having but little to divert my mind from current happenings the impressionable events of the early days of our city, remains with me to the present time. So it has been with others, passing through the same stirring era.

In April 1835, my father with his family came to Columbus, Ga., by stage coach, from Augusta, Ga. Columbus was laid out in 1828, hence the town was only seven years old on our arrival. I have literally "grown up with the town."

We found the usual border population, composed of whites, Indians, and negroes. It must have been a pretty village as its pet or nickname was Sodom, while Girard, just across the river was known as Gomorrah, these names endured for many years.

Population grew faster than houses, the same difficulty of housing the people as at present. Fortunately, we found temporary quarters with Mr. Elisha Tarver, (grandfather of Monte Moore, the present city clerk of council), located on the southwest corner of Ninth and Broad street.

The stage coach stopped with us on our arrival at McIntosh Hall, located where now stands the Rankin House, kept by Mrs. Love, who was the great-grandmother of the late Sam Spencer, railroad magnate. His good wife, lately deceased, was a charter member of Oglethorpe chapter.

The Indians lived on the Alabama side of the river, mainly at Coweta Town. They were not permitted to remain in the town after dark. I saw much of them in their passing and repassing. Crossing the river bridge on Dillingham street which was quite near our boarding place.

Paddy Carr, a friendly Indian, lived on the Alabama side. His cabin was about 200 yards south of the western abutment of Dillingham Street bridge. He was a man of considerable ability and importance—was U. S. interpreter, owned many slaves and land; had three wives, one of them a daughter of Gen. Wm. McIntosh. Carr's first born children were twin girls. He named one Ari and one Adne after Col. Crowell's son's daughter, Ariadne Crowell. (Col. Crowell was the red Indian agent.) When the Creeks revolted Carr raised an army of 500 Creeks and marched to Florida. He, with his family, went west with the balance of Creeks, when they were deported.

My negro nurse took me over the river to see the Carr family. We found Carr and the twins at home. I can see him now, as he stood in his door, hand resting on each side, pipe in his mouth, swart of visage, tall and of athletic mould. The twins made much of me. Held me in their laps. Carr took me in his arms, tossed me up in a civilized fashion, made my visit not only rememberable, but a desire to repeat it. I was always fond of the Indian in spite of the bad reputation given them.

The Indians were a constant source of apprehension, quickened from time to time by their retaliating raids and murders. Major Dade, but a little while after we came to Columbus, with his command of one hundred were waylaid in Florida, near Warhoo swamp. When I was a lad, I was traveling in Florida with an old gentleman when we passed the battle ground, he pointed out how the Indians disposed their force so as to achieve a complete victory, his whole command of one hundred killed.

I well remember the night that news was received from Jim Henry, the hostile Creek, that he was coming to burn Columbus. This proved to be a diversion as he went below burning, pillaging and murdering as he went, burnt Roanoke (now Florence), fired on the St. Hyperion, killing the pilot, a brother of the late Chas. Brockway. The citizens had every reason to believe Henry would come as promised. They organized a company of citizens, placed the women and children in safety in the Oglethorpe Hotel, an unfinished and unfurnished four-story brick building located where now stands the Masonic Temple. It was a sorrowful night, for the anxious mothers, husbands, soldiering. No lights, save that furnished by homemade tallow candles. No matches. But in spite of the serious conditions, the children treated it as a frolic. Next day we returned to our home with a sigh of relief, that Jim Henry had headed his Indians the other way.

Dr. Ware's Drug Store was next north of the present Kirven Store, the doctor was first lieutenant of the Columbus Guards. My father's place of business was next door. A tall, fine-looking Indian was talking in a very earnest way to a group of citizens. My father was of the crowd, and stood near the speaker, who was Jim Henry. As Henry spoke, from time to time he would reach out and pat me on my head and shoulder. I asked the doctor a short while before his death if he remembered the scene and he replied: "As well as tho' it was but yesterday." Dr. Ware was the father of the late lamented Mrs. Jane Ware, a charter member of your chapter.

I saw the Indians who burnt the stage and murdered some of the passengers, brought down Second Avenue in charge of Sgt. John D. Carter and a squad of Columbus guards. They had been surrendered by the Creeks. Were tried and hanged in Girard. The wheel of the burnt stage hung in the Summer House at the public garden for many years. The garden was located at the Reich place, lower Broad and Front. General Scott's headquarters were on the southwest corner of Fifteenth Avenue and Thirteenth Street. I lived just across the street, and was there every day, attracted by the "spirit stirring drum and ear piercing fife." I well remember the general's appearance; large and military looking, he remained here but a short while. The house until torn down, was known as Kellet's Corner.

Our school house was the old Baptist church, moved from the corner, west of present church. It faced Third Avenue on the land between the Methodist and Baptist churches. Miss Hannah Briggs was our teacher, she married Jack Johnson, probate judge. The present Miss Mary Johnson was their daughter. A young dapper looking officer appeared in the door, saluted teacher and scholars and stated his company, with her permission would be glad to occupy the school house. The request was promptly complied with, much to the delight of we youngsters, who saw ahead a week's holiday to visit headquarters. At that time there was about 50 companies here.

I was on the river for a number of years. Sitting watch one night was joined by Engineer Dan Fry; in the conversation asked him how long he had been on the river. He replied, "since the Indians were hung"—a local fixed the date. He said he was the carpenter on the Hyperion when the Indians fired on the boat, killing Pilot Brockway. Tell me all about it, for I am anxious to know.

"James Y. Smith was the captain when the Indians fired on the boat. The mulatto cook seized a musket to fire on the Indians. Capt. Smith took the gun away from him and threw it overboard. 'Don't you know,' says Smith, 'if you shot at them and they take the boat they will kill and scalp the last one of us.' Well," says Fry, "it was a serious occasion, but it was [a] laughable scene, to see the crew jump overboard to go ashore, the boat had drifted to a sand bar and the water was about waist deep. Some of them would try and swim—these run with much splashing. The yellow cook was in the lead, and he told me when he reached the road, near Davis Andrews' place he heard the crowd coming. Behind a big pine, wrapped his big red bandanna handkerchief around his head as the crowd appeared, sprang into the road with a war whoop—Eustis Chatte Hola—Wagus Cha—(Band Indian). They just melted down in the road as they supposed they had run into the gang that fired on the Hyperion. I saw they were very badly scared and walked nearer to them, calling Mr. Sam, the cook. It took some time to understand, but when they 'come too,' chunked me all the way to town."

The Indians called the river Chata. The falls at the west end of Twelfth Street Wetumpka—Troubled Waters (a name I suppose applied to all falls.) Seminoles, Wanderers or refugees from other tribes. Creeks from their settling in well watered hilly lands.

While the National Door was thrown wide open to the "downtrodden" and degenerated of foreign countries, no organized effort was made by our church or state, in behalf of our native Americans, to lead them in the paths of civilization. In the light of recent events the Indian has proven a citizen's capability. Robbed of lands, demoralized with free drink, their homes invaded, treaties made at the point of the bayonet. Yet, the public opinion was expressed in the saying, "the only good Indian is a dead Indian."

The city's first radio station, WRBL, was heard on the air in 1928. It was established by William Lewis and Monte Moore, a motion picture operator for Roy E. Martin, Sr., who had just opened his magnificent Royal Theater. The most commonly-held belief is that the call letters of the tiny station, operating out of a dressing room at the theater that was hung with croker sacks for acoustical effect, were the "W" being a Federal Communications Commission designation and the "RBL" standing for Radio Bill Lewis, as he was known. As a teenager, Lewis had built his own little radio transmitter and "sneaked" on the air through unlicensed broadcasts sometime between 1920 and 1925. By the time the accompanying 1932 photo was taken, the station had been (1) sold to the Columbus Junior Chamber of Commerce, (2) closed, (3) sold to David Parmer and back on the air by November of 1929, and (4) sold again (to J. W. Woodruff, Sr.) in 1931. On March 15, 1939, WRBL joined the CBS network of stations from its location in the former Woodruff family home at 1420 Second Avenue. The lady in the middle of the photo is Gertrude Handley, an early radio personality and beloved local pianist, and the menfolk surrounding her are, (left to right), Thurston Bennett, John Henderson, David Parmer, Hubert N. Caraway, Dr. W. Laird Miller, Noel Moore, and Bill Lewis. Photograph courtesy of the Columbus Ledger-Enquirer newspapers

Mrs. Irwin Rothschild, third from left on the front row, was president of the Muscogee County Council of the Parent-Teacher Association when the council held its first 1928 meeting with Mrs. J. D. Miller of Atlanta, the state PTA president, as honored guest. Front row, left to right, are, Mrs. M. James Calloway, Mrs. duPont Kirven, Mrs. Rothschild, Mrs. Miller, Mrs. Cooper Campbell, Mrs. Lester Slade, Mrs. J. L. Peed. Second row, left to right, Mrs. John Gallagher, Mrs. J. W. Coppock, Mrs. Reynolds Flournoy, Mrs. Walter Drane, Mrs. W. H. Moon, Mrs. J. C. Batcheldof, Mrs. L. H. Crowell, Mrs. Emil Ausfields, Mrs. Josiah Flournoy, (unidentified), Mrs. Wheeler Tolbert, Mrs. Jeff Kelly, Mrs. Fred M. Schomburg, Mrs. J. B. Knight. Third row, Mrs. O. D. Smith, Mrs. Albert Wade, Mrs. B. E. Pulliam, Mrs. Arthur Lynch, Mrs. Walter Cargill, Mrs. S. C. Harris, Mrs. Annie Mae Walters, Mrs. Clifford Boland, Mrs. T. L. Bowden, Mrs. Clarence Tigner. They are pictured on the front steps of the First Baptist Church. Photograph courtesy of the Columbus Ledger-Enquirer *newspapers*

A permanent theater in the town by 1832 (albeit of crude logs), a lecture by Oscar Wilde in the 1880s, and a music conservatory established in 1892 indicate that culture was not a new thing to Columbus when the Three Arts League was formed in 1927. Mrs. William de L. Worsley (the Columbus historian Etta Blanchard Worsley) was its first president. The premier season was ambitious, featuring performances by Suzanne Keener, soprano of the Metropolitan Opera Company, and Margaret Matzenauer, contralto of the company; the New York Theatre Guild's classic production of Mr. Pim Passes By, *and world traveler-journalist Lowell Thomas delivering his famous* With Lawrence in Arabia *lecture. The site of the first season was the New High School Auditorium (Columbus High School) in Wynnton. Later affiliated with Community Concerts Corporation of New York, the Three Arts League presented concerts well into the 1960s, bringing many famous performers to the enjoyment and enlightenment of appreciative audiences. When* Mr. Pim Passes By *was seen in Columbus on February 14, 1928, George Gaul and Florence Eldridge (in photo at right) played the leads that had been originated by Hortense Alden and Frederic March in New York. Both photographs courtesy of the* Columbus Ledger-Enquirer *newspapers*

When Franklin Delano Roosevelt spoke at the Springer Opera House on October 4, 1928, he was promoting the candidacy of Alfred E. Smith, a Roman Catholic and the nominee of the Democratic Party for the presidency. Roosevelt himself was a candidate at the time, but his Columbus audience wasn't eligible to vote as he was running for the office of governor of the Empire State of the North (New York) and not the Empire State of the South (Georgia). It was reported that the local speech received a great ovation, but Smith still lost in the general election. Roosevelt came down to Columbus for his speech from Warm Springs where he was receiving treatment for his body that had been ravaged by polio. Extreme left: Jack Ellis; next, a delegation from Opelika, Alabama. Center to right: Franklin D. Roosevelt, Walker R. Flournoy, Wm. De L. Worsley, Mrs. Perry Burrus, Bentley H. Chappell, Mrs. Bentley H. Chappell, Leighton MacPherson, Henrietta Worsley and Mrs. Wm. de L. Worsley, Mrs. William Hart and two unidentified persons at the end. Photograph from Etta Blanchard Worsley's Columbus on the Chattahoochee *(1951)*

Downtown Columbus was a solid block of buildings in this 1928 photo. If the entire photo is regarded as a clock, then stretching from 6 o'clock to 10 o'clock along the river was a solid string of cotton warehouses. At 1 o'clock can be seen the Ralston Hotel, and at 3 o'clock there is the Springer Opera House. Between the Springer and the Ralston, the white structure is the YMCA, with a tennis court on the west side. The City market extends more than halfway down First Avenue and there is a transportation transfer station clearly visible at the intersection of Tenth Street and Broad. Less discernible are stations at the Twelfth Street and Broad intersection and at Ninth Street and Broad. Yes, that's the Eagle and Phenix Mill at 11 o'clock and, at high noon, the Waverly Hotel shows. Photograph courtesy of the Columbus Ledger-Enquirer *newspapers*

In 1929, a correspondent for the New York Herald *toured the South, reporting on fine Southern dishes in such gastronomically-renowned cities as Memphis and New Orleans. She did not leave out Columbus. The restaurant with which the reporter fell in love was the Cricket. Opened in 1918 by Gordon Flournoy and his wife, Suzette Joerg, the sign for the Cricket can easily be seen in this Twelfth Street and Broadway photo. Note that the stop-and-go signal is hand operated by the policeman who judges the amount of traffic flow in any particular direction. It is fall, but not cold, as the lady at the extreme left has her fur-collared coat open. The automobile making a turn east onto Twelfth Street, permissable in the good old days, is identified as a Hudson. The Yankee reporter waxed eloquent about the Cricket, saying: "I never hoped to eat such good food and positively home-cooked. The place was plain and immaculate; creamy as to walls, the only decoration being shelves to hold flower vases, which were always full of fresh flowers. In fact, the place fairly blossomed daily, the tables plentifully supplied, and one day I counted 14 varieties. The waitresses are pretty as pictures, their uniforms the green of the leaves of lily-of-the-valley, all flower skirts and trim." A Cricket recipe was included: 1 quart milk, 2 cups waterground meal, 2 tablespoons butter, 2 teaspoons salt, 2 eggs. Beat the eggs until light, boil the milk, add salt, then the meal, slowly, stirring until perfectly smooth. Then add the other ingredients and stir well. Put into a greased pan and brown. Cut in six-inch squares, split with butter. Over this eggbread, chicken was placed, so that it really became a chicken-eggbread sandwich. The Cricket was also noted for its butterscotch pies. Photograph courtesy of the* Columbus Ledger-Enquirer *newspapers*

The inscription on a monument in Linwood Cemetery reads "To one whose life was brief but whose influence is lasting." Indeed, Noble Leslie DeVotie did have a short life, from January 24, 1838, to February 12, 1861: a total of twenty-five years and nineteen days. Born in Tuscaloosa, Alabama, DeVotie was a candidate for the ministry and the most brilliant student at the University of Alabama, his grade average being the highest ever made by anyone up to that time. Eight close friends, under his leadership, gave birth to Sigma Alpha Epsilon, holding that fraternity's first official meeting on March 9, 1856. As a minister of the Gospel, it was fitting and proper that DeVotie would serve as chaplain in the Confederate Army until he drowned at Fort Morgan near Mobile.

"Greater love had no man than this, that a man lay down his life for his friends," reads a second inscription on the memorial, erected in 1929 by the SAE fraternity to honor its founder. Noble's brother Howard, a surgeon in the Confederate Army, also died during the conflict and the two brothers share a common gravestone. From 1856 to 1985, SAE has grown from eight members to over 160,000, with 195 active chapters on campuses in forty-eight states. *Photograph courtesy of the* Columbus Ledger-Enquirer *newspapers*

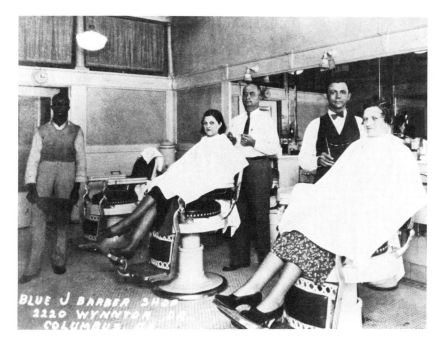

The around-the-stove camaraderie of the rural country store compares in social importance to that of the peaceful gatherings in neighborhood barbershops. Traditionally thought of as predominantly male territory, the Blue J Barber Shop, which opened in September of 1928, clearly was breaking into brave new worlds by providing service to female customers, as witnessed by this 1929 photo. The Blue J founder, Marvin Jones (right), who died in 1982, is seen in this photo with fellow tonsorialist Thomas A. Gay. Still located at 2220 Wynnton Road, the Blue J contains many of its original architectural fixtures and probably is the oldest barbershop in the city in continuous operation at the same location, now serving a fourth generation of some Columbus families. Many of its first customers, like the author, are now its middle-aged customers, also like the author. Photograph from the author's collection

Herbert Clark Hoover was inaugurated as the thirty-first president of the United States on March 4, 1929, when it began to rain in the Columbus, Georgia, area. And it rained. And it rained. The creeks flooded first, then the river began to rise. And rise. And rise. Soon, the Chattahoochee was no longer accepting its bed, narrow or wide. Nor were the willful waterweeds holding it thrall. It was out of its banks and encroaching upon residential and commercial sections of the community that had previously been high and dry. Since Gen. John Pershing was not at Fort Benning for an inspection tour, the name of the first Quaker and mining engineer president seemed the most likely one to be attached to the flood. Eleven days passed. And the river again rose over flood stage, reaching this time a record high water mark of 53.3 feet on March 16, 1929. Naturally, this in local parlance became known as the Second Hoover Flood. Photographs courtesy of the Columbus Ledger-Enquirer *newspapers*

Fort Benning truly was beginning to take on the appearance of a permanent military post by 1930, as indicated by these new officers' quarters, specifically "Block 15, 8-15-30." Such quarters continue to serve in the present as residences for personnel with the designation of major and colonel. In the early 30s, the Main Post Chapel (of all faiths), the Officers' Club and the Infantry School building were also built. Photograph courtesy of the Columbus Ledger-Enquirer *newspapers*

A stock exchange is an organized market for the sale and purchase of securities such as shares, stocks and bonds. This country's first exchange was established in Philadelphia in 1791. A year later, under a tree at 68 Wall Street in New York, twenty-four merchants and brokers credited the New York Stock Exchange, where, since 1953, membership has been limited to 1,366. This is how Fenner and Beane looked in Columbus in the early 1930s. The location is probably 13 West Eleventh Street. Note that the board is clean and the markers are ready to chalk up sales. Customers have even assembled and the time is ten minutes to nine o'clock. Identified are, left to right, (unknown), Harry Reich, Joe Flowers, Sr., Charles Foley, (unknown), and Ben Wardlaw who, in 1931, was the brokerage office's manager. According to the city directory of 1934, Fenner, Beane and Ungerleider's local office had telephone numbers 2272, 2273, 2274 and 2275, plus long distance 9962. A Eufaula native, Flowers ran the brokerage office called Livingston and Company at 1207 First Avenue before he became an investor-realtor, purchasing the Masonic Temple at Twelfth Street and First Avenue in 1940 for $90,000. Flowers died in 1951 at the age of fifty-seven. Photograph courtesy of the Columbus Ledger-Enquirer *newspapers*

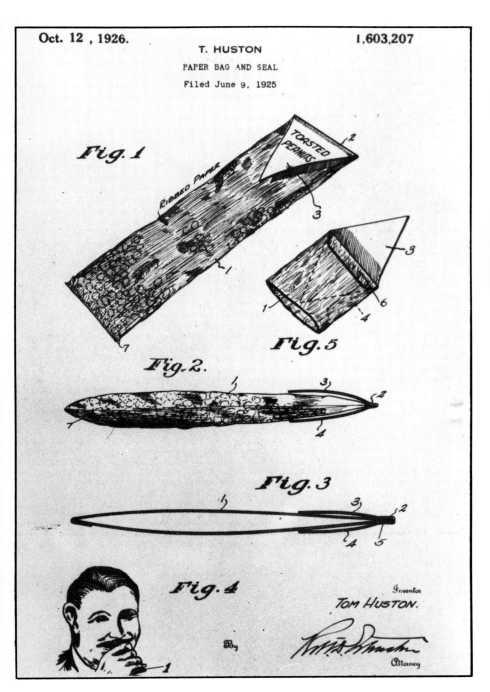

Alabama-born and Texas-raised, Tom Huston learned early in life that, while he liked peanuts, he disliked shelling them. So he invented a machine to remove the meat of the nuts, free and unbroken. The market for such $5,000 machines was limited. But, say, what about a snack-sized bag full of "Tom's Toasted Peanuts," in a narrow cellophane package with a red triangular label selling at five cents? He began packaging such items in a frame shed in his north Columbus machine factory. Four years later, Time magazine of August 25, 1930, featured his arrival as the peanut tycoon on Wall Street's Curb Market. A subsequent venture into freezing Georgia peaches was disastrously defrosted by the Stock Market Crash and the Depression that followed. Disheartened and devalued, Huston departed Columbus in 1931, never to return until 1970 in his casket. Between those dates, he made another fortune, this time merchandising pet products, and further displayed his inventiveness by artistically-stunning excursions into abstract photography. Both photographs courtesy of the Columbus Ledger-Enquirer *newspapers*

An advertisement for the motion picture Disraeli, *starring the celebrated actor George Arliss, appeared in the* Enquirer-Sun *of September 1931. Listed as his co-star was Louise Huff, who was born in Columbus in 1895 and moved with her family to New York at the age of thirteen. Her dramatic studies began there and led her to a diversified line of parts in stock in New York. This experience, according to the* Enquirer-Sun, *directed Miss Huff to Philadelphia to perform in two and three-reel pictures. Her first film was* The Old Homestead *where "she acquitted herself with so much glory...that her future in motion pictures was assured." She was featured in many pictures, and she "afterwards co-starred with Jack Pickford in a series of pictures that proved one of the most satisfying groups of recent years," added the* Enquirer-Sun. *She died in 1973. Her older-by-two-years sister, Justina, also had a brief movie career before settling down to married life. Photograph courtesy of the* Columbus Ledger-Enquirer *newspapers*

She was less than six months from becoming the first woman to fly solo across the Atlantic, but slight, sandy-haired Amelia Earhart was already a famed aviatrix when she autogyroed into Columbus on November 28, 1931, landing at the Municipal Air Field on Victory Drive. Earhart was endeavoring to interest women in flying, and a large female delegation, headed by Mrs. Walter Richards, met her at the airport (now largely an industrial site composed of a banking company, a machine factory, a mill outlet store, a bottling plant, a national guard armory and a golf driving range). She was feted at a luncheon at the country club where she made a speech. Mrs. Richards and city manager Henry B. Crawford were given a ride in her plane. Later she wrote to Mrs. Edith Kyle Harrison about establishing landmark designations for planes coming into the city. On May 22, 1932, she flew non-stop from New Foundland to Ireland. A few years later (1935), she soloed to Hawaii and, in June of 1937, commenced a round-the-worlder, planning to keep near the equator. On July 1st, she and her navigator took off from New Guinea for Howland Island, occupied by the Japanese, and they were never heard from or seen again, despite a massive air and sea search. Photographed in 1931 with Miss Earhart were, left to right, Mrs. Jefferson Box, Mrs. Frank D. Foley, Mrs. Charlton Battle, Mrs. J. Homer Dimon, Mrs. J. Ralston Cargill, Mrs. William de L. Worsley, Mrs. Leighton MacPherson, Amelia Earhart, Mrs. Walter Richards, Mrs. Edith Kyle Harrison, Miss Latimer Watson, Mrs. Edmond Page, and Mrs. Frank G. Lumpkin. Photograph courtesy of the Columbus Ledger-Enquirer *newspapers*

The Depression was still an economic reality when this photo was taken on October 19, 1933. But children were frequently spared the brutal facts by parents who thought that one's childhood is the time to be happy and sans souci. *Thus, Margie Thrasher (nee Graves) celebrated her fifth birthday with a Halloween party in the company of cousins, neighbors, and friends. She is number nine in the photo; the other children are (1) Marian Hicks (2) June Ballou (3) Peggy Ryan (4) Erie Sue Bloodworth (5) John Cozart (6) Walter Miller (7) Sue Walters (8) Joe Walters (9) Marjorie Graves (10) Nancy Storey (11) Mary Alice McDonald (12) Billy Cunningham (13) Memory Richards (14) Dorothy Wells (15) Patsy Butts (16) Margaret Ann Richards (17) Peggy Miller (18) Mary Lou Illges (19) unidentified (20) Julia Pitts DeGraffenreid (21) Tom Cook (22) Barbara Bullock (23) Susan Cooper (24) Frank Bullock (25) Lucile Cooper (26) Caroline Nuckolls (27) Bobby Burts (28) Edward Bouchard (29) Hugh Roberts, Jr. (30) Tommy Tuggle (31) Bettie Jean Garrett (32) Sally Bradley (33) Frank Bradley (34) Frances Reeves (35) Clason Kyle (36) Kyle Spencer (37) Patsy Layfield (38) Annette Garrett (39) Tina Wells (40) Virgil McDowell (41) Tom Phillips (42) Sara Ann Proffitt (43) Elizabeth Hunter (44) Isla Hunter (45) Martha Howard (46) Frank Billings, Jr., and (47) Tommy Latta. Photograph courtesy of the Marjorie Graves Thrasher collection*

Parties with a theme such as costumes are great fun, particularly if everyone participates. The 1930s in Columbus was an era when money was short but talent was long. Therefore, more ingenuity went into costumes than anything else. For example, the Theo Goldens borrowed a Western Union uniform (for him) and a flower box (for her). Add some roses spilling from the top of the box, and ribbon around her head and you had an animated "Flowers by Wire." They probably won first prize. Photograph courtesy of the Bettie Golden Tyler collection

The South may have lost the war but a secret terrorist organization known as the Ku Klux Klan was organized at Pulaski, Tennessee, after the hostilities. The KKK was determined to revive the authority of the planter aristocracy and to avoid sharing political power with the newly enfranchised former slaves. The army of "The Invisible Empire of the South" had a grand wizard and dressed in robes and sheets to frighten the superstitious and to disguise their identity. It was disbanded in 1869 by order of the Grand Wizard, former Confederate Gen. Bedford Forrest. However, the Klan remained locally active in numerous locations and enjoyed various periods of popularity, particularly after its reorganization in nearby Atlanta in 1915 when its bias was increased to include Roman Catholics, Jews, foreigners and organized labor and, in the mid-1960s, the Civil Rights Act of 1964. This 1933 application for citizenship in the Invisible Empire begins, "I, the undersigned, a native born, true and loyal citizen of the United States of America, being a white male Gentile person of temperate habits, sound in mind and a believer in the tenents of the Christian religion, the maintenance of White Supremacy and the principles of a 'pure Americanism' do most respectfully apply for membership in the Knights of the Ku Klux Klan through Klan No., Realm of." Photograph courtesy of the Columbus Ledger-Enquirer *newspapers*

A program utilizing unemployed architects, draftsmen and photographers to record the architecture of the United States was born in 1933 with Roosevelt's New Deal. A HABS (acronym for Historic American Building Survey) team visited the Columbus area in 1936, recording ten houses, such as this Greek Revival mansion located on what was known as Golden Row. Built by John Fontaine, the first elected mayor of Columbus (1836-1837), the house, on the corner of Eleventh Street and Front Avenue, facing Fontaine's cotton warehouse, was demolished in the 1940s. Through the 1934 agreement of the American Institute of Architects, the Library of Congress and the National Park Service, the survey continued until just before World War II, with more than 23,000 sheets of measured drawings and more than 25,000 photographic negatives of some 6,389 structures having been recorded. Photograph courtesy of the Historic American Building Survey

Not friendly rivals, but allies on the same team. That was the case in 1935 when the Columbus High School "Blue Devils" were a bi-school team, the players being chosen from Columbus High and from Industrial High School (later Jordan Vocational High School). Those pictured are, front row (left to right): Marion Page, Herbert Rosser, (?) Casper, Johnnie Jones, John Barfield, Harold Monroe, Bill Whitehead, Sumpter Blackmon; second row (left to right): Richard Parks, Billy Woodall, Alva Norris, Harry Jackson, Billy King, Franklin (Buddy) Horton, Charles Heldreth, Allen Jones; back row (left to right): Frank Johnson (manager), Judson T. Mayfield (coach), Wood King, Walter Chandler, Dan Odom, James Skipworth, Warren Boswell, R. G. Jones, LeRoy Burnham, Paul Kennon, Henry (Red) Wadsworth (assistant coach).

"Be prepared:" is the motto of the Boy Scouts of America. On the day that this photo was taken in 1936, Troop Six had been victorious in a council-wide field meet. Holding the Schomburg Trophy was Scout Dick Munn. Behind him in the front row were: left to right, John Harris (with flag), Leslie Lilienthal, John T. Miller, Fred Durham, Steve Richards, Jack McGee, Edward Jackson, Denton Johnson, Dean Inglis, David Barton, Billy McDougal (with flag); second row, left to right, Randolph Townsend, Beverly Mobley, Grey Carter, Bill Ogletree, John Deignan; third row, left to right, Gordon Hunter, Billy Romeo, Frank Wadsworth, Bob Huff; fourth row, left to right, Bert Smith, Hugh Martin, Oscar Smith; fifth row, left to right, Paul Kennon, Bob Clarke, Louis McElroy. Troop Six has been active and chartered continuously since its inception in 1932 and its chartering in 1933. Begun by the PTA at Saint Elmo School, the troop has, since 1972, been sponsored by Trinity Episcopal Church. The Thirteenth Street landmark cabin was started in the fall of 1935 and completed in the spring of 1936. Members of the troop not present for the photo were Leonard Allen, Edgar Johnson, Bill Jones, and Cadwallader Jones. Since 1910 when the Boy Scout movement came to the United States, more than seventy million American boys and young men have taken the pledge to do their best, to do their duty to God and country, to obey Scout law, to help other people at all times, and to keep themselves physically strong, mentally awake and morally straight. Photograph courtesy of the Columbus Ledger-Enquirer newspapers

The name of the game is poker, and the hand must be a crucial one, even though the stacks of chips upon the table don't indicate a loser. The dealer, with a pipe in his mouth, is Jeff Kelly, Sr., and he's about to turn over a card which considerably interests the pair of kibitzers standing behind him, especially J. Linton White in the dark shirt. The second player from the left is Tom Wade, and at the right end of the table in a rocking chair is Walter A. Richards, with a cigar jammed into the corner of his mouth. The identities of the other players/watchers weren't determined, nor of the bartender who obviously isn't pouring from an original formula Coca-Cola bottle. The place? The porch of the Thronoteeska Club in Florida. The time? A good one which was being had by all. Photograph courtesy of the Columbus Ledger-Enquirer newspapers

In 1936 the Ladies Memorial Association recognized with appropriate ceremony the unveiling of a marker and bronze plaque that commemorated the spot where the association had been organized, the now-demolished John Tyler residence at the corner of Fourteenth Street and Fourth Avenue. The marker reads: "Tyler Home, where in March 1866 the Ladies Aid Society organized the first memorial association honoring Confederate heroes. 'One day' each year is theirs." Miss Lizzie Rutherford is credited with the idea for the memorial day, and Mrs. Robert Carter was the first president. Shown in this photo at the dedication ceremonies are (left to right) T. G. Reeves, Sterling Albrecht, Robert Elliott, (unidentified), Mrs. M. J. Stone, (unidentified), Mrs. J. B. Knight, Mrs. Elizabeth Jones, Mrs. Charles Meredith, Mrs. Mark Mote, Roland B. Daniel, Mrs. Louis Garrard, Mary Florence McKee. The four youths kneeling are, left to right, Porter Pease, Patsy Ann Huffman, Albert Woolfolk, and Sally Davis. Photograph courtesy of the Columbus Ledger-Enquirer *newspapers*

Celebrated cooks who just happened to be sisters, or, maybe its the other way around, sisters who just happened to be celebrated cooks were Misses Fannie and Mamie Schnell. They opened the Corridor Tea Room in 1937. Novices to restauranteuring they were not, for they had operated the Cozy Tea Room for Trinity Episcopal Church since 1916. The challenge to the Cozy, started by Trinity's Women's Auxiliary, was to raise enough money to purchase the Victorian house next door to Trinity for use by its rector, S. Alston Wragge, his wife and their three daughters. Having met its goal, the Cozy closed and the Schnells opened the Corridor, opposite Kirven's Twelfth Street entrance. Shown here are Elise Wallace, Inez Hanson, Patty Revels and Jetta Patterson, whose duty it was to deliver the Cozy's and the Corridor's specialty of the house—Lemon Ice Cream,—to eager customers. Unlike Profumo's ice cream, that dessert has been included in various editions of the Junior League of Columbus's cookbooks. Photograph courtesy of the Columbus Ledger-Enquirer *newspapers*

Columbus had been ten years without a representative in baseball's major leagues when Skeeter Newsome signed with the Philadelphia Athletics. In August of 1938, Newsome became the first major league player to wear a helmet while batting. Twice hit in the head by pitched balls, the second time almost fatally, Newsome was required by the "A's" manager, Connie Mack, to wear protective headgear, a revolutionary step in baseball, but now mandatory from the majors down to the Little League. Newsome later played for the Boston Red Sox and the Philadelphia Phillies. Photograph courtesy of the Columbus Ledger-Enquirer newspapers

To Isabelle Garrard Patterson should go the credit for exciting Columbus residents about their rich Indian heritage. Widely known in archaeological circles, she was vitally interested in the early history of the Indian tribes of this area, spending many years studying the migration of the Creeks to this region. More than just a dusty-tomed scholar, she "dug" (in the vernacular) her work, making a series of important discoveries near the mouth of Bull Creek. One of these was Folsom Point, a projectile so-called because it was of a type found first in Folsom, New Mexico, but later in the mid-west and in Georgia. In the summer of 1936, Dr. A. R. Kelly of the University of Georgia's Department of Archaeology headed a team of archaeologists here. Among their findings from Bull Creek were three rare effigy dog pots which were put on public exhibition in the lobby of the Merchants and Mechanics Bank on Broadway. Early in 1937, Mrs. Patterson presented a paper on the Columbus project dig to the Society of American Archaeology at the Smithsonian, being introduced by Frank R. Swanton, highly respected ethnologist. In May of 1954, the Museum of Indian Arts and Civilization in the Chattahoochee Valley, located in the basement of the newly-organized Columbus Museum of Arts and Crafts, was dedicated to Mrs. Patterson, who died in 1955. Photograph courtesy of the Columbus Ledger-Enquirer newspapers

Franklin Delano Roosevelt, at the last minute accompanied by wife Eleanor, visited Columbus and Fort Benning on March 30, 1938, being received by a large crowd in front of the Muscogee County Courthouse. Already into his second term as president, Roosevelt was becoming an increasingly familiar sight locally as he continued to find increased benefits from exercising in the waters of nearby Warm Springs, where he had built a cottage which became known worldwide as the Little White House. Photograph courtesy of the Columbus Ledger-Enquirer newspapers

Death came to George Foster Peabody on March 4th at Pine Glade, only a few hundred yards from his friend Franklin D. Roosevelt's Warm Springs cottage. Born in Columbus, Peabody had moved north with his family when he was thirteen and attended Deerfield Academy. However, family finances forced him to go to work (at eight dollars a month) and his formal education was acquired largely through night courses at the YMCA, to such an extent that he always referred to the YMCA as his alma mater. However, Peabody's financial circumstances did not remain strained. He became "eminently successful as a financier and business leader" and "made numerous bequests to churches, schools and humanitarian causes; giving away practically all of his fortune in his lifetime." A partner in a leading New York banking investment firm which had a highly useful role in the financing of railroads, mines and industries in America, Peabody was one of the oustanding laymen of the Protestant Episcopal Church and was National Treasurer of the Democratic Party. A generous contributor to education locally and on the state level (the George Foster Peabody School of Forestry at the University of Georgia is named in his honor), Peabody's ashes were scattered at "Yaddo," a nationally important retreat for writers and artists in New York State. Since 1941, the University of Georgia has given awards in the field of radio and television for excellence; these awards also are named in honor of Peabody. Both photographs courtesy of the Columbus Ledger-Enquirer *newspapers*

Built originally as a ferry for service on the Mississippi River, the George W. Miller *was the last of nearly two hundred steamboats which braved the waters of the Chattahoochee from the founding of Columbus until April 1, 1939, when the* Miller *arrived in the local port. Owned by Thurston C. Crawford, the* Miller *had an overall length of 165 feet and an overall width of 44 feet, its boilers being allowed 212 pounds of steam. With deck accomodations for 736 passengers, the ship was operated as an excursion boat until it was dismantled in the late '40s and its steel hull sold as a barge. Photograph courtesy of the* Columbus Ledger-Enquirer *newspapers*

It was in the fall of 1939 that this group of business and civic leaders gathered in the Oak Room of the Ralston Hotel for the organizational meeting of the Army-Navy YMCA. Although several faces around the table are unfortunately unidentified, the majority of them are. They are, standing (left to right): Dr. J. Calvin Reid, Jim Woodruff, Jr., Solon Davis, (unknown), (unknown), Frederick Porter, Jim Thomas, (unknown), (unknown), Tom Fowler, Walter Pike, (unknown), Hugh Bentley, Dr. Osgood F. Cook; seated (left to right): Floyd Francisco, D. Abbott Turner, Alvah H. Chapman, Pop Amerson, (unknown), J. DuPont Kirven, (unknown), Ira Moyer, Harbin K. Park, (unknown), (unknown), Jessie H. Cutler. Photograph courtesy of the Columbus Ledger-Enquirer *newspapers*

She was born Gertrude Pridgett in Columbus in 1886, but she didn't acquire her lasting fame with that name. At age fourteen she made her singing debut at a Springer talent show, appearing in a group called "A Bunch of Blackberries." Eighteen years later, in 1904, she married Will (Pa) Rainey and became the main attraction in his travelling "Rabbit Foot Minstrels." In 1923, she began making recordings, a total of ninety-two of which are known. Paramount Records advertised her as "Ma Rainey—Mother of the Blues." A talented musician who is credited with transforming rural black folk music into urban jazz, she retired to her birth city, dying here on December 22, 1939. She is buried in Porterdale Cemetery, where her headstone reads simply "Gertrude Rainey," without either the Pridgett name or the sobriquet, "Ma." Photograph courtesy of the Columbus Ledger-Enquirer *newspapers*

Her family called her "Tartie," but the world knew her as Carson McCullers. However, she was born Lula Carson Smith here in 1917. After spending her childhood and adolescence wishing and hoping to become a concert pianist, McCullers—shortly after her graduation from Columbus High School at age seventeen—left Columbus for New York where her love and talent for writing became evident. In 1940, at the age of twenty-three, her first novel, The Heart is a Lonely Hunter, brought McCullers to the forefront of the American Literary scene, garnering for her praise from among the nation's literati. The New York Times Book Review claimed that "No matter what the age of its author, The Heart is a Lonely Hunter would be a remarkable book. When one reads that Carson McCullers is a girl of 23 it becomes more than that. Maturity does not cover the quality of her work. It is something beyond that, something more akin to the vocation of pain to which a great poet is born." The pain of which this reviewer spoke would remain one of the most shattering influences on McCullers' personal and professional life, although in spite of it she was able to produce an impressive canon of fiction and non-fiction works by the time of her death in 1967. (See Chapter VII for more information regarding McCullers' life.) She is seen here with her husband, James Reeves McCullers, Jr., in a photo taken in 1950s Paris by noted photographer Louise Dahl-Wolf. Photograph by Louise Dahl-Wolfe; courtesy of the Roger T. Harris collection

From 1941 to 1945, the Cincinnati Reds (and Columbus) had a brother battery in pitchers Elmer and John Riddle. Elmer established an all-time Cincinnati won-and-lost record in '41 with a percentage of .826 for nineteen victories and four defeats, also leading the National League with a 2.24 ERA. Two years later he tied for most wins in the National League with twenty-one. And he set a major league record in 1943 for pitchers by going 102 games without an error before his first miscue. Asked once by Cecil Darby, sports editor, what his biggest moments were, he said, "I guess I'd have to say pitching in the World Series of 1940 and being chosen on the National League All-Star team in 1948 were tops." In the accompanying photo, Elmer Riddle is on the left and brother John on the right. The fellow in the middle was Bing Crosby, who described Elmer's 1948 performance as "the greatest comeback since (Al) Jolson!" Photograph courtesy of the Columbus Ledger-Enquirer newspapers

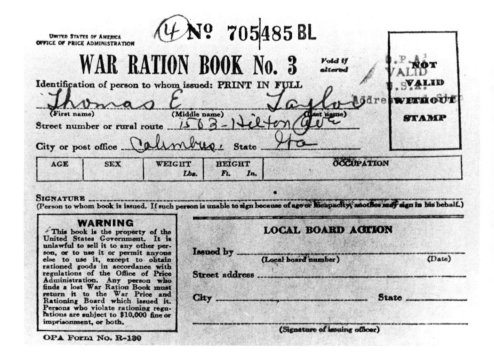

"A date that will live in infamy." Thus did Franklin D. Roosevelt describe the events of December 7, 1941, when the Japanese made a sneak attack upon the U.S. fleet anchored at Pearl Harbor in the Hawaiian Islands. Within a few weeks' time, every home in Columbus had been furnished the Civil Defense Air Raid instructions sheet for posting in a conspicuous place in each dwelling; and wallet-sized cards had been issued for individual members of each family. Note there were two kinds of signals: the "Alert Signal" which was "A steady three-minute blast of the sirens, repeated after one minute of silence" and the "Take Cover Signal, a wailing or rising and falling blast on the siren for three minutes." Fortunately, Columbus citizens never heard these signals, except in practice exercises! Food rationing, however, was all too much of a reality for civilians in World War II. While Americans never suffered real deprivation, they were vividly conscious of wartime shortages. Pictured is the cover of a World War II ration book and a sheet of the stamps which the book contained. Housewives carefully counted their stamps and shopped with ration books in hand. Poster from the author's collection; ration book photographs courtesy of the T. Earl Taylor collection

At the start of World War II, the commandant of the Infantry School at Fort Benning was Omar Nelson Bradley. Born February 12, 1893 in Clark, Missouri, Bradley was to die in New York on April 8, 1981, after an illustrious career in the U.S. Army, graduating from West Point Military Academy in 1915. He rose through the ranks from second lieutenant to General of the Army, a glittering rank that carries with it five stars on each epaulet. This promotion came in 1950 while he held the delicate position as first chairman of the Joints Chiefs of Staff. During World War II, Bradley and his troops captured Bizerte, Tunisia, in May of 1943 (accepting the surrender of more than 250,000 troops), recaptured Sicily for the Allied cause and was on hand for the liberation of Paris in August of 1944. He headed the largest force—the U. S. 12th Army Group—ever placed under an American group commander. No stars, however, glisten on the shoulders of Bradley in this post-World War II photo, seen as he prepared to leave the Tom Butts residence on Third Avenue for a bird hunt. Photograph courtesy of the Columbus Ledger-Enquirer *newspapers*

As if World War II wasn't generating enough excitement in Columbus, the presence of a movie star of such silver-screen wattage as actress Bette Davis at the annual Georgia-Auburn football game in 1942 was electrifying. Not only did she appear with Fort Benning-stationed Sgt. Lewis Riley (with whom Hollywood gossip columnists had her romantically linked), but she and Mrs. Ellis Arnall, wife of the Georgia governor, were wearing nearly identical leopard skin coats and hats. In 1942, four-footed animals were happily slaughtered for m'lady's fashionable backs, with the only truly endangered species being the two-footed Allies. Photograph courtesy of the Columbus Ledger-Enquirer newspapers

For years, it had stood in a commanding position at the intersection of Twelfth Street and Broadway. For years, it had been a Mount Everest to youngsters whose mothers were shopping, a summit to scale before the kindly policeman on the block shooed them off. For years, it had been a reminder of World War I, and of the exceptional work done by the Charles S. Harrison Post of the American Legion in exceeding Columbus' quota in the endowment funds raised in 1925 for orphans of World War I veterans and disabled comrades of that hostility. In 1942, this Austrian 88 field piece was sent to a smelting factory to be melted down for use in World War II, along with the facade of the West Eleventh Street USO. Photograph courtesy of the Columbus Ledger-Enquirer *newspapers*

More than one glamorous movie star glimmered about Columbus during 1942. Actress Veronica Lake visited the city as a part of a War Bond selling tour. Known as much for her one-eyed hair style as her thespian abilities, Miss Lake received a gift of towels from officers of the Muscogee Manufacturing Company, clockwise, left to right: Allen Jones, George S. Kyle, Sr., R. A. Ward, William D. Swift, Edward W. Swift, Sr., and George P. Swift, Jr. Photograph from the author's collection

Columbus' oldest church, Saint Luke Methodist, dates to the city's charter year of 1828. The state of Georgia had set aside a downtown city block to be used by Methodist and Baptist denominations. Including the present structure, Saint Luke's congregation has worshipped in five different buldings. The photo shows Saint Luke's fourth church, constructed between 1897 and 1900. That completed edifice burned on Mother's Day, May 9, 1942. Photograph courtesy of the Columbus Ledger-Enquirer *newspapers*

Columbusites had begun going off into the wild blue yonder as early as October 1, 1931 when private planes had started landing at the primitive Victory Drive airstrip and scheduled airmail service had commenced there in 1936. But it was not until August 1, 1944, that the first commercial passenger plane ever landed in Columbus. An Eastern Airline D-3 named the "Houston Flyer," part of Eastern's Great Silver Fleet, took on Columbus's first passenger, a youthful Ray Saffold. The War Production Board had set a ceiling of $1,000 for the construction of the Muscogee County Airport, and it was said that "one more nail and it would have cost more than $1,000 and if there had been one nail less, it would have fallen down." Photograph courtesy of the Columbus Ledger-Enquirer newspapers

The first Woman of the Year award by the Columbus Business and Professional Women's Club was made in 1945 to Latimer Watson, longtime woman's editor of the Ledger-Enquirer newspapers. This prestigious award annually has gone to an outstanding local woman whose activities in various fields of endeavor during the past year have warranted special recognition. Former recipients, from left to right, are Mrs. Shelby Compton (1951), Mrs. S. P. Wright (1950), Mrs. Lee Snow (1953), Mrs. T. K. Kendrick (1955), the winner for 1958, Mrs. Arthur Berry, Mrs. Joseph Spano (1957), Mrs. W. H. Glenn (1949), Miss Latimer Watson (1945), Mrs. T. Charlton Hudson (1952), Miss Edwina Wood (1948) and Mrs. Helen K. Smothers (1954). The presentation is annually awarded at the Christian Fellowship Association. Photograph courtesy of the Columbus Ledger-Enquirer newspapers

Self-styled the "Jolly Boys," a group of Columbus businessmen were enthusiastic entertainers. They gave the rehearsal party for Miss Caroline Dykes and Frank Kibler on November 23, 1945, at the Ralston Hotel. For the occasion, there was a printed program that listed the hosts (Frank D. Foley, A. McWilliams, Tom Lamar, J. A. S. Bradley, H. Joerg, T. T. Cook, George Woodruff, Forest Carson, Claude Scarbrough, George Swift, R. B. Hicks, Lem Hill, Gray Worsley, Milton Hofflin, Andrew Prather, Theo Foley) and the leviathan menu of seven courses. Posed before an exhibit featuring photos of the happy bride and groom-to-be were, left to right, Alfred Young, Elliott S. Waddell, Dr. A. N. Dykes (father of the bride), Tom Tuggle, Arthur Lynch, Frank Foley, Jim Barfield, and Oscar Betts and, in the insert, George Woodruff, Sr. Photograph courtesy of the Columbus Ledger-Enquirer *newspapers*

FDR? Dead? Incredulity followed by dismay was the popular reaction to the somber news that issued forth from the nation's radios on the afternoon of the 12th of April, 1945. As World War II was drawing to a close, the four-term President of the United States was sitting for Mme. Elizabeth Shoumatoff, New York artist, when he was fatally stricken with a massive cerebral hemmorhage. Roosevelt had been coming to Warm Springs for health reasons since contracting infantile paralysis in 1921. During the ensuing decades, he had made friends with people in the area and especially with a number of Columbusites, such as Miss Georgia Wilkins, the William Harts, and the Joseph family, who had summer cottages in the popular nineteenth and early twentieth century spa. The copy of the Atlanta Constitution *that accompanied FDR's last breakfast tray proclaimed the good news that the "9th Army was only 57 Miles from Berlin." Both photographs courtesy of the* Columbus Ledger-Enquirer *newspapers*

Modeled after the YMCA, but originally for young women, the Christian Fellowship Association was granted a charter on June 14, 1946 by Superior Court Judge T. Hicks Fort. It obtained a membership of over one thousand and was "at home" (1425 Third Avenue) when Mrs. W. H. Glenn hosted a tea there on August 5, 1946. The founder, Mrs. C. A. Cutler, was also the CFA's first president. A private community organization, the CFA provides educational and recreational activities for the whole family and serves as a meeting place for various community clubs, groups and organizations. One of the CFA's earliest theatrical efforts was a 1951 production of I Remember Mama, *in which the following cast members (bottom to top of stairs) appeared: Jack Scott, Bill Ford, Rozelle Fabiani, Pat King, Cecilia Andrews, Sue Andrews, and Don Fabiani. Photograph courtesy of the* Columbus Ledger-Enquirer *newspapers*

The formula for Coca-Cola had been devised by a Columbus-moved-to-Atlanta druggist, Dr. John S. Pemberton. But it was to be the talents, wisdom, and busines acumen of another Columbusite, William Clark Bradley, (pictured here), to put the soft drink on the national and world map. Bradley was born in Oswichee in Russell County, Alabama, on June 28, 1863, and he died July 26, 1947 at his Wynn's Hill Estate (property eventually donated to the city of Columbus and now occupied by the Columbus Museum of Arts and Sciences, the Bradley Memorial Library, and the Muscogee County School System offices). Planter, steamboats owner, banker, industrialist, Bradley was part of the group that, for $25 million, purchased Coca-Cola from Asa G. Chandler in 1919. He served as chairman of the board of directors of the cola firm from 1919 until 1941. Photograph courtesy of the Columbus Ledger-Enquirer *newspapers*

In 1947 a group of fifteen gentlemen organized a literary and discussion society under the name of the "Candun Club," the name being derived from "candor unlimited" and with all discussions to be free, frank and candid. William Henry Shaw, superintendent of Columbus public schools, can probably be regarded as the founder as he had observed to the Rev. Mack Anthony, J. Q. Davidson and M. G. Murray, Jr., that he missed membership in the Fortnightly Club, a literary club in Sumter, South Carolina, where he had formerly lived. On March 17, 1947, an organizational meeting was held at the Ralston Hotel and the Candun Club came into being, with the stipulation that each member serve in alphabetical order as host in providing dinner and there be the presentation of an original stimulating paper on any subject deemed appropriate to the interest of debate by club members. The bylaws provided there should be only one officer, a president, and Theo J. McGee was elected to serve as first president. A Candun group in 1969 consisted of front row, left to right, McGee, Howell Hollis, Shaw, Edward S. Shorter, Murray, (unidentified), and Hiram Stanley; back row, left to right, Thomas Y. Whitley, G. Othell Hand, John Kinnett, Jr., Howard Callaway, LeGrand Elebash, Dr. Luther Wolff, James W. Woodruff, Jr., Judge J. Robert Elliott, (unidentified), Dr. John Anderson, Dr. P. C. Graffagnino, and Maynard R. Ashworth. The present president is Jacob L. Riley, Jr. Photograph courtesy of the Columbus Ledger-Enquirer *newspapers*

A group of local women met at the public library in May of 1927 to discuss the establishment of a Woman's Club House Association. The consensus was that the idea was a sound one and should be pursued. When another meeting was held, on September 24 of that same year, there were 128 charter members, and Mrs. Frederick B. Gordon was elected the first president. No doubt, she was influential in having the residence of the Otis family on Wynnton Road purchased a couple of years later as the club's permanent home, as it was located directly across the street from her ante-bellum home, Gordonido. The clubhouse served the organization through continued enlargement and beautification for more than fifty years before an early morning fire gutted the building in 1980. Besides being the new officers of the Woman's Club House Association in 1947, these mesdames were certainly well-chapeaued. They are, standing, left to right, Mrs. Homer McClatchey, Mrs. Charles McLaughlin, Mrs. Crawford Jenkins, Mrs. S. S. Scott, Mrs. Evelyn McGehee and Mrs. Herbert

Fay Gaffney. Seated, left to right, Mrs. Eugene Smith and Miss Julia Traylor. Both photographs courtesy of the Columbus Ledger-Enquirer *newspapers*

Ships of the air receive the same christening treatment as ships of the sea. Here, Benning Burgard, the great-great-granddaughter of Maj. Gen. Henry L. Benning, C.S.A., smashed a bottle of champagne against the propeller of a DC3 named in honor of her ancestor. Lookers-on Hazel Hubbell and brother Herbert Hull, both of Fort Worth, Texas, were also descendants of the Confederate general. The other participant in the scene, directly behind Miss Burgard, is Frank Hulse, founder of Southern Airways. When queried in 1983 as to the fate or whereabouts of the Benning, *Hulse (now Vice Chairman of Republic Airlines) remembered that the plane had been sold to an underdeveloped country, but not which country. Knowing the legendary longevity of DC3s, the* Benning *is probably flying from Manila via Batangas and Iloilo to Cebu. For a Southern Airways christening, it is interesting to a note that Miss Burgard is standing on a box with a Delta logo on it, and she and Hulse both are standing on a Delta baggage cart. The year? No one remembers, but it must be after 1947, the year Southern commenced flights into Columbus! Photograph courtesy of the* Columbus Ledger-Enquirer *newspapers*

The inscription reads, "Camp Benning established on this site in 1918 as the U.S. Army Infantry School. Originally embracing eighty-five adjoining acres, in 1919 the garrison was permanently located nine miles southeast of Columbus and is now designated Fort Benning. This tablet presented by Columbus Chamber of Commerce 1947." The site is three miles from the heart of the city off the Macon Road, near Columbus Square. Pictured, from left to right at the tablet's unveiling are: Maj. Andrew W. Petrosky, J. Homer Dimon, Brig. Gen. Reuben W. Jenkins, Frank G. Lumpkin, Lt. Col. William Shure, Maynard R. Ashworth, Maj. Gen. John W. O'Daniel, J. Arthur Lynch, Col. John Blizzard, L. W. MacPherson, Maj. Elevin A. Kreilick, and Rev. William E. McTier. Photograph courtesy of the Columbus Ledger-Enquirer *newspapers*

Columbus Airport officials were awaiting eight Delta Airline executives on the morning of April 22, 1947, dignitaries who were coming to prepare for the opening of the new terminal office. An eyewitness said businessman J. C. Fussell took off in his private plane and settled down on the tail of the incoming Delta plane. Feeling the impact, the Delta pilot pulled the nose of his aircraft up and began to turn right, as did Fussell. The tangled planes fell to earth on the airfield. Nine people were killed. Photograph courtesy of the Columbus Ledger-Enquirer *newspapers*

The commencing of Robert W. Service's poem "The Shooting of Dan McGrew" goes like this: "A bunch of the boys were whooping it up in the Malamute Saloon." These lines establish the epic's setting as the Yukon Territory in Alaska as surely as this photo of a bunch of local boys establishes that they were in front of the then-rustic mantel of the Big Eddy Club in 1947. Freshmen that year in various southern institutions of higher learning were, left to right, back row: Philip Byrne, Tommy Butts, Mote Andrews, Jr., Billy Wickham, and John Dorn; second row, left to right: Rosser Jones, Gene Woolfolk, George Woodruff, Jr., Herby Murray, Johnnie Myrick, and Bobby Rowe. The lone figure in the front row was Chick (Charles) Autry. The Big Eddy was founded as a catfish club (one invitation to membership is framed at the club and bears the date of May 17, 1920), but it was reorganized in 1960 as a private club—without tennis, swimming, or golf facilities—dedicated to haute cuisine. Fashion note of the time: brown and white saddle shoes, white socks and wide ties. The Columbus light-o'-love, the lady that's known as Lou, is nowhere to be seen. Photograph courtesy of the Columbus Ledger-Enquirer *newspapers*

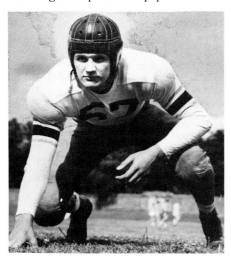

The playing of six sixty-minute football games in this final college season at Georgia Tech probably won for Robert T. (Bobby) Davis his All-American lineman designation in 1947. Team captain of both Tech's football and basketball teams, Davis won four varsity letters, plus he had the experience of being coached by the Atlanta-based school's famed Bill Alexander and Bobby Dodd. Becoming the first Columbusite to play in the National Football League (a season with the Boston Yanks in 1948), Davis gave up football in favor of a successful business career as a textile executive. Photograph courtesy of the Columbus Ledger-Enquirer *newspapers*

Since the weight of one's personal opinion is determined by the respect that is held for the speaker, it was clearly evident that when George Gingell first voiced his views on radio in 1951, and later in 1953 on television, people were going to listen. Born in France, raised in England, schooled in New York, manager (and poetry contributor) to Sammy Kaye's nationally famous orchestra, Gingell came to Columbus after World War II. By the time of his death in 1977, at age sixty-three, Gingell had become a most ardent Columbus booster via affiliation and participation in many civic activities, such as the American Cancer Society, the Springer Theater Company, Christian Fellowship Association and was the first president of the Columbus Symphony Guild when it was founded in 1949. Photograph courtesy of the Columbus Ledger-Enquirer *newspapers*

Fort Benning was not a totally mechanized post when it opened for business in 1922. Many an infantryman must have Shakespearized, "My kingdom for a horse" as he saw mounted officers galloping down shaded bridle paths, parading around the show ring or engaged in a spirited game of polo on Sunday afternoons on French Field. The post's most famous horse was named "Blue Point," after the famous Maryland marine mollusk, and, in this picture, is being presented by Capt. Marshall Bullock. "Blue Point" was a jumper whose celebrated stunt was to circle a ring two or three times while various jumps were constantly being raised to test the horse's ability. And this stunt was done without the benefit of a rider! The local photo was made at the show ring on the Fairgrounds, behind where is now located the Naval Armory. Bullock retired to the Pine Mountain Valley where he owned and operated the Valley Meat Packing Company. He retired "Blue Point" after a final championship at the Fulton-DeKalb Shrine Horse Show in Atlanta in 1949. Photograph courtesy of the Columbus Ledger-Enquirer *newspapers*

Only thirteen years after the founding of the oldest orchestra in continuous service in America—the New York Philharmonic—Columbus, with a population of six thousand inhabitants, had one too. The year was 1855 and it was the first such musical aggregation in the state of Georgia. The earliest orchestra was founded by a German composer-conductor and student of Felix Mendelssohn, Hermann S. Saroni. In much the same manner as the War Between the States had dealt a death blow to Hermann Saroni's group, the lives of orchestras two and three (founded in 1908 and 1936, respectively) had been snuffed out by World Wars I and II. Columbus' fourth symphony orchestra, pictured here, was formed in 1948-49 with Jordan High School Band Director Robert Barr as its first conductor. Since 1965, Harry Kruger, of Columbus College's music faculty, has been the symphony's maestro and, since 1978, the orchestra has given its seasons of concerts at the Three Arts Theatre. Photograph courtesy of the Columbus Ledger-Enquirer *newspapers*

She was the easy winner of the Miss Georgia Pageant, and the Columbus Jaycees, a valuable community service organization founded in 1928 with Jack Key, Sr., as its first president, were confident that she was going to be the next Miss America. And they were right! A student at Wesleyan College in Macon, Neva Jane Langley was a music major and played the piano for her talent competition, winning that segment of the Atlantic City pageant as well. In case you don't instantly recognize it, that is a Nash Rambler in which she is riding in her Welcome Back parade up Broadway in 1952. Photograph courtesy of the Columbus Ledger-Enquirer *newspapers*

Once upon a time, both Girard and Columbus erected toll booths at opposite ends of the Dillingham Street bridge and waged a small "collections" war for a few months. A similar war exists between the Georgia city of Fort Gaines and the Alabama city of Eufaula over the name of the body of water behind the Walter F. George Lock and Dam. Fort Gainesians call it Lake George and Eufaulans call it Lake Eufaula. On a visit to Columbus in 1948, the venerated senator from Georgia for whom the project is named is shown here with Jim Woodruff, Jr., (left), who, like his father, was a staunch advocate of the river system. The son of a Georgia sharecropper, George was a former dean of the Senate and the U. S. Ambassador to NATO during the Eisenhower administration, and has been called "one of the twentieth century's most respected and influential members of the United States Senate." Photograph courtesy of the Columbus Ledger-Enquirer *newspapers*

J. Tom Morgan, Jr., invented a better mousetrap by developing a system to better reproduce full-color photographs. Since 1949, when Morgan reproduced Victor Keppler's famous Wine and Cheese *photo so successfully that the Smithsonian Institution dubbed it the premier example of modern color lithography, the world has beat a path to his family-owned corporation. In 1960, he improved on black and white lithographs by printing two impressions instead of one. A Columbus native, Morgan went to work for Commercial Printers in 1933 and became president of the firm in 1942. In 1947, he developed Litho-Krome Company and, in 1964, the two companies became one. A major customer of Morgan's, Hallmark of Kansas City, Missouri, saw fit to arrange a merger with the local firm on December 17, 1979. The Morgan portrait was painted by A. Henry Nordhausen, noted New York artist now residing in Columbus. Photograph courtesy of the* Columbus Ledger-Enquirer *newspapers*

Chapter VII
1950-1985
To the Present

The Muscogee County School District did not, like Topsy, spring full blown into existence. For the Columbus Public Schools, founded in 1866, and for the Muscogee County School System, founded in 1872, to unite required: (1) a Constitutional Amendment signed by Gov. Ellis Arnold on November 26, 1948; (2) an Enabling Act passed by the Georgia Legislature on February 25, 1949; and (3) approval by the citizens of the city and the citizens of the county, voting in separate elections. Commencing operation on January 1, 1950, the consolidated system became the first of its kind in the State of Georgia. Dr. William Henry Shaw was named the first superintendent, serving until his retirement in 1972-73. Left to right in this 1950 photo are Miss Annie V. Massey, Dr. Roland B. Daniel and Shaw. Dr. Daniel, who served for twenty-eight years, from 1907 to 1937, as superintendent of Columbus Public Schools, seems to be particularly enjoying what must have been an in-house joke. In 1973, Dr. Braxton A. Nail succeeded Dr. Shaw as Superintendent of Education in Muscogee County and continues to serve in that capacity. Photograph courtesy of the Columbus Ledger-Enquirer *newspapers*

The town had a dubious distinction after World War II. As more and more superhighways, the American version of the German *Autobahn*, were built, Columbus became the largest city in the United States not on an interstate. Now, that was some honor. And it was not until 1979 that Interstate 185 would be finished, connecting Fort Benning-Columbus with Interstate 85 which extends from Montgomery to Atlanta. At this writing, Interstate 185 still has a strip of some forty miles between the northern city limits and its junction with Interstate 85 that is devoid of emergency telephone service, a lovely but lonesome strip to drivers fearful of their automobiles breaking down.

On the other hand, other elements of the city were making progress. As previously noted, the school systems of the city and county merged in order to give quality education, and the city and county governments followed suit on January 1, 1971. Culturally, Edward S. Shorter, the dean of art interests in this area, served without remuneration as the director of the Columbus Museum of Arts and Crafts (now Columbus Museum of Arts and Sciences) when it was established in 1952. That same year, May 21, to be exact, saw the opening of "the prettiest garden that will ever be seen on earth till Gabriel blows his horn." The words were those of the late Cason J. Callaway, referring to the exceptional recreational facility that he founded, located just north of Columbus and between Hamilton and Pine Mountain, then known as Chipley, Georgia.

Also, in the field of education, Columbus acquired a junior college in 1958, one that soon outgrew this two-year designation. Columbus College became a full-fledged four-year institution in 1970.

In the field of transportation, the Tri-Rivers Association was formed in 1959 to push river development and is still at it, ever seeking to maintain the deeper channels that would permit the Chattahoochee, Flint and Apalachicola rivers to be utilized to their fullest for economic benefit to the city and to west Georgia, north Florida and east Alabama. With the arrival of the river boat *Jubilee* in 1983, area residents are getting a firsthand look at the reaches just below the Columbus fall line, a look not available since the departure of the steamboat *George W. Miller*, the last of nearly two hundred boats that plied the Chattahoochee since 1828.

Also in the field of transportation, the formerly rural setting of the Muscogee County Airport (now called Columbus Metropolitan Airport), an area where cows grazed and boys hunted rabbits, seemingly overnight turned into an area surrounded by shopping centers and residences. In the late 1960s and early '70s, much debate occurred over moving the airport to east Alabama, to the flat lands around Crawford or Smiths. Civic pride on both sides of the river, coupled with the designation of Columbus as a "feeder" to the Hartsfield International Airport in Atlanta, probably will result in the airport's retaining its present site, with monies being spent in strengthening its runways, making its approaches safer and replacing its 1950 terminal. In 1977, more than 169,000 passengers—approximately the population of Columbus—boarded planes here, compared to the first-year (1944) figure of 556 when Delta was the only carrier. In 1977, two other airlines, Southern and Eastern, also operated out of the local airport. Today, Delta, ASA and a new commuter called the Eastern Connection expect approximately 95,400 boardings.

The local newspapers, each of which has won the most coveted award in journalism, the Pulitzer Prize, for distinguished and meritorious public service, became members of the Knight newspaper family on October 1, 1973, when Knight Newspapers, acquired the R. W. Page Corporation. The acquisition came two days after a Columbus native, Alvah H. Chapman, Jr., was elected president of the out-of-town newspaper group. Chapman, whose family had been associated with the local papers for three generations, was once business manager of the *Ledger-Enquirer* newspapers. A year later, Knight merged with Ridder Newspapers to form Knight-Ridder, the combined chain publishing thirty-three dailies in twenty one cities, selling 24.4 million newspapers in a typical week. It is the largest newspaper chain in America in terms of number of readers. Among its larger-than-Columbus news-sheets are the *Miami Herald*, the *Philadelphia Inquirer* and the *Detroit Free Press*.

Reorganized in 1956, the Columbus Little Theater had been without a permanent home for nearly ten years when the Springer Opera House was warranted as suitable for demolition. The property on the Tenth Street-First Avenue corner was to be used for the United States' chief contribution to transportational culture, a parking lot. "Rescue the building and restore it as a home for the CLT" became the cry of a small group of Columbus citizens. Fortunately, their cry was heard, for on October 6, 1965, not only did the Springer reopen in style, but it reopened with an original musical production of one of the best-known novels of the Victorian era, *St. Elmo*, and, appropriately enough, one written by a Columbus native, Augusta Evans Wilson (see page 29). In 1971, then-Georgia Governor Jimmy Carter officially designated the one-hundred-year-old Springer the State Theater of Georgia.

Two years after the Springer reopened, arrangements were made to purchase the "Fair of 1850" and move it from Jonesboro, Georgia to its new site, Lumpkin. This relic of the past, "The Fair of 1850," had been a private folk culture museum created by John Ward West, a Georgia education and history professor and one-time president of North Georgia College at Dahlonega. Under a new name honoring the collector West, the fair's time frame would be 1850, and it would be a living history museum that would preserve, research and teach the handicrafts and skills common to the people of Georgia in the pre-industrial era. "Westville" officially opened to the public on April 1, 1970, with more than $2 million spent on Westville's development by 1978, monies coming from public and private sources and from admission fees. Dr. Joseph Mahan served as Westville's first executive director, a position today held by Matthew Moye.

The most momentous news event in southwest Georgia in 1974, of course, concerned the Lochinvar that had come unheralded out of the South and not of the West, a "Jimmy Who" who would wind up on the covers of all the national weeklies, the fronts of all the daily newspapers and the lead story on the nightly television newscasts. This lion was more like a David who knocked off his opponents with a peanut and a few well-chosen homilies. He added "Fritz" to "grits," and the result was a dish that had been bought by the voting public.

On a cold November day in 1976, the peanut farmer from Plains, Jimmy Carter, was elected the thirty-ninth president of the United States of America.

Good times and bad times in Columbus seemed to coincide with extremes in the weather. During the

When Saint Francis Hospital opened its doors in March of 1950, a new era in health care dawned for Columbus. It was the first private hospital to open here, and its construction was the culmination of a massive effort on the part of local citizens and the Sisters of the Third Order of Saint Francis, a Roman Catholic nursing order. The J. W. Woodruff family donated the twenty-one acre site at the corner of Woodruff and Yarbrough roads. A local fund drive, of which Jack B. Key was chairman, raised $500,000, which was matched by the Sisters of Saint Francis. Hill-Burton funds were also used in the construction of the $2 million, fifty-four bed hospital. The story of Saint Francis actually began in 1947, when Sister M. Laurentine and Sister M. Evelyn came to Columbus from Pittsburgh, Pennsylvania, where the order's motherhouse is located, to begin plans for the hospital. The two sisters—Sister Laurentine is in the center—are pictured here in 1949 with hospital architect J. W. Jeffries as the structure neared completion. Sister Laurentine became the hospital's first administrator. Saint Francis underwent a major expansion beginning in 1971. The $6.5 million expansion added intensive care facilities and a coronary unit and almost doubled the hospital's capacity. Recently, a multi-story parking facility has been added adjacent to the original structure. Photograph courtesy of the Columbus Ledger-Enquirer newspapers

One of the persons honored when the new public library within the grounds of the former W. C. Bradley estate was dedicated in 1950 was Miss Loretto Lamar Chappell, left, who graduated cum laude from Bryn Mawr College prior to serving as librarian at the public library's former location on Mott's Green. She joined the library staff in 1915, is well-remembered for her "story hours," and was named librarian in December of 1942, a post she held until August 12, 1962. The Junto Study Club presented a portrait in her honor at the W. C. Bradley Memorial Library which reads "In recognition of her charm, love of humanity and cultural contribution to Columbus through her many years of dedicated library service." Also shown are John R. Bannister, Director of Libraries for the Chattahoochee Valley Regional Library, and Mrs. Roy Smisson, Sr., right. Photograph courtesy of the Columbus Ledger-Enquirer newspapers

While-in-office U.S. presidential visits to Columbus began with Harding in 1921. Roosevelt visited Fort Benning in 1938, and then in April of 1950 came Harry S Truman, who inherited the post of Commander in Chief when FDR died and who went on in 1946 to amaze the pollsters and the Chicago Tribune, *whose now famous-but-inaccurate headline proclaimed his opponent to be the winner. The President seems to be enjoying the* Ledger's *headline which read, "President Awed by Benning Might; Hopes It Helps Keep Peace Secure." Christened with middle initial of "S" but which did not stand for a particular name so that, diplomatically, both his grandfathers could claim that he was named for them, Truman wanted to go to West Point but his eyesight didn't meet military standards. However, he helped organize a field artillery regiment in 1917, was discharged a major in 1919 and later became a colonel in the reserves. A career in politics began in 1922 with election as a county judge, followed by election to the U.S. Senate in 1934. He had only been vice-president for eighty-three days when fourth-term Roosevelt died at Warm Springs. Photograph courtesy of the* Columbus Ledger-Enquirer *newspapers*

long, hot summer of 1971 there was racial unrest in the city. At the other end of the thermometer the best time that the city has ever had was in February of 1973 when a freak winter storm blanketed Columbus with more than a foot of snow. In the first case, civic leadership accomplished a cooling of tempers and in the second, the cold white stuff caused neighbors to warm to each other as never before.

The Springer's restoration effort in 1963-65 began what has become a major current in the community's economic life. Local preservationists agree that, had the Springer's revitalization not moved from being a dream to being a reality, the resulting activity wouldn't have been labeled feasible or probable. One Columbus mover and shaker described the difficulty of preserving old houses and buildings into adaptable reuse as "akin to pushing a snowball uphill in Georgia and the first difficulty isn't locating a hill."

Organized in 1966, the Historic Columbus Foundation has been the guiding force in the local movement. Its initial accomplishment was the creation and redevelopment of a Historic District, located east and west of Lower Broad in southwest Columbus. In 1984, it shifted its former residential focus to mount a successful "Save the Station" campaign, the station being the 1890s Central of Georgia Railroad passenger terminal that was threatened with demolition.

Columbus Mayor B. F. Register took to the nation's airways in 1951 when he was the guest of Tallulah Bankhead, smokey-voiced actress from Alabama. The occasion was the fall premier of her weekly radio show, appropriately called the "Big Show." Miss Bankhead, celebrated performer on stage and screen, is clutching what appears to be a minature bale of cotton and a statuette of Vulcan, the symbol of Birmingham's steel industry. Our mayor was sporting a silk, hand-painted tie that bore the battle flag of the Confederacy. Naturally, Miss Bankhead admired the tie, being from a powerful political family not only in the Deep South but nationally as well. Photograph courtesy of the Columbus Ledger-Enquirer *newspapers*

As well-known as is Art Linkletter, television viewers in the Columbus area probably would more quickly identify the television personality on the left. A native of Cleveland, Tennessee, Rozell Fair Fabiani has been coming into the living rooms, kitchens and bedrooms of local homes with the "Rozell Show" since 1953. Among the many awards that she has received during some three decades are three Gold Mikes for public service programming in television, the highest recognition given to women broadcasters. Linkletter is but one of the many celebrities, and just plain folks, who have appeared on her morning and noon programs and chatted informally with the warm and gracious hostess. Photograph courtesy of the Columbus Ledger-Enquirer *newspapers*

The city of Columbus embraced the preservation ethic when it adapted the southern section of the former Columbus Iron Works into its Convention and Trade Center. This highly attractive renovation was accomplished for $7 million, considerably less than what a new facility would have cost, and has won the plaudits of many visiting conventioneers and exhibitors. Most recently, a number of private organizations have rehabilitated praiseworthy structures listed on the National Register of Historic Places (U.S. Department of the Interior) via the Economic Recovery Tax Act of 1981, wherein the law provided a 25 percent investment tax credit for rehabilitations of historic, commercial, industrial and rental residential buildings. Since 1982 a revitalization of the downtown business district has been sparked by an organization called Uptown Columbus, which is headed by Rozier Dedwylder, who was the architect for the Iron Works Convention and Trade Center and the Hilton Hotel.

The first cooperative effort to enhance the arts in Columbus was celebrated on November 3, 1985, with the first annual Columbus Steeplechase at Callaway Gardens. The proceeds from this festive sporting event, originated by Mason Lampton, president of the Columbus Chamber of Commerce, were designated to benefit five non-profit organizations: the Ida Cason Callaway Garden Foundation, the Columbus Symphony, the Historic Columbus Foundation, the Columbus Museum of Arts and Sciences, and the Springer Opera House. The Steeplechase, one of thirty-five such meets held in cities throughout the United States and sanctioned by the National Steeplechase and Hunt Association, continues a sporting tradition that was begun in 1752 when two Irishmen matched their horses in a four-mile race from church steeple to church steeple.

Columbus art and artists, a vibrant force on the local cultural scene have received an economic hand-up in the past couple of years. When the largest automated forging facility in the Free World's aerospace industry, the $200 million Pratt and Whitney aircraft parts plant, was dedicated here on April 19, 1984, distinguished guests, employees and company officials were greeted by a display of local artists' work. Located on the Macon Road in the Midland area, the Pratt and Whitney plant is the largest capital expenditure ever made by United Technologies for a single facility.

In 1985 the W. C. Bradley Company commissioned twenty noted U.S. artists to paint works commemorating the company's one hundredth birthday and sponsored an art show for local artists in May at the Columbus Museum of Arts and Sciences, setting aside $10,000 for purchase awards.

Both companies, Pratt and Whitney and the Bradley Company, were honored in 1985 by the Georgia Business Community for the Arts for their interest in and support of art.

When coupled with the Steeplechase, the business community's commitment to the arts could spell a bright future for the industrial growth of Columbus as art seems to attract industry and vice versa.

Miss Chappell ended her "history" in that centennial edition with an account of the last battle of the War Between the States in this manner: "On this, the page of violence and despair, the history of old-time Columbus ends. Though grieve we must for the sorrow of the city sixty-three years ago, we must also rejoice, knowing with that grace and spirit the townspeople adapted themselves to a new order."

There seems to be "a new order" present in Columbus today, 157 years after its unique beginning. That "new order" seems to be coming to grips with what it means to be a twentieth century Sun Belt city, one where business and industry happily co-exist with respect for human rights and admiration for the arts.

The gates to Ida Cason Callaway Gardens opened with simple ceremonies on the morning of May 21, 1952. Three years in preparation, the gardens were the dream of Cason J. Callaway, Georgia farmer, textile executive, corporate board director, philanthropist and presidential advisor, who had a vision for west central Georgia. "What we want to do is build the prettiest garden that ever can be seen on earth till Gabriel blows his horn." Governor Herman Talmadge came unannounced to see what eventually would attract more than half a million people a year seeking recreation and inspirational beauty. Named for Callaway's mother, the gardens are located thirty-five miles north of Columbus. With a beach that can accommodate twenty thousand bathers, Robin Lake opened the next year and is annually the scene of the Master Water Ski Tournament. Mrs. Callaway (pictured here) has carried on her husband's philanthropies and his interest in the gardens. In 1972, the Cason J. Callaway Memorial Forest was designated a registered national landmark, "possessing exceptional value in illustrating the natural history of the United States." Both photographs courtesy of the Columbus Ledger-Enquirer *newspapers*

Columbus acquired two television stations within a period of forty days in 1953. The first station to get on the air, on October 6, 1953, was WDAK-TV on Channel 28, a joint venture between radio station WDAK, owned and operated by Allen Woodall, Sr., and Martin Theaters. The second station, also a partnership between the Page Corporation (owners of WGBA) and Jim Woodruffs, Sr., and Jr., (owners of WRBL) went on the air November 15, 1953. WDAK-TV was initially an NBC affiliate, broadcasting out of studios in the Martin Building downtown, whereas WRBL-TV was a CBS affiliate, with studios on Thirteenth Avenue. It was not until 1970 that the city acquired a third television station, with WYEA (owned by Eagle Broadcasting Company) going on the air as an all-color NBC affiliate. Here Woodall inspects the television camera while RCA television engineer R. B. Spivey (left) and John E. Minter, Jr., of Columbus, look on. Photograph courtesy of the Columbus Ledger-Enquirer *newspapers*

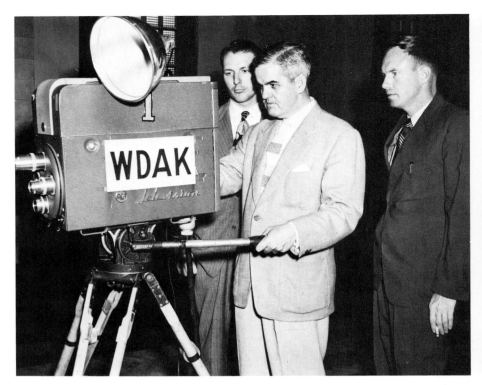

In a car sponsored by the Ledger-Enquirer *newspapers, Joe Lunn won the 1952 National Soap Box Derby at Akron, Ohio. Lunn won his first heat easily, but lost control of his sleek black racer and smashed into the foot-high board fence surrounding the track. The car was hastily patched together with tin and cardboard, wood screws and cellophane tape, and Lunn went back out onto the track and won the remaining four heats for the title. Smiling broadly as he emerges from the Eastern Airline plane, he was given a true hero's welcome upon his return to Columbus. Photograph courtesy of the* Columbus Ledger-Enquirer *newspapers*

"The fact that it wasn't an ordinary tornado doesn't mean it wasn't as much or more destructive than a tornado would have been," said weatherman Tom Floyd. He added, "The idea seems to be going around that a tornado is terrifically destructive whereas a storm not named a tornado is not so bad. That isn't necessarily true." To judge from the statistics tallied by the April 18, 1953 storm that struck the bi-city area in the early afternoon, it was destructive. Two men in Columbus and one woman in Phenix City died and more than four hundred persons were injured. The extent of damage to homes was even more extensive, with some four hundred being destroyed and an additional 2,700 damaged by the storm which cut a swath some two miles wide, appearing first at Auburn, then continuing through Smith's and on to Phenix City and Columbus. Auto dealers and repairmen estimated that more than two thousand cars were damaged. Photograph courtesy of the Columbus Ledger-Enquirer *newspapers*

Just a scant eighteen days after an extensive campaign based on a vice cleanup pledge that netted him the Democratic nomination for attorney general of the state of Alabama, Phenix City lawyer Albert L. Patterson was murdered on June 18, 1954, in the alley between his office and the Elite Cafe on Fifth Avenue. This murder set off cries for justice across the nation as well as the state of Alabama, and Patterson was made a martyr. Supported by the Russell Betterment Association, Patterson's son, John, took up the good fight where his father left off and was elected attorney general. Later, he served two terms as governor of Alabama. Photograph courtesy of the Columbus Ledger-Enquirer *newspapers*

Gen. W.L. (Crack) Hannah Confiscates Slot Machines in Phenix City in 1954

Under the leadership of Maj. Gen. W. J. ("Crack") Hanna, left, and the Alabama National Guard, a multi-million dollar gambling-and-drug-and-prostitution ring in Phenix City was systematically destroyed. The Cleanup, as it became known, started with the July 24, 1954 raid on D. O. ("Head") Revel's Bridge Grocery Store on Dillingham Street, just two days after Hanna put the city under martial law. It concluded with a Blue Ribbon Grand Jury handing down over six hundred indictments, the beginning of the end of an era of open lawlessness that had reigned in Phenix City for many years. Photograph courtesy of the Columbus Ledger-Enquirer *newspapers*

"A lot of people didn't believe it was possible. They were very much surprised. I fooled myself," said Love McDuffie (Mrs. Wheeler) Tolbert, in reference to being the first woman to represent Muscogee County in the Georgia General Assembly, winning a special election on January 16, 1933, over three men opponents. This 1954 photo of Mrs. Tolbert was made on the occasion of her being named "American Mother of the Year" by the Golden Rule Foundation of New York City. A mother of six sons, a journalist, a vigorous civic worker and a church leader, Mrs. Tolbert died in 1979. Photograph courtesy of the Columbus Ledger-Enquirer *newspapers*

A pair of celebrated clowns were together in Columbus in 1954, Joe E. Brown, right and Emmett Leo Kelly. The latter, born in Kansas in 1898, gained fame as a sad-faced hobo dressed in tatters. This wistful tramp, known as Weary Willie, was created by Kelly not long after he became a circus performer in 1921. Featured in a number of movies and guest appearances on television, Kelly was six years younger than his friend Brown, who became a circus acrobat in 1902, later was a headliner in burlesque and vaudeville and in motion pictures beginning in 1927. In 1959, after his appearance here, Brown would have his greatest success in a film called Some Like it Hot, *in the acting company of Tony Curtis, Marilyn Monroe and Jack Lemmon. Photograph courtesy of the* Columbus Ledger-Enquirer *newspapers*

Simon Schwob, a native of the Alsace-Lorraine, immigrated first to Maryland and later settled in Columbus, where he opened a tailoring shop in 1912. Success followed, and the Schwob Manufacturing Company, with its motto "Schwobilt Suits the South," grew into the south's largest manufacturer and retailer of menswear. After Schwob's death in 1954 at the age of sixty-seven, his nephew, Henry Schwob, headed the company until its sale to Waico Investments, ironically a concern based in the state that Schwob passed up to come to Georgia. Schwob and his wife, Ruth, were philanthropists who were involved in a wide range of community activities. But because of their being at the forefront of developmental growth at Columbus College, the Schwobs are probably most readily identified with cultural growth in this area; the college's Simon Schwob Memorial Library was named in honor of Schwob, and Mrs. Schwob established the Ruth S. Schwob Music Scholarship Trust Fund to provide annual financial assistance to talented students. Photograph courtesy of the Columbus Ledger-Enquirer *newspapers*

The year 1956 was the first time Fred Haskins retired at the Country Club of Columbus, this time after thirty-three years as its golf professional. Known as the Englishman who had made the Scottish game a way of life in Columbus, Haskins had arrived in 1922 at a course that had only twelve completed holes, less than fifty regular golfers and no youngsters playing at all. He took on the double task of finishing the links and developing a youth program. So successful were his free Saturday morning clinics for children that Haskins came to be regarded as one of the country's finest teaching pros. Fifteen years later Haskins again retired, this time from the position of head greenskeeper. That same year, 1971, local golf enthusiasts established the "Fred Haskins Award," to be annually presented to the top collegiate golfer in the country, as prestigious in its field as winning the Heisman or Naismith trophies. In this mid-1940s photo, Haskins is shown with four of his star linksmen: left to right, Bryan Rust, John Dorn, Billy Key, and Jere Pound. Photograph courtesy of the Columbus Ledger-Enquirer *newspapers*

No other newspapers of similar size in the country had ever undertaken a project as extensive as "Operation Birmingham," the name given to the Ledger-Enquirer's *coverage of the trials of the three Phenix City men charged with the murder of Albert Patterson. For its vigorous reportage and editorial coverage of the murder, the trials and the cleanup of Phenix City (so complete that in December of 1955, the National Municipal League awarded Phenix City one of its coveted All American Cities Awards), the* Columbus Ledger *and the Sunday* Ledger-Enquirer *were awarded the Pulitzer Prize for 1955. Carlton M. Johnson, then* Ledger *city editor, is shown holding the framed award from Columbia University, while in the foreground can be seen a number of state and national recognitions of merit won by the local afternoon newspaper. Photograph courtesy of the* Columbus Ledger-Enquirer *newspapers*

In 1956, a pair of world-famous entertainers, the madcap comedy team of Dean Martin and Jerry Lewis, came to Fort Benning to film Jumping Jacks. *Relying heavily for plot and laughs on the zany antics and clumsiness of fall-guy Lewis, the film utilized the jump towers (250 feet high, costing $86,000) that had been purchased from the Safe Parachute Jump Company and were similar to the popular parachute jump ride from the 1939 World's Fair held in New York City. Two years earlier, a tornado had destroyed one of the four towers. Photograph courtesy of the* Columbus Ledger-Enquirer *newspapers*

Broadway was packed with patriotic citizens for the 1957 Armed Forces Day Parade and the marching soldiers had just done "eyes, left" for the reviewing stand erected at the intersection of Twelfth and Broad. American flags flew in front of the businesses on the west side of Broad, a list of enterprises and locations on the west side of Broad, a list of enterprises and locations well-remembered by citizens over fifty years old, i.e., Montgomery Ward, the Merchants and Mechanics Bank, Patterson's, the White Company, Sealy's, WGBA, Days Credit Clothing, Humes, the Chickasaw Club (occupying the former site of the old Muscogee Club), Martin Furniture Company, Sears (Roebuck and Company), Rothschild Furniture, The Rialto, Miller and Taylor, Max Rosenberg's, The Bradley Theater and Maxwell Brothers on the end. Obviously, the era of the shopping mall had not arrived. Photograph courtesy of the Columbus Ledger-Enquirer *newspapers*

A civic and industrial leader, Charlie Frank Williams died August 21, 1957, at the age of sixty-six. His forte was the construction business and World War II was the impetus that thrust him into the category of major contractor, building camps and cantonments for thousands of troops, notably at Camp Shelby, Mississippi, Camp Gordon Johnston and Tyndall Field in Florida and at Fort Benning. First president of the Columbus Quarterback Club, Williams served as president of the Gas Light Company of Columbus, chief executive of two firms bearing the Williams name and on a number of boards of directors. Shown posing for his portrait by the noted artist Robert Brackman, Williams donated the new chapel to the First Baptist Church. Photograph courtesy of the Columbus Ledger-Enquirer *newspapers*

The twin bill presented for the dedication of Memorial Stadium on November 7, 1925 consisted of a football game (Georgia beating Auburn 34 to 0) in the afternoon and a boxing match in the evening where Macon's Young Stribling decisioned the Australian George Cook. So, boxing had been and still was a popular sport in 1957 when former Olympic gold medal winner Pete Rademacher challenged World Heavyweight Champion Floyd Patterson. Rademacher trained at Lake Huston and his entourage grew each day. Columbus, if not the rest of the world, was in his corner. Seventeen thousand fans were in Sicks Stadium in Seattle, Washington, on the evening of August 22, 1957, including Mike Jennings and the group of adventurous Columbus businessmen who had financed Rademacher's bid for pugilistic glory. In the second round, Rademacher (left) decked Patterson. But two minutes and fifty-six seconds into the sixth round, the referee stopped the fight. Patterson had knocked Rademacher down seven times, four of them in the fifth round. Two years later, Rademacher lost a bout to Zora Foley and quietly retired from professional boxing in 1962, with a record of fifteen victories, seven defeats and one draw. He and his family live in Medina, Ohio, and he is in the plastics business. Photograph courtesy of the Columbus Ledger-Enquirer *newspapers*

Born in 1888, son of a prominent cotton dealer, Mercer Blanchard decided after he had graduated from the University of Georgia that he wanted to be a doctor, particularly a pediatrician. In 1918, he was appointed Columbus school physician, a position he would hold for more than forty years. A portrait by noted artist Frank Bensing of New York was unveiled in 1957 at the Medical Center, where Blanchard created a pediatric department in 1948. Blanchard died in 1976. With him are his wife, the former Katherine Neill McDuffie, and young admirers, some of whom are his grandchildren. Left to right are Betsy Blanchard, Peggy Blanchard, Marianna Swift, Belle Blanchard, Sue Coley and Stephanie Swift. Dr. Blanchard is holding granddaughter Susan Blanchard. Fittingly enough, an elementary school was named for Dr. Blanchard and dedicated on November 24, 1968. Photograph courtesy of the Columbus Ledger-Enquirer *newspapers*

Known for his bone-crushing handshake and quiet philanthropies, James Waldo Woodruff was born in Columbus on March 9, 1879. Despite a variety of business interests, "Mr. Jim" will be remembered as a vigorous waterway advocate, perhaps influenced by his birthplace, a house at the corner of First Avenue and Sixth Street not far from the banks of the Chattahoochee. Throughout his life, he visualized and worked for a navigable Chattahoochee-Flint-Appalachicola rivers system. On March 23, 1957, the first of a series of navigation/power dams built on the Georgia-Florida line at a cost of $47 million was named in his honor. "Mr. Chattahoochee" died on February 3, 1963, not living to see the completion of either the Walter F. George Lock (the highest single-life lock in the United States) or the Columbia (both dedicated at ceremonies in Phenix City later in the year) but leaving behind an impressive river development project which he conceived and spearheaded. The Tri-Rivers Waterway Development Association, established in 1959, is a modern-day successor to the organization that Woodruff formed in 1935 to promote river development. Woodruff is seen here

(at left) chatting with Florida Governor Leroy Collins at the dedication of the Jim Woodruff Dam in 1957. Photograph courtesy of the Columbus Ledger-Enquirer *newspapers*

"Country Captain" is Columbus's most famous dish. Mrs. W. L. Bullard is credited with the recipe generally used by local hosts and hostesses. Traditionally, it was born on a summer's eve in nearby Warm Springs where the Bullards had a summer home and was first served at a dinner party in honor of Franklin D. Roosevelt who was recovering there from polio. The concoction was an immediate success that evening and its fame quickly spread to Columbus and Fort Benning. It has remained a favorite buffet repast and is one always served to visitors, sometimes more than once if menus aren't carefully coordinated.

Country Captain

1-3½ to 4 pound hen
2 finely chopped onions
2 green peppers
2 cans tomatoes
¼ pound roasted almonds
3 large tablespoons currants
½ teaspoon chopped parsley
2 cups rice
small garlic bean
1 good teaspoon salt
½ teaspoon white pepper
1 good teaspoon curry powder
½ teaspoon powdered thyme
black pepper

  Cut up young tender hen to fry. Remove the skin and roll chicken in flour, salt and black pepper and fry. Now remove the chicken from the pan but keep it hot. (This is a secret of the dish's success.) Into the lard in which the chicken has been fried add onions and green peppers and garlic beans. Cook very slowly, stirring constantly. Season with salt, white pepper and curry powder. (Test curry to suit taste of your family.) Add tomatoes, chopped parsley, and thyme. Now put chicken in roaster and pour mixture over it. If it does not cover the chicken rinse out skillet in which mixture has been cooked and pour over chicken also. Place top on roaster very tight. Put in oven and cook about 45 minutes until the chicken is tender. Now have ready almonds (scalded, roasted to a golden brown) and currants. Put chicken in middle of a platter and pile 2 cups rice, cooked very dry around it. Now drop currants into the sauce mixture and pour over rice. Scatter almonds over top of rice. Garnish with parsley and you have food for the gods. Mrs. L. W. McPherson

Anyone over thirty years of age likely will remember the once-a-year excitement surrounding the annual local confrontation between the Bulldogs of the University of Georgia and the Tigers of Auburn University. Since 1925, the second oldest rivalry in college football (Harvard-Yale is older) had been played at Memorial Stadium. This neutral ground site ended in 1958 with Auburn winning the finale by a score of 21-6. Now the annual gridiron contest is played on a home-to-home basis, in stadiums seating fifty thousand more than the modest twenty-five thousand shown gathered here. And the social life of Columbus has not been the same since! Here are two of the most famous coaches in modern day football, Wally Butts of Georgia and "Shug" Jordan of Auburn, leaving Memorial Stadium after "the" game. Both photographs courtesy of the Columbus Ledger-Enquirer newspapers

Her "Strut, Miss Lizzie, Strut" always brought down the house, as did her "Saint Louis Blues." But when she wasn't performing for every civic and social club that demanded her talents, Pauline Mitchum Lamar (1900-1964) had another life, a life far different from that of a blues singer. At the age of thirty-two, Mrs. Lamar was admitted to the bar. Later, she served as Juvenile Court judge until ill health forced her retirement. During 1958, all Columbus watched as the town's torch-singing judge appeared on national television, winning first prize on the "Revlon Show" and then $16,000 on the "$64,000 Question," answering questions pertaining to American jazz and in particular to the jazz composer W. C. Handy. Judge Lamar is shown here with master of ceremonies Hal March. Photograph courtesy of the Columbus Ledger-Enquirer *newspapers*

In the tradition of the Flournoy family (See Chapter V), Mr. and Mrs. J. Linton White gathered their progeny together for a formal family portrait at their residence, 1604 Twelfth Street. The occasion was the marriage in October of 1958 of their granddaughter Betty Brinson to Brian Bush. The bride is perched on the top row, upper steps rampart right, and the senior Whites are seated in the top row on either side of the hand rail. Their children and grandchildren are divided by the rail into four families: the O. R. Coppages and the Ritchie Whites on the left and the J. Park Brinsons and the junior J. L. Whites on the right. Photograph courtesy of The White Company

During the first twenty-eight years of its existence, the Junior League of Columbus donated more than $260,000 to health, welfare, recreational, educational and cultural activities in the city. On an irregularly regular basis, this group of Columbus women, along with talented friends, presents a musical "Follies" to raise money to support these local charities. One of the acts of the 1959 edition was entitled "Surprise, Surprise, Surprise" starring Adelaide Hutto and the Red Hot Mamas, left. Left to right, mesdames Ruth King, Martha Thwaite, Patsy Martin, Josephine Mullin, Adelaide Hutto, Ruth Hempstead, Eula Williams, Josephine Jordan and Frances Cole. Equal time for the Red Hot Mamas was demanded by these kickers, right. From left to right: Sarah Louise Butler, Frances Woolfolk, Margie Thrasher, Alice Metcalf, Dot Knight, Fleming Venable, Cathryn Kilgore, Barbara Henkel, Betty Kinnett, Dot Young, Peggy Love, and Ruth Woolfolk. The showgirls seen behind the chorus line are, left to right, Shirley Kirven, Connie Van Dorn, Mary Margaret Byrne, and Sara Rowe. Both photographs courtesy of the Columbus Ledger-Enquirer newspapers

Service to the community was the idea which drew fifty-nine Columbus women together in 1931 as, appropriately, the Community Service League. With Mrs. Willis Battle as its first president, CSL well earned its name by donating some 4,505 hours of voluntary service to the city of Columbus, chiefly to the thirty-four orphans at the Anne Elizabeth Shepherd Orphans Home. It was during the 1936 term of Mrs. William H. Young, Jr., that the CSL was accepted into the Association of Junior Leagues of America, founded in New York in 1921. During its first thirty years of existence, the local league performed more than 600,000 hours of voluntary service to the community. Its administrative expenses are supported from membership dues, and all monies collected from the community are placed in a community trust fund and 100 percent are expended in the community to further League projects. The primary source of money raised for these projects comes from an annual attic sale, follies and the league's Columbus cookbook. This 1959 photo taken at the Country Club of Columbus contains twelve past presidents of the local league. Seated, left to right are, Mrs. Tracy Davis, Mrs. Ben Hurt Hardaway, Mrs. William H. Young, Mrs. Henry Watson, and Mrs. James Jenkins. Standing, left to right, are, Mrs. Edward Swift, Mrs. Charles Dimon, Mrs. Willis Battle, Mrs. C. F. Williams, Mrs. Arechavala Tyler, Mrs. Charlton Williams, and Mrs. Frank Martin. Photograph courtesy of the Columbus Ledger-Enquirer *newspapers*

To the strains of "If I Ever Cease to Love," a Mardi Gras waltz air imported from New Orleans, Miss Vera Swift and Jack B. Key entered the Country Club of Columbus ballroom as the queen and king of a tradition new to Columbus, but one that has been especially popular in the gulf-ports of Mobile and New Orleans for two centuries or more. Introduced in 1959 by Mr. and Mrs. L. H. Morrison, former residents of that Louisiana crescent city, and sponsored by the Saint Francis Hospital Auxiliary, the first Mardi Gras Ball (to benefit the local Catholic-run hospital) quickly became the social event of the year. The identity of the new king and queen is a closely guarded

secret until the new royal couple enters the scene of the lavishly decorated soiree. She is chosen from the current crop of debutantes, and he is always a prominent business or professional man who has been active in community affairs. Photograph courtesy of the Columbus Ledger-Enquirer *newspapers*

Voting chiefly by proxy, the shareholders of the Nehi Corporation voted on March 24, 1959, at its annual meeting in Wilmington, Deleware, to change its corporate name to Royal Crown Cola, taking the name from its principal product. On March 31, the New York Stock Exchange began trading the stock under the ticker tape code of RCC. Shown with Wilbur H. Glenn (holding the bottle), the cola company president, are, (left to right), Jerome Frankel, stock specialist of the exchange; G. Keith Funston, president of the exchange; and Fred C. Whaley, New York stock specialist. The listing on the big board became the first such for a Columbus-based company. Photograph courtesy of the Columbus Ledger-Enquirer *newspapers*

The early 1960s had a different look on Twelfth Street. Unlike today, traffic was permitted to go both east and west. The Ralston is still the tallest structure in sight, but the large four-story building on the north side of the street is the new branch of Davison's. And on the right, the Columbus Bank and Trust Company has a modernized glass and marble front. There now is only one billiard hall, the "Palace," on Twelfth Street, not two. You can't get a shine any more, but the sign proclaiming "Hamburgers" spells out the arrival of the fast-food era. The spire of the Church of the Holy Family is barely visible at the exact middle of the picture, and just to the right of it is the Federal Building, better known locally as the Downton Post Office. Photograph courtesy of the Columbus Ledger-Enquirer *newspapers*

It was natural that, while campaigning for the presidency, John F. Kennedy made a pilgrimage to the Democratically "holy" ground of the Little White House at Warm Springs. On a sunny October 10 morning in 1960, fifteen thousand people jammed their way into the oval area in front of the FDR cottage. After his speech, the viewers surged forward to shake Kennedy's hand or touch him. Predictably, the crowd turned unruly mob and demolished a section of wood-rail fence and trampled shrubbery in its frenzied efforts to surge after the candidate. The Georgia State Patrol finally had to lock arms and hustle Kennedy out of the grounds to the open convertible that was waiting for him. He also made a short address and shook hands with a more orderly multitude assembled at the Muscogee County airport. Photograph courtesy of the Columbus Ledger-Enquirer *newspapers*

Begun in 1960, the 1,749-foot television tower near Cusseta was to bear a proud title: the tallest manmade structure in the world. Jointly enabling WRBL-TV and WTVM to widen their primary and secondary transmission coverage, the tower initially was to be 1,260 feet tall, ten feet taller than the Empire State Building in New York City, but not taller than the 225-foot television antenna atop the Manhattan structure. After negotiations, the Federal Communications Commission allowed an additional 489 feet to be added to its height. Transmission began May 25, 1962, along with the world recognition as tallest among the tall. But fame is fleeting. A tower in Chattanooga was constructed one foot taller and one in Fargo, North Dakota claimed a height of two thousand feet. The current tallest manmade structure is the Warszawa Radio guyed mast at Konstantynow, Poland, located approximately sixty miles northwest of Warsaw, reaching a cloud-tickling 2,120 feet and eight inches. Photograph courtesy of the Columbus Ledger-Enquirer *newspapers*

Son of parents whose religious beliefs were to oppose war or any kind of violence, he grew up to be the commander of the greatest army in history, after graduating sixty-first in a class of 164 at West Point. Predicted by his high school yearbook to be a professor of history at Yale, he served two years as president of Columbia University. Four years after insisting that a life-long professional soldier should never enter politics, he was nominated on the first ballot as the presidential standard bearer of the Republican Party. As commander in chief, he visited Fort Benning and reviewed troops in 1960. That was quite a different station in life from that of major as Dwight David Eisenhower had been in 1926, when he was one (second from right) of the two coaches for the All Army football team at Benning or even when, as chief of staff, he was General Eisenhower on an inspection tour of the post in 1947. Both photographs courtesy of the Columbus Ledger-Enquirer *newspapers*

Helen Joerg and her Villula Tea Garden had to be experienced to be appreciated. It was virtually impossible to describe either. You could say both were delightful, both slightly eccentric, both institutions in the Chattahoochee Valley. But you would be a long way from a true picture of either. You would be nearer the mark if you explained that both Mrs. Joerg and the popular restaurant near Seale in Russell County that she founded and operated were uniquely and particularly southern. You could have found neither in any other part of the country. Helen Dudley Joerg, eighty-seven when she died in 1981, was one of a long line of southern women who took the regional cuisine and raised it to an art form. A meal at her Villula was a leisurely experience to be cherished and savored. Establishments like Villula and even the kind of food they serve are disappearing in a flood of fast-food outlets, absence of help and the general homogenization of our culture. A generation is growing up that will have no memory of them, and that's a pity. Villula, which Mrs. Joerg opened in the late 1940s, was the last of a long line of restaurants with which she had been associated, including the Country Club of Columbus, where she was hostess in the early 1930s. Mrs. Joerg is pictured at Villula in 1961. Photograph courtesy of the Columbus Ledger-Enquirer *newspapers*

Theatricals, both amateur and professional, had been a part of Columbus life since its founding days. There had been a Columbus Dramatics Club in the early 1900s, and another Little Theater group in the late twenties gave productions, including one that travelled to Warm Springs to entertain the newly-elected Franklin D. Roosevelt. Stimulated by interest shown following operettas presented by the Christian Fellowship Association, a formal charter was granted in 1961 to the Columbus Little Theater, whose first production was Happy Birthday, *followed by* My Three Angels. *These first two productions were performed in the auditorium of Jordan Vocational High School for limited runs, i.e., two nights each. Photograph from the author's collection*

In mid-June of 1962, the city commission voted to provide a solid foundation (i.e., a reinforced concrete slab) for the new acoustical band shell of the Columbus Symphony Orchestra. Designed by local architect Thomas Brookbank, the shell was built at a cost of $6,000 and was dedicated at a pops concert on August 30 in Weracoba Park before a crowd of over five thousand music lovers: music lovers who were reclining on blankets or sitting in folding chairs. Only once since has the shell ever been ported; that was in an effort to meet the ticket demand for a Three Arts League-sponsored recital by pianist Van Cliburn. For that November 8, 1962 occasion (pictured here), the shell was inserted into (but barely minimized) the cavernous Municipal Auditorium. Upon viewing the physical problem of awesome space before the concert, the youthful and obviously cheerful keyboard artist observed, "Well, there's one good thing. It's too late to do anything about it!" Photograph courtesy of the Columbus Ledger-Enquirer *newspapers*

One of the top female journalists in the south, Latimer Watson, died September 16, 1962, at the age of seventy-three, having gone to work in 1927 for the Enquirer-Sun. *While Columbus' readers regarded her as an institution, her fellow workers regarded her as a glass of champagne. She had verve, charm, energy, enthusiasm, style and the push required to get a story when a push was needed. About the highest compliment one journalist can pay to another is this: "She never wrote a bad story." With equal effervescence, she wrote about fashion or food or the college boy who had just won an honor. After she suffered a heart attack, the newspaper installed an elevator to her office floor. Naturally, it was dubbed "Latimer's Lift." She's shown here in a 1962 photo with a youthful Richard M. Nixon, future president of the United States. Photograph courtesy of the* Columbus Ledger-Enquirer *newspapers*

Governor Ernest Vandiver did double duty on July 25, 1962. First, he accepted a deed on behalf of the state of Georgia to the future Confederate Naval Museum and then he assisted in the symbolic breaking ground of the third inland-barge port operated by Georgia Ports Authority, pictured here. A severe thunderstorm forced both ceremonies to move into the Municipal Auditorium and the dirt for the groundbreaking ceremony was brought indoors in a bucket. Electrical power failed in the auditorium, and the governor had to use a battery-powered microphone for his two speeches. In one, he predicted that "this inland port will soon make itself strongly felt in your economy" and, in the other, that the "CSS Muscogee is at home in Columbus and has become, for the second time, visible evidence of this community's active determination and dedication to a believed-in-cause." Photograph courtesy of the Columbus Ledger-Enquirer *newspapers*

The South rose again in 1961, a century after it began its fall. A community project by the Civil War Centennial Committee of the Columbus Historical Society, The Gallant City, *was an historical drama written by Clay Lacy and Tom Sellers. The story line traced the exciting and occasionally tragic story of Columbus during the War Between the States. Staged on the floor of the Municipal Auditorium where horses and carriages and other elements of spectacle could be utilized to great advantage, the pageant featured, among many other groups, the reactivated Columbus Guards. Seen here, in their authentic costumes tailored by Schwobilt Clothes, the guards received a last-minute inspection from Ben Penton before the troops went on stage to perform a masterful close-order drill.* Gallant City *was repeated in 1962, but was not the rousing success that it had been the previous year. Photograph courtesy of the* Columbus Ledger-Enquirer *newspapers*

A harmonic lament of a fictitious prisoner put a Seventh Avenue and Tenth Street structure on the musical map in 1927. The structure was the Columbus Stockade and the song was written by Thomas P. Darby, (right), a Columbus native, and his partner, Jimmy Tarlton, a famous guitar-picking and singing duo of the day. Although the song "Columbus Stockade Blues" netted them little financial gain, it became famous. After many years apart, the team of Darby and Tarlton was reunited in the summer of 1963 when they agreed to be a part of the Columbus Symphony Orchestra's opening pops concert in Weracoba Park. Many famous musicians, including Jimmy Davis, Lenny Dee, Pete Fountain, Woody Guthrie, Bill Monroe, the Nashville Brass and Webb Pierce, have recorded versions of the "Columbus Stockade Blues." At the concert, Tarlton and Darby also performed some of their other compositions, such as "Longest Train I Ever Saw" and "Lonesome in the Pines." Photograph courtesy of the Columbus Ledger-Enquirer *newspapers*

"American Traditionalists of the 20th Century" was its title and when it opened officially on the fiftieth anniversary of the famous New York Armory Show, crowds of art lovers jammed the new $250,000 wing of the Columbus Museum of Arts and Crafts, viewing an exhibition valued at over half a million dollars. The traditionalists collection featured paintings by the immortal "Eight" of the "Ashcan School," a term applied to a group of realistic American artists who painted bars, prizefights, and street scenes rather than traditional "pretty pictures." It was believed to have been the largest such exhibition assembled in America since World War II. The 1963 addition, financed by a gift of $100,000 from the W. C. and Sarah Hall Bradley Foundation and matched by gifts from other local foundations, corporations, and individuals, contains an octagonal auditorium-gallery, four smaller galleries and a large gallery of Indian arts, depicting Indian life in the southeast from ten thousand years ago to the present. Shown left to right are Mr. and Mrs. D. A. Turner, Mr. and Mrs. Edward S. Shorter, and Mr. and Mrs. C. Dexter Jordan. Not only has the museum continued to grow in physical size, but also it has recognized, with group and individual shows, the strong artistic abilities of many local inhabitants, some native-born and some imports. The Columbus art colony, too numerous to name, plays a prominent role in the cultural life of this community. *Photograph courtesy of the* Columbus Ledger-Enquirer *newspapers*

An oceangoing barge named Sun Coaster and a tug named Swamp Angel caused commerce to be reborn on the Chattahoochee on Saturday, August 24, 1963, by docking at the Columbus wharf. Owned by Thurston Crawford, a local transportation executive, the Sun Coaster was a 56-foot-wide, 285-foot-long, self-unloading barge that had been designed by Crawford to carry phosphate rock, sulphur, potash and other dry bulk materials and was built in Pascagoula, Mississippi, by the Ingalls Shipbuilding Corporation. With a capacity of six thousand tons, the barge was probably the largest vessel that has ever been on the river, that is if one doesn't count the time when the U.S. battleship Missouri was anchored behind the Eagle and Phenix Mills between the Fourteenth and Dillingham Street bridges. The latter event was an April 1st joke of the Ledger accomplished by superimposing a photograph of the battleship on the millpond and which brought thousands of gullible people to the river bank for a look-see. *Photograph courtesy of the* Columbus Ledger-Enquirer *newspapers*

For the Three Arts League, a mountain as high as Everest was crested in early September 1963 when Mrs. A. Illges, concert series president, announced that the league had closed its purchase agreement with Martin Theaters for the 2,200-seat Royal Theater. This climaxed a fund-raising campaign begun in March of 1963 to buy and renovate the Royal which, for the past couple of years, had served as the concert hall for the league. The campaign was launched after the city commission agreed to maintain and operate the Royal if the League raised approximately $200,000. Substantial donations by the owners of the theater, E. D. and Roy Martin, and Columbus and Atlanta descendants of pioneer Columbus citizen George Waldo Woodruff made the purchase possible as a center for the performing arts. The Royal was one of the south's largest theaters when it was constructed in 1929. Photograph courtesy of the Columbus Ledger-Enquirer *newspapers*

The reunion, if you will pardon the expression, of the prow and stern sections of the Confederate gunboat Muscogee *occurred in late July of 1963, just one year, four months and sixteen days short of a century after the whole vessel had sunk into the mud of the Chattahoochee and, for all practical purposes, had disappeared into the mist of memory. A Confederate history class under Dr. Joseph Mahan at the Columbus Museum of Arts and Crafts in 1959 had sparked interest in the lost warboat. When its burnt-out hull was located twenty-five miles south of Columbus in 1960, salvage operations commenced that eventually would enlist the entire membership of the Columbus Junior Chamber of Commerce, assistance from the Georgia Historical Commission, state funds matching appropriations from the city and county commissions, plus assistance and resources from countless individuals, all combining to free the remains of the* Muscogee *from its watery grave and leading to the establishment of the only Confederate Naval Museum in the United States of America. Robert Holcombe, curator of the museum, stands in the shadow of the C.S.S.* Muscogee. *Photograph courtesy of the* Columbus Ledger-Enquirer *newspapers*

Festival Days was part of a community-wide tourist promotion that won for Columbus the 1963 "Stay and See Georgia" contest, sponsored by the state Chamber of Commerce Travel Council. A part of those June 21-30 Festival Days was the "green corn" and other ceremonial Yuchi dances, performed by descendants of that Indian tribe who had been removed from what is now east Alabama in 1836. Dressed in period costumes are Addie and Rufus George, who came from Sapulpa, Oklahoma, to assist with the preparation of the dancecamp site on the one hundred acres of land, donated locally to the tribe, just south of Phenix City. The Georges also aided in the exhibit installation of the new Indian wing of the Columbus Museum of Arts and Sciences, which was dedicated and opened by the present Yuchi queen, Mrs. Jewell Brown Caton, who inherited the leadership of the tribe at the death in 1957 of her father, Chief Samuel W. Brown, Jr. Photograph courtesy of the Columbus Ledger-Enquirer *newspapers*

"The greatest thing that can happen to a person is to be a first-generation American." And, luckily for Columbus, Georgia, these quoted words are from a distinguished native son, Aaron Cohn, who grew up on Second Avenue in the 1920s. Aaron's father, Sam Cohn, immigrated to America at the turn of the century and operated a successful livery stable on Front Avenue. Aaron Cohn received his law degree from the University of Georgia in 1938 and practices law with his son, Leslie. Their office is located at 831 Second Avenue—the same building that Cohn knew as home as a young boy. In addition to the practice of law, Aaron Cohn has served as Muscogee Juvenile Court Judge since 1964. Judge Cohn is known throughout the country as a man of impeccable integrity who has built and served a strong juvenile justice system in Columbus for over twenty years. He is pictured on the far right taking his oath of office on December 29, 1964. Pictured with Cohn are Judge John Land (left) and Judge Alvan Davis. Photograph courtesy of the Columbus Ledger-Enquirer *newspapers*

The grand reopening of the Springer Opera House took place October 6, 1965, with an original musical based on the famous nineteenth century novel, St. Elmo, *written by a Columbus native, Augusta Evans Wilson. Music for the twentieth century production also was by Columbus native Don Tucker, at the piano at right, and the lavish show was directed by Charles Jones, another talented local. The hotel portion of the Springer had operated through World War II and the picture house had shown films until 1964, when the Springer's fate—demolition—seemed certain. Then, a group of influential Columbusites headed by Robert M. Lewis, Jr., banded together with the avowed goal of saving the building and restoring it for use, not only as the home of the Columbus Little Theatre but as a repository of history and a showcase for the lively arts. Photograph courtesy of the* Columbus Ledger-Enquirer *newspapers*

Born at Fort Benning in 1922 where his father was stationed as a career serviceman, Albert Thompson attended post and local schools, graduating from Spencer High School. He obtained a bachelor of science in business from Savannah State College, served in the U.S. Army as a sergeant with the Forty-first Engineer Regiment, and then entered Howard University Law School in Washington, D. C., graduating in 1950. He hung out his law shingle in Columbus in 1951, and his first legal work was the preparation of a deed for which he was paid five dollars. In 1965, Thompson was elected to the Georgia House of Representatives, becoming the first black office-holder in Columbus in the twentieth century. He was re-elected seven times in a district with a substantial white majority. He was appointed by Governor George Busbee in January of 1981 to the six-county Chattahoochee Judicial Circuit, when Superior Court Judge Oscar Smith resigned. "It was the proudest day of my life," recalled Thompson. Photograph courtesy of the Columbus Ledger-Enquirer *newspapers*

Water, water, everywhere and not a place to park. Such was the lament of regular Ledger-Enquirer *and Eagle and Phenix Mills employees as they viewed what normally was their parking lot adjacent to their respective places of employment. The beginning of 1964 had seen an ice storm hit the area, causing damage mostly to tree limbs and power lines. The ice soon melted and the river returned to its normal banks. Photograph courtesy of the* Columbus Ledger-Enquirer *newspapers*

The end of an era was flown through Columbus by a native son on a sparkling cold Sunday night, January 31, 1965. At the controls of Southern's flight #207-208 was Capt. Otis Cabiness, a former Columbus airport manager. That evening's flight was the last scheduled DC-3 flight through Columbus for any of the three airlines servicing the area, as Delta and Eastern had removed their DC-3's several years before. That flight finished more than two decades of DC-3 service in and out of Muscogee. With a shape similar to an unpregnant guppy, the DC-3 was born in 1933 and soon became the workhorse of aviation. Renamed the C-47, these planes are credited with the Allied victory in World War II by none less than Gen. D. D. Eisenhower. Photograph courtesy of the Columbus Ledger-Enquirer *newspapers*

Although four were absent for this formal portrait taken of the directors of the Fourth National Bank, present were (front row, left to right): Jack M. Passailaigue, Andrew Prather, William R. Bowdoin, George P. Swift, (chairman of the board), Charles S. Daley (president), Judge Frank D. Foley, and Oscar L. Betts, Jr., (back row, left to right): W. Evans Bruner, Rupert A. Triplett, W. T. Heard, Jr., Leon K. Camp, Howell Hollis, J. W. Oliver, Robert T. Davis, Jr., Jac H. Rothschild, Jack A. Bell, William D. Swift, Henry W. Swift, George P. Swift, Jr., and W. L. Haines, (secretary). Those directors not photographed were Cason J. Callaway, Jr., C. William Curry, Frank D. Foley, Jr., and John P. Illges, III. Nine years after this photo, the Fourth National Bank had a name change and became the National Bank and Trust Company. This designation remained until 1985 when it became the Trust Company Bank of Columbus. Photograph courtesy of the Columbus Ledger-Enquirer *newspapers*

Domiciled in dust and debris at Jonesboro, the Fair of 1850 was a disheartened and ill-tended complex of buildings ranging from a camp-meeting arbor to a cotton press, and sleeping inside these structures was a valuable collection of Georgiana, ranging from a cobbler's kit to carriages. Owned by the estate of John W. West, a Georgia education and history professor and one-time president of North George College at Dahlonega, the West Foundation's collection was acquired by a non-profit corporation, Westville Historic Handicrafts, in December of 1966. The purpose of WHH was (and is) to preserve, research and teach (such as the quilter, Mrs. Dan Ware, is doing here) pre-industrial era handicrafts and skills common to the people of this area via a living outdoor history museum. The motto of Westville is "Where it's always 1850." And so it is in this recreated village on the outskirts of Lumpkin. To this site have been brought houses, buildings and artifacts, with more than $2 million having been expended in the development of Westville, which officially opened on April 1, 1970. Its first director was Dr. Joseph Mahan. Early Westville supporters include, left to right, Miss Pattie Pearson, Mrs. L. M. Moye and Mrs. Sam Singer. Photographs courtesy of the Columbus Ledger-Enquirer newspapers

From being the mascot of the Columbus High baseball team as a young boy (center, in photo at left) to having the new baseball field at the University of Georgia named in his honor was the logical finale to the life of Frank D. Foley, Sr. Born August 17, 1888, Foley was descended from both the founder of the Springer Opera House and from the architect of the Church of the Holy Family. He received his bachelor of law degree from the University of Georgia in 1910 and was a trustee of the Athens school from 1920 to 1944. Affectionately called "Judge" in recognition of the judicial era of his life, Foley was honored in 1965 with a varsity "G" for his contributions to the university. Two years after his death in 1966, a statue of Foley was unveiled on the campus. Photographs courtesy of the Columbus Ledger-Enquirer *newspapers*

In 1966, city council adopted a new motto for Columbus: "Fountain City." In previous years it had been the "Electric City," "Lowell of the South," and "Port City." Because of the many marriages that Columbus girls have made to boys stationed at Fort Benning, it has more accurately been called the "Mother-in-law of the Army." An affectionate name for the handsome white marble statue-fountain at the intersection of Wynnton-Buena Vista-Dinglewood and Peachtree is "A Columbus mother looking for a son-in-law at Fort Benning." However, it is officially a landmark of Sarling Park, dedicated to the memory of Mrs. Leonora Sarling, who died in an automobile wreck in 1928. One of the pioneers in the Christian Science First Church of Christ, Scientist, Mrs. Sarling was active in civic, social, and religious concerns. Donated in her honor by family members, the statue is a more modest version of the bare-breasted Lost Pleiad by Randolph Rogers. Photograph from the author's collection

Spearheading the preservation movement in Columbus was Sarah Turner Butler, who joined with other interested citizens to form the Historic Columbus Foundation in 1966 and who has continued to be involved in every aspect of preservation-related activities in the area. As one of the foundation's early presidents, she was instrumental in establishing HCF's revolving redevelopment fund, which, over the last twenty years, has helped to preserve over thirty significant historic properties. She was also at the forefront of the acquisition, restoration, and interior decoration of the foundation's present headquarters at 700 Broadway. The Sarah Turner Butler Award, to be given only when "an individual's efforts are so meritous or a project so outstanding that the contribution to preservation cannot be ignored," was established in her honor in November of 1984. Shown here at the spring 1981 dedication of the Walker-Peters-Langdon House historic marker (the house being the first office of the Historic Columbus Foundation) are (left to right): then-Mayor Harry C. Jackson; Mrs. Butler; Douglas C. Purcell, executive director of the Historic Chattahoochee Commission; and George Wade, then-president of HCF. Photographs courtesy of the Columbus Ledger-Enquirer newspapers

Several weeks after Arthur Fiedler (and the Boston Pops) had given an April 1967 concert in Columbus under the auspices of the Three Arts Theater, the Associated Press syndicated a photo of Fiedler doing the twist with a bosomy blonde in a San Francisco nightclub. The accompanying cutlines pointed out how quickly Fiedler had learned the current dance craze. The real reason he was so adept was that he had practiced with Columbusite Ruth Woolfolk at a post-concert party, while fellow Columbus concert-goer Henry Watson (left) and Mrs. Fiedler provided encouragement. Photograph from the author's collection

"To extend its labors upon the broad fields of Charity and Benevolence." So resolved the Ladies' Purim Association on July 5, 1874, who became the Daughters of Israel. Flourishing under several other names, the group finally adopted the title of Jewish Ladies Aid Society in 1907 and has indeed met its resolve, having reached far beyond the Temple Israel congregation to leave its mark upon the whole city. Among its most widely known and respected projects is the Milk Fund, which began just before the Great Depression and, during that period of economic low ebb, distributed milk to hundreds of needy children throughout the city. Its founder, Mrs. Laura F. (Max) Rosenberg, was honored in 1931 by the Lions Club as Columbus' best citizen of the year. In this 1967 photo, left to right, Mrs. Irving Zyskind, Mrs. Harry Kruger and Mrs. Nathan Schultz prepare bags for the American Red Cross. Photographs courtesy of the Columbus Ledger-Enquirer *newspapers*

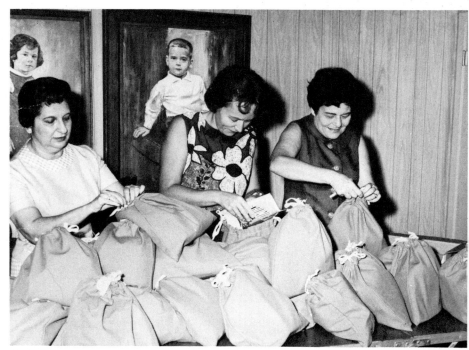

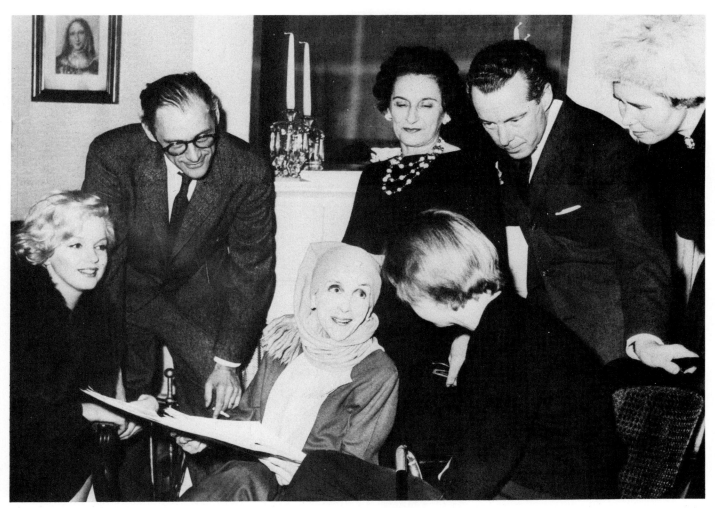

It was in 1959 that this colorful group of personalities gathered in Nyack, New York, at Columbus-born Carson McCullers' home overlooking the Hudson River for a luncheon given in honor of Isak Dinesen (Baroness Karen Blixen-Finecke), the Danish author whom McCullers had so greatly admired from her first reading of Out of Africa. *Miss Dinesen had expressed special interest in meeting Marilyn Monroe, and it was McCullers who arranged the introduction over a feast of oysters, white grapes, and champagne. McCullers, whose back is unfortunately turned to the camera, is flanked by (left to right) Miss Monroe; her then-husband, playwright Arthur Miller; Miss Dinesen; Felicia Geffen, executive secretary of the National Institute and National Academy of Arts and Letters; Jordan Massee (McCullers' favorite cousin); and Clara Svendsen, Miss Dinesen's secretary. Eight years later, on September 29, 1967, McCullers died after what had been a lifetime of physical and emotional suffering, highlighted, however, by towering artistic achievements which included her four novels:* The Heart is a Lonely Hunter, Reflections in a Golden Eye, The Member of the Wedding, *and* Clock Without Hands; *a novella,* The Ballad of the Sad Cafe; *numerous short stories, poems, and essays.* Member, *which was later produced as a play, enjoyed a successful Broadway run of 501 performances and won the prestigious New York Drama Critics' Circle Award for the best play of the season.* The Square Root of Wonderful, *her second play, and Edward Albee's adaptation of* Ballad *also played before Broadway audiences. In addition, major motion pictures were produced from* Heart, Member, *and* Reflections *and included in lead roles such film stars as Alan Alda, Ethel Waters, Julie Harris, Elizabeth Taylor, and Marlon Brando. In November of 1967, just two months after her death, Columbus paid homage to McCullers—doubtless the most celebrated literary figure ever to be born here—by staging* The Lonely Hunting: A Memory of Carson McCullers *at the Springer Opera House. Local players presented scenes from the author's principal works. Photographs courtesy of the* Columbus Ledger-Enquirer *newspapers*

Can a little show from Dixie find happiness on the Great White Way? Clive Barnes, reviewer for the New York Times *wrote, "Yes. Despite its failings, believe me,* Red, White and Maddox *is fun in the first place and significant in the second. Who needs a third place?" The composer, lyricist and co-author of "RWAM," Don Tucker, became the third Columbus native—Nunnally Johnson (see page 276) and McCullers had preceded him—to have a show on Broadway when the show opened at the Cort Theater on January 26, 1967. Known for his satirical revues and the musical version of* St. Elmo *which opened the restored Springer Opera House, Tucker's musical was transferred from its fall debut in Atlanta en toto to New York after a successful run in the state capital. Tucker graduated from Jordan High School and attended the University of Georgia. Photograph from the author's collection*

After two years in the Georgia State Legislature, Jack Brinkley made a grab for the brass ring and was elected to the U. S. Congress in 1967, becoming the first member of that august body from Columbus in the twentieth century. (Rep. Thomas Wingfield Grimes had been the last Columbusite to serve, 1887-1891.) Born December 22, 1930, Brinkley was a U.S. Air Force pilot during the Korean War and served for five years. Married to Lois Kite and the father of two sons, Brinkley decided to come back to Georgia in 1982 after eight elections to congress, a term which would rank as the second longest served by a Georgia Third District representative since the War Between the States. In addition to acting as dean of the Georgia Congressional Delegation, he was also a member of the House Armed Services Committee and chairman of the Military Installations and Facilities Subcommittee. Surrounding the youthful congressman in his office in Washington, D. C., was a group of Columbus supporters: back row, left to right, J. R. Allen, Maynard Ashworth, B. Ed Johnson, Norman Bishop, Jim Woodruff; and front row, left to right, T. G. Reeves, Brinkley, Oscar Betts and George Woodruff. Photograph courtesy of the Columbus Ledger-Enquirer *newspapers*

Opening with the "Lord's Prayer," sung from behind the curtain to a darkened theater audience, Columbus-born Fredye Marshall commenced her triumphant "Evening of Song" on April 22, 1967. A benefit for the Springer Opera House, this was the first time that home folks had heard her four-and-a-half-octave-range voice in concert, although she had become a headliner on five continents. Photographed some ten years before the Columbus benefit at a party given by the Ira Gershwins while the Porgy and Bess *cast was performing in Los Angeles, Miss Marshall's chums can easily be identified as, left to right, Humphrey Bogart, Judy Garland, Miss Marshall, Lauren Bacall and Louis Calhern. Highlights of her career include three command performances (before England's Royal Family; the Lord Mayor of Melbourne, Australia; and Argentina's Juan and Eva Peron); making the first-ever recording of "Witchcraft" (later made famous by Frank Sinatra); Broadway appearances (*Carmen Jones, My Darling Aida, Cabin in the Sky*) and singing the role of Bess at La Scala Opera House in Milan. Since 1967, she has busied herself with many appearances on local television and frequent singing engagements in the Columbus area. Photograph courtesy of the* Columbus Ledger-Enquirer *newspapers*

The matron turned from the cashier, bumped a gentleman with her pocketbook, then looked up in apology. "Oh, excuse me, Mr. Glenn." Although the scene was the Ralston Hotel, the Mr. Glenn to whom she begged pardon wasn't Wilbur, president of Royal Crown Cola, but John, the astronaut and space pioneer who also just happened to be with the same local cola company. Glenn, seen here with Lt. Gen. John M. Wright in July of 1967, was elected vice president for corporate development and RC director in 1962, a position he held until 1974. Since 1975 he has been a U.S. senator from Ohio. Photograph courtesy of the Columbus Ledger-Enquirer *newspapers*

An 1898 Enquirer-Sun *newspaper article described the home of Mr. and Mrs. James Rankin, both Scotland-born, as the most expensive house in Columbus, placing its value at $18,500. The Rankins' home features a divided walnut staircase and spaciously, graciously appointed rooms. After the War Between the States, the Rankins spent a number of years in Scotland, where their sons attended the University of Edinburgh. Donated to the Historic Columbus Foundation in 1969 in memory of the late James Waldo Woodruff, Sr., the brick, Second Empire mansion was opened in 1970 as a historic house museum of the 1850-1879 period. Begun just prior to 1861 but not completed until the war had ended, the house has notable features which include exquisite iron grillwork on its verandah and flying balcony, wide heart-of-pine floor boards and hand-carved cornices and door frames. The spacious downstairs rooms, restored and furnished in the appropriate high Victorian Style, are open to the public, while the upstairs rooms are occupied as offices by the Junior League of Columbus. In the accompanying 1982 photo, Royal Crown Cola Companies board member Cason J. Callaway, Jr., presents a check representing the international firm's gift to Mrs. L. Neill Bickerstaff, Rankin House Special Projects Coordinator, and C. Dexter Jordan, Jr., then HCF president. Photograph courtesy of the* Columbus Ledger-Enquirer *newspapers; Roger T. Harris and the Historic Columbus Foundation collection*

The honored lady to whom Historic Columbus Foundation's first annual Heritage Ball was dedicated was Mrs. Ethel Illges Woodruff, and the scene of the charity ball was the old Illges home at 1428 Second Avenue. Spurred on by the success of the trustees of the Springer Opera House in their efforts to restore that historic structure, the Historic Columbus Foundation was organized in June of 1966 by seventy-five initial members who were deeply committed to the preservation of the city's architectural legacy, the recognized value of tourism, the revitalization of downtown and to the overall betterment of the city as a whole. The Heritage Ball, held annually at a different historic site, also introduces new debutante members of the Cotillion Club. The author is seen presenting the dedication scroll to Mrs. Woodruff, while her sons, James W. (left) and J. Barnett smile their approval. Photograph courtesy of the Columbus Ledger-Enquirer *newspapers*

Rufe Edwards McCombs was born in Decatur, Georgia, and knew at the age of ten that she wanted to be a lawyer. She passed the state bar exam in her first year of law school at the University of Georgia. After graduating in 1942, she obtained a job in the legal department of the U.S. Department of Agriculture in Washington D.C. Moving to Columbus where her husband was in the insurance business, in 1962, she served as a volunteer in the Legal Aid department for six months until she was placed on salary. Six years later, she announced her candidacy for a vacant Muscogee County judgeship and, in the election, defeated three other candidates without a run-off to become the first woman to be elected to a judgeship in Columbus. Three years later, 1972, she was elected to fill a vacancy in the state court judgeship and in 1982 successfully ran for Superior Court judgeship. Photograph courtesy of the Columbus Ledger-Enquirer *newspapers*

Construction executive Ben H. Hardaway III (foreground) has become known for his superb fox hound pack, not only in the south but in the traditional hunt areas of England and Ireland as well. Recognized as a master of the Fox Hounds Association of America, Hardaway, along with his brother-in-law, noted orthopedic surgeon Dr. Jack Hughston, founded the Midland, Georgia, hunt after World War II. All the foxes pursued are wild and native to Hardaway Hall property. His well-trained pack is composed of legendary bloodlines like the Tipperary, Tiverton and Taunton Valed, mixed with West War Waterford, Penn Mary Dell and July, the latter being a celebrated hound bred by the late George J. Garrett, often called the dean of southern fox hunters. Photograph courtesy of the Columbus Ledger-Enquirer *newspapers*

John Wayne, one of the most famous actors in the world, arrived in Columbus in the summer of 1968 to shoot a film based upon the book by Robin Moore, The Green Berets. *This story of Vietnam was shot, naturally, at Fort Benning, on a distant site near Cusseta. But Wayne also needed a Southeast Asia plantation for the scene of a kidnapping, and he found such a setting on the grounds of the ante-bellum estate called Hilton (on Hilton Avenue at Macon Road). Shooting there took several days, and because the home is not nearly as remote as Fort Benning, tremendous traffic jams were caused by curious sightseers. Also in the movie was David Jannsen (left, in photo at right), whose last installment of the popular television series, "The Fugitive," was being shown at the WTVM studio while the actor was on location here. Thus another traffic jam was created, this time in downtown Columbus. Rounding out the all-star cast was Jim Hutton. Photograph courtesy of the* Columbus Ledger-Enquirer *newspapers*

It wouldn't be until the 1960s that Columbus would adopt the motto of the "Fountain City" as a way of describing itself. But as far back as the late 1880s, its citizens had had a romantic yearning for splashing waters in a controlled space. One of the terms of a contract between the Water Works Company and the city was that the city would be provided with an ornamental fountain. However, the decision as to where to place the fountain took several years. When the eleven-foot acanthus-leaf and scroll-based fountain was finally mounted in 1890 in front of the Muscogee County Courthouse, the additional ornaments of two Pans, a girl and a swan were stripped before the final installation. The originator of the "Fountain City" motto was G. Othell Hand. The pastor of the First Baptist Church of Columbus, he is seen here in a 1969 photo at dedication ceremonies for the church's new fountain, which was originally designed for a federal building in Washington D.C. Hand later left the ministry for the market place, becoming an executive with the American Family Life Assurance Company. Photograph courtesy of the Columbus Ledger-Enquirer *newspapers*

When the Columbus Round Table assembled in July of 1960, it was to honor one of their "knights." In this case, publisher of the Columbus Ledger-Enquirer *newspapers, Maynard Ashworth, on his seventy-fifth birthday. His wellwishers included: seated, left to right, Oscar McCollister, Tom Sikes, Frank Lumpkin, Jr., Ashworth, waitress Lottie Gregory, Theo McGee, Henry Reeves, Rev. Norman Lovein, Dr. Joseph Serrato, and John K. Hart. Standing, left to right, are Arnold Thompson, Richard Bickerstaff, Ritchie White, Dr. John T. Miller, Irvin Rosenberg, Frank Schley, Dr. Brent Fox, Jim Woodruff and Oscar Betts, the hotel's manager. Unlike King Arthur's Round Table where the bravest knights of the realm were invited to join, the local branch had an informal membership; anyone who gravitated at lunch time to the round table in the rear of the Ralston's Coffee Shop found good food and better conversation! Photograph courtesy of the* Columbus Ledger-Enquirer *newspapers*

"Except for Carnegie Hall, it (the Three Arts Theater) is the finest acoustically in which we have played in America," said Jascha Horenstein, maestro of the London Symphony Orchestra. This accolade came after the orchestra gave a concert to benefit the restoration of the Springer Opera House. The August 18, 1969 performance climaxed with a post-concert party atop the Columbus Car Park, transformed into a simulated English pub called the "Paw and the Claw." This party site was almost destroyed a few hours earlier by a violent thunderstorm, an ill-tempered squall born of Hurricane Camille passing nearby in Alabama. The co-chairman of the party, Frances Ellis, viewed the debris and suggested "that we just leave it and call it bomb damage." Actually, the devastation was repaired and the party, along with the concert, was judged a great success. Here, Mrs. Charles McClure, left, and Miss Ellis are surrounded by members of the orchestra. Photograph courtesy of the Columbus Ledger-Enquirer newspapers

One of the original seventeen incorporators of the Columbus Museum of Arts and Crafts, (now the Columbus Museum of Arts and Sciences) was Edward Swift Shorter. He also was the first director of the museum, a position he held for more than a decade without remuneration. A graduate of Macon's Mercer University, from which he received an honorary doctor of laws degree in 1969, Shorter was to be recognized as the "dean of artistic interests in the Columbus area" when he became the recipient of the prestigous Gari Melchers Award in 1965. Presented annually since 1944 by the trustees of the Artist's Fellowship to "the American who has furthered the interests of fine arts and culture in America," the Melchers award is named for the celebrated American artist Gari Melchers, a member of the "Ashcan School," who was born in 1860 and who died in 1932. Previous recipients of the award have included such prominent persons in the field of art as Chester Dale, Rush Harrison Kress, Huntington Hartford and Norman Rockwell. Here Shorter, right, is seen receiving his degree from Dr. Rufus Harris, Mercer University president. Photograph courtesy of the Columbus Ledger-Enquirer newspapers

At the tender age of fifteen, Nicholas ("Nick") Spano's five feet and eight inch frame was toting 120 pounds. Two years later, through weightlifting at the YMCA, he had gained forty-five pounds of solid muscle, had seventeen inch biceps, a forty-seven inch chest and was no longer the puniest kid on the block. Three years after that, the Columbus native had been named "Mr. Georgia," "Mr. East Coast," and "Mr. South," plus runner-up in the Mr. Teenage America contest. Then came "Mr. Dixie" and a dozen or so more body-building titles. After college and a graduate degree, Spano was a teacher at Baker High School and dean of men at Columbus High. He returned to the world of exercise and physical culture when he opened the Columbus Health Club in 1967. Spano followed this venture in 1975 by building the Olympic Health Spa, which was exclusively for men before a facility for women was added nearby. This is how "Mr. Dixie" looked in 1970 at the age of twenty-eight. Photograph courtesy of the Columbus Ledger-Enquirer *newspapers*

"I remember Buffalo Bill when his Indians and cowboys had their show on the South Common...(and) Annie Oakley riding horse and breaking glass balls with her Winchester rifle as the balls were thrown up into the air." The quote is from a slim volume of recollections published by Fred H. Schomburg, Sr., who was born October 17, 1881, at 510 Front Avenue and who grew up to be a prominent jeweler in Columbus. "Buffalo Bill" of course was the nickname for William F. Cody, the celebrated buffalo hunter, scout and actor who formed a lively Wild West exhibition in 1883 and kept it on the road for thirty years. The show, which gained international fame when it played at Queen Victoria's diamond jubilee in 1887, provided employment for Indians and preserved America's buffalo herd, in addition to creating entertainment and birthing the romantic image of the West. As an actor, Cody appeared at the Springer in two plays, The Widow's Victim *and* Life on the Border. *He died in 1917, whereas Schomburg lived until age ninty-three, still active in the business that his father, a native of Germany, founded here in 1872. In this 1970 photograph, Schomburg is seen with the Seth Thomas clock which his father installed in front of the Broadway store in 1906. Photograph courtesy of the* Columbus Ledger-Enquirer *newspapers*

The last victor of the Southern Open, before it was revived in 1970, was Mr. Golf himself, Bobby Jones. This famous Georgian won the tourney in 1927. Since its rebirth after a 43-year hiatus, first as the Green Island Open (a PGA satellite event) when Mason Rudolph was the champion, its winners have been a who's who in the links world, winners such as Johnny Miller, Gary Player (pictured here) and Jerry Pate, to name just a few. The final hole of the course draws the largest crowd and frequently provides the real drama of the tourney, with the winner being decided there. Gunby Jordan, Columbus businessman and civic leader, has championed the popular "new" sports event to where it is, to a large degree, making up for social, athletic and national attention that was attached to the Georgia-Auburn football games in the years when they were played here. Photograph courtesy of the Columbus Ledger-Enquirer *newspapers*

Out of Fred Haskins' free Saturday morning youth clinics at the Country Club of Columbus came golfers like George Swift, George Hamer, Jack and Billy Key, all of whom played any-league championship golf. To that list must be added Hugh Royer, Jr., (pictured here), the first Columbusite to go on the professional golf circuit. He began touring in 1966 and continued for six years, until he retired because its lifestyle did not please him. He became and still is the pro at the Bull Creek Golf Course in Columbus, but his moment of golfing glory came in 1970 when he won the prestigious Western Open being played in Chicago. Photograph courtesy of the Columbus Ledger-Enquirer *newspapers*

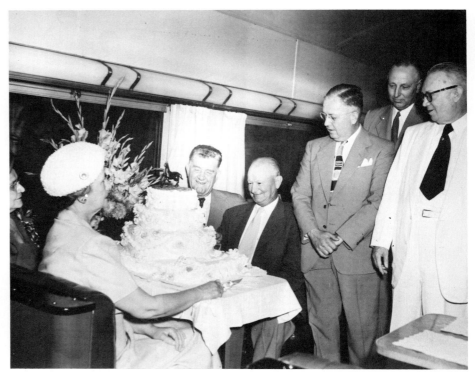

One by one, they died. The trains, that is. For a century plus nineteen years, Columbus had had railroad passenger service. Then by 1971, they were all gone. The sleek, modern Man O'War *that had been born after World War II offered businessmen, female shoppers and school children on daily outings round-trip service to Atlanta. After first cutting the frequency of its runs and later dropping its lounge car, the* Man *failed to complete its race in 1969. Two sleepers passed through each evening providing access to more distant horizons, the south-bound* Seminole *to Miami and the north-bound* City of Miami *to Chicago. The* Seminole *made its last war whoop in 1968, and the* City of Miami *lumbered through for the last time in 1971. Columbus, as well as the nation, ended its romance with railroading with hardly more than a nostalgic whimper. It was a far cry from the civic enthusiasm that had greeted rail connection to Savannah in the spring of 1853. Or the enthusiasm shown in this fourth birthday celebration aboard the* Man O'War *with, left to right, Mrs. S. C. Harris, Mrs. W. E. Dillard, W. T. Bennett, T. J. Stewart, George Stradtman, W. E. Dillard and S. C. Harris. Photograph courtesy of the* Columbus Ledger-Enquirer *newspapers*

With the stroke of the gubernatorial pen, the century-old Springer Opera House became the State Theater of Georgia on September 7, 1971. The pen belonged to Jimmy Carter. Seen that day in Atlanta with the governor was a Springer delegation composed of, left to right, Clason Kyle, Allen Perry, Betty Britto, Eleanor Jones, Marie Kemp, Mary Gregory Jewett (Executive Director of the Georgia Historical Commission), J. E. Slaughter, Jr., Charles Jones and Sue Slaughter. The local group was augmented by members of the state legislature from Columbus, including Senator Harry Jackson, who initiated the request which sparked such a designation. Georgia became the ninth state having a state theater, with the first being Barter Theater in Virginia, which was founded by Robert Porterfield, who was active in his support of the rescue of the local opera house. A few years later, Carter was elected president of the United States and Jackson was elected mayor of Columbus. The Springer was named a National Historic Landmark in 1978 in part because of the notables who had played the stage. Photographs courtesy of the Columbus Ledger-Enquirer *newspapers*

Altogether, the Bull Creek Watershed Project cost approximately $7,000,000 and took thirteen years to complete. It consists of eleven dams and lakes, the channelization of two miles along Lindsay Creek and erosion control measurers along roads throughout Muscogee County. In 1971 the project was recognized by the National Watershed Congress as the most outstanding flood control effort of its kind in the nation. A former member of the Muscogee County Commission and of the Columbus Council, John Rigdon is credited with the chief role in the flood control effort, the first Soil Conservation Service-sponsored project in an urban area in the United States. In 1962, Lake Heath Park was named for Rigdon's wife, the late Heath Cooper Rigdon. Security from flood damage, new subdivisions, beautiful parks, a golf course, tennis courts, and playgrounds have been additional rewards from Rigdon's forward thinking. Rigdon is seen here closing the valve on a flood control dam. Photograph courtesy of the Columbus Ledger-Enquirer *newspapers*

You can bet that the subject under discussion wasn't roses but politics instead when these two gentlemen, sartorially elegant in their double-breasted suits, relaxed on this sofa in the foyer of the Ralston Hotel ballroom. On the left is Richard Brevard Russell, who was born in Winder, Georgia, in 1897 and twenty-two years later was elected to the state legislature. Nine years after that, he became the youngest governor in the state's history. In 1932, he assumed his U.S. senator's seat in Washington where he served until his death there in 1971, numbering among his accomplishments chairmanship of the all-important Armed Services Committee. Perhaps he was telling Columbus Mayor B. Ed Johnson how he was going to throw his hat into the ring as a presidential candidate at the 1952 Democratic Convention, a nomination he lost to Adlai E. Stevenson of Illinois. Highly respected in character and for his awesome institutional power, Russell's finest tribute came from among his colleagues who regarded him as the "senator's senator." Photograph courtesy of the Columbus Ledger-Enquirer *newspapers*

Good things come in small packages, it has been said. Here, William ("Bill") Zimmerman displays the trophy he won for being the International Seniors champion, a tournament played over the testy courses of Gleneagles in Scotland. Actually, he has a pair of these trophies, having won first in 1971 and again in 1974. In real life, these prizes have a use. Called quaichs, the Scots use them as a toasting cup. A native of Augusta, Georgia, and a stockbroker with Johnson, Lane, Space and Smith Company since 1937, Zimmerman and his family have lived in Columbus since 1949. Besides being on two International Seniors teams that played against Holland, Belgium and Japan, he has won the Georgia Amateur Championship and four times has been the Georgia Seniors champion. In 1980, Zimmerman won the U.S. Seniors Golf Association in Rye, New York. Photograph courtesy of the Columbus Ledger-Enquirer newspapers

At the age of ninety-three, William Clyde Woodall died in February of 1971 in Columbus, the city which he adopted at the age of ten and about which he wrote for all of his adult life. A native of Talbot County, where he was born in 1878, Woodall moved to Columbus as a child when his father, William Hardy Woodall, came here to become principal of Tenth Street School (Sixteenth Street School was later renamed Woodall School in honor of the Elder Woodall). W. C. Woodall was best known as a local journalist, his columns "Vanity Fair," "Good Morning," and "Our Town" being favorites of the Ledger-Enquirer newspapers' readership for decades. In addition, he was known in the publishing world as cofounder of the Industrial Index (a magazine devoted to construction, industrial and business news in the southeast) and of the Woodall Press, a Columbus printing firm. His membership on the board of education and his love of writing and history led to his being commissioned by the board to write—along with his daughter, Mrs. John Nilan, and Katherine Mahan—a social history of education in Muscogee County, a book which was published in 1977, six years after his death. Regarded as the city's unofficial historian, Woodall was also the author of Home Town, a collection of his memoirs which was published in 1937. The portrait pictured here, the work of Columbus artist Wyndell Taylor, hangs in the Woodall Building at Columbus College. Photograph courtesy of the Columbus Ledger-Enquirer newspapers

In the summer of 1971 race relations in Columbus, usually reasonably good, turned sour. Six black Columbus policemen, members of the Afro-American Patrolmen's League, in protest over what they termed the Columbus Police Department's racially discriminatory practices, removed the American flag emblems from their uniforms and picketed the department. They were fired May 31. The firings prompted four nights of violence, including several firebombings. A state of emergency was declared, the sale of liquor and firearms was banned and state troupers were brought in. Pictured here is a group of black citizens marching in support of the fired policemen. Marches and unrest continued throughout the summer. Several court cases resulted from the summer's events. Now, fourteen years later, only one of these cases is still in the courts. White and black citizens emerged from the affair realizing that good relations between the races is something that must be worked at. There have been no serious racial disturbances in Columbus since the summer of 1971. Photograph courtesy of the Columbus Ledger-Enquirer newspapers

The city commission on Wednesday, December 28, 1966, voted to recommend to the county commission the creation of a joint eleven-member study committee to recommend consolidation of city and county functions and elimination of duplicate services. A dramatic symbol of the new unity in Columbus and Muscogee County is illustrated in this 1971 photo of the new government building looming up behind the half-razed county courthouse, the old and the new, the outdated and the modern. The most tangible result of the election on May 27, 1970, was the approval to construct a new government center, replacing the 1896 Muscogee County Courthouse with an $11,000,000 complex consisting of a fourteen-story main tower and two three-story wings. Voters that day gave overwhelming approval to a consolidation of city and county offices and services, the first such merger in the state of Georgia. The government center was designed by Columbus architect Edward W. Neal. Photograph courtesy of the Columbus Ledger-Enquirer *newspapers*

While attempting to jump thirty compact cars and break a 171-foot record, twenty-two-year-old Bob Pleso of Ocala, Florida was killed August 4, 1972, at Phenix Dragway. Pleso left the five-foot-high takeoff ramp at an estimated ninety-five miles per hour. Traveling more than one hundred fifty feet, he cleared the first twenty-seven cars before crashing onto the windshield of the twenty-eighth vehicle. He was thrown from the motorcycle and flew through the air for at least one hundred feet before striking the asphalt drag strip. A veteran of sixty-three jumps in his three-year career, Pleso often bragged that he had suffered four major crashes but had walked away from each one. This photo won a first place award for Al Alexander, photographer for the Ledger-Enquirer *from the Georgia Press Association. Photograph courtesy of the* Columbus Ledger-Enquirer *newspapers*

A Spencer High School graduate, Otis Sistrunk made it to the National Football League in 1972 after the Oakland Raiders bought his contract from the Los Angeles Rams. At the time, he was a twenty-six-year-old rookie with no collegiate experience. Sistrunk arrived in the majors after three years in the Continental League where, in 1971, he was the league's Player of the Year while tackling in Virginia for the Norfolk Neptunes. A fixture in the Raider line, Sistrunk has appeared in several movies and wears a Super Bowl championship rating as a result of the Raiders' crunching of the Minnesota Vikings in January of 1977. In high school, Sistrunk preferred basketball to football, but received no scholarship offers for basketball. *Photograph courtesy of the* Columbus Ledger-Enquirer *newspapers*

One day before his scheduled separation from active duty, Lt. William L. Calley was formally charged by the U. S. Army for the murder of 102 Vietnamese civilians during a combat assault on an obscure hamlet. The date of the military operation was March 16, 1968. The trial ended with the jury finding Calley guilty and, on March 31, 1971, he was given a life sentence coupled with dismissal from the service and forfeiture of all pay and allowances. To many of the general public, this was an unpopular and controversial verdict. The longest trial in U.S. military history, the court hearing had lasted four and one-half months (including thirteen days of deliberation) and was covered by press from all over the world. Calley's original sentence to a life of hard labor in prison was finally reduced to a ten year term by the secretary of the army in 1974. He was released that year, however, after four and one-half months in the military prison at Fort Leavenworth, Kansas, following about three years of house arrest at Fort Benning. He now lives in Columbus and is affiliated with his father-in-law's jewelry store. *Photograph courtesy of the* Columbus Ledger-Enquirer *newspapers*

In 1972, this simple four-room cottage was given to the Historic Columbus Foundation and dedicated to the memory of a Columbus pharmacist who had invented a formula for a soft drink that would become an international beverage, Coca-Cola. It was here that Dr. John Stith Pemberton lived with his family from 1855 to 1860. This house was then located at 1017 Third Avenue. In 1869, he moved his family to Atlanta, where poor health and meager finances made him sell two-thirds of his formula for $1,200 and the ramaining third a few months later for $550 or $200 less than he had paid for this house. He died on August 16, 1888, and is buried in Columbus's Linwood Cemetery. The Pemberton House and Apothecary Shop, donated by the Coca-Cola Company and restored with donations from "friends of Coca-Cola," is on the National Register of Historic Places. Seen here at dedication ceremonies are Joseph W. Jones of Atlanta, Mrs. Francis Norman, and James W. Woodruff, Jr. (Although the marker says "John Styth Pemberton," the family spells it "Stith.") (See Chapter IV for more information.) *Photograph courtesy of the* Columbus Ledger-Enquirer *newspapers*

Celebrated for taking his comic routines to front-line U.S. troops in all hostilities since and including World War II is Bob ("Ski Nose") Hope. His appearance in Columbus was in February of 1972 in support of an ongoing national campaign to raise $6,000,000 for a new National Infantry Museum at Fort Benning. The local performance by the famous jokester, dubbed "a friend of the soldier all his life," was similar in one way to Hope's overseas visits. It became a bit of a battlefield. Protesting the glorification of combat, a group of "peace-niks" demonstrated outside the Municipal Auditorium during Hope's act. Many of the protesters held signs that advised one and all to "Preserve People, Not Weapons." Photograph courtesy of the Columbus Ledger-Enquirer *newspapers*

About seven o'clock in the morning, the pre-dawn sleet began to turn to snow. Schoolchildren were already on their way to their classes. Businesses were beginning to open. Several hours later, it was still snowing. By now, hard. At noon, with the white stuff still descending, schools were dismissed as roads were becoming impassable. (The city of Columbus has no specifically designated snow-moving equipment.) And still it snowed. Into the late afternoon. When it finally ceased, a total of fourteen inches had fallen, to the amazement (and general delight) of the majority of the city's citizenry. Naturally, it is the record snowfall for any year in weather-keeping or recorded memory. The date? February 9, 1973. Photograph courtesy of the Columbus Ledger-Enquirer *newspapers*

"I see a new city...one that is born in hope and dedicated to progress." The speaker was J. R. Allen, first mayor of Columbus under its new consolidated government form. Allen brought the same kind of vigorous leadership to this position of city official that had distinguished him in business and civic life, setting out to give Columbus not only a new image but a change from the inside out. A plane crash in 1973 took Allen's life, thus ending a meteoric political career that had promised higher state or national positions. Photograph courtesy of the Columbus Ledger-Enquirer *newspapers*

Born in Cuthbert in 1898, Philip Harris Giddens moved with his family to Columbus when he was three years old and later said that "Columbus has always been my only real home, although I have literally lived all over the world." A graduate of Columbus High School and Georgia Tech, Giddens received a commission for his work as part of the architectural team of New York architects responsible for designing the new high school in 1926. He studied at the famous Ecole Superieure Nationale des Beaux Arts in Paris, became interested in etching, and later was internationally known both as an etcher and a portrait painter, children being his forte. Widely collected, his works have been purchased by institutions such as the British Museum. Giddens died in 1973. The bust of Giddens and the engraving belong to the Columbus Museum of Arts and Sciences. Both photographs courtesy of the Columbus Ledger-Enquirer *newspapers*

L. R. Burnham owned a furniture store at 1029 Broadway, and the store owned a truck to deliver furniture that customers had bought. Frequently, townspeople asked for the truck to assist in their personal moving situations. Eventually the requests for moving outnumbered the furniture customers, and Burnham Van Service was founded in 1921. In 1938, "grandfather" authority was granted to the growing firm for operation in the thirty-five states east of the Rockies. Two years later, it became the first company to handle a shipment of household goods via air transport. By 1977 the one-truck company had grown into a business ranked ninth among the largest of the nation's moving and storage companies. Burnham completed a $2 million office and warehouse complex near the Manchester Expressway in 1973. In the words of its chief executive officer, Ray Crowley, "Our home base has always been in Columbus, and we're very proud of that." Photograph courtesy of the Columbus Ledger-Enquirer *newspapers*

Aspiring to the presidency was Hubert Horatio Humphrey when he gave a campaign speech here at Municipal Auditorium in 1973. Former vice president under Lyndon Johnson, Humphrey was a U.S. senator who was a liberal and strong civil rights champion. He lost to Richard Nixon in the 1968 election, with Alabama's George Wallace running third as the independent party candidate. In 1976, he didn't challenge the front runner Jimmy Carter for the nomination. Two years later, he died of cancer and was given a head-of-state funeral. Of him, Carter eulogized, "From time to time, our nation is blessed by the presence of men and women who bear the mark of greatness, who help us see a better vision of what we can become. Hubert Humphrey was such a man." Photograph courtesy of the Columbus Ledger-Enquirer *newspapers*

Accomplishments shouldn't stop just because one is named Woman of the Year (1956), or so thought Lucy Page, the publisher of the neighborhood newspaper, the Tattler. *Therefore, finding idle time on her hands, she founded the first multi-arts camp in the southeast. Trees should rock to Bach, snakes should slither to Drigo, and dramatic declamations should compete with bullfrogs. And that is exactly what happened when Musemont opened in 1963. Located first at Pine Mountain and later at Jekyll Island, Musemont was sponsored initally by the Guild of the Columbus Symphony Orchestra. The arts camp closed in 1974, but not before proving that the arts can coexist with nature and the study of nature can benefit the promising young artist. Here, Nancy Fowler, woodwind instructor, conducts nine of her class of fourteen students, all housed in a four-person cabin. "It was crowded," they said, "but no one seemed to mind." Photograph courtesy of the* Columbus Ledger-Enquirer *newspapers*

DJH Industries, Inc., announced in New York City on February 1, 1974, that it had made a more than $10,000,000 purchase of a textile operation here that had begun modestly in old Temperance Hall. Known as Excelsior Mills, its founders had been William A. Swift and G. Mote Williams, who incorporated it in 1883 as Swift Manufacturing Company. As Swift, it remained a successful, locally-owned firm until 1961 when it was acquired by Glen Alden Corporation, a New York conglomerate which changed the mill's name in 1965 to Swift Textiles. Glen Alden sold Swift in January of 1972 to Johnston Industries of New York. Swift is the nation's leading producer of denim, and its annual indigo-dyed output is equivalent to twenty-five million pairs of blue jeans. John A. Boland is chairman of the board of the local DJH division, located along the marshalling yards of the railroad on Sixth Avenue. Photograph courtesy of the Columbus Ledger-Enquirer *newspapers*

Dr. William J. Murtagh, keeper of the National Register, United States Department of the Interior, was the speaker when the Folly was dedicated on November 8, 1974, as a National Historic Landmark, the city's first. A dwelling has existed at 527 First Avenue since 1831 when Julia Forsyth, the daughter of the governor of Georgia, married a Columbus attorney, Alfred Iverson, who later became a U.S. congressman and senator. One of their sons became a brigadier general in the Confederate Army and the other a colonel. Just prior to (or in the early days of) the War Between the States, a carpenter-contractor, Leander May, converted the original cottage into the present flamboyant neo-gothic double-octagonal. This "remodeling" was in keeping with the architectural fashion that had been touched off by Orson Squire Fowler when he published a book in 1848 advocating double-square houses. The Folly is believed to be the only double-octagonal house in the United States. It is owned by the author. Photograph courtesy of the Columbus Ledger-Enquirer *newspapers*

In April of 1975, the war waifs of An Lac Orphanage were threatened by the imminent fall of Saigon, South Vietnam. "They must be rescued," resolved Columbus housewife Betty Tisdale who, a dozen years before, had started a non-profit organization to support these hapless children. Against unbelievable odds of battle and bureaucratic red tape, evacuation permission was finally secured. And, on April 12, 1975, a United Airlines DC-8 touched down at Fort Benning's Lawson Field, bearing 219 children from the orphanage. Wife of Dr. Patrick Tisdale, Mrs. Tisdale was widely applauded for her humanitarian perseverance and the children were eventually adopted into homes in Pennsylvania and Georgia, some fifteen growing up in the Columbus area. Mme. Vu Thi Ngai, the orphanage's founder-directress, also escaped and arrived at Columbus's Metro Airport on April 30, 1975, to be greeted by Mrs. Tisdale and one of her adopted Vietnamese children. Aided by the late Dr. Tom Dooley, Mme. Ngai had set up An Lac in Saigon after fleeing North Vietnam in the 1954 Communist takeover. With many regrets,

the Tisdales moved to Seattle, Washington, in 1982 where she directs a free program which provides motivational videotapes to non-profit organizations such as United Way, battered spouse groups and prison fellowships. Photograph courtesy of the Columbus Ledger-Enquirer *newspapers*

Little Michael Lord is no longer little. The Rev. Michael Lord, Jr., is now eighteen years old and he and his father, Michael Lord, Sr., are co-pastors of the Love Cathedral that meets in a downtown Cleveland, Ohio, hotel because the congregation lacks a church building. As a blond five-year-old, Columbus-born tot, Little Michael had a big reputation and a sizeable following as a faith healer. In 1972, his family billed him as "one of the world's youngest singing, recording and TV performers" and also as "one of the world's largest gospel singers." (He had made several records and recorded a tune he conceived called "Up in Heaven.") A July 1975 Newsweek *article called Little Michael, then eight, "a commanding preacher, gospel singer and faith healer." A year later, a child evangelist named Rev. Jimmy Joe Jeter appeared as a character on the television adult soap "Mary Hartman, Mary Hartman," with the show's producers readily admitting that Little Michael had been the inspiration for Jimmy Joe. Photograph courtesy of the* Columbus Ledger-Enquirer *newspapers*

The thirty-eighth president of the United States, Gerald Ford, sipped a soft drink as he sat with his box lunch in his lap while viewing Ranger exercises at Fort Benning during a summer visit in 1975. The civilian with the gray sideburns, second person to Ford's left, is Howard (Bo) Callaway, former congressman for the third district and former secretary of the army. At the time of the visit, Callaway was Ford's presidential campaign manager. Later Callaway would resign after there were allegations that he had used his office of army secretary to obtain a favorable ruling for expansion of his Crested Butte (Colorado) ski area. These charges were dropped by the Justice Department on January 11, 1977. Callaway had predicted all along that the matter was politically motivated and that he would be vindicated. Under another campaign manager, Ford lost his bid for the presidency to a Georgia peanut farmer, Jimmy Carter of Plains. Photograph courtesy of the Columbus Ledger-Enquirer *newspapers*

In the beginning, Columbus was a simple trading post. Textile and grist mills, attracted by the city's abundant water power, were our first major industries, and textiles continue to employ thousands in the bi-cities. The establishment of Fort Benning in 1918 added another component to the economy and its payroll over the decades has grown into many millions. Beginning with a trickle in the 1960s, growing into a stream in the 1970s and becoming a flood in the 1980s, other types of businesses have come into Columbus, diversifying the economic base and assuring that local prosperity will no longer be dependent on just one or two industries. Abundant water, clean air, excellent schools and large labor pool have all helped to attract them. So has the establishment of modern industrial parks where sufficient acreage for expansion is available. Held back for several years because of the city's lack of access to the U.S. interstate road system, that hurdle was passed with the opening of I-185 in 1979. Pictured here is a ribbon-cutting at the Union Carbide plant in 1976. The company makes solid tantalum capacitors that are used in a variety of electronic devices. Helping to wield the giant scissors are, left to right: George Busbee, then-governor of Georgia; Dave Maquire of Union Carbide; then-mayor Jack Mickle; and W. E. Gross, Jr., then-president of the Columbus Chamber of Commerce

Columbus-born, Dartmouth-educated junk dealer Harry Kamensky was a member of a trade convention center committee that went in January of 1976 to see how western metropolitan cities had successfully adapted historic old buildings into modern uses. On his return, he saw that the Rankin Hotel block of Broadway between Tenth and Eleventh Streets could become Rankin Square, a future complex of shops, offices and apartments, and a major impetus toward downtown redevelopment. Here, Kamensky points out aspects of a former livery and inner courtyard of the ambitious project. Photograph courtesy of the Columbus Ledger-Enquirer *newspapers*

Columbus' celebration of the U.S. Bicentennial focused on the establishment of the Chattahoochee Promenade, an outdoor historical museum on Front Avenue between Fifth and Ninth streets. Designated in the original town plan as a buffer space between the city and the river, it features a Promenade Center which is currently the home of the Columbus Arts Council. A history walk encompasses various aspects of Columbus' development: from religious freedom to industry, from military involvements to cultural accomplishments. The Riverfront Amphitheatre hosts a wide range of activities, predominantly marriage ceremonies. Donated to the Promenade and hanging in a gazebo is an exact replica of the nation's original Liberty Bell. In celebrating America's Bicentennial, White-Chapel Bell Foundry in London (the original caster) made one hundred full-size copies, two for each of the fifty states. Public funds, contributions from organizations and foundations, and nickles saved from childrens' lunch monies combined to create this fitting Bicentennial observance. Photograph courtesy of the Columbus Ledger-Enquirer *newspapers*

Since 1976 this lady has been unbeatable. State Representative Mary Jane Galer is currently serving her fifth two-year term in the House of Representatives from District ninety-seven. A resident of Columbus since 1960, Rep. Galer was a librarian and associate professor at Columbus College prior to her election to the Georgia General Assembly. She has been particularly interested in improved transportation facilities for jobs, economic development, improvements in education, income tax reduction, improved worker's compensation and equal rights. She has been active in civic, cultural and professional organizations on a national, state and local level and in 1979 was named one of the five most influential women in Columbus. Galer was the first woman elected to the Georgia General Assembly from Muscogee County since the election of Love Tolbert in 1933. (See page 225.) Photograph courtesy of the Columbus Ledger-Enquirer *newspapers*

He didn't want to play football or basketball, not when he was a ninth grader at Central High School in Phenix City. His sport was track, an under-appreciated athletic endeavor in these parts. But he had a dream: he wanted to run in the 1976 Olympics in Montreal, Canada. And he did, while a freshman at Auburn University. Harvey Glance won the NCAA indoor and the outdoor sixty-meter championships. He also tied the world record for the one hundred meters. But he did more than that; he realized his dreams. He was a member of the United States 440 relay team that won a gold medal at Montreal! Here Glance, left, joins John Jones, Millard Hampton and Steven Riddick as they take their victory lap after winning the Olympic event. Photograph courtesy of the Columbus Ledger-Enquirer *newspapers*

The peanut farmer from Plains, Georgia, Jimmy Carter, flashed his famous smile as he held up the November 3, 1976 issue of the Columbus Enquirer *with the exciting banner proclaiming that he had been elected president of the United States. Standing on the platform of the town's depot that had served as his campaign headquarters, the former governor of the state had accomplished the impossible. He had gone from "Jimmy Who?" to become the future occupant of the Oval Office and tenant of the nation's most prestigious address, 1600 Pennsylvania Avenue, Washington, D.C. Photograph courtesy of the* Columbus Ledger-Enquirer *newspapers*

An urban fair with an 1880s flair, the Salisbury Fair has become a major spring event for residents of the Chattahoochee Valley. Now in its seventeenth year, it was initially held on the median of the 700 block of Broadway, an area originally called Salisbury Park for noted resident Col. William Salisbury. Sponsored by the Historic Columbus Foundation, it serves as a fun and fund raising event for many participating service clubs and organizations. Featuring rain-or-shine fun, it is now held in and around the Columbus Iron Works Convention and Trade Center. Arts and crafts, antique dealers, a children's carnival, continuous entertainment by bands and dancers, food from hot dogs to gourmet delights, displays, foot and bike races and excursions on the Jubilee *combine to draw approximately thirty thousand visitors per year. Former Third District Congressman Jack Brinkley and Salisbury Fair Chairman Mrs. Roy E. Martin III eagerly watch then Governor George Busbee cut the ribbon to open the 1976 Fair festivities. Photograph courtesy of the* Columbus Ledger-Enquirer *newspapers*

Dig those Indians! In the literal sense, it is forbidden by the Antiquities Act of 1906. However, if you "dig" in the appreciation sense, there is plenty of opportunity along the Chattahoochee River, a stream that for at least two thousand years was a highway for the "First Americans." Within view of Walter F. George Dam, Columbus Museum of Arts and Sciences archaeologist Frank Schnell led a summer excavation in 1977. The bluff mound yielded displayable material such as a dog and human effigy pot, more than a dozen decorated mugs and pieces of a copper headdress. Evidences of houses and buildings were found, and Schnell suggested restoring this village "in order to give the public an idea of the rather advanced construction methods that the Indians had." Not far away is Rood Landing, near Omaha, which was a village level with the river, rather than being built on a bluff. Rood with its nine mounds is regarded as the most eastern outpost of the prehistoric Mississippian Empire and the largest known site in the Chattahoochee Valley. Schnell reported that "agri was their general culture with three-fifths of the crops that we know today having been domesticated by the Indians. They cultivated all the usual things like corn, beans, and squash, but most folks are surprised to know that they (the Indians) had the so-called Hawaiian pineapple and the so-called Irish potato also!" With Schnell, left in the second photo, is Walter Smalling, photographer with the Department of the Interior, National Register division of the National Parks service. In Cemochechobee—Archaeology of a Mississippian Ceremonial Center on the Chattahoochee River, which was published in 1982, Schnell determined that the village mounds were built around 900 A.D., and abandoned about 400 years later, around 1350 A.D.

But for three votes, John Beverly Amos today would be a politician and not the founder of a financial empire selling supplementary cancer insurance called the American Family Life Assurance Company. Born June 5, 1924, in Enterprise, Alabama, Amos was a University of Florida law graduate running for district attorney when he was defeated. The year was 1952. Four years later, he and his two brothers commenced "Am Fam" on a $50,000 investment. Today, the firm's assets are in excess of one billion dollars, with annual revenues exceeding $700,000,000. Am Fam became one of only fourteen insurance holding companies to hold a listing on the New York Stock Exchange in 1974, and a year later the company constructed an eighteen-floor tower on Wynnton Road to serve as its home office and international headquarters. Amos, however, may not have become an elected politician, but he has stayed close to politics as evidenced by this 1977 photo of him and his Cuban-born wife, Elena, as they attended one of the Carter inaugural balls in Washington, D.C. Photograph courtesy of the Columbus Ledger-Enquirer *newspapers*

Late in 1977, a murder was committed of a sixty-year-old woman, Ferne Jackson, a prominent local Health Department executive. For the next seven months, the community was stunned and horrified as six more elderly women, all living alone, were also brutally killed. The anonymous murderer was locally dubbed the "Stocking Strangler." The other victims were Martha Thurmond, Jean Dimenstein, Florence Sheible, Kathleen Woodruff, Mildred Borom and Janet Cofer. The community had never known such general panic as it fearfully wondered who would be the next victim. A special Task Force was organized by the police and helicopters patrolled the Wynnton area where all of the murders took place. A suspect in two of the slayings is now awaiting trial. Photograph courtesy of the Columbus Ledger-Enquirer *newspapers*

With a mission to honor the infantryman and his two centuries of service to our nation, the National Infantry Museum was established in October of 1959. For its first eighteen years, the museum was housed in a collection of World War II wooden buildings. But on July 1, 1977, it acquired a permanent home. Assisted by the museum's director, Col. Richard "Dick" Grube, General of the Army Omar Nelson Bradley, in his wheelchair, used a saber to cut the ribbon opening the new facility, located in the fort's former hospital, one of the oldest buildings on post, built in 1923. In October of 1982, federal funds in the amount of $100,000 were allocated to the renovation of the third floor and the completion of the museum, which contains fifty thousand square feet of floor space. Six years to the day from the original ribbon-cutting by General Bradley, the Honorable John O. March, secretary of the army, cut the ribbon opening the third floor. The collection contains some thirty thousand artifacts which range from the atomic "Davy Crockett" to War Between the States dominos and Revolutionary War pay slips, from Harry Truman's World War I breeches to U. S. Grant's liquor cabinet, and from Herman Goering's shotgun to George Marshall's field boots. Photograph courtesy of the National Infantry Museum.

The president and publisher of the Ledger-Enquirer *newspapers received his first journalistic experience as a reporter for the Albany, Georgia* Herald, *from 1952 to 1955. Next, Newton County-born Glenn Vaughn came to the* Ledger *as copy editor for two years before service as a reporter for the* Atlanta Journal. *Then he commenced a series of employments with the* Ledger *and with the* Enquirer, *each position being just a bit higher up the editorial or corporate ladder. Interspersed were tenures with the* Atlanta Journal, *the Phenix City (Alabama)* Citizen *and four years as editor-publisher of the Athens, Georgia,* Daily News. *Beginning in 1977, he became president and publisher of the local newspapers. Vaughn, born May 19, 1929, and his wife Nancy have four children. Photograph courtesy of the Columbus* Ledger-Enquirer *newspapers*

Long one of the screen's top (and highest paid) writers, Nunnally Johnson (1897-1977) began his writing career with the Enquirer-Sun *in his native Columbus, graduating from Columbus High School in 1915. After military service and a stint in journalism that took him north to Brooklyn and New York, Johnson began a short-story career that ultimately won him three O. Henry Memorial awards in the late 1920s. (In some of his satirical and humorous pieces, Columbus appears as the town of Riverside.) As did many writers, Johnson moved to Hollywood where his first film assignment was* A Bedtime Story, *a Paramount film which starred Maurice Chevalier. He ultimately became a triple threat, writing such movies as* Papa Loves Mama *and* Cardinal Richelieu, The Man Who Broke the Bank at Monte Carlo *and* The Grapes of Wrath; *writing and directing such films as* Night People *and* How to Be Very, Very Popular; *and producing such successes as* The Three Faces of Eve *and* Temptation. *He was the father of Nora Johnson whose bestseller* The World of Henry Orient *also was a hit as a motion picture with Peter Sellers. (The screen script was co-authored by the father-and-daughter team.) This novel again served as the plot for the 1967 musical* Henry, Sweet Henry *which starred Don Ameche and Carol Bruce, set to music and lyrics by Bob Merrill, whose more memorable tunes can be heard in* Carnival, Take Me Along *and* New Girl in Town. *The photos show Johnson with his mother, a member of the Columbus Board of Education, and on his first job, selling the* Saturday Evening Post *with other young hawkers in 1910. He is in the first row, second from right. Both photographs courtesy of the* Columbus Ledger-Enquirer *newspapers*

"Country Captain" has already been mentioned as a Columbus concoction that has travelled around the world. Another famous Columbus dish can only be had at Dinglewood Pharmacy, in its third location on Wynnton Road. Now being enjoyed by the fourth generation of youngsters, the Dinglewood hotdog, smothered in chili, was invented by Sport Brown who shared the secret recipe with Lieutenant Stevens, here seen celebrating his thirty-fourth year as custodian of the chili pot, an integral part of the hotdog. One Columbus girl had hotdogs flown to her wedding reception in Naples, Italy, such was her fondness for the specialite du chef. Photograph courtesy of the Columbus Ledger-Enquirer *newspapers.*

With a daytime enrollment of 285 students, Columbus College opened its doors on September 30, 1958, in the former Shannon Hosiery Mill in North Highlands. For prior thirteen years, the community and its leaders had sought a higher education facility. The University of Georgia had opened a night school in 1947, but the citizens of Muscogee County wanted more, voting affirmatively in five different elections pertaining to the development of Columbus College. In May of 1958, the junior college and its proposed site were approved by the state's board of regents, and Dr. Thomas Y. Whitley was named the first president of the college which, to that time, had existed only on paper. Its permanent campus was dedicated on January 6, 1963, its senior unit status approved two years later, and its first graduating class was in the spring of 1970. By 1978, its enrollment was over five thousand students, with a faculty that had grown from its original fifteen members to more than two hundred. In 1980, Dr. Francis J. Brooke, pictured here, was named the college's second president. Both photographs courtesy of the Columbus Ledger-Enquirer *newspapers*

After a twenty-year singing career with the Metropolitan Opera Company in New York, Phenix City native Osie Hawkins moved into stage management, ultimately advancing to executive stage manager, a position of commanding responsibility. In 1978, Hawkins, left, a graduate of Columbus High School, became the second recipient of the prestigious Verdi Memorial Award for Achievement, the award being presented by the late Rudolf Bing, the Met impresario. Hawkins also was the recipient of the Met's first-ever scholarship, given to him for opera training. He made his debut in the 1941-42 opera season as Donner in Das Rheingold *and ultimately sang an impressive number of bass-baritone roles. Photograph courtesy of the Metropolitan Opera Company*

Sporting a Greek sailor's cap which he wore at Princess Caroline's wedding in Monaco, author Truman Capote almost stole King John Kinnett's and Queen Winn Venable's thunder with his appearance at Saint Francis Hospital Auxiliary's Annual Mardi Gras Ball on the evening of February 27, 1979, at the Country Club of Columbus. In December of the same year he returned to Columbus for An Evening with Capote *at the Springer Opera House, a reading which he delivered of selected passages from his prose fiction works. Capote, born Truman Streckfus Persons on September 30, 1924, was a native of New Orleans who spent his boyhood in Monroeville, Alabama, and in New York City. It was in New York that he achieved his first notoriety with the publication of* Other Voices, Other Rooms *(1948), his celebrated first novel, and it was also there that he would maintain his United Nations Plaza apartment until his untimely death in the summer of 1984. Capote's literary career was nearly eclipsed by his increased participation in the world of the international jet set, the best-known proof of his* savoir vivre *being the lavish "Black and White Ball" which he hosted at the Plaza Hotel—a gathering of 540 guests that* New York Times *society reporters called "as spectacular a group as has ever been assembled for a private party in New York, an international Who's Who of notables." Shown with Capote (right) at Saint Francis' Mardi Gras Ball are first cousin Janice Persons Biggers and her husband, James J. W. Biggers, Jr. Also shown is an overhead view of the onstage party which followed Capote's Springer appearance. Photograph courtesy of the* Columbus Ledger-Enquirer *newspapers; photograph from the author's collection*

1. James Blanchard 2. William B. Turner
3. John B. Amos 4. D. Abbott Turner 5. G. Gunby Jordan II 6. J. W. Feighner
7. Harry Jackson 8. John Henry Land 9. Harry Kamensky 10. George Woodruff

In 1979 Nolan Walters, staff writer for the Columbus Enquirer, *published the results of a six-month-long study which the* Enquirer *conducted to arrive at the names of the ten most powerful personalities in Columbus. The top ten were chosen after votes were received from an electorate of one hundred "important" local people, after votes were counted from a telephone poll made by randomly calling area residents, and after facts relative to community leaders' involvement in city endeavors were reviewed. Prefacing the publication of the biographical sketches devoted to the ten most powerful was the remark that "it should be remembered that the findings are at best well-grounded opinions. No further findings are possible." Called "Profiles in Power," the series featured the men who are pictured here. The men and their titles at the time of the selection—listed from one to ten in order of their amount of power—were: (1) James H. Blanchard, president of Columbus Bank and Trust Company; (2) William B. Turner, president and chief executive of the W. C. Bradley Company; (3) John B. Amos, president and chief executive of the American Family Corporation; (4) D. Abbott Turner, chairman of CB & T Bancshares Company; (5) G. Gunby Jordan, II, president and chief executive of the Jordan Company; (6) J. W. Feighner, president of Tom's Foods Limited; (7) Harry Jackson, mayor of Columbus; (8) John Henry Land, superior court senior judge; (9) Harry Kamensky, developer of Rankin Square; and (10) George C. Woodruff, Jr., president and chief executive of the Woodruff-Brown Company. Photograph courtesy of the* Columbus Ledger-Enquirer *newspapers*

Local optometrist Dr. Isaac (Ike) Maxwell is so expert in camping and canoeing that for him one thousand miles of paddling and a total of two-and-a-half months annually of sleeping on the ground are not unusual. In 1979, Maxwell and two others stroked the 421-mile-long Copper Mine River at the Arctic Circle in the Northwest Territories of Canada, becoming the first persons to do so in single-occupant boats. A dream of his is to paddle Canada's Back River, a river that reportedly has been paddled only three times in this century. Photograph courtesy of the Columbus Ledger-Enquirer *newspapers*

The city's new pride and joy, the Iron Works Convention and Trade Center, opened in September of 1979. Established in 1853, the former foundry complex had manufactured a wide range of products, from agricultural implements to ice machines, particularly a very successful line of ammonia-absorption machines which were among the earliest commercial air conditioners. In 1975, the city was able to purchase the southern portion of the Iron Works through a generous contribution from its owners, the W. C. Bradley Company, and commenced rehabilitating the structures into its new community function. Rozier Dedwylder of the firm of Pound, Flowers and Dedwylder was the principal architect for the successful conversion. The convention center complex is shown in the 1982 photograph. Photograph courtesy of the Columbus Ledger-Enguirer newspapers

The coming of an interstate link to Columbus was so long delayed that some citizens were convinced it would never happen. It took more than twenty years of frustration, thwarted efforts and political maneuvering. For years Columbus had the dubious honor of being the largest city in the United States without an interstate connection. By 1968, however, the outlook began to improve. Columbus was finally added to the federal interstate network, showing up on the plan as dotted lines indicating the future construction of Interstate 185. But then a landmark environmental battle, led by Mrs. Cason J. Callaway, delayed the road for two years and resulted in a new route through Harris County. Mrs. Callaway, to her credit, perceived the damage the planned route, which would have sliced into the crest of Pine Mountain, would have done. Hers was the major voice in persuading the state to find an alternate route. Then the economic crunch of 1974, which caused the impoundment of highway funds, threatened indefinite postponement. But Governor George Busbee came to the rescue with a plan to finance completion of Georgia's interstates with state bond issue funding. The first contracts were finally let in July of 1975, and the 43.6 mile, $100,000,000 roadway opened in July of 1979. The highway extends from the end of the Lindsay Creek Bypass in Columbus to Interstate 85 near LaGrange. Photograph courtesy of the Columbus Ledger-Enquirer newspapers

Ground breaking ceremonies occurred in 1979 for the new Columbus Hilton, the supporting facility for the Iron Works Convention and Trade Center. The $12,250,000 hotel was financed through combined public and private sources, including $4,500,000 in revenue bonds issued by the Columbus Development Authority purchased by Citizens & Southern Bank, $3,500,000 in private investment, a $1,900,000 federal Urban Development Action Grant, and more than $2,000,000 provided through the local government. The site for the 180-room Hilton is a full block, across from the trade center and incorporating the historic Empire Mills into the overall structure. Photograph from the author's collection

The painted memories of Jessie DuBose Rhoads, such as this "Family Dinner," evoke a rural childhood spent on a family farm in Coffee County, Alabama, between the year 1900 and the death of her father in 1913. Mrs. Rhoads first tried her brushes while living in Pennsylvania in the late 1940s. Around 1961, she returned to painting for therapy in attempting to recover from a serious illness. Her subject matter, treated in her basically self-taught and always naively direct manner, was of box suppers, family dinners, watermelon cuttings, square dancing and numerous farm activities such as syrup making, wood cutting, hog killings and lamp cleaning. In 1982, ten years after her death, Fred C. Fussell, curator of the Columbus Museum of Arts and Sciences, organized a touring exhibition of Mrs. Rhoads' works to ten other southeastern institutions. And in 1983, the Historic Chattahoochee Commission and CMAS cosponsored a book of Mrs. Rhoads' paintings and her taped recollections, edited by Fussell. In recalling her career as a painter, she wrote of her work, "Each painting is a brainchild which I try to express on canvas as I have known and experienced it, not by rule or regulation, but born from memories of growing up on an Alabama farm and in a small town. What a joy it has been!" Photograph courtesy of the Columbus Ledger-Enquirer *newspapers*

Once thought not worth their face value, a gold coin minted by Templeton Reid in Gainesville in 1830 was bought by an Atlanta rare coin investment firm for $199,995 more than the face value of the $5 coin. Private minting of coins was legal in 1830 and Reid reportedly minted about $15,000 worth of Georgia gold into coins. But he failed to make a profit and closed his mint within a year. Reid lived in Columbus from 1836 to his death in 1851. A silversmith as well as a gold and gunsmith, Reid operated a gin manufacturing plant at what is now Eleventh Street and First Avenue. That plant was destroyed in the Big Fire of 1845. However, Reid built at another location, apparently operating the plant until his death. The sum of $200,000 for a $5 coin? Just shows how 150 years can change values! Photograph courtesy of the Columbus Ledger-Enquirer *newspapers*

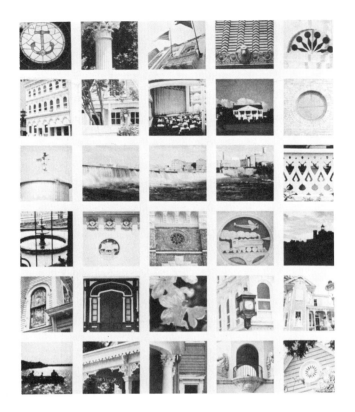

Here's a puzzle for you. Identify these bits and pieces of Columbus. Start with the three "free" spaces in the middle of the picture, which are views of the Eagle and Phenix Mill complex fall line taken from the Alabama side of the Chattahoochee River. Eighteen or more makes you a native son or daughter; twelve to seventeen and you must be a newcomer to town! This little challenge was developed by the downtown Rotary Club (which was founded in 1915 and carries national club number 200) for their members' bulletin known as "The Rote-A-Bit" and was first used on their July 30, 1980, issue.

Going for Guinness—the Guinness Book of World Records, *that is—was Nora Bickerstaff (Mrs. Robert) Eakle whose fourteen-foot-plus decorated live cedar stood proud through six Christmases in her ante-bellum mansion, Hilton, before being dismantled and laid to rest. The tree, which was adorned with precious family ornaments for its "first" holiday season in December of 1976, had lost surprisingly few of its cinnamon-colored needles when friends and local television cameras stopped by on the evening of March 6, 1982, to see its wheat-lights flicker for the last time at the "de-decorating" party given in its honor. "Anything after this will be an anticlimax," Mrs. Eakle said, adding, "I've satisfied a long-time whim, and I've broken my previous record." Sixteen months later, on July 24, 1983, an early Sunday morning fire would do extensive damage to Hilton. Columbus newspapers carried front-page stories on the fire, recounting memorable moments in the 140-year-old home's colorful history. Photograph from the Roger Haris collection*

The accolade of "America's greatest living classical architect" was awarded to Columbus native Philip Trammell Shutze by the board of directors of Classical America. Shutze was born here in 1890, but upon the death of his father, his mother moved the family to Atlanta. A graduate of both Georgia Tech's and Columbia University's schools of architecture, Shutze won the prestigious Prix to Rome competition in 1915 and spent three years at the American Academy in Rome. After employment in New York, Shutze elected to return to Atlanta in 1923 and by 1926 was a full partner in the firm of Hentz, Adler and Shutze. Among his many noteworthy efforts is the Swan House, pictured at left. Designed in 1926 for Mr. and Mrs. Edward H. Inman, it is regarded as Shutze's most outstanding achievement. Called a master of proportion, Shutze considered it his chosen mission to keep burning the candle of classicism in architecture. He felt a "restless dissatisfaction with the (current) cold, cruel, concrete and glass approach to architecture," but sensed a "renaissance of interest in classical architecture and its traditions among the very young (architects)." Shutze died in Atlanta at the age of 92 in 1982 and is buried in Linwood Cemetery. Another Columbus architect, James J. W. Biggers, Sr., a fellow of the American Institute of Architects, has also been recognized in Classical America's publication where his design for a bank in Eufaula was featured. Photograph by Gittings; courtesy of Walter L. Roberts and the Atlanta Historical Society. Swan House photograph courtesy of the Atlanta Historical Society

Columbus's loss was Miami's gain when Alvah H. Chapman, Jr., settled there. Chapman did return to his hometown after being a major, commander of a squadron and a thirty-seven-combat-missions pilot over Nazi-held Europe during World War II. He didn't stay long, but did stay in the newspaper business where his grandfather and father had also been newspapermen. "I love the business. I've never known anything else. I've never aspired to be anything else." However, he's more than just a newspaperman; he's the chairman of the board of Knight-Ridder Newspapers which owns, among other important city dailies, the Philadelphia Inquirer, the Detroit Free Press, the Miami Herald and, you guessed it, the Columbus Ledger and Enquirer. He has made his home in Miami for the past twenty-four years, and has led its business community on a string of community betterment campaigns that range from developing downtown to fighting the crime wave there in the early 1980s. The city of Miami named a street after him in November of 1984. And in China, he and his wife Betty (pictured here) were greeted by Vice Premier Deng Xiaoping in the Great Hall of the People in Peking during a recent visit. Photograph courtesy of the Columbus Ledger-Enquirer newspapers

At the podium is his honor, the mayor of Columbus, J. W. Feighner. To the right of the mayor (his left) are Dr. and Mrs. Jack C. Hughston. The physician was about to have his dream come true on September 30, 1984: the dedication of the $18,300,000 sports hospital seen in the background and named in his honor. Third from the left, Georgia's Lieutenant Governor Zell Miller termed it, "A hospital that is unique in the nation and represents a giant step forward in orthopedic care." A pioneer in the field of sports medicine and developer of surgical techniques that bear his name, Hughston was the founder of the Hughston Orthopedic Clinic. the Columbus Crippled Children's Clinic, and is the orthopedic surgeon for athletics at Auburn University. He holds memberships in more than a dozen professional societies and was a former office holder in many of them. In 1967, he founded the Institute of Athletic Health Care and Research. The institute supervises the physical screening, both medical and dental, of every potential high school athlete in every sport in Muscogee, Marion and Harris counties in Georgia and Russell and Lee counties in Alabama. In the second photo, Mr. and Mrs. Cason J. Callaway, Jr., are waiting to congratulate Dr. Hughston. Photograph courtesy of the Columbus Ledger-Enquirer newspapers

A long-sought industrial plum came to Columbus in 1980 with the announcement that United Technologies, parent company of Pratt & Whitney—one of the world's premier suppliers of jet aircraft parts—would locate a Pratt & Whitney plant here. In this photograph of a news conference in Atlanta on November 6, 1980, at which the plant's location was announced, Harry Gray (far right), president of United Technologies, shakes hands with Harry C. Jackson, then-mayor of Columbus. George Busbee (center), who was at that time governor of Georgia, beams his approval, while Dennis Calhoun (far left), then-president of the Columbus Chamber of Commerce, chats with Georgia's senior senator, Sam Nunn. The high-tech manufacturing prize has made Columbus the envy of the state. The $200,000,000 seven-hundred-thousand-square-foot plant, located on Macon Road in the Midland area, was dedicated Thursday, April 19, 1984. The plant opened with 325 employees and will have 800 on the payroll in 1986 or 1987. The plant, the largest automated forging facility in the free world's aerospace industry, makes compressor blades and discs for jet engines. Associated Press photograph courtesy of the Columbus Ledger-Enquirer *newspapers*

Hand-to-hand combat for leadership in ancient tribes is probably the origin of what is spelled "wrestling" but what is locally pronounced "rassling." And the Municipal Auditorium version is probably closer to survival of the fittest than to the pristine collegiate and Olympic contests. (Non-fans would add survival of the fittest but strong acting ability and careful physical choreography.) Probably the most popular "sport" in Columbus, weekly sell-outs at the 5,200-seat auditorium were the rule rather than the exception during the 1970s. Fred Ward (in photo at right) has been the chief promoter of professional wrestling in Columbus and in Macon and Albany as well. In a field where charges have been made that combatants are told when to bleed and when to win, former professional wrestler Eddy Mansfield of Columbus recently has urged that certain reforms be made. Known as the villainous "Continental Lover," Mansfield used to boast that "I'm a rich girl's lover and a poor girl's dream." The late First Mother Lillian Carter (pictured at right) was one of the area's most avid "rassling" fans. Photograph courtesy of the Columbus Ledger-Enquirer *newspapers*

Greenbelt: a string of parkways or farmlands around a planned town or community that prevents undesirable encroachments. Such a greenbelt or common existed in the early planning of Columbus. One hundred fifty-seven years later, only the South Common remains committed to ornament or recreation. The north has gone to residential, the east to the railroad's marshalling yards and the west is now industrial, save for a small promenade along the riverbank below the Dillingham Street Bridge. On the South Common can be seen Golden Park (to the west) and the Municipal Auditorium (to the east), with the Confederate Naval Museum and a parking lot sandwiched in between. In the lower right hand corner are the exhibit buildings of the Chattahoochee Valley Exposition. The east-west boulevard is Fourth Street, connecting to the Oglethorpe Bridge. In the upper right corner can be seen the Metro Government Center and the business district of downtown Columbus. Photograph courtesy of the Columbus Ledger-Enquirer *newspapers*

Bibliography

Albaugh, William A., III. *Confederate Edged Weapons*. New York: Harper & Brothers, 1960.

Angle, Paul M. *A Pictorial History of the Civil War Years*. New York: Doubleday, 1967.

Bain, Robert, Joseph M. Flora, and Louis D. Rubin, Jr., eds. *Southern Writers: A Biographical Dictionary*. Baton Rouge: L.S.U. Press, 1979.

Barfield, Louise Calhoun. *The History of Harris County, Georgia, 1827-1961*. Columbus: Columbus Office Supply, 1961.

Bartlett, John. *Familiar Quotations*. Boston: Little, Brown & Company, 1946.

Bartram, William. *Travels Through North and South Carolina, Georgia, East and West Florida*. (Facsimile of 1792 London edition.) Savannah: Beehive Press, 1973.

Biographical Souvenir of the States of Georgia and Florida. Chicago: F. A. Battey & Company, 1889.

Blum, Daniel. *A Pictorial History of the American Theatre: 1900-1956*. New York: Greenberg, 1956.

Blum, Daniel. *A Pictorial History of the Silent Screen*. New York: Putnam's, 1953.

"Building Columbus: A Special Report to the Columbus-Phenix City-Fort Benning Community from the Columbus Chamber of Commerce." (Supplement to *The Sunday Ledger-Enquirer*, January 1, 1978.) Columbus: The *Columbus Ledger-Enquirer* Newspapers.

Burgard, Augusta C., Frank U. Garrard, Jr., and W. S. Jenkins, eds. *Columbus, Georgia, Fort Benning and Vicinity*. n.p.: n.p., 1941.

Burke, James Wakefield. "The Black Eagle." *The Retired Officer*, May 1984, pp.28-31.

Burney, Eugenia and Clifford Sheats Capps. *Colonial Georgia*. New York: Thomas Nelson, Inc., 1972.

Callaway, Howard H. *The Story of a Man and a Garden*. (An address at Pine Mountain, Georgia, April 4, 1965.) New York: The Newcomer Society in North America, 1965.

Carr, Virginia Spencer. *The Lonely Hunter: A Biography of Carson McCullers*. New York: Doubleday, 1975.

Carse, Robert. *Department of the South: Hilton Head Island in the Civil War*. Columbia, S.C.: State Printing, 1961.

Carson McCullers in the Theater. (A scrapbook of McCullers-related memorabilia, in possession of F. Clason Kyle.)

Carson McCullers: A Scrapbook. (A scrapbook of McCullers-related memorabilia, in possession of F. Clason Kyle.)

Catton, Bruce. *The Civil War*. New York: American Heritage Press, 1971.

Chappell, J. Harris. *Georgia History Stories*. New York: Silver, Burdette and Company, 1905.

Cheney, Sarah. "Francis Orray Ticknor." *The Georgia Historical Quarterly*. June 1938, pp. 138-59.

"Civil War Centennial Edition." (Supplement to *The Sunday Ledger-Enquirer*, April 16, 1961.) Columbus: The *Columbus Ledger-Enquirer* Newspapers.

Coggins, Jack. *Arms: Equipment of the Civil War*. New York: Fairfax Press, 1983.

Coleman, Kenneth and Charles Stephen Gurr. *Dictionary of Georgia Biography*. Vols. I & II. Athens: Univ. of Georgia Press. 1983.

Coleman, Kenneth. *Georgia History in Outline*. Athens: Univ. of Georgia Press, 1960.

"Columbus Centennial Edition." (Special feature of the *Columbus Ledger* and the *Columbus Enquirer-Sun* Newspapers.) Columbus: the *Columbus Ledger* and the *Columbus Enquirer-Sun*, 1928.

Cooper, Walter G. *The Story of Georgia* Vols. I, II & III. New York: American Historical Society, 1938.

Corkran, David H. *The Creek Frontier, 1540-1783*. Norman: Univ. of Oklahoma Press, 1967.

Counties of the State of Georgia, The. Savannah: Georgia Historical Society, 1974.

Crawford, Richard, ed. *The Civil War Songbook*. New York: Dover Publications, 1977.

DeBolt, Margaret W. and Emma R. Law. *Savannah Sampler Cookbook*. Norfolk: Donning, 1978

Drimmer, Frederick. *Very Special People: The Struggles, Loves and Triumphs of Human Oddities*. New York: Bantam, 1976.

Duckett, Alvin Laroy. *John Forsyth: Political Tactician*. Athens: Univ. of Georgia Press, 1962.

Fretwell, Mark E. *This So Remote Frontier: The Chattahoochee Country of Alabama and Georgia*. Tallahassee: Rose Printing, 1980.

Fundaburk, Emma Lila. *Southeastern Indians, Life Portraits: A Catalogue of Pictures, 1564-1860*. Birmingham: Birmingham Printing, 1958.

Gallant City, The. (Program for "an historical drama with music" commemorating "The Last Land Battle of the Civil War.") Columbus: Columbus Productions, 1965.

Georgia Civil War Historical Markers. Atlanta: Georgia Historical Commission, 1964.

Gilbert, James. *A History of the First Presbyterian Church of Columbus, Georgia During the First 100 Years of Its Existence*. Columbus: Gilbert Printing, 1930.

Gray, Lewis Cecil. *History of Agriculture in the Southern United States to 1860*. Vols. I & II. Gloucester, Mass.: Peter Smith, 1958.

Guernsey, Alfred H. and Henry M. Alden. *Harper's Pictorial History of the Civil War*. (Reprint of 1866 edition). New York: Fairfax Press, n.d.

Hardee, Charles Seton. *Reminiscences and Recollections of Old Savannah*. n.p.: n.p., n.d.

Hardesty, Von and Dominick Pisano. *Black Wings: The American Black in Aviation*. Washington, D. C.: Smithsonian Institution, 1984.

Harper, Eugenia Flournoy and Lucile Moore Johnston. *Beside These Waters: The Story of Warm Springs, Meriwether County, Georgia*. Columbus: Columbus Office Supply, 1967.

Harris, Joel Chandler. *Uncle Remus: His Songs and His Sayings*. New York: D. Appleton and Company, 1925.

Harris, Walter A. *Here the Creeks Sat Down*. Macon: J. W. Burke, 1958.

History of Columbus. (A history of Columbus compiled by the Georgia History Class of Columbus High School in 1912.) Columbus: Gilbert Printing, 1912.

Hoffman, Donald. *The Meanings of Architecture: The Writings of J. W. Root*. New York: Horizon Press, 1961.

Home Book, The. (A photographic report on Columbus, particularly development of Waverly Terrace.) Columbus: The Jordan Company, n.d.

Horan, James D. *"C.S.S. Shenandoah": The Memoirs of Lieutenant Commander James I. Waddell*. New York: Crown, 1960.

Horan, James D. *The McKenney-Hall Portrait Gallery of American Indians*. New York: Crown Publishers, 1972.

Horn, Stanley F. *Gallant Rebel*. New Brunswick: Rutgers Univ. Press, 1947.

Howard, Robert M. *Reminiscences*. Columbus: Gilbert Printing, 1912.

Hunt, William Dudley, Jr. *American Architecture: A Field Guide to the Most Important Examples*. New York: Harper & Row, 1984.

Information Please Almanac 1985. Boston: Houghton Mifflin, 1985.

Johnson, Dorris and Ellen Leventhal, eds. *The Letters of Nunally Johnson*. New York: Alfred A. Knopf, 1981.

Kane, Harnett T. *Gentlemen, Swords and Pistols*. New York: William Morrow and Company, 1951.

Krakow, Kenneth. *Georgia Place-Names*. Macon: Winship Press, 1975.

Lane, Mills. ed. *The Rambler in Georgia*. Savannah: Beehive Press, 1973.

Lane, Mills. *The People of Georgia*. Savannah: Beehive Press, 1973.

Lanier, Mary D., ed. *The Poems of Sidney Lanier*. New York: Scribner's, 1913.

Lewis, Lloyd and Henry Justin Smith. *Oscar Wilde Discovers America [1882]*. New York: Benjamin Blom, 1967.

Lief, Alfred. *Metering for America: 125 Years of the Gas Industry and American Meter Company*. New York: Appleton-Century-Crofts, 1961.

Logue, Mickey and Jack Simms. *Auburn...The Loveliest Village: A Pictorial History*. Virginia Beach: Donning, 1981.

Lord, Walter. *A Time to Stand: The Epic of the Alamo.* Lincoln: Univ. of Nebraska Press, 1961.

Lovell, Caroline Couper. *The Golden Isles of Georgia.* Boston: Little Brown and Company, 1933.

Lupold, John S. *Industrial Archeology of Columbus, Georgia: A Tour Guide for the 8th Annual Conference of the Society for Industrial Archeology, April 1979.*

Lupold, John S. *Columbus, Georgia, 1828-1978.* Columbus: Columbus Productions, 1978.

Mahan, Katherine Hines and William Clyde Woodall. *A History of Public Education in Muscogee County and the City of Columbus, Georgia, 1828-1976.* Columbus: Muscogee County Board of Education, 1977.

Mahan, Katherine Hines. *Showboats to Soft Shoes: A Century of Musical Development in Columbus, Georgia, 1828-1928.* Columbus: Columbus Office Supply, 1968.

Major, Howard. *The Domestic Architecture of the Early American Republic: The Greek Revival.* Philadelphia: J. B. Lippincott, 1926.

Malone, Henry Thompson. *The Episcopal Church in Georgia, 1733-1957.* Atlanta: The Protestant Episcopal Church in the Diocese of Atlanta, 1960.

Martin, John H. *Columbus, Georgia, 1827-1865.* Columbus: Thomas Gilbert, 1874.

Marzio, Peter C. *A Nation of Nations.* New York: Harper & Row, 1976.

Morley, Sheridan. *Oscar Wilde.* New York: Holt, Rinehart and Winston, 1976.

Mott, Frank Luther. *American Journalism: A History of Newspapers in the United States Through 260 Years, 1690-1950.* New York: Macmillan, 1953.

Neville, Bert. *Directory of Steamboats on the Chattahoochee-Apalachicola River System.* Selma, Ala.: Coffee Printing, 1961.

Orpheus Club of Columbus' Handbook, 1981-1982. n.p., n.p., 1981.

Pachter, Marc. *A Gallery of Presidents.* Washington: Smithsonian Institution Press, 1979.

Pageant Book Celebrating the 200th Anniversary of the Founding of the Colony of Georgia, February 12th 1733. (Issued by the 200th Anniversary Commission of the City of Savannah.) Savannah: Review Printing Company, n.d.

Parrish, Robert. *Growing Up in Hollywood.* New York: Harcourt Brace Jovanovich, 1976.

Perkerson, Medora Field. *White Columns in Georgia.* New York: Rinehart & Company, 1952.

Phillips, Sidney C. *The Life and Works of Augusta Evans Wilson.* Thesis, Auburn University, 1937.

Pictorial History of the Battle of Gettysburg. A. Gettysburg: L. E. Smith, 1978.

Presidents of the United States. Chicago: Field Enterprises Educational Corp., 1968.

Purcell, Douglas C., ed. *Chattahoochee Trace Historical Markers in Alabama and Georgia.* Eufaula: Historic Chattahoochee Commission, 1983.

Richards, J. M., ed. *Who's Who in Architecture from 1400 to the Present.* New York: Holt, Rinehart and Winston, 1977.

Richardson, John. "The Life and Times of 'Mr. Taste.'" *House & Garden.* May 1983, pp. 8-12.

Schubert, Paul. *Cason Callaway of Blue Springs.* Atlanta: Foote & Davies, 1964.

Scruggs, Carroll, ed. *Georgia Historical Markers.* Valdosta: Bay Tree Grove, 1973.

Sesquicentennial Collection. Editions I, II, III, IV. (Supplements to four consecutive editions of *The Sunday Ledger-Enquirer.*) Columbus: The *Ledger-Enquirer* Newspapers, April 16-May 7, 1978.

Sheppard, Peggy and Kit Corley. "A Salute to Columbus on the Occasion of Her Sesquicentennial." *Georgia Life,* Summer 1978, pp. 12-16.

Smith, J. Frazer. *White Pillars: Early Life and Architecture of the Lower Mississippi Valley Country.* New York: Bramhall House, 1941.

Spalding, Phinizy. *Oglethorpe in America.* Chicago: Univ. of Chicago Press, 1977.

Standard, William Diffee. *Columbus, Georgia in the Confederacy: The Social and Industrial Life of the Chattahoochee River Port.* New York: William-Frederick Press, 1954.

Stempel, Tom. *Screenwriter: The Life and Times of Nunally Johnson.* New York: A. S. Barnes & Company, 1980.

Stern, Philip Van Doren. *The Confederate Navy.* New York: Bonanza Books, 1962.

Student's Photobook of Georgia. Atlanta: Georgia State Chamber of Commerce, 1961.

Swift, Charles Jewett. *The Last Battle of the Civil War.* (A paper read at the organizing of the first meeting of the Columbus Historical Society, Wednesday night, February 10th 1915.) Columbus: Gilbert Printing, 1915.

Telfair, Nancy. *The Columbus, Georgia Centenary: A History of Columbus, Georgia, 1828-1928.* Columbus: Columbus Office Supply, 1929.

Thompson, C. Mildred. *Reconstruction in Georgia: Economic, Social, Political, 1865-1872.* Savannah: Beehive Press, 1972.

Turner, Maxine. *Naval Operations on the Apalachicola and Chattahoochee Rivers, 1861-1865.* Reprint from *The Alabama Historical Quarterly,* No. 36, Fall/Winter 1974-1975.

Wells, Tom Henderson. *The Slave Ship 'Wanderer.'* Athens: Univ. of Georgia Press, 1967.

Whitehead, Margaret Laney and Barbara Bogart. *City of Progress: A History of Columbus, Georgia.* Columbus: Columbus Office Supply, 1978.

Wiley, Bell I. and Hirst D. Milhollen. *Embattled Confederates: An Illustrated History of Southerners at War.* New York: Harper & Row, 1964.

William A. Flamm & Company's Pocket Map and Business Guide of Columbus, Ga., Lively and Girard, Ala. Baltimore: William A. Flamm & Co., n.d.

Williams, Joan. "Waverly Terrace Historic District." *Columbus Magazine,* July/August 1983, pp. 60-63.

Williams, T. Harry, Richard N. Current and Frank Freidel, eds. *A History of the United States [to 1876].* New York: Alfred A. Knopf, 1962.

Windham, Donald. *Footnote to a Friendship: A Memoir of Truman Capote and Others.* Verona: n.p., 1983.

Windham, Kathryn Tucker. *Thirteen Georgia Ghosts and Jeffrey.* Huntsville, Ala.: Strode Publishers, 1973.

Winn, Billy. *The First Georgians: The History of This Area's First Families.* (A series of ten articles written for and published by *The Atlanta Journal.* April 1968.

Wintermute, H. Ogden. *Daniel Decatur Emmett.* Columbus, Ohio: Heer Printing, 1955.

Woodall, William C. *Home Town and Other Sketches.* Columbus: Columbus Office Supply, 1935.

Worsley, Etta Blanchard. *Columbus on the Chattahoochee.* Columbus: Columbus Office Supply, 1951.

Wright, Buster W. *Burials and Deaths Reported in "The Columbus [GA] Enquirer," 1832-1972.* n.p.: n.p., 1984.

EDITOR'S NOTE:
In addition to the sources listed here, various issues of *The Industrial Index* and *The Columbus Magazine,* both long-time publications of Columbus' now-defunct Woodall Press, were consulted in the compilation of historical facts for this volume.

Index

Index of Images: A Pictorial History of Columbus, Georgia featuring the principal Columbus people, places, events, banks, businesses, churches, organizations, and material generally associated with them.

A

Adams, Pres. John Quincy, 5
Alabama, State of, 17, 27, 31, 33
Albaugh, W. A., III, 53
Albertson, Rev. Ralph, 111
Albrecht, Sterling, 199
Alexander, Al, 262
Allen, Charles E., 133
Allen, Emmie, 117
Allen, J. R., 250, 265
Allen, Leonard, 198
Alston, Philip H., 14, 15
American Expeditionary Force, 165, 166
American Family Life Assurance Company, 254, 274
American Institute of Architects, 197
American-LaFrance Company (fire truck), 175
American Legion, Columbus Post #35, 166
American Red Cross, Muscogee Chapter of, 160
American Revolution, 34
American Theater, 158
Amerson, Pop, 202
Amos, Elena (Mrs. John), 274
Amos Hays (steamboat), 148
Amos, John B., 274, 279
Anderson, Dr. John, 210
Andrews, Cecilia, 209
Andrews, Mote, 212
Andrews, Mrs. Barschall, 160
Andrews, Sue, 209
An Lac Orphanage, 268
Anne Elizabeth Shepherd Orphans Home, 181, 234
Anne (ship), 21
Anthony, Susan B., 106
Anthony, The Rev. Mack, 210
Apalachicola, 157
Appomattox Court House, 28, 60
Arfwedson, C. D., 21, 22
Argyle (horse), 30
Army of Virginia, 77
Arnall, Mrs. Ellis, 205
Arsenal, 49
Ashburn, George W., 68
Ashworth, Maynard, 250, 255
"At Evening on the Banks of the Chattahoochee" (poem), 25, 26
Atkinson, George F., 100
Atlanta Constitution, 93
Atlanta Exposition, 109
Atlantic Steel, 178
Auburn University, 100, 231
Ausfields, Mrs. Emil, 188
Austrian 88 Field Piece, 206
Autry, Charles (Chick), 212
Avant, Sarah Ann Samantha (Mrs. James H. Hawkins), 101, 102
Avery, Col. I. W., 47

B

Bacall, Lauren, 251
Bachelors, The, 153
Bailey, Capt. S. Armstrong, 28
Ball, Emmie, 140
Ball, Kathleen, 140
Ball, Lucile, 140
Ballou, June, 195
Bandshell at Weracoba Park, 238
Banister, John R., 219
Bankhead, Tallulah, 221
Bank of Chattahooche, 28
Bank of Columbus, 39
Banks, John, 35
Barber, Mrs. J. W., 113
Barfield, Jim, 208
Barfield, John, 197
Barlow, Winfred, 130
Barnes, Robert H., 167
Barnett, Nathan, 21
Barnum, P. T., 28, 78
Barnwell, C. H. Professor, 100
Barr, Robert, 213
Barrett, Mrs. Thomas, 240
Barrymores, The, 71
Bartlett Ferry Dam, 123, 183
Bartlett, Minnie Lee, 117
Bartlett, T. D., 101
Barton, David, 198
Batcheldof, Mrs. J. C., 188
Bates, Asa, 24
Battle Flag of the Confederacy, 21
Battle, Mrs. Charlton, 172, 194
Battle, Mrs. Willis, 160, 234
Battle of Buena Vista, 38
Battle of Caleto, 31
Battle of Columbus, 47
Battle of Hitchiti, 22
Beahn, J. R., 101
Beall, Elias, 14, 15
Beallwood Home, 39
Bell, Alexander Graham, 81
Bell, Jack A., 244
Bell Tower, 107, 132
Belt Line, 91
Bennett, C. W., 101
Bennett, James Gordon, 169
Bennett, Thurston, 187
Bennett, W. T., 258
Benning, Anna Caroline, 64, 173
Benning, General Henry Lewis, 61, 77, 136, 166, 173, 211
Bensing, Frank, 230
Bently, Hugh, 202
Berlin Work, 116
Berry, George, 154
Berry, Gertrude, 140
Berry, Mrs. Arthur, 207
Bethune Plantation, 138
Betjeman, John A., 124
Betts, Oscar L., Jr., 185, 208, 244, 250, 255
Bibb City, 144
Bibb Manufacturing Company, 49, 127
Bickerstaff, Howard, 146
Bickerstaff, Nora Walton, 119, 146
Bickerstaff, Richard, 255
Bickerstaff, Sarah Bussey, 184, 252
Big Eddy Club, 212
Biggers, Bascom Hill, 111
Biggers, Carrie, 111
Biggers, Helen Pease, 111
Biggers, James J. W., Jr., 278
Biggers, James J. W., Sr., 111, 283
Biggers, James Norman, 111
Biggers, Janice Persons (Mrs. James J. W., Jr.), 10, 278
Biggers, Susie Lee, 111
Biggers, William Pease, 111
Billings, Frank, Jr., 195
Billings, Louise, 140
Bing, Rudolph, 278
Birdsong, Louise, 117
Bishop, Norman, 250
Black, J. T., 159
Blackmar, A. O., II, 182, 186
Blackmar, Betsy, 186
Blackmar, Dana, 123
Blackmar, Mary (Mrs. A. A. Drake), 123
Blackmar, Mary Ann Blood (Mrs. A. O., II), 182, 186
Blackmar, Susie, 146
Blackmon, Sumpter, 197
Blain, Charles, 126
Blanchard and Booth's Dry Goods Store, 123
Blanchard, Belle, 230
Blanchard, Betsy, 230
Blanchard, Emmie, 117, 129
Blanchard, Etta, 117, 129
Blanchard, James H., 278
Blanchard, Katherine McDuffie, 230
Blanchard, Mercer, 123, 230
Blanchard, Mrs. Thomas, 172
Blanchard, Paul, 123
Blanchard, Peggy, 230
Blanchard, Susan, 230
Blanchard, T. E., 133
Blankenship, Josie, 128
Blizzard, Col. John, 211
Bloodworth, Erie Sue, 195
Blue J. Barber Shop, 191
Blue Point (horse), 213
Bogart, Barbara, 7, 9
Bogart, Humphrey, 251
Boland, John A., 267
Boland, Mrs. Clifford, 188
Bonita Theatre, 151
Bonsoir (social club), 94
Booth, Edwin, 71, 78
Booth, John Wilkes, 44, 71
Borom, Mildred, 274
Boston-Savannah Steamship Company, 87
Boswell, Warren, 197
Bouchard, Edward, 195
Bowden, T. L. Mrs., 188
Bowdoin, William R., 244
Bowers, Lloyd G., 19, 118, 142
Box, Mrs. Jefferson, 194
Boykin, F. M., 100
Brackman, Robert, 229
Bradley, Alice, 117
Bradley, Frank, 195
Bradley, Gen. Omar N., 174, 205, 275
Bradley, J. A. S., 208
Bradley, Mrs. W. C., 37
Bradley, Sally, 195
Bradley Theater, 228
Bradley, W. C. Company, 74
Bradley, W. C. Memorial Library, 10, 209
Bradley, William Clark, 129, 209, 219
Brady, Matthew (photographer), 51
Brannon, Peter, 30
Brescia, Joseph, 177
Brescia, Mary Agnes (Mrs. Joseph), 177
Brinkley, Jack, 250, 272
Brinkley, Lois Kite (Mrs. Jack), 250
Brinson, Betty, 232
Brinson, B. O., 117
Brinson, J. Park, 232
Britt, Berta, 117
Britt, W., 101
Britto, Betty, 259
Brookbank, Thomas, 238
Brooke, Dr. Francis J., 277
Brooke, John Mercer, 113
Brown, A. B., 159
Brown, Chief Samuel W. Jr., 242
Browne, J. Rhodes, 82, 139
Browne, Mrs. Rhodes, 160
Brown, J. B., 159
Brown, Joe E., 226
Brown, Sport, 277
Brown Thrasher (state bird), 21
Bruce, Harry, 129
Bruce, Misses, 119, 120
Bruner, W. Evans, 244
Bryant, Marie Brescia (Mrs. John T.), 177
Bryan, William Jennings, 71
Bryant's Ferry, 22
Buckalew, S. J., 100
Buckingham, James Silk, 34
Buckner, Gen. Simon B., 174
Bullard, Dr. William Lewis, 94
Bullard, Eugene Jacques, 165
Bullard-Hart Home, 94
Bullard, Mrs. W. L., 231
Bullard, Myra, 117
Bull Creek Watershed Project, 260
Bulloch, Dr. Richard, 10
Bullock, Barbara, 195
Bullock, Capt. Marshall, 213
Bullock, Frank, 195
Bullock, Rufus B., 73
Bullock, Sarah Nisbet, 119
Burdock's Landing, 168
Burgard, Benning, 211
Burnham, LeRoy, 197, 266
Burnham Van Service, 266
Burnside, Thomas E., 38
Burrus, Charles, 41
Burrus, George, 48, 49
Burrus, Marie, 128
Burts, Bobby, 195
Busbee, Gov. George, 270, 272, 285
Bush, Brian, 232
Bussey, Arthur, 124, 163, 172
Bussey, Brannon, 120
Butler, Sarah Turner (Mrs. Clarence C.), 233, 247
Butterflies Social Club, 128
Butts, Jamie, 128
Butts, Patsy, 195
Butts, Tom, 205
Butts, Tommy, 211
Butts, Wally, 231
Byington, Edward T., 146
Byington, Elia Goode, 146
Byrne, Mary Margaret, 10, 233
Byrne, Philip, 212

C

Cabiness, Capt. Otis, 244
Caffey, Lizzie-Olive Hunt, 119
Calculator, 177
Calhern, Louis, 251
Calhoun, Dennis, 285
Calhoun, John C., 37
Calhoun, Mrs. James S. (Nancy Howard), 61
Callaway, Cason J., 174, 217, 222
Callaway, Cason J., Jr., 244, 252, 284
Callaway, Mrs. Cason J., 280
Callaway Gardens, Ida Cason, 217, 222
Callaway, Howard (Bo), 210, 269
Calley, William L., 263
Camp, Leon A., 131
Camp, Wilson, 131, 163
Candler, Asa G., 209
Candun Club, The, 210
Canning Dramatic Company, 44
Cannon, G. W., 101
Cannon, Lula Belle, 146
Capote, Truman, 278
Carache, Juan, 24
Caraway, Hubert N., 187
Cargill, E. K., 141
Cargill, J. Ralston, 185
Cargill, Mrs. J. Ralston, 194
Cargill, Mrs. Walter, 188
Carpenter, J. H., 159
Carson, Forest, 208
Carson, Lilly, 140
Carter, Betty, 160
Carter, Caroline, 111
Carter, Grey, 198
Carter, Lillian, 285
Carter, Mrs. Robert, 199
Carter, Pres. Jimmy, 218, 259, 266, 269, 272
Carter, Robert, 137
Carter, Rosalyn, 285
Caton, Jewell Brown, 242
Catton, Bruce, 58, 62
Cawthorne, Herb, 42, 121
Central Fire Station, 125
Central Line of Steamers, 81
Central of Georgia Passenger Terminal, 220
Central of Georgia Railway, 9, 49, 167, 184
Chambers, James, 35
Chancellor, Alexander C., 76
Chancellor Company, 69, 74, 76
Chancellor, J. Edgar, 76, 163
Chandler, Walter, 197
Chang and Eng (Siamese twins), 28
Chapman, Alvah H., 202
Chapman, Alvah H., Jr., 218, 284
Chapman, Betty (Mrs. Alvah H., Jr.), 284
Chapman, Lydia Belle, 161
Chappell, J. Harris (educator), 78
Chappell, Loretto Lamar, 14, 22, 219, 222
Chappell, Lucius Henry, 113
Chappell, Thomas J., 115
Chappell, Virginia, 160
Chase Conservatory of Music, 132
Chase, George, 132
Chase, George Williams, 132
Chase, Louis, 132
Chattahoochee Choo Choo, 171
Chattahoochee Circuit Superior Court, 73
Chattahoochee Falls Company, 139
Chattahoochee (gunboat), 54
Chattahoochee Promenade, 271
Chattahoochee Regional Library, 137
Chattahoochee River, 13, 14, 15, 19, 25, 27, 37, 38, 45, 56, 60, 123, 162
Chattahoochee Valley Emancipation Proclamation Association, 108
Chattahoochee Valley Exposition, 93, 287
Chero-Cola Company, 179
Cherokee Indians, 31
Cherokee Rose (state flower), 21
Chickasaw Club, 228
Christian Fellowship Association, 207, 209, 237
Christian Science First Church of Christ Scientist, 247
Christie, The Rev. L. R., 163
Christmas, Richard, 34
Church of the Holy Family, 80, 235
City Auditorium, 105
City Council, 35, 40
City Directory, 43
City Federation of Woman's Clubs, 172
City Hospital, 105
City Mills, 19, 49, 77, 89, 104, 123, 153, 185, 189
City of Columbus, 14, 15, 16, 17, 19, 21, 22, 23, 29, 47, 87
City of Columbus (steamboat), 87
City of Eufaula (ship), 157

City of Miami, The (passenger train), 258
Civil War, 48, 52
Clapp's Factory, 49, 82, 139, 162
Clapp, J. R., 82
Clark, Gen. Mark, 174
Clarke, Bob, 198
Clason, Dorothy, 161
Clason, Milo, 163
Clay, Henry, 27, 37
Cleveland, Pres. Grover, 180
Cliburn, Van, 238
Coart, Sgt. Jon C., 120
Cobb, General Howell, 51, 58
Cobb, Thomas R. R., 51
Coca-Cola, 124, 209
Coca-Cola Company, 93
Cody, William S. (Buffalo Bill), 257
Cofer, Janet, 274
Cohn, Aaron, 242
Cohn, Leslie, 242
Cohn, Sam, 242
Cole, Mrs. Burrell, 38, 233
Coleman, Ralph, 120
Coley, Florence Banks, 184
Coley, Sue, 230
Collins, Gen. J. Lawton, 174
Colquitt, Peyton H., 53
Columbus Ambulance Corps, 55
Columbus Arts Council, 271
Columbus Bank and Trust Company, 129, 235
Columbus BPW Club, 207
Columbus Chamber of Commerce, 166, 222
Columbus College, 10, 212, 217, 226, 271, 277
Columbus College Archives, 104, 111, 175
Columbus Daily Sun, 75, 182
Columbus Dramatic Club, 129, 237
Columbus Electric and Power Company, 139, 182, 185
Columbus Enquirer, 34, 56, 79, 182
Columbus Enquirer-Sun, 66, 103
Columbus Episcopal Association, 28
Columbus Factory, 82
Columbus Female College, 78
Columbus Foundries, 95
Columbus Guards, 22, 28, 86, 140, 239
Columbus Gun Club, 179
Columbus High School, 116, 146, 197, 200
Columbus Hilton, 281
Columbus Historical Society, 50, 239
Columbus Hook and Ladder Company, 36, 175
Columbus Hospitals, 105
Columbus Hotel, 21
Columbus Industrial Index, 133, 179
Columbus Iron Works, 49, 54, 56, 95, 131, 222
Columbus Iron Works Convention and Trade, 175, 222, 280
Columbus Junior Chamber of Commerce, 187, 241
Columbus Ledger, 13, 103
Columbus Ledger-Enquirer, 9, 10
Columbus Little Theater, 129, 218, 237, 243
Columbus Male Public Number One School, 65, 88
Columbus Manufacturing Company, 49, 82
Columbus Mills, 66
Columbus Museum of Arts and Crafts, 149, 217, 240, 241
Columbus Museum of Arts and Sciences, 33, 107, 181, 209, 217, 222, 265, 273
Columbus Musicians Protective Assoc., 152
Columbus, Original City Map by Thomas, 102
Columbus Police Department, 100, 101, 113, 261
Columbus Public Library, 87, 92, 137, 149
Columbus Railroad Company, 49, 104
Columbus Railway Station, 104
Columbus Rose Hill Lodge No. 480, 159
Columbus Round Table, 255
Columbus Savings Bank, 129
Columbus Steeplechase at Callaway Gardens, 222
Columbus Stockade, 239
Columbus Stockade Blues, 239
Columbus Symphony Guild, 266
Columbus Symphony Orchestra, 213, 222, 238, 239
Columbus Times, 53
Columbus Town Committee, Colonial Dames, 38
Columbus Water Works, 139, 162
Commercial Hotel, 49
Commons in Columbus (*see also* Greenbelt), 15, 21, 49, 105, 184
Commonwealth Georgia, 111

Community Service League, 234
Compton, Ann, 140
Compton, Ellen, 160
Compton, John M., 101
Compton, Mrs. Shelby, 207
Con. T. Kennedy Shows, 158
Concert Hall Theater, 44
Conde West Publications and House and Garden, 88
Confederate Army, 50
Confederate Cabinet, 57
Confederate Hospitals, 55, 86
Confederate Memorial Day, 64, 185
Confederate Monument, 80
Confederate Naval Museum, 54, 56, 113, 238, 241, 287
Confederate Navy, 54
Cook, Dr. Osgood F., 202
Cook, George, 229
Cook, H. W., 175
Cook, Hatch, 138
Cook, Mrs. James C., 97
Cook's Hotel, 138
Cook, Tom, 195
Cook, T. T., 208
Cooley, C. R., 101
Cooper, Lucile, 195
Cooper, Newsome, 161
Cooper, Samuel, 34
Cooper, Susan, 195
Copeland, J. E., 101
Coppage, O. R., 232
Coppock, Mrs. J. W., 188
Corley, L. Y., 159
Corn, Lovick Pierce (Mr. and Mrs.), 32
Cornett, J. R., 101
Corridor Tea Room, 199
Cotillion Club of Columbus, 184, 256
Country Captain (recipe), 231
Country Club of Columbus, 142, 185, 227, 237
Courthouses, 110
Cowdery Home, 154
Coweta Falls, 14
Coweta Manufacturing Plant, 66
Coweta Reserve, 14, 186
Coweta Town (Creek Indian capital), 33
Cozart, John, 195
Cozy Tea Room, 199
Cranton, Peter R., 41
Crawford, Gov. George Washington, 38
Crawford, Henry B., 194
Crawford, Martin J., 51, 53, 57
Crawford, Mrs. Henry B., 81
Crawford Street Theater, 44
Crawford, Thurston C., 200, 240
Creek Confederacy, 30, 33, 47
Creek Indians, 13, 22, 24, 30, 31, 154, 170, 186, 200
Creek War of 1836, 22, 28
Cricket, The (restaurant), 190
Crosby, Bing, 203
Cross Country-Columbus Square, 166
Crowell, Jenny, 160
Crowell, John, 30
Crowell, Mrs. L. H., 188
Crowley, Ray, 266
CSS *Alabama,* The, 28
CSS *Columbia* (ironclad boat), 113
Culbreath, U.A., 100
Cullinan, Michael Father, 80
Culver, 100
Cummings, Charlotte Storey, 184
Cunningham, Billy, 194
Curry, C. William, 244
Cutler, Jesse H., 202, 209

D
Daley, Charles S., 244
Dallas Historical Society, 31
Dalquist, Gen. J. E., 174
Daniel, Dr. Roland B., 163, 197, 217
Dantzler, G. W., 100
Darby, Cecil, 145
Darby, Thomas P., 239
Dartmouth, 109
Daughters of Israel, 248
Daughters of the American Revolution, Oglethorpe Chapter, 175
David Rothchild and Company, 107
Davidson, J. Q., 210
Davidson, W. J., 101
Davis, Alvan, 242
Davis, Bette, 205
Davis, Capt. John E., 28

Davis Construction Company of Atlanta, 184
Davis, Jefferson, 28, 60, 62, 86
Davis, John T., 121
Davis, Mrs. Tracy, 234
Davis, Robert (Bobby) T., Jr., 212, 244
Davis, Sally, 199
Davis, Solon, 202
Davis, Theodore R., 69
Davis Wagon Factory, 121
Dawson, William Crosby, 51
Day's Credit Clothing, 228
Debardeleben, H. T., 100
Debating Society, 22, 24
DeBrabant Family, 111
DeDwylder, Rozier, 280
de Graffenried, Baron Christopher, 15
de Graffenried, Dr. Edwin L., 9, 14, 15
de Graffenried, Julia Pitts, 195
DeWolfe, Florence Kling, 176
Deignan, John, 198
Deignan, Richard, 120
Depression of 1929 in Columbus, 118
Des Portes, Margaret Garrard, 160
Devore, Jim, 120
Devotie, Howard, 190
Devotie, Noble Leslie, 190
deWolfe, Thomas, 75
Dews, George M., 66
Dexter, MacDougald, 129
Dexter, Park, 117
Dickey, James, 82
Dillard, George W. K., 23
Dillard, W. E., 258
Dillard, Mrs. W. E., 258
Dillingham Street Bridge, 69
Dimon, J. Homer, 211
Dimon, Mrs. Charles, 116, 234
Dimon, Mrs. J. Homer, 194
Dinesen, Isak (Baroness Karen Blixen-Finecke), 249
Dinglewood (Home), 53
Dinglewood Hotdog, 277
Dinglewood Pharmacy, 277
Dinner Toters, 156
Dismuke, Frederick Mr. and Mrs., 138
District Nurse Committee, 160
"Dixie" (song), 109
Dixie Chip and Flapper Food, 96
Dixon, John, 147
Dixon, Marshall, 147
Dixon, Maude Flournoy, 147
DJH Industries, Inc., 267
Dolcater, John, 146
Donning Company Publishers, 10
Dooley, Dr. Tom, 268
Dorn, John, 212, 227
Dorsey, Jasper, 81
Doughboy Stadium, 181
Dowd, Coach W. L., 145
Downing, Mary Lou, 146
Dozier, Albert, 123
Dozier, Alonzo, 145
Dozier, Anna, 161
Dozier, Susie, 140
Dozier, Vera, 128
Drane, Mrs. Walter, 188
Drew, Mrs. John, 71
Drimmers, 28
Dudley, Peter, 21
Dukes, W., 101
Dummy Line, 74
Durham, Fred, 198
Dusenberry, Mrs. Ethel, 172
Duy, Mr. and Mrs. George C., 130
Dykes, Dr. A. N., 208
Dykes, Carolyn, 208

E
Eagle and Phenix Cotton and Woolen Mills, 84
Eagle and Phenix Mill, 64, 136, 156, 282
Eagle and Phoenix Manufacturing Company, 39, 49, 189
Eagle Broadcasting Company, 222
Eagle Drug and Chemical Company, 92
Eagle Manufacturing Company, 39, 49
Eakle, Nora Bickerstaff (Mrs. Robert), 119, 146, 282
Eames, Col. Henry E., 124
Earhart, Amelia, 194
Eddy, Gen. Manton S., 174
Eelbeck Mills, 19
Eisenhower, Pres. Dwight D., 174, 236, 244
Eldorado (*see also* St. Elmo), 27

Eldridge, Florence, 188
Elebash, LeGrand, 210
Electricity, 104
Elks Lodge, 31
Elliott, Bishop Stephen, 59
Elliott, J. Robert, 199, 210
Ellis, Frances, 256
Ellis, Virginia Garrett, 83
Ellison, Sar., 101
Elms, The (Home), 142
Emancipation Proclamation, 108
Emens, Joan, 10
Emmett, Daniel Decatur, 109
Emory College, 16, 32, 93
Empire Building, 86
Empire Mills, 49, 93, 281
Enquirer-Sun, The (Columbus), 13, 21, 25, 50, 93, 182, 194
Ephesus Baptist Church, 140
Esquiline (Moses family home), 71
Evans, Augusta Jane (*see* Wilson, A. Jane), 27, 29
Evans, Matthew, 29
Evelyn, Sister M., 219
Everidge, James B., 163
Excelsior Mills, 86, 267

F
Fabiani, Don, 209
Fabiani, Rozell Fair, 209, 221
Fannin, James Walker, Jr., 31, 38
Fanny Ferne (steamboat), 104
Farrish, Robert, 117
Federal Wire Road, 33
Feighner, J. W., 279, 284
Feimster, Pauline Johnson (Mrs. E. A.), 161
Fenner and Beane Brokers, 192
Festival Days, 242
Few, Ignatius, 14, 15, 16
Few, William, 16
Fiedler, Arthur, 248
Fiedler, Mrs. Arthur, 248
Fieldcrest Mills, 61, 64
Fields, Al G., 169
Fillingim, Henry, 133
Fillmore, Millard, 27, 40
Fire Bell Tower, 85
Fire Department, 36, 48, 65
Fire Station Number Four, 49, 175
First African Baptist Church, 42
First Baptist Church of Columbus, 15, 42, 64, 84, 140, 158, 161, 183, 188, 229, 254
First Georgia Regiment, U.S. Volunteers, 115
First National Bank, 67
First Pershing Flood, 168
First Presbyterian Church, 49, 65, 69, 84, 85, 89, 98, 148
First World War, 28
Fitch, Capt. A. B., 63
Fletcher, Mrs. John T., 160
Flewellen, A. H., 35
Flint River, 271
Florist Transworld Delivery, 178
Flournoy, Frank, 147
Flournoy, Gordon, 147, 190
Flournoy, Hatcher, 147, 161
Flournoy, John F., 147
Flournoy, John Manley, 147
Flournoy, Josiah, 147
Flournoy, J. Reynolds, 124, 147
Flournoy, Leila Priestly, 147
Flournoy, Mary Hannah, 147
Flournoy, Mary Reynolds, 147
Flournoy, Mattie Hatcher, 147
Flournoy, Mrs. Josiah (Jeanette Martin), 147, 188
Flournoy, Mrs. Reynolds, 188
Flournoy, Priestly, 147
Flournoy Realty, 183
Flournoy, Suzette Joerg, 190
Flournoy, Walker, 147
Flowers Building, 34, 185
Flowers, Joe, Sr., 192
Floyd, Tom, 224
Foley, Charles, 192
Foley, Daniel Matthew, 80
Foley, Frank D., 63, 83, 184, 208, 244, 246
Foley, Frank D., Jr., 41, 244
Foley, Mrs. Frank D., 189
Foley, Theo M., 87, 208
Folly, The (home), 268
Fontaine, John, 29, 82, 197

291

Foran, John, 101
Ford, Bill, 209
Ford, Hamlin, 154
Ford, Pres. Gerald, 269
Forrest, Gen. Bedford, 196
Forsyth, Gov. John, 13, 15, 88
Forsyth, John, Jr., 28, 53
Forsyth, Julia, 268
Fort Benning, 77, 126, 168, 169, 171, 173, 174, 177, 181, 185, 191, 192, 200, 213, 243, 270
Fort Benning Infantry School, 173
Fort Gaines, Georgia, 37
Fort Mitchell, 30, 33, 38
Fort Sumter, 53
Fort, T. Hicks, 209
Fortson, Glennie Mae, 146
Fourth National Bank of Columbus, 74, 107, 244
Fowler, Nancy, 267
Fowler, Orson Squire, 268
Fowler, Tom, 202
Fox, Dr. Brent, 255
Fox, Jim (James Claudius), 139
Foxhounds in Columbus area, 254
Francisco, Floyd, 202
Franklin College, 77
Franklin, Sam O., III, 11
Fraternal Order of Odd Fellows, 180
Frazier, Bob, 100
Freeman, Janie Bruce, 119
French Field, 169
French Wine Coca, 92
French, Daniel Chester, 136
Friedlander, Julius, 94
Fulford, Hallie, 117
Fuller, Dozier, 129
Funston, G. Keith, 235
Fuqua Industries, 151
Fussell, Fred C., 281
Fussell, J. C., 211

G
Gaffney, Mrs. Herbert Fay, 210
Gaines, Pastor Wesley J., 55
Galer, Mary Jane, 271
Gallagher, Mrs. John, 188
Gallant City, The (historical drama), 239
Garland, Judy, 251
Garrard, Annie Leonard, 118
Garrard Building, 49
Garrard, Guy, 117, 129
Garrard, Helen, 128
Garrard, Louis, 142
Garrard, Mrs. Louis, 199
Garrard, Spencer, 121
Garret, Hettie, 140
Garrett and Sons, 83
Garrett, Annette, 195
Garrett, Bettie Jean, 195
Garrett, George J., 83
Garrett, Joseph Simpson, 83
Garrett, Lyra, 128
Gas Light Company of Columbus, 53, 148, 229
Gaul, George, 188
Gay, Thomas A., 191
Geeslin, Florence, 161
Geffen, Felicia, 249
George II, 14, 40
George, Addie, 142
George, Rufus, 142
George, Walter F., 214, 273
George W. Miller (steamboat), 218
Georgia-Auburn Football Game, 205, 231
Georgia, Colony of 14, 21, 177
Georgia Department of Archives and History, 90
Georgia Historical Commission, 214, 259
Georgia Home Building, 67, 114
Georgia Midland and Gulf Railroad, 106
Georgia Militia, 30
Georgia Seal, 21
Georgia Secession Convention, 38, 51
Georgia Teachers Association, 109
Georgia Woman Suffrage Association, 106
Georgia's National Democratic Committee, 175
Georgia, State of, 13, 14, 15, 17, 21
Gettysburg, 28
Gibson, Carlton B., 134
Gibson, Charles Dana, 128
Gibson, Gladys, 140
Giddens, Philip Harris, 265
Giffen, Isaac, 55
Giglio's, 180
Giglio, Frank, 180
Gilbert, Thomas, 43, 75
Gingell, George, 212
Girard Cemetery, 68
Girard Cotton Mills, 136

Girard-Phenix City, 27, 49, 50
Glance, Harvey, 272
Glen Alden Corporation, 267
Glenn, G. R., 78
Glenn, John, 251
Glenn, Lillian, 146
Glenn, Mrs. W. H., 207, 209
Glenn, Wilbur H., 255
Gloer, Dorothy, 185
Glorie, The (ironclad warship), 56
Goat Rock Dam, 123, 153, 183
Goater, Walter, 84
Godwin Cemetery (Phenix City), 27
Godwin, John, 27, 35, 69
Goff, John, 154
Going, R. B., 100
Golden Park, 105, 139, 287
Golden Row, 29, 197
Golden, J. P., 95
Golden, Lyda Mae, 196
Golden, T. E., 95, 139
Golden, Theo, 196
Goodwill Industries, 130, 158, 183
Gordon, Brig. Gen. Walter H., 176
Gordon, Frederick B., 142
Gordon, Mary, 128
Gordon, Mrs. Frederick B., 210
Gordon, Thomas G., 23
Gordonido (home), 210
Gordy, Eunice, 140
Gowdy Field, 181
Gowdy, Hank, 181
Graffagnino, Dr. P. E., 210
Grand Theater, 49
Grant, Gen. Ulysses S., 47, 60
Graves, E. H., 100
Graves, Marjorie, 195
Gray, Harry, 285
Gray, William, 101
Green Berets, The, 254
Green, C. C., 101
Greenbelt in Columbus (*see also* Commons), 15, 21, 184, 287
Greene, R. W., 100
Gregory, Lottie, 255
Griffin, Anna H., 92, 175
Griffin, Daniel, 38, 59, 61, 175
Griffin, Theresa, 92
Grimes, Thomas Wingfield, 99, 250
Gross, Wilfred E., Jr., 270
Grube, Col. Dick, 275
Gruppe, Charles P., 149
Guerry, M. M., 175
Guest, D. J., 163
Gunby, R. B., 82
Gunby, R. M., 38, 64
Guttinger, P. A., 63

H
Hadley, J. J., 63
Haiman, Elias, 53
Haiman, Louis, 53, 95
Haiman Swords, 49, 53
Haines, W. L., 244
Hall, Capt. Basil, 13, 16, 17, 18, 21
Hall, Henry T., 36, 37
Hall, Mrs. Basil, 9, 16
Hallam, James, 14, 15
Hamburger, Flournoy, 147
Hamburger, George, 147
Hamburger, Isabel, 147
Hamburger, Rebecca, 147
Hamer, George, 258
Hammond, Elaine, 172
Hampton, Gen. Wade, 30
Hampton, Millard, 272
Hand, G. Othell, 210, 255
Handley, Gertrude, 90, 187
Hanna, W.J. (Crack), 225
Hannah, Ermine Trulock, 184
Hanserd Home (Muscogee Club), 153, 183
Hanson, Inez, 199
Hardaway, Ben H., III, 254
Hardaway Construction Company, 123, 125, 153, 183
Hardaway Contracting Company, 148
Hardaway, Mrs. Ben, 235
Harding, Mrs. Warren G., 172
Harding, Pres. Warren G., 172, 176, 220
Harding, R. M., 183
Hardy, Patricia, 10
Hare, C. L., 100
Harmony Circle, 94
Harmony Club, 94
Harper, R. C., 101
Harris, Herbert, 120
Harris, Joel Chandler, 182
Harris, John, 198
Harris, Julian L., 182

Harris, Mrs. S. C., 188, 258
Harris, Roger T., 11, 102, 159, 203, 252
Harris, S. C., 185, 258
Harrison, Edith Kyle, 194
Harrison Freshet, 35
Harrison, Lt. Charles S., 166, 206
Harrison, Pres. William, 99
Hart, John K., 255
Hart, William (Mr. and Mrs.), 208
Harvard University, 109
Harvey Lumber Company, 74
Haskins, Fred, 227, 258
Hatcher, Carrie Estides Biggers, 111
Hatcher, Claud, 124, 151
Hatcher Grocery Company, 124
Hatcher, Samuel, 67
Hawkins, Annie, 102
Hawkins, Belle, 102
Hawkins, Evans, 102
Hawkins, James H., 102
Hawkins, John Clifford, 102
Hawkins, Leola, 102
Hawkins, Mary Elizabeth, 102
Hawkins, Osie, 278
Head, Samuel B., 23
Heard, W. T., Jr., 244
Heath, Annie Forest, 146
Heldreth, Charles, 197
Hempstead, Ruth, 233
Henderson, John, 187
Hendrix, R. Howard, 159
Henkle, Barbara, 233
Hennis, Sgt. Louis, 120
Henry, Eula, 117
Henry, Jessie, 128
Heritage Ball, 253
Hero's Memorial, 130
Herren, A. W., 100
Herrick, Robert, 119
Hicks, Herman, 117, 163
Hicks, Marian, 195
Hicks, R. B., 208
Higdon, Daniel, 34
Hill, Helena Dismukes, 165
Hill, Lem, 208
Hill, Terrell Wingfield, 165
Hillhouse, 181
Hilton (Bickerstaff/Eakle family home), 254, 282
Historic American Building Survey, 197
Historic Chattahoochee Commission, 247
Historic Columbus Foundation, 10, 116, 118, 220, 247, 252, 253, 263, 273
Hocker, Katherine, 172
Hodges, Gen. Courtney H., 174
Hodges, Philemon, 34
Hofflin, Milton, 208
Hoffman, Donald, 129
Hoffman, Henrietta, 145
Hofflin, Maude, 129
Holcombe, Robert, 241
Holden, Mrs. Walter, 160
Hollis, Howell, 163, 210, 244
Holstead, Willis, 120
Holt, Col. Hines, 37
Holt, Mary Lewis, 146
Home Federal, 86
Homer, Winslow, 51
Hoover, Pres. Herbert Clark, 191
Hope, Bob, 264
Horenstein, Jascha, 256
Horton, Franklin (Buddy), 197
Houston Flier (airplane), 207
Houston, Sam, 25
Howard Manufacturing Company, 39
Howard, Colonel Robert M., 146
Howard, Ethel Holden, 184
Howard, Helen Augusta, 106
Howard, John, 29
Howard, Martha, 195
Howard, Nan, 140
Howard, Nicholas, 21
Howard, T. Michael, 83
Howard, Toombs, 154, 163
Hubbell, Miss Hazel, 211
Hudson, Betty Chipley, 184
Hudson, Helen Flournoy Huff, 128, 147
Hudson, Mrs. T. Charlton, 160, 207
Hudson, Tom, 129
Huff, Bob, 198
Huff, Edwin, 123
Huff, Louise, 194
Huff, William, 123
Huffman, Patsy Ann, 199
Hughston Orthopaedic Clinic, 284
Hughston, Dr. Jack C., 254, 284
Hughston, Mrs. Jack C., 284
Hull, Anna, 92
Hull, Herbert, 211

Hulse, Frank, 210
Hume's Company, 228
Humphrey, Hubert H., 266
Hunt, Mrs. Charles, 120
Hunt, Odelle Pearce, 119
Hunt, Sadie, 117
Hunter, Elizabeth, 195
Hunter, Gordon, 198
Hunter, Isla, 195
Hunter, Judge and Mrs. Henry Hall, Jr., 37
Hurt, Joel Early, 53
Hurt, Julia, 53
Huston, Minnie Bullock (Mrs. Tom), 176
Huston, Tom, 176, 193
Hutto, Adelaide, 233

I
I-185, 217
Ida Cason Callaway Gardens Foundation, 222
Illges, A., 82, 95, 239
Illges, Abram, 146
Illges, Ethel, 128
Illges, John P., 129, 154, 163
Illges, John P., III, 244
Illges, Mary Lou, 195
Illges, Mrs. A., 241
Indian culture in Columbus area, 22, 23, 33
Indian War, 28
Industrial High School, 123, 197
Infantry School, The, 124, 167, 174, 194, 211
Ingersoll Hill, 50
Ingersoll, Stephen M., 38
Inglis, Dean, 198
Inman, Mr. and Mrs. Edward H., 283
Iverson, Alfred, 51, 268

J
Jackson, Pres. Andrew, 15
Jackson, Edward, 198
Jackson, Ferne (Mrs. Herndon), 274
Jackson, Harry C., 197, 247, 259, 279, 285
Jackson, the (ironclad warship), 56, 113
James Shivers and Company, 82
James W. Woodruff, Jr., Confederate Naval Museum, 54, 56, 113, 238, 241, 287
Jannsen, David, 254
Jefferson, Joseph, 71, 87
Jeffries, J. W., 219
Jenkins, Brig. Gen. Reuben W., 211
Jenkins, Clifford, 163
Jenkins, Mrs. Crawford, 210
Jenkins, Mrs. James, 234
Jennings, M. C., 229
Jennings, Mrs. M. C., 181
Jewett, Mary Gregory, 259
Jewish Ladies Aid Society, 248
Joerg, H., 208
Joerg, Helen, 237
John Bascomb (horse), 30
John D. Gray Construction Company, 148
John Edward, The (bateau), 154
Johns Hopkins University, 82
Johnson, Alice, 128
Johnson, B. Ed., 250, 260
Johnson, Carlton M., 227
Johnson, Charles A., 163
Johnson, Denton, 198
Johnson, Don, 133
Johnson, Edgar, 198
Johnson, Eiver, 128
Johnson, James, 163, 197
Johnson, Nunnally, 276
Johnson, Pres. Lyndon, 266
Johnston Industries of New York, 267
Joines, Edmund Wesley, 74
Jolly Boys, The, 208
Jones, Allen, 197, 206
Jones, Bill, 198
Jones, Bobby, 258
Jones, Cadwallader, 198
Jones, Charles, 243, 259
Jones, Clara Bruce, 119
Jones, Eleanor, 259
Jones, Elizabeth, 199
Jones, John, 272
Jones, Johnnie, 197
Jones, Joseph W., 263
Jones, Lt. Catesby ap R., 54
Jones, Maj. J. Paul, 124
Jones, Marvin, 191
Jones, Mary Howard, 77
Jones, R. G., 197
Jones, Rosser, 212
Jones, Seaborn, 16, 19, 25, 27, 29, 123
Jordan, C. Dexter, Jr., 252
Jordan, C. Dexter, Sr., 4, 136, 240
Jordan Company, 135
Jordan, G. Gunby, 106, 129, 134, 135, 163
Jordan, G. Gunby, II, 106, 258, 279

Jordan High School, 197, 237
Jordan, Mrs. C. Dexter, Sr., 233, 240
Jordan, R. Curtis, 163
Jordan, Ralph (Shug), 231
Joseph, Dan, 163
Joseph family, 93, 104, 208
Joseph, Fannie, 93
Joseph House, 93
Joseph, Isaac, 93
Joseph, Jake, 133
Joy, William E., 178
J. T. Knight Scrap Metal Company, 148
Jubilee (riverboat), 217
Jungermann Studio, 147
Julius, Joe, 163
Julius, M., 94
Jugerman, Annie, 146
Junior League Follies, 233
Junior League of Columbus, 199, 233, 234, 241, 252
Junto Study Club, 219

K
Kamensky, Harry, 270, 279
Kamm, Rufus, 124
Kaufman, Lillie, 117
Kaufman, Marjorie, 146
Kaul, Florence, 117
Keene, Jean, 146
Keener, Suzanne, 188
Keller, John, 49
Kelly, Denney, Pease, and Allison, 146
Kelly, Emmett Leo, 226
Kelly, Jeff, Sr., 198
Kelly, Mrs. Jeff, 188
Kemp, Marie, 259
Kendrick, Clarence, 161
Kendrick, Mrs. T. K., 175, 207
Kennard's Trail, 177
Kennedy, John P., 40
Kennedy, Pres. John F., 235
Kennon, Paul, 197, 198
Key, Billy, 227
Key, Jack B., Jr., 258
Key, Jack B., Sr., 71, 214, 234
Key, James Biggers, 71
Key, James W. (Billy), 71, 258
Key, J. B., 71, 101
Key, Rev. Howard W., 78
Kibler, Frank, 208
Kilcrease, Dana, 145
Kilgore, Cathryn, 233
King George V, 165
King, Billy, 197
King, Horace, 19, 27, 45, 69, 125, 148
King, Pat, 209
King, Ruth, 233
King, Wood, 197
King-Godwin (Marker), 178
Kinnett, Betty, 233
Kinnett, John, 278
Kinnett, John, Jr., 210
Kirven, Annie, 117
Kirven, Eula, 128
Kirven, J. Albert, 77
Kirven, J. DuPont, 202
Kirven, Mrs. duPont, 188
Kirven, Richard, 77
Kirven, Shirley, 233
Kirven's, 49, 74, 77, 199
Kivlin, Miss Mary Unity, 107
Knight, Dot, 233
Knight, Mrs. J. B., 172, 188, 199
Knight-Ridder Newspapers, 218, 284
Knights of Pythias, 140
Kravtin's Novelty Shop, 115
Kreilick, Maj. Elevin A., 211
Kruger, Harry, 213
Kruger, Mrs. Harry, 248
Ku Klux Klan, 182, 196
Kunsberg, Phillip, 120
Kunsberg, R., 101
Kunze, Al F., 128, 163
Kurniker, Daisy, 117
Kurtz, Wilbur G., 27
Kyle, F. Clason, 195, 253, 259
Kyle, George S., Sr., 123, 206

L
Lacy, Clay, 239
Ladies Defender (gun), 113, 131
Ladies Education & Benevolent Society of the City of Columbus, 181
Ladies Memorial Association, 28, 198
Ladies Purim Association, 64, 248
Lafayette Flying Corps, 165

Lafayette, Marquis de, 30
Lafollette, Robert M., 37
Lake Oliver, 139
Lake, Veronica, 206
Lakebottom, 238, 239
Lamar, Lucius Quintus Cincinnatus, 25
Lamar, Mirabeau Buonaparte, 25, 38, 182
Lamar, Polly Mitchell, 232
Lamar, Tabitha Jordan (Mrs. Mirabeau B.), 25
Lamar, Tom, 208
Lampton, Mason, 222
Land, Frederick, 133
Land, John Henry, 242, 279
Landers, M. L., 175
Lane Cake (recipe), 116
Lane, Emma, 116
Langley, Neva Jane, 214
Lanier, Sidney, 44, 82, 126
Last Battle of the Civil War, 50, 52, 59
Latta, Georgia Howard, 184
Latta, Tommy, 195
Laurentine, Sister M., 219
Law, Emma, 116
Lawhorn, Allen, 223
Lawhorn, Samuel, 23
Lawrence, Roberta, 4
Lawson, L. L., 101
Layfield, J. P., 101
Layfield, Patsy, 195
LeRolle Company, 94
Ledger-Enquirer Newspapers, 9, 10, 137, 147, 218, 224, 227
Lee, Gen. Robert E., 28, 47, 58, 60
Leonard Springs, 162
Leonard, Van, 35
Levy, Arthur, 120
Levy, Edna, 128
Lewis, Ann Eliza Clifford, 92
Lewis, Betty Washington, 23
Lewis, Fielding, 23
Lewis, Jerry, 228
Lewis, Robert M., Jr., 243
Lewis, Sport, 277
Lewis, Tom, 145
Lewis, Ulysses S., 23
Lewis, William, 187
Liberty Bell (replica in Columbus), 271
Liberty Hall, 57
Lilienthal, Leslie, 198
Lincoln, Pres. Abraham, 53, 57, 108, 136
Lindsey, Annie, 117
Linkletter, Art, 221
Linwood Cemetery, 10, 28, 49, 51, 64, 92, 105, 106, 113, 185, 190, 263
Lion House, 184
Lions Club, 248
Litho-Krome Company, 215
"Little Giffen of Tennessee" (poem), 55, 56, 77
Little, Judge William Augustus, 180
Little White House, The, 200, 235
Live Oak (state tree), 21
Lockwood, T. Firth, 176
Loeb, Sadie, 117
Loeb, Sol, 49, 94
Lord, The Rev. Michael, Jr., 269
Lord, The Rev. Michael, Sr., 269
Lorenz, Charles E., 163
Lott, Louise, 128
Love Cathedral, The, 269
Lovein, The Rev. Norman, 255
Love, Peggy, 233
Lowe, J. C., 101
Lowell (steamboat), 37
Lowell of the South, 37, 123
L. Straus and Son's, 150
L. Thornton and Company, 94
Lucas, William D., 14
Lummus, F. Edward, 163
Lummus, Franklin L., 73
Lummus Industries, 73
Lummus, Jeanette Baldwin, 184
Lumpkin, Frank G., 118, 141, 211
Lumpkin, Frank G., Jr., 255
Lumpkin, Mrs. Frank G., 194
Lunn, Joe, 224
Lupold, Dr. John, 7, 9
Lupton, 100
Lyceum Theater, 44
Lynch, J. Arthur, 208, 211
Lynch, Mrs. Arthur, 188
Lyon, Harold, 145
Lyric Theater, 185

M
McClatchey, Mrs. Homer, 210
McClure, Dorothy (Mrs. Charles), 256
McCollister, Oscar, 255
McCollum, John B., 163
McCollum Studio, 147

McCombs, Rufe E., 253
McCullers, Carson, 203, 249
McCullers, James Reeves, Jr., 203
McDonald, Effie, 140
McDonald, Lucy, 120
McDonald, Mary Alice, 195
McDougal, Billy, 198
McDougal, Maj. Gen. Daniel, 28
McDowell, Virgil, 195
McEachern, Dan, 120
McEachern, Ed, 101, 117
McElroy, Louis, 198
McGee, Jack, 198
McGee, Theo, 210, 255
McGehee, Allen C., 79
McGehee, Capt. C. C., 50
McGehee, Leonora Watkins, 79
McGehee, Mrs. Cassy Ann, 105
McGehee, Mrs. Evelyn, 210
McGinnis, Callie B., 10
McGruder, Florence, 117
McIlhenny, John, 65
McIntosh, Gen. William, 186
Mack, Connie, 200
McKee, Mary Florence, 199
McKenzie, W. W., 163
McKissick, A. F., 100
McLaughlin, Lt. Augustus, 54
McLaughlin, Mrs. Charles, 210
McLaughlin, O. E., 175
McLennan, A. D., 100
McMicheal, W., 101
McPherson, L. W., 211
MacPherson, Mrs. Leighton, 194
McPherson, Mrs. L. W., 194
McRae, R. Y., 100
McTier, The Rev. William E., 211
McWilliams, A., 208
Macy, R. H. Company, 42
Maddern, Minnie, 87
Maguire, Dave, 270
Mahan, Dr. Joseph, 218, 241, 245
Mahan, Dr. Katherine Hines, 7, 9, 132, 152, 261
Maher, Joe, 10
Main Post Chapel, 192
Mallory, Edith Berry, 184
Man-O'-War (train), 258
Mansfield, Eddy, 285
March, Frederic, 188
March, Hal, 232
Marcum, Capt. A. A., 157
Mardi Gras Ball, 234
Marsh, John O., 275
Marshall, Fredye, 251
Marshall, Gen. George C., 129, 174
Marshall Junior High, 108
Marshall, Mrs. George (Catherine Tupper), 129
Marshell, S. R., 108
Martin, Dean, 228
Martin, E. D., 151, 241
Martin, Ella, 117
Martin Furniture Company, 188, 228
Martin, Hugh, 198
Martin, Jeanette, 128
Martin, John C., 133, 163
Martin, John H., 7, 9, 21, 22, 24, 35, 36, 39, 40, 55, 103
Martin, Kilpatrick and Davidson, 93
Martin, Mrs. Frank, 234
Martin, Mrs. Roy E., III, 272
Martin, Patsy, 233
Martin, Roy E., 151, 241
Martin, Roy E., Jr., 151, 176
Martin, Ruth, 128
Martin Theaters, Inc., 222, 241
Masonic Hall and Lodges, 43, 45
Masons, 86, 192
Massee, Jordan, 249
Massey, "Bud," 145
Massey, Miss Annie V., 217
Mathews, George W., Jr., 95
Matson, Carrie, 146
Matzenauer, Margaret, 188
Maxwell Brothers Furniture Company, 228
Maxwell, Dr. John, 7, 9
Maxwell, Dr. Isaac, 279
Mayfield, Judson T., 197
May, Leander, 268
Medlock, G. B. S., 159
Meigs, Henry D., 82
Memminger, C. G., 39
Memorial Stadium, 100, 105, 139, 181, 185, 229
Merchants and Mechanics Bank, 71, 183, 200, 228
Meredith, Charles, 199
Meriwether Inn, 170
Merrimac, The, 56
Metcalf, Alice, 233

Methodism, 32
Metro Government Center, 287
Metropolitan Opera Company, 278
Mickle, Jack, 270
Mid-South Steel Building Company, 178
Mike Rose's Italian Orchestra, 177
Military Maids, 140
Milledgeville, Georgia, 13, 14, 19, 24
Miller and Taylor, 228
Miller, Angie Mae, 146
Miller, Arthur, 249
Miller, Dr. John T., 198, 255
Miller, Dr. W. Laird, 187
Miller, Johnny, 248
Miller, Peggy, 195
Miller, Walter, 195
Miller, Zell, 284
Minter, John E., Jr., 224
Minter, Mrs. J. E., 173
Mitchell, Alexander, 96
Mitchell, Evans, 96
Mitchell, Gov. David Brydie, 30
Mitchell, Katherine, 117
Mobile Register, 53
Mobley, Beverly, 198
Monitor, The (ship), 54
Monroe, Harold, 197
Monroe, Marilyn, 249
Monroe, Pres. James, 30
Montarella, Mike, 34
Montgomery and West Point RR, 49
Montgomery Ward, 228
Moon, M., 101
Moon, Mrs. W. H., 188
Mooney, Edward L., 181
Moore, J. T., 101
Moore, Montague, M., 80, 171
Moore, Monte, 187
Moore, Noel, 187
Moore, T. E., 101
Morgan, J. Tom, Jr., 215
Morrison, Mr. and Mrs. L. H., 234
Morse, Samuel F. B., 31, 38
Morse Telegraph Line, 38
Morton Realty Company, 157
Morton, Marshall, 163
Morton, Mrs. Marshall, 160
Mosen, Hans, 163
Mote, Mrs. Mark, 199
Mott House, 61, 64
Mott's Green, 137
Mott, Randolph Lawler, 61
Moye, Matthew, 218
Moye, Mrs. L. M., 245
Moyer, Ira, 202
Mullin, Josephine, 233
Municipal Air Field, 194
Municipal Auditorium, 238, 239
Munn, Dick, 198
Murtagh, William J., 268, 296
Muscogee County Council of the Parent-Teacher Assoc., 188
Muscogee County Courthouse, 74, 110, 113, 131, 200, 255
Muscogee County School District, 2
Muscogee County School System, 176, 209
Muscogee Manufacturing Company, 61, 64, 137, 206
Muscogee Mills, 66
Muscogee, The (gunboat), 56, 113, 238, 241
Musemont, 267
M. W. Kelly, The (steamboat), 157
Myrick, Johnnie, 212

N
Naegele, Charles Frederick, 149
Naid, The (steamboat), 126
Nail, Dr. Braxton, A., 217
National American Woman Suffrage Association, 106
National Bank and Trust Company, 244
National Bank of Columbus, 71
National Historic Landmarks in Columbus, 268
National Infantry Museum at Ft. Bennings, 39, 40, 264
National Park Services, 273
National Register of Historic Places, 67, 108, 222, 268
Neal, Ann Deaton, 184
Neal, Charles, 161
Neal, Edward W., 262
Neal, Roy, 163
Nehi Corporation, 235
Nehi Drinks, 179
Neigs, Henry D., 82
Neill, Adelaide Koonce, 184
New York Herald, 169, 190
New York Times, 182
Newman, Chester, 145

Newman, Judge William T., 99
Newman, W. F., 120
Newsom, H., 101
Newsome, Skeeter, 200
Ngai, Mme Vu Thi, 268
Nilan, Leonora Woodall (Mrs. John), 79, 261
Nixon, Pres. Richard M., 238
Nolen, John, 184
Nordhausen, A. Henry, 215
Norman, Virginia I. (Mrs. Francis), 263
Norris, Alva, 197
North Highland Dam, 104, 123, 127, 153, 183
North Highlands Casino, 120
Nucholls, Caroline, 195
Nunn, Sen. Sam, 285

O

O'Daniel, Maj. Gen. John W., 211
O'Neal, Clyde, 140
O'Neill, Eugene, 71
O'Neill, James, 71
O'Tool, W. J., 175
Oakley, Annie, 257
Odd Fellows, 45, 86, 180
Odom, Dan, 197
Odom, William, 88
Offenbach, Jacques, 179
Officers' Club, 169, 174, 192
Oglethorpe Bridge, 56, 287
Oglethorpe Chapter of the DAR, 177
Oglethorpe, Gen. James Edward, 21, 33, 88, 177
Oglethorpe Hotel, 31, 186
Oglethorpe House, 34, 37, 39
Oglethorpe Marker, 177
Oglethorpe University, 82
Ogletree, Bill, 198
Oklahoma Territory, 33
Old Asbury, 53
Oliver, J. W., 244
Olmstead, Fredrick Law, 41, 48
Orpheus Club, 107
Owens, Hubert Bond, 59
Oxford, Town of, 16, 17

P

Pactolus, The (steamboat), 90
Page (R. W.) Corporation, 218, 224
Page, Celia G., 10
Page, Edmond Mrs., 194
Page, Lucy Q. (Mrs. Marion), 267
Page, Marion, 197
Page, R. W., 101
Page, Rinaldo William, 147
Palace, The, 235
Palmer, James, 101
Parham, Eliza Ott, 184
Park, Harbin, 202
Parks, Richard, 197
Parmer, David, 187
Parsons, Frank A., 88
Parsons School, 88
Passailaigue, Jack M., 244
Passailaigue, Mary, 147
Patch, Gen. Alexander M., 174
Pate, Jerry
Patrick, William, 34
Patterson, Albert L., 225
Patterson, Floyd, 229
Patterson, Isabelle Garrard, 200
Patterson, Jetta, 199
Patterson, John, 225
Patterson, Robert, 120
Patterson's, 228
Patton, Gen. George S., 174
Paw and Claw, 256
Payne Clothing Company, 183
Peabody, George Foster, 128, 200
Peacock, Albert, 146
Peacock, Lucile, 140
Pearce, G. A., 19
Pearce, Katherine, 128
Pearson, Pattie, 245
Pease, Leonard, 145
Pease, Porter, 199
Pease, William G., 141
Peddy, Capt. Tippo, 145
Peed, Mrs. J. L., 188
Pemberton, Ann Clifford Lewis, 92
Pemberton, Dr. John Stith, 92, 209, 263
Pemberton House, 263
Pennsylvania, State of, 32
Perkins, Bessie, 140
Perry, Allen, 259
Perry House, 45, 68
Perry, Sar, 101
Pershing, Gen. John J., 124, 168, 191
Pest House, 105
Peters, Thomas W., 163
Petri, Marjorie Cargill, 184

Petrie, Dr. George, 100
Petrosky, Maj. Andrew W., 211
Phenix City, Alabama, 27, 29, 225
Phenix Dragway, 195
Phillips, Tom, 194
Pickford, Jack, 194
Piedmont Park, 100
Pierce, Dr. George F., 32
Pierce, Dr. Lovick, 32
Pierce, Pres. Franklin, 62
Pike, Walter, 202
Player, Gary, 258
Pleso, Bob, 252
Polk, James Knox, 27, 39
Polo in Columbus/Ft. Benning area, 169
Population Statistics in Columbus area (1830), 22
Porter, Frederick, 202
Porterdale Cemetery, 130, 200
Porterfield, Robert, 259
Post Boy (horse), 30
Post, W. Merritt, 149
Potuznik, Laura, 10
Pou, Felder, 133
Pou Harness Company, 133
Pou, Mrs. Dozier, 160
Pou, R. E., 129
Pound, Flowers and Dedwyler, 280
Pound, Jere, 227
Powell, Charles Frederick, 75
Power, Tyrone, 22, 29
Prather, Andrew, 208, 244
Pratt & Whitney, 222, 285
Preer, Peter, 120, 129
Price, Shelton, 146
Pridgett, Gertrude, 202
Proffitt, Sara Ann, 195
Profiles in Power, 279
Profomo, Mary, 145
Profumo, Francis Xavier, 145
Profumo's, 145, 180, 199
Promenade, The Chattahoochee, 177
Public Health Nurse Association, 160
Pulitzer Prize (1955), 182
Pulliam, B. E., Mrs., 188
Purcell, Douglas C., 247
Putnam, Katie, 72

Q

Queen City (steamboat), 148
Queen Theater, 180

R

Race Course, 103
Racine Hotel, 68, 136, 270
Rademacher, Pete, 229
Radio Station WRBL, 90, 187
Rainey, Gertrude (Ma), 202
Ralph B. Draughon Library, 29
Ralston Hotel, 177, 185, 189, 200, 208, 210, 235
Ralston Towers, 185
Ramsey, James N., 64
Randall, Louise, 172
Rankin Hotel, 107, 115
Rankin House, 116, 138, 186, 252
Rankin, James, 252
Rankin Square, 169, 270
Rebecca Everingham (steamboat), 81
Red Jacket, The (cannon), 28, 86, 93, 113
Reed, W. A., 29
Reese, F. R., 101
Reese, Joe, 117
Reeves Brothers, 64
Reeves, Frances, 195
Reeves, Henry, 255
Reeves, T. G., 199, 250
Refrigeration, 105
Register, Mayor B. F., 221
Reich, Frederick, 22, 83
Reich, Harry, 192
Reich, Mamie Vent, 146
Reid, A., 138
Reid, Alex, 124
Reid, Edge R., 9, 248
Reid, Dr. J. Calvin, 202
Reid, R., 138
Reid, Templeton, 281
Republic Airlines, 211
Revel, D. O. ("Head"), 225
Revels, Patty, 199
Revolutionary War, 14
Revolutionary War Soldiers, 34
Reynold's, Lt., 101
Rhoads, Jessie DuBose, 281
Rialto Theater, 158
Richards, Margaret Ann, 195
Richards, Memory, 195
Richards, Mrs. Walter, 194
Richards, Steve, 198

Richards, Walter A., 198, 255
Richards, W. E., 100
Richardson, H. H., 125
Richmond, Virginia, 47, 48
Riddick, Steven, 272
Riddle, Elmer, 203
Riddle, John, 203
Rigby, Walter, 144
Rigdon, Heath Cooper (Mrs. John), 260
Rigdon, John, 260
Riley, Jacob L., 210
Riley, Sgt. Lewis, 205
Riverdale Cemetery, 158
Riverfront Amphitheater, 271
Riverside (home), 124, 172
Roach, John and Son, 87
Roberts, Hugh, Jr., 195
Rock Island Paper Mill Company, 49
Rogers, Ethel, 146
Romeo, Billy, 198
Rood Landing (Omaha), 273
Roosevelt, Eleanor, 169, 174, 200
Roosevelt, Pres. Franklin D., 104, 170, 174, 189, 200, 204, 208, 220, 237
Roosevelt, Pres. Theodore, 74
Root, John Wellborn, 99
Root, Sidney, 99
Roran, A. B., 53
Rose Hill Baptist Church, 120
Rose Hill School, 97
Rose, Mike (Michele Fiedarone), 91, 152, 177
Rosebuds, The, 119
Rosemont Home, 97
Rosenberg, Irvin, 198
Rosenberg, Laura F. (Mrs. Max), 248
Rosenberg's, 74, 228
Rosser, Herbert, 197
Rotary Club of Columbus, 163, 282
Rothchild, Rosa, 146
Rothschild, David, 74, 115, 163
Rothschild Furniture, 228
Rothschild, Irwin, 115
Rothschild, Irwin Mrs., 188
Rothschild, Jac H., 244
Rothschild, Nathan, 115
Rowe, Bobby, 212
Rowe, Sara, 233
Royal Crown Cola, 124, 179
Royal Crown Cola Company, 162, 235, 252
Royal Crown Ginger Ale, 124
Royal Theater (Three Arts Theater), 151, 174, 176, 187, 241
Royer, Hugh, Jr., 258
Ruby Restaurant, 138
Rudolph, Mason, 258
Rutherford, Lizzie, 199
Russell County, Alabama, 49, 50
Russell, Richard B., 260
Rust, Bryan, 227
Rutherford, Lizzie, 199
Ryan, J. W., 138
Ryan, Peggy, 195
Ryckeley, Lt. 101

S

Safford, Ray, 207
Salisbury, Belle, 128
Salisbury, Col. William, 272
Salisbury Fair, 272
Salisbury, William E., 79
Sampson, Dr. and Mrs. Lloyd, 94
Sandoval, Gladys, 10
Santa Anna, Gen. Antonio Lopez, 31, 38
Sarling, Leonora, 247
Sarling Park, 247
Saroni, Hermann, 213
Scarbrough, Claude, 152, 208
Scarbrough, Ethel, 140
Scheible, Florence, 274
Scherenschnitte, 79
Schield, A., 94
Schley, Dr. and Mrs. Philip T., 27
Schley, Frank, 255
Schley, Philip T., 28, 86
Schnell, Fannie, 198
Schnell, Frank, 273
Schnell, Mammie, 199
Schomburg, Carl Frederick, 75, 85, 98
Schomburg, C. L., 120
Schomburg, Frederick Collins, 75
Schomburg, Frederick Herman, Jr., 75
Schomburg, Frederick Herman, Sr., 75
Schomburg, Fred H., 98, 117, 120, 140, 163
Schomburg, Fred H., Sr., 85, 120, 179, 257
Schomburg, Mrs. Fred, 188
Schultz, Mrs. Nathan, 248
Schwob, Henry, 226
Schwob, Mrs. Ruth, 226

Schwob, Simon, 226
Schwobilt Clothes, 226, 239
Scott, Gen. Winfield, 23, 27, 31
Scott, Ira, 23
Scott, Jack, 209
Scott, Mrs. S. S., 210
Scurlock, William, 34
Sealy's, 228
Sears, C. A., 163
Sears Roebuck and Company, 228
Second Empire Architecture, 252
Second Hoover Flood, 191
Second Pershing Flood, 168
Sellers, Peter, 276
Sellers, Tom, 289
Seminole, The (train), 258
Semmes, Paul J., 28
Semmes, Raphael, 28
Serrato, Dr. Joseph, 255
Service Club Number One, 173
Service, Robert W., 212
Seven Hundred Broadway, 247
Seventh Regiment of the Georgia Infantry, 77
Seward, William H., 53, 57
Shakespeake, William, 107
Shannon Hosiery Mill, 277
Shaw, Dr. William Henry, 210, 217
Shearith Israel Synagogue, 164
Shepherd, Albert Hillhouse, 181
Shepherd, Anne Elizabeth Smythe (Mrs. Albert Hillhouse), 181
Shepherd, W. S., 28, 81
Sheram, George L., 120
Sherwood Hall, 106
Shiver's Wrecking Company, 121
Sho-Place, The, 178
Shorter, Edward S., 210, 217, 240, 256
Shorter, Mrs. Edward S., 240
Shoumatoff, Elizabeth, 208
Shure, Lt. Col. William, 211
Shutze, Philip Trammell, 283
Sigma Alpha Epsilon Fraternity, 190
Sikes, Tom, 255
Simon Schwob Memorial Library, 10
Singer, Mrs. Sam, 245
Sistrunk, Otis, 263
Skelton, Clarkie Davis, 120, 121, 162
Skipworth, James, 197
Slade, Capt. J. J., 96
Slade, Mary, 160
Slade, Mrs. Lester, 188
Slade, Rev. Thomas B., 96
Slade, Richard, 146
Sladeville Hall, 96
Slaughter, J. E., Jr., 259
Slaughter, Sue, 259
Small, Brownie, 161
Smalling, Walter, 273
Smisson, Mrs. Roy, Sr., 219
Smith, Al, 189
Smith, Alva C., 86
Smith, Bert, 198
Smith, Bragg, 130, 178
Smith, C. H., 100
Smith, C. T., 159
Smith, Gen. W. Bedell, 174
Smith, H. H., 100
Smith, James Milton, 73
Smith, Lula Carson (Carson McCullers), 203
Smith, Mrs. Eugene, 210
Smith, O. D. Mrs., 188
Smith, Oscar, 198, 243
Smith, Simon L., 23
Smith, Sol, 24, 44
Smith, Thomas W., 135
Smith, W. G., 101
Smithsonian Institution, 165
Smothers, Mrs. Helen K., 207
Smythe, Anne Elizabeth, 181
Snell, H. M., 101
Snow, Mrs. Lee, 207
Snowfall in Columbus, 264
Society Circus, 140
Society of American Archaeology, 200
Society of Industrial Archeology, The, 7
Sodom (Phenix City), 22, 29, 186
Soldiers' Aid Society, 67, 74, 114
Sommerkamp, Alberta, 146
Sommerkamp, F. M., 120
"Song of the Chattahoochee" (poem), 82, 84
Songs of Malta, 45
Sons of Temperance and Cadets, 86
Sousa, John Philip, 179
South Atlantic League, 139
Southern Airways, 211
Southern Open, 258
Southern Overall Company, 49
Southern Railway Company, 49, 74, 106, 136
Spanish-American War, 28, 74, 114

Spano, Angelo, 169
Spano, Angelo, Jr., 169
Spano, Mrs. Joseph, 207
Spano, Nicholas (Nick), 257
Spano's Restaurant, 169, 180
Spencer High School, 108, 243
Spencer, Helen L. (Mrs. Samuel), 92, 186
Spencer, Kyle, 195
Spencer, Samuel, 106, 136, 186
Spencer, W. H., 108
Spivey, R. B., 224
Sprang, Henry, 135
Springer, Francis Joseph, 52, 71
Springer Opera House, 44, 54, 71, 72, 78, 85, 87, 109, 140, 169, 176, 179, 185, 200, 218, 220, 222, 243, 250, 251, 256, 259
Springer Theater Company, 129
St. Elmo (book), 29
St. Elmo (*see also* Eldorado) (home), 27
St. Elmo School, 96, 198
St. Francis Hospital, 219, 234
St. James African Methodist Episcopal Church, 55
St. James A.M.E. Church, 55, 86
St. Louis Cardinals, 139
St. Luke United Methodist Church, 16, 32, 42, 64, 84, 112, 206
St. Paul Methodist Church, 155
Staffordshire China, 18
Staffordshire, England, 18
Stag Billard Hall, 184
Stage Coach Road, 27
Standard, Diffie W., 48
Stanley, Hiram, 210
"Stars and Stripes Forever" (song), 179
Stephens, Alexander, 57, 68
Stephens, Barbara (Mrs. Edward), 10
Sternberg Carpet House, 87
Stevens, 100
Stevens, Lieutenant, 277
Stevenson, Adlai E., 260
Stewart, Charles D., 82
Stewart, George, 82
Stewart, S. C., 175
Stewart, T. J., 258
Stilwell, Gen. Joseph, 174
Stocking Strangler, 274
Stone and Webster Company, 82, 104, 123, 139
Stone, Mrs. M. J., 199
Storey, Fred G., 163
Storey, Nancy, 195
Stradtman, George, 258
Stratton, Charles "Tom Thumb" Sherwood, 78
Stratton, H. D., 95
Straus Home, 150
Straus, Isidor, 42, 150
Straus, Jack, 150
Straus, Lazarus, 42, 150
Straus, Nathan, 42, 150
Straus, Oscar, 42
Street Fairs, 114, 118, 123
Stribling, Young, 229
Sts. Philips and James, Church of, 80
Sullivan, John L., 71, 72
Svendsen, Clara, 249
Swan House, 283
Swanton, Frank R., 200
Swift, Charles Jewett, 52
Swift, Clifford, 129, 154
Swift, Edward W., Sr., 206
Swift, George P., III, 66, 206, 208, 244
Swift, George Parker, 9, 66
Swift, George P. V., 66
Swift, George (Sonny), 66, 258
Swift, Henry W., 244
Swift, Leonora, 129
Swift Manufacturing Company, 86, 267
Swift, Marianna, 230
Swift, Mrs. Edward, 234
Swift, Stephanie, 230
Swift Textiles, Inc., 267
Swift, Vera, 234
Swift, William A., 86, 267
Swift, William D., 206

T
Taft, Robert A., 37
Talmadge, Herman, 220, 222
Tarlton, Jimmy, 239
Tarver, Elisha, 186
Tattler, The, 267
Tavern on the Square, 133
Taylor, Beverly S. (Mrs. T. Earl), 10
Taylor, Pres. Zachary, 38
Taylor, Wendell, 261
Temperance Hall, 40, 44, 45, 86, 180
Temperance Society, 15, 21, 25, 28

Temple Israel, 42, 248
Tenth Street School (*see also* Woodall School), 89
Texas, State of, 25, 31, 38, 176
Thackeray, William Makepeace, 40, 133
Third Georgia Cavalry Regiment, 51
Third National Bank, 129
Thomas, Edward Lloyd, 14, 17, 88, 103, 184
Thomas Gilbert and Company, 43
Thomas, Jim, 202
Thomas, Rev. L. L., 55
Thomas, Seth, 98
Thomas, The Rev. Joseph A., 163
Thomas, Truman, 17
Thomason, Richard, 175
Thompson, Albert, 243
Thompson, Arnold, 255
Thompson, J. R., 101
Thronateeska Fishing Club, 154, 198
Thornton and Acee, 76
Thrasher, Margie, 195, 233
Three Arts League, 188
Three Arts Theater, 213, 214, 248, 256
Thurmond, Martha, 274
Thwaite, Martha, 233
Thweatt, Shep, 117
Tibbets, Ret. Col. Ralph, 87
Tichnor, Stewart, 123
Ticknor, Daisy, 172
Ticknor, Dr. Francis Orray, 55, 77
Tigner, Mrs. Clarence, 188
Tillery, W. E., 101
Time (magazine), 5
Tisdale, Betty (Mrs. Patrick), 268
Tisdale, Dr. Patrick, 268
Titanic, The, 150
Tolbert, Love McDuffie (Mrs. Wheeler), 188, 225, 271
Tom Huston Peanut Company, 193
Tom's Foods Ltd., 121
Toombs, General Robert, 57
Torch Hill Home, 55, 77
Tornado (1953), 224
Townsend, Randolph, 198
Trail of Tears, 31, 32, 33
Traylor, Miss Julia, 210
Treaty of 1832, 31
Tri-Rivers Association, 217
Trinity Episcopal Church, 15, 53, 59, 72, 84, 99, 198
Triplett, Rupert A., 244
Triune Mills, 66
Troup, Gov. George, 19, 88
Truman, Harry S., 220
Trust Company Bank of Columbus, 10, 244
Tucker, Don, 243, 250
Tuggle, Tom, 208
Tuggle, Tommy, 195
Tupper, Allene, 129
Tupper, Catherine, 129
Turner, Charles E., 161
Turner, D. Abbott, 202, 240, 279
Turner, Eunice, 161
Turner, John, 146
Turner, Mrs. D. Abbott, 240
Turner, T. C., 175
Turner, William B., 279
Tuskegee Institute, 109
Tutherow, W. Presley, 135
Twining, Gen. N. F., 174
Tyler, Bettie Golden, 196
Tyler home (marker), 199
Tyler, John, 199
Tyler, Mrs. Arechavala, 234

U
Union Bottling Works, 124, 179
Union Carbide, 270
United Daughters of the Confederacy, 80, 173
United States Army, 33
United Technologies (Pratt & Whitney), 222
University of Georgia, 32, 77, 100, 200, 230, 246
University of Georgia Libraries, 156
University of the South, 59
Upatoi Creek, 168, 173
Uptown Columbus, 222
Urquhart, John A., 28

V
Van Buren, Pres. Martin, 15
Van Dorn, Connie, 233
Van Ness, James, 23
Vandiver, Ernest, 238
Vaughn, Glenn, 11, 275
Vaughn, Nancy (Mrs. Glenn), 275
Vaux, Calvin, 41
Venable, Fleming, 233
Venable, Winn, 278

Verandah Hotel, 125
Victorian Gothic Revival, 55
Villa Reich, 72, 83, 91
Villula Tea Garden, 237
Virginia, The (ironclad warship), 54, 56
Voight, C. H., 101
Volney, 30
Von Zinken, Leon Colonel, 59

W
Waddell, Elliott S., 154, 167, 208
Waddell, George, 129
Waddell, Major James Fleming, 53
Waddell's Battery, 50
Wade, George E., Jr., 247
Wade, Mrs. Albert, 188
Wade, Thomas P., 163
Wade, Tom, 154, 167, 198
Wadsworth, Frank, 198
Wadsworth, Henry (Red), 197
Walker-Peters-Langdon House, 17, 247
Walker, Willie Bell, 120
Wallace, Elise, 199
Wallace, George, 266
Walters, Joe, 195
Walters, Mrs. Annie Mae, 188
Walters, Nolan, 279
Walters, Sue, 195
War Between the States, 28, 29, 34, 39, 40, 42, 44, 47, 51, 53, 56, 57
Ward, Fred, 285
Ward, R. A., 206
Wardlaw, Ben, 192
Warm Springs, Georgia, 104, 170, 171, 200, 208, 235
Warner, James H., 49, 54
Warren, Lavinia "Mrs. Tom Thumb," 78
Washington, Booker Taliaferro, 109
Washington, George, 23, 30, 88
Waters, T. E., 117
Watkins, L. F., 101
Watson, Henry, 248
Watson, James C., 23
Watson, Latimer, 194, 207, 238
Watson, Mrs. Henry, 234
Watson, Rev. Henry, 42
Watt, Placie, 120
Waverly Hotel, 189
Waverly Terrace, 135
Wave, The (steamboat), 37
Wayne, John, 254
W. C. and Sarah Hall Bradley Foundation, 240
W. C. Bradley, (steamboat), 155
WDAK-TV, 224
Webster, Daniel, 15, 37
Wedemeyer, Gen. A. C., 174
Weekley, Ruth, 146
Weems, Gen. G. H., 174
Wells, Dorothy, 195
Wells, L. C., 163
Wells, Lt. Ed., 120
Wells, Tina, 195
Weracoba (*see also* Lakebottom and Wildwood Park), 238, 239
Weracoba Creek, 162
Wesleyan College, 32, 132
West, John Ward, 218, 245
Westmoreland Estate, 138
West Point, 14
Westville Historic Handicrafts, Inc., 218, 245
WGBA, 228
Whaley, Fred C., 235
White Bank, The, 115, 167
White Company, The, 157, 232
White, J. Linton, 157, 232
White, J. L., Jr., 232
White, Ritchie, 232, 255
White, The J. Linton Family, 232
White's Book Store, 49, 157, 184, 228
Whitehead, Bill, 190
Whitehead, Captain S. J., 90
Whitehead, Margaret, 7, 9
Whiteside, George B., 81
Whiteside, Samuel J., 81
Whitley, Dr. Thomas Y., 210, 277
Wickam, Lon, 117
Wickham, Billy, 212
Wickham, Fred L., 117, 148, 157
Wiggins, Thomas (Blind Tom), 138
Willcox, D. F. Company, 141
Wilde, Oscar O'Flahertie Wills, 40, 71, 85
Wildwood (birthplace of Augusta Evans), 29, 137
Wildwood Park (*see also* Weracoba and Lake Bottom), 74, 91
Wilkins, Miss Georgia, 208
Williams, Charlie Frank, 139, 229
Williams, Chief Wiley, 101
Williams, Eula, 233

Williams, George, 123
Williams, G. Mote, 86, 267
Williams, Harry L., 163
Williams, Mrs. C. F., 234
Williams, Mrs. Charlton, 234
Williams, Susie, 117
Willis, B. H., 101
Willis, C. J., 101
Willman, City Manager, J. A., 38
Wilson's Raid, 53, 54, 56, 58
Wilson, Augusta Jane Evans, 27, 29, 218, 243
Wilson, Brady, 10
Wilson, D. E., 100
Wilson, Gen. James H., 47, 49, 50, 59, 60, 61, 62, 64, 66, 69, 74, 82, 86, 114, 123
Wilson, Kent, 35
Wilson, Lorenzo Madison, 29
Windsor Castle, 165
Winslow, General Edward F., 60
Wise, Will, 120
Wolff, Dr. Luther, 210
Wolfson, Emmie, 117
Wolfson, Louis, 120
Wolfson, Sadie, 117
Woman of the Year Award, 207
Woman's Club House Association, 210
Woman's Reading Club, 92
Woodall, Allen, Sr., 224
Woodall, Billy, 197
Woodall Building, 261
Woodall, C. H., 159
Woodall Press, The, 261
Woodall School (*see also* Tenth Street School), 89
Woodall, William Clyde, 90, 101, 261
Woodall, William Hardy, 261
Wood, Enoch, 18
Wood, Edwina, 129, 207
Wood, W. J., 163
Woodruff, Edith, 130
Woodruff, Ethel Illges (Mrs. James W.), 253
Woodruff, George C., 208, 250
Woodruff, George C., Jr., 212, 279
Woodruff, George Waldo, 49, 93, 241
Woodruff, J. Barnett, 253
Woodruff, James (Jim) W., Jr., 9, 187, 202, 210, 214, 219, 224, 250, 253, 255, 263
Woodruff, James Waldo, Sr., 129, 154, 230, 252
Woodruff, Kathleen (Mrs. George), 274
Woodruff, Robert Winship, 93
Wood, W. J., 163
Woolfolk, Albert, 199
Woolfolk-Bussey Plantations, 166
Woolfolk, Charles M., 163
Woolfolk, Frances, 233
Woolfolk, Gene, 212
Woolfolk Plantation, 35
Woolfolk, Ruth, 233, 248
Woolfolk, Sowell, 14, 23
Woolridge, Charles, 120
Woolworth Store, 178
World War I, 28
World War II, 173
World War II Ration Book, 204
Worrill, Judge Edmund H., 41
Worsley, Etta Blanchard, 7, 9, 59, 188, 194
Worsley, Gray, 208
Wragge, Rector S. Alston, 199
WRBL-TV, 224, 236
Wrestling in Columbus, 285
Wright, Lt. Gen. John M., 251
Wright, Mrs. S. P., 207
Wright, Paul, 154
WTVM, 236, 254
WYEA-TV, 236, 254
Wynn and Shivers, 138
Wynn's Hill, 49, 209
Wynnton Elementary School, 35, 185
Wynnton School, 161
Wynn, William, 35

X
Xiaoping, Vice Premier Deng (of China), 284

Y
Yonge-Key-Tyler House, 59
Young Men's Christian Association, 45, 49, 128, 140, 145, 189
Young, Alfred, 208
Young, Dot, 233
Younge, Wattie, 117
Young, Mrs. William H., 234
Young, William H., 39, 52, 64, 133
Yuchi (tribe of Creek Confederacy), 33, 242

Z
Zimmerman, William (Bill), 261
Zyskind, Mrs. Irving, 248

About the Author

Photo by Peter Cranton

A former newsman-turned-historian, F. Clason Kyle did not work on the Columbus High School *Blue Streak* when he was a student there. His first print media experience came as a senior when he edited the 1953 *Tomokan*, the yearbook of Rollins College in Winter Park, Florida. This hands-on training fueled his interest in the field of journalism, a graduate masters program that he pursued at Stanford University in Palo Alto, California.

Upon his return to Columbus, Mr. Kyle still did not go to work for the local newspapers but, along with a college classmate, founded the Monogramming Company.

However, his articles on the history of the Columbus textile industry, local banking and Fort Benning that appeared in the *Columbus Ledger's* Seventy-fifth Anniversary Edition in 1961 led to his joining the staff of the *Columbus Enquirer* later that same year. In 1978, he came full circle as editor of the *Columbus Ledger-Enquirer's* Sesquicentennial Edition and "retired" from the newspaper business. During these seventeen years at the *Ledger-Enquirer*, Mr. Kyle ran the gamut from police reporter to music and drama critic, from travel writer to Sunday Magazine co-editor, and from a one-week's stint as "society editor" (while the late Miss Latimer Watson was on vacation) to writing a pair of free-wheeling weekly columns called (appropriately enough) "Kylestyle" and "On the Go."

Born in Columbus in 1929 and descended from one of the five original commissioners of Columbus, Dr. Edwin L. de Graffenried; and from George Parker Swift, a pioneer textile mill owner in Georgia, Mr. Kyle has had a lifelong association and identification with the local area.

One of the original trustees of the Springer Opera House and currently chairman of the Springer Opera House Arts Association, Mr. Kyle has been active in civic and cultural affairs, having served on the boards of the Columbus Museum of Arts and Sciences, the Columbus Symphony Orchestra and the Historic Columbus Foundation. He also has been a vigorous advocate in the field of historic preservation, having been one of the founders and/or officers of the Georgia Trust for Historic Preservation, the League of Historic American Theaters, the Historic House Association and the Victorian Society in America. In the latter organization, he currently serves as a vice-president.

He is the owner of the double octagonal dwelling at 527 First Avenue in Columbus that is known as "The Folly." This Historic District structure was named a National Historic Landmark for architecture in 1973 by Dr. William J. Murtagh, Keeper of the National Register, United States Department of the Interior.